Adventures in Art

Teacher's Edition
Level 3

Laura H. Chapman

Davis Publications, Inc.
Worcester, Massachusetts

Program Author
Laura H. Chapman, Cincinnati, Ohio

Reading Consultant
Dr. JoAnn Canales, University of North Texas,
Denton, Texas

Extensions
Dr. Lila G. Crespin, California State University,
Long Beach, California

Overhead Transparencies
Bill MacDonald, Art Education Consultant,
Vancouver, British Columbia, Canada

Dr. Connie Newton, University of North Texas,
Denton, Texas

Sandra Noble, Cleveland Public Schools,
Cleveland, Ohio

Large Reproductions
Dr. Cynthia Colbert, University of South Carolina,
Columbia, South Carolina

Unit Planners
Kaye Passmore, Notre Dame Academy,
Worcester, Massachusetts

National Standards correlations
Judith Stross Haynes, Cincinnati, Ohio

John Howell White, Kutztown University,
Kutztown, Pennsylvania

© 1998 Davis Publications, Inc.
Worcester, Massachusetts, U.S.A.

Printed in U.S.A.

ISBN: 0-87192-325-4

10 9 8 7 6 5 4 3 2

Publisher: Wyatt Wade

Editorial Director: Claire Mowbray Golding

Production Editors: Nancy Burnett, Carol Harley

Production/Manufacturing: Steven Vogelsang

Design Assistance: Karen Durlach

Editorial Assistance: Robin Banas, Jane DeVore,
Colleen Fitzpatrick, Michelle Johnson, Stacie Moffat,
Mary Ellen Wilson

Design: Douglass Scott, Cathleen Damplo,
Tong-Mei Chan, Ellen Dessloch, WGBH Design

Electronic page makeup: Glassman/Mayerchak

Illustrator: Mary Anne Lloyd

Front cover: Student artwork by Holly Dyer,
Bethel-Tate School, Bethel, Ohio. From the Crayola®
Dream-Makers® Collection, courtesy of Binney &
Smith Inc.

Teacher's Edition Contents

Assessment Masters

Davis Publications, Inc.

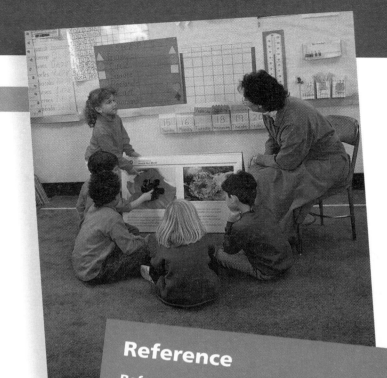

Reference

Wilton Series
Elements of Design
Davis CD-ROM Library

Welcome...

to a proven classroom
tool for inspiring students
to perceive, create, and
appreciate the visual arts.

to a comprehensive curriculum
that interweaves art appreciation,
history, criticism and production.

to art explorations that encourage
critical and creative thinking while
building an awareness of art in
everyday life.

to a presentation of art
from around the world and
examinations which integrate
other disciplines.

to the means for promoting
a mastery of basic art
concepts and encouraging
creative expression.

to a rich visual environment
in which students create,
read, write, listen, talk and
learn about art.

...and congratulations on
selecting *Adventures in
Art,* the leading program
for creating meaningful
learning experiences,
and fostering a lifelong
interest in art.

The *Adventures in Art* team

Program Author

Laura H. Chapman, Ph.D.

noted art educator, scholar and author, is recognized as being among the foremost authorities on, and contributors to art curriculum development nationwide.

Dr. Chapman has served as an advisor to many leading arts and education institutions and organizations, and is a Distinguished Fellow of the National Art Education Association. She is the 1997 recipient of the NAEA Educator of the Year award.

"Art is one of many important ways for children and young people to express what they see, know, feel and imagine.

Art is also a subject for study; a legacy of visual images from around the world, past and present. *Adventures in Art* provides a foundation for students to develop a lifelong interest in art."

Dr. JoAnn Canales

Reading Consultant
College of Art Education
University of North Texas,
Denton

Learning about art is like learning to speak another language. Both require ways of knowing and talking that draw on specific knowledge and skills. Each provides us with an orientation that can broaden our field of vision, open windows to new possibilities and persepctives, and foster an understanding and appreciation for diversity.

Dr. Lila G. Crespin

Contributing Author
Teacher's Edition Extensions
College of Fine Art
California State University, Long Beach

Students who acquire sophisticated sources of imagery in art education evidence expanded vocabularies in both oral and written language. A comprehensive art education nurtures students' abilities to access vital thinking processes, and it allows them to do so with increasing desire, confidence and success.

Dr. Cynthia Colbert

Author, Large Reproductions
Chair of Art Education, Professor of Art
University of South Carolina, Columbia

The works of art chosen specifically to support the units of study are unique because most are not readily available from other commercial sources. Great care was taken to select images that would be interesting to children, and that would support age-appropriate art instruction as well as address concepts common to the teaching of other disciplines.

Dr. Connie Newton

Author, Overhead Transparencies
Grades 3–4
Associate Professor of Art
School of Visual Art
University of North Texas, Denton

Designed to enrich the learning
experience, supplementary
materials encourage students to
apply core concepts from the text
to other works of art. Students
receive information about artists
from many different cultures,
detailed questions for critical analysis, historical context and aesthetic
issues concerning the images, and correlations to other areas of the
curriculum.

Sandra Noble

Author, Overhead Transparencies
Grades 5–6
Cleveland Public Schools, Ohio

Additional images provide an expanded
opportunity to view, study, compare
and assess artworks. From these activities, students are likely to develop
meaningful relationships with works
of art, which can also be built upon to
support the study of other subjects.
Short of a museum visit, there is no better way to present students
with such a diverse range and inspiring collection of art images.

Bill MacDonald

Author, Overhead Transparencies
Grades 1–2
Art Education Consultant
Vancouver, British Columbia, Canada

Visual resources for learning the language
of art give children important avenues
of communication and expression that
help them know themselves and their
world. Working with the visual language
of art helps provide a necessary link to developing
children's literacy in our school programs.

Program Contributors

Judi Haynes, Cincinnati, Ohio
David Henley, Hampton, New Jersey
Barbara Ivy, Denton, Texas
Lianne Morrison, Berkeley, California
Donna Pauler, Austin, Texas
Carolyn Sherburn, Fort Worth, Texas
Sharla Snider, Denton, Texas
Kim Solga, Mt. Shasta, California
Nancy Walkup, Denton, Texas
John Howell White, Kutztown, Pennsylvania

Davis Publications, Inc. also wishes to thank:

Diann Berry, Binney & Smith, Inc.
Emmy Casey, Pitt County Schools, Greenville, North Carolina
Sara Chapman, Alief ISD, Houston, Texas
Deborah Cooper, Charlotte-Mecklenburg Schools, Charlotte, North Carolina
Beverly Fletcher, Fort Worth ISD, Fort Worth, Texas
Juan Garcia, Brownsville ISD, Brownsville, Texas
Eldon Katter, Kutztown University, Kutztown, Pennsylvania
William McCarter, North Texas Institute for Educators in the Visual Arts, Denton, Texas
David McIntyre, El Paso ISD, El Paso, Texas
Kaye Passmore, Notre Dame Academy, Worcester, Massachusetts
Diane Spears, Edgewood ISD, San Antonio, Texas
Jerry Tollifson, Columbus, Ohio
Eric C. Zebley, Binney & Smith, Inc.

Giving you the most...

Thematic and sequential organization within and across grade levels, along with the most extensive array of corresponding visual and support resources you'll find anywhere, makes *Adventures in Art* the single solution for comprehensive art instruction.

means giving you more...

Student Textbook

Designed to inform and inspire, the high-interest student books present large, colorful works with corresponding details and diagrams to clarify art concepts.

Clear and concise text speaks to students and builds art vocabulary, while thoughtful questions foster a deeper understanding.

Multicultural comparisons further extend the learning experience to visual expressions from around the world.

Big Book

For ease of instruction in group settings, large-sized versions (34" x 22") of the student textbooks are available for grades 1 and 2, and come with a bound-in, self-standing easel.

Teacher's Wraparound Edition

Complete control and unparalleled teacher support is in your hands with this newly redesigned guide.

A three step teaching sequence is applied to all sixty lessons in an easy-to-follow format which also includes pointers for cooperative learning, interdisciplinary, individual needs and other strategic options.

The four units are preceded by unit openers which provide a quick overview and assist you in tailoring the program to your specific curriculum needs.

More options...

CD-ROM Library

Six art appreciation CD-ROMs designed for the classroom provide enrichment and expand the study of art with interactive explorations.

Correlated to the text, they can be used for all levels of learners as lesson reinforcement, for independent study, or in any manner you integrate technology into the classroom.

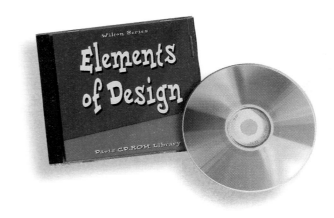

Large Reproductions

Twenty-four large (18" x 24") laminated color reproductions provide additional images that support the textbook.

A guide is also included which provides you with quick access to the images available, while also offering background information and supplemental lesson ideas.

The two sets are designed for use at grades 1–3, and 4–6.

Assessment Masters

A collection of reproducible resources challenge student understanding of art concepts.

Students are called upon to use interpretive, writing, illustrative and various other skills in demonstrating their art knowledge, allowing you to measure their progress throughout the program.

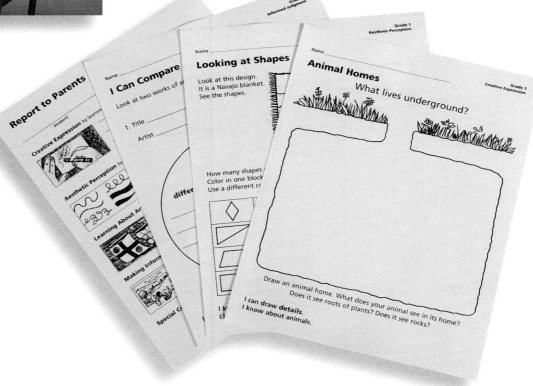

and more support...

Art Safety

Use all tools carefully.

Wash your hands after art lessons.

The labels on your art materials should say non-toxic.

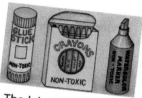
If you spill something, help to clean it up.

Art Safety & Technique Posters

Eight large (18" x 24") posters clearly illustrate for students proper methods and precautions for working with various art materials and media.

Slide Sets

Sets of thirty slides for each level add even more complimentary art images.

Also adding to the variety of media, styles, periods and cultures presented throughout the program, these sets are keyed to the lessons for ease of use.

Overhead Transparencies

Twenty-four color transparencies offer additional images to compliment the textbooks.

The included guide provides you with quick access to the images available, while also offering background information and supplemental lesson ideas.

The three sets are designed for use at grades 1–2, 3–4, and 5–6.

Complete control is always in your grasp with the **Teacher's Wraparound Edition** that allows you to effortlessly integrate all of the program components in a mix you create to meet your instructional needs.

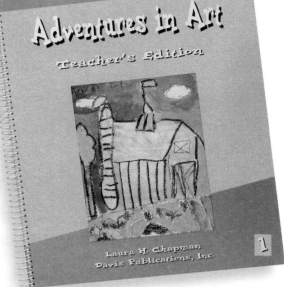

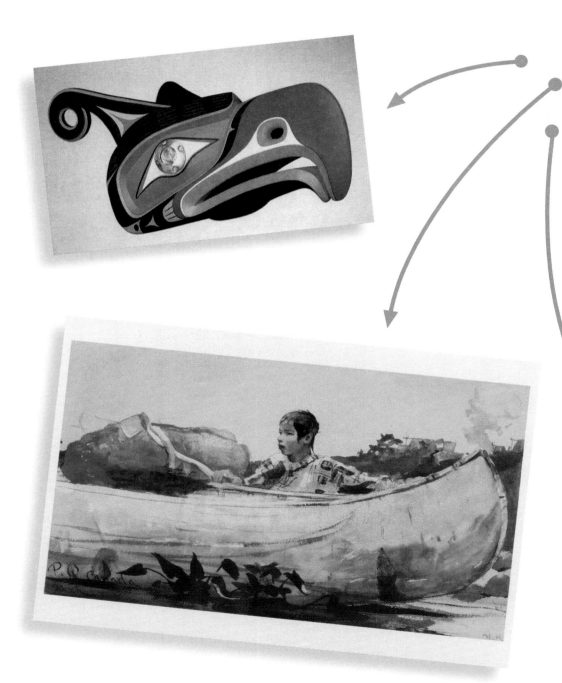

Adding even more supporting art images to lessons, use of the **Overhead Transparency, Large Reproduction** and **Slide Set** images are all referenced in the Teacher's Edition.

Art works for you.

Correlated use of the **Assessment Masters** provides an additional means of measuring student performance, while the **CD-ROM Library** takes advantage of the latest in instructional technology.

Comprehensive content is balanced with multiple materials and approaches, yielding the single, simple solution for Art Teachers and Classroom Teachers, working individually or in tandem.

Sixty full lesson plans direct the use of the **Student Textbooks** at the very core of this curriculum.

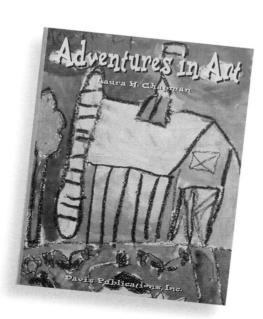

The picture of organization...

Lesson Structure

This Teacher's Wraparound Edition surrounds reproductions of the student textbook pages with the information you need in a format that allows you to keep the bulk of your concentration and effort directed towards your students.

PREPARE

You're always ready with this look at what's to be covered in the lesson, and what materials to have handy.

Objectives

let you know what to expect, and what's to be accomplished.

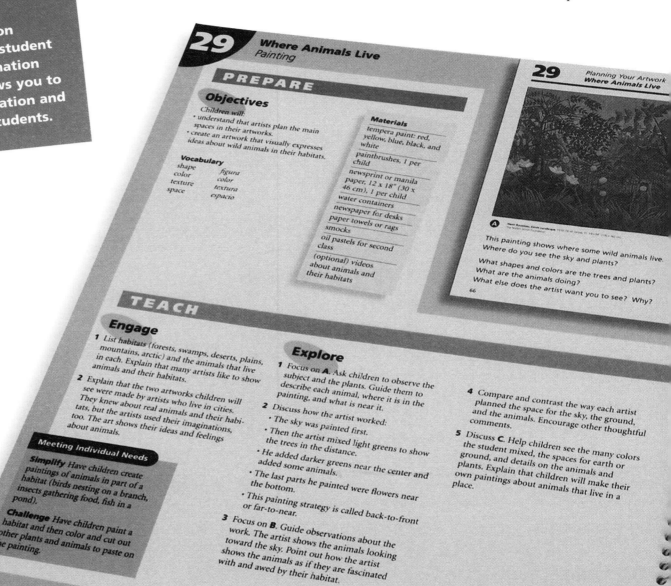

TEACH

Here's the core of your lesson, with discussion points, questions and instruction in a quick-scan format.

Engage

The classroom action starts here with the introduction of the lesson concept. Concise teacher points keep you focused on your students, and keep the lesson flowing.

Explore

Here you're given some questioning strategies and interpretive information to help students interact with the images in their textbooks and understand the art concept being presented.

Create

The studio activity is presented here, including suggestions for enabling students to put the lesson's art concept into practice.

Unit Planners

Preceding each of the four units is a Unit Planner which provides a **detailed overview** of all of the lessons, giving you the means to identify the **key program elements**. Quickly scan each lesson activity, concept and objective. Correlations are provided to the resource materials and **The National Visual Arts Standards**. Special Features, Cultural Representations and **Interdisciplinary Extensions** are also highlighted here, enabling you to easily incorporate this complete curriculum into your specific classroom environment.

B *Monica Miller, Northern Lights.*

Look at picture B.
What does the artist show you?

What painting can you make?
What animals will you show?

C

67

Create

1 Distribute supplies. Have children visualize a place and the plants and animals there. They can use both what they know and what they imagine.

2 Encourage children to think about colors that suggest weather and time of day. Have them mix colors and paint the sky and background.

3 When children have covered most or all of the paper, conclude the painting session with the assurance that the work will be completed using oil pastels.

4 When children resume work, have them gather in groups to discuss how they will finish their work. Ask each group member to share a plan and listen to others' ideas.

5 Have children finish independently. Circulate and ask questions such as: What textures or patterns can you show? How can you show the many greens or browns in this place?

CLOSE

Assess

1 Ask children to form conversation groups. Review the main ideas for thoughtful statements about art. Let children take turns showing their work and inviting comments from peers.

2 Call the class together. Ask volunteers to offer reasons why some artists create paintings about animals. Accept varied answers.

Reminder
Have children's portfolios available for the next lesson, a review of Unit 2.

RESOURCES

Large Reproductions
Carolina Parrots, Audubon, 8
Overhead Transparencies
Raven, Reid, 1
Zunoqua, Carr, 7
CD-ROM
2, *Elements of Design,* Lesson 2
Slide Set
Bear Cub, Charushin, 7
Assessment Masters
Animal Homes, 10
I Can Compare, 20

Critical Thinking

Display photographs of some of the animals shown in **A** and **B**. Have children compare and contrast the purposes of the photos and the expressive art qualities of the paintings in this lesson.

67

CLOSE

Wrap it up and reinforce the concepts at hand with clearly defined assessment exercises.

Assess

Close the lesson with suggestions for evaluating the students' artwork as well as initiating discussions to measure their understanding.

...and the model of instruction.

Essential Extras

All the support you need is here, clearly presented and instantly accessible.

Titles

A quick look at any lesson page, and you've got the **general lesson concept** and type of **studio activity**.

What Will I Need?

Check ahead to see exactly what art **materials** you'll need for the lesson's studio activity.

Vocabulary

Key words are identified here, along with their **Spanish** counterparts. You'll find the definitions, just like your students, in the glossary found in the back.

Special Features

These blue boxes pop-up to give you options for tailoring the program to your classroom. **Cooperative learning** opportunities are often highlighted, as well as methods for **meeting** your students' **individual needs**.

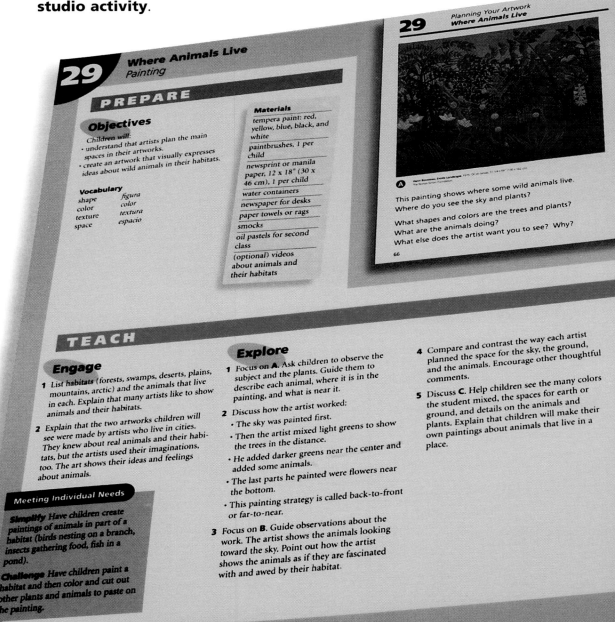

Going Further

Extensions give you quick ideas for modifying or extending lessons to incorporate a more interdisciplinary approach. Icons at the top of the page provide an immediate visual reference to the subject areas covered, including Language Arts, Social Studies, Mathematics, Science, and the Performing Arts.

Children's Books

 Look to the **Literature Link icon** for some suggestions of titles which can be incorporated directly into or implemented as supplemental reading for the lesson.

Resources

Here is your correlated list of the many support resources which are available to offer more visual examples or activities that relate to the lesson concept. The **technology icon** alerts you to related lessons from the CD-ROM Library.

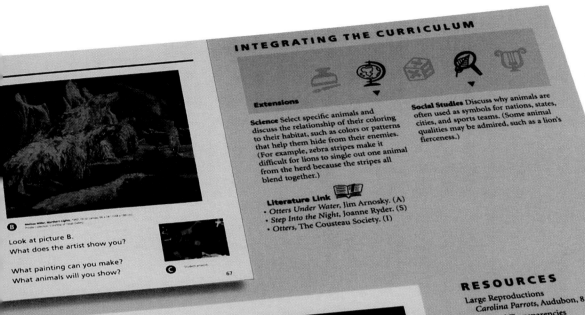

INTEGRATING THE CURRICULUM

Extensions

Science Select specific animals and discuss the relationship of their coloring to their habitat, such as colors or patterns that help them hide from their enemies. (For example, zebra stripes make it difficult for lions to single out one animal from the herd because the stripes all blend together.)

Social Studies Discuss why animals are often used as symbols for nations, states, cities, and sports teams. (Some animal qualities may be admired, such as a lion's fierceness.)

Literature Link
• *Otters Under Water*, Jim Arnosky. (A)
• *Step Into the Night*, Joanne Ryder. (S)
• *Otters*, The Cousteau Society. (I)

Look at picture B.
What does the artist show you?

What painting can you make?
What animals will you show?

CLOSE

Create

1 Distribute supplies. Have children visualize a place and the plants and animals there. They can use both what they know and what they imagine.

2 Encourage children to think about colors that suggest weather and time of day. Have them mix colors and paint the sky and background.

3 When children have covered most or all of the paper, conclude the painting session with the assurance that the work will be completed using oil pastels.

4 When children resume work, have them gather in groups to discuss how they will finish their work. Ask each group member to share a plan and listen to others' ideas.

5 Have children finish independently. Circulate and ask questions such as: What textures or patterns can you show? How can you show the many greens or browns in this place?

Assess

1 Ask children to form conversation groups. Review the main ideas for thoughtful statements about art. Let children take turns showing their work and inviting comments from peers.

2 Call the class together. Ask volunteers to offer reasons why some artists create paintings about animals. Accept varied answers.

Reminder Have children's portfolios available for the next lesson, a review of Unit 2.

RESOURCES

Large Reproductions
Carolina Parrots, Audubon, 8
Overhead Transparencies
Raven, Reid, 1
Zunoqua, Carr, 7
CD-ROM
2, Elements of Design, Lesson 2
Slide Set
Bear Cub, Charushin, 7
Assessment Masters
Animal Homes, 10
I Can Compare, 20

Critical Thinking

Display photographs of some of the animals shown in **A** and **B**. Have children compare and contrast the purposes of the photos and the expressive art qualities of the paintings in this lesson.

67

More Special Features

Critical and **Creative Thinking** exercises hone students' visual and cognitive skills.
Art History and **Cultural Awareness** boxes provide fascinating background.

Scope and Sequence

	Perception			Creative Expression		Culture and Heritage				Informed Judgment		Integrating the Curriculum
Lesson	Elements of Design	Principles of Design	Perceive Design Qualities in ...	Subject/Theme	Forms/Media/Techniques	Artists	Cultures	Time Periods	Styles/Purposes	Evaluation	Apply Knowledge	Subject Areas
U1	Line, Shape, Color, Texture, Space	Emphasis	Own and others' art, Constructed world, Nature	Environment, Animals	Drawing, Drawing media				Representational, Expressive, Imaginative, Practical	Own and others' art, Art in everyday life		(icons)
1		Proportion	Own and others' art, Works by major artists, Nature	Portraits, Work or play, Nature, Feelings	Drawing, Pencils, Sketching	Bonheur, Millet	France	19th c.	Representational, Expressive	Own and others' art, Works by major artists, Art in everyday life	Aesthetic Awareness	(icons)
2	Line, Shape	Proportion, Emphasis	Own and others' art, Works by major artists	Fantasy, Humor, Feelings	Drawing, Crayons or oil pastels	Miró, Calder	Spain, U.S.A.	20th c.	Expressive, Imaginative	Own and others' art, Works by major artists	Aesthetic Awareness	(icons)
3	Line, Forms, Space	Movement, Rhythm	Own and others' art, Works by major artists, Constructed world	Fantasy, Feelings, Abstract images	Drawing, Crayons or oil pastels	Macdonald, Randall	Canada, U.S.A.	20th c.	Expressive, Imaginative	Own and others' art, Works by major artists, Art in everyday life	Aesthetic Awareness	(icons)
4	Shape, Space	Pattern, Emphasis, Unity/variety	Own and others' art, Works by major artists, Nature	Animals, Abstract images	Drawing, Drawing media, Optical illusion	Escher	Netherlands	20th c.	Expressive, Imaginative	Own and others' art, Works by major artists	Cooperative Learning	(icons)
5	Shape, Space	Emphasis, Pattern	Own and others' art, Constructed world, Nature	Places, Feelings, Past and present	Printing, Tempera, Stencils				Expressive, Imaginative	Own and others' art, Art in everyday life	Community Awareness	(icons)
6	Shape, Color	Pattern, Rhythm, Unity/variety	Own and others' art, Works by major artists	Feelings, Abstract images	Collage, Colored paper	Matisse	France	20th c.	Expressive, Imaginative	Own and others' art, Works by major artists		(icons)
7	Texture	Emphasis	Own and others' art, Works by major artists, Constructed world	Objects, Fantasy, Moods	Collage rubbing, Oil pastels or crayons	Ernst, Ruiz	Germany, U.S.A.	20th c.	Expressive, Imaginative	Own and others' art, Works by major artists	Aesthetic Awareness	(icons)
8	Line, Texture	Pattern, Unity/variety	Own and others' art, Works by major artists, Nature	Animals, Fantasy	Drawing, Drawing media	Rembrandt, Larras	Netherlands, U.S.A., Russia	17th c., 19th c., 20th c.	Representational, Expressive, Imaginative	Own and others' art, Works by major artists	Cooperative Learning	(icons)
9	Line, Shape, Texture	Emphasis	Own and others' art, Works by major artists, Nature	Animals, Cultural symbols	Printmaking, Tempera, Monoprinting	Lomahaftewa	U.S.A.	20th c.	Expressive, Imaginative, Ceremonial	Own and others' art, Works by major artists, Art of varied cultures	Art Criticism	(icons)
10	Shape, Color	Pattern, Rhythm	Own and others' art, Constructed world	Art in everyday life	Printmaking, Tempera, Stamp printing				Decorative, Practical	Own and others' art, Art in everyday life	Cultural Awareness	(icons)
11	Shape, Color, Space	Pattern, Rhythm, Unity/variety	Own and others' art, Works by major artists	Work or play, Animals, Feelings	Drawing, Crayons or oil pastels	Orozco, Doriani	Mexico, U.S.A.	20th c.	Expressive, Imaginative	Own and others' art, Works by major artists	Creative Thinking	(icons)
12	Color, Value	Unity/variety, Emphasis	Own and others' art, Works by major artists, Nature	Nature, Flowers	Drawing, Crayons or oil pastels	Nolde, Leone	Germany, U.S.A.	20th c.	Representational, Expressive, Imaginative	Own and others' art, Works by major artists		(icons)
13	Color, Texture, Value	Unity/variety	Own and others' art, Works by major artists, Nature	Landscape, Nature	Painting, Tempera, Color mixing	Monet	France	19th c.	Representational, Expressive, Imaginative	Own and others' art, Works by major artists		(icons)

Lesson	Elements of Design	Principles of Design	Perceive Design Qualities in...	Subject/Theme	Forms/Media/Techniques	Artists	Cultures	Time Periods	Styles/Purposes	Evaluation	Apply Knowledge
14	Shape, Color	Unity/variety	Own and others' art, Works by major artists	Abstract ideas, Feelings	Painting, Tempera, Explore fluid qualities	Frankenthaler, Louis	U.S.A.	20th c.	Expressive, Imaginative	Own and others' art, Works by major artists	Art History
15	Line, Shape, Texture	Pattern, Rhythm	Own and others' art, Works by major artists, Constructed world, Nature	Portraits, Feelings, Abstract images	Painting, Tempera, Explore brushstrokes	Indji, Matisse	Australia (Aboriginal), France	20th c.	Expressive, Imaginative, Ceremonial	Own and others' art, Works by major artists, Art of varied cultures	Cultural Awareness
R1	Line, Shape, Color, Texture, Value, Form, Space	Emphasis	Own and others' art, Works by major artists, Nature	Landscape, Nature, Fantasy, Feelings	Drawing, Drawing media	van Gogh, Burchfield, Marin	Netherlands, U.S.A.	19th c., 20th c.	Expressive, Imaginative	**Portfolio review** Own and others' art, Works by major artists	
U2	Line, Shape, Space	Emphasis, Unity/variety	Own and others' art, Works by major artists, Constructed world, Nature	Landscape	Drawing, Pencils	Carr, Davis	Canada, U.S.A.	20th c.	Representational, Expressive	Own and others' art, Works by major artists, Art in everyday life	Art History
16	Color, Value	Emphasis	Own and others' art, Works by major artists, Constructed world	Landscape, Weather, Fantasy, Feeling	Painting, Tempera, Mixing tints and shades	Bonnard, Monet	France	19th c., 20th c.	Expressive, Imaginative	Own and others' art, Works by major artists	Art History
17	Color, Value, Space	Movement	Own and others' art, Works by major artists, Nature	Landscape, Weather	Painting, Watercolors	Jeffreys, Homer	Canada, U.S.A.	19th c., 20th c.	Representational, Expressive	Own and others' art, Works by major artists	
18	Color, Space	Emphasis, Unity/variety	Own and others' art, Works by major artists, Nature	Landscape, Seasons	Drawing, Oil pastels, Color schemes	MacDonald, Monet, Storm	Canada, France, U.S.A.	19th c., 20th c.	Representational, Expressive	Own and others' art, Works by major artists	Aesthetic Awareness
19	Color, Texture, Value	Emphasis, Unity/variety	Own and others' art, Works by major artists, Nature	Landscape, Seasons	Painting, Oil pastels, Shading and detail	Pissarro	France	19th c.	Representational, Expressive	Own and others' art, Works by major artists	Aesthetic Awareness
20	Color, Texture, Value	Emphasis	Own and others' art, Works by major artists, Nature	Animals, Fantasy, Feelings	Painting, Tempera, Mixing tints and shades	Bonheur, Audubon	France, U.S.A.	19th c.	Representational, Expressive	Own and others' art, Works by major artists	Aesthetic Awareness, Critical Thinking
21	Shape	Balance, Emphasis	Own and others' art, Works by major artists, Nature	Animals, Cultural symbols, Fantasy, Abstract Ideas	Drawing, Drawing media, Mural		India	16th c.	Expressive, Imaginative	Own and others' art, Art of varied cultures	Art History
22	Line, Shape, Texture	Emphasis	Own and others' art, Nature	Nature, Fantasy, Animals	Printmaking, Clay blocks, Relief printing				Expressive, Imaginative	Own and others' art	
23	Line	Proportion	Own and others' art, Works by major artists, Nature	Portraits	Drawing, Pencils, Sketching from poses	van Gogh, Bellows, Brown	Netherlands, U.S.A.	19th c., 20th c.	Representational, Expressive	Own and others' art, Works by major artists	
24	Shape, Space	Proportion	Own and others' art, Works by major artists, Constructed world, Nature	Places, Special events, Activities, Feelings	Drawing, Drawing media, Perspective	Glackens, Shahn	U.S.A.	20th c.	Representational, Expressive	Own and others' art, Works by major artists	
25	Shape, Space	Emphasis, Proportion	Own and others' art, Works by major artists, Constructed world	People, Places, Special events	Drawing, Drawing media, Perspective	Lawrence, Shinn	U.S.A. (African American)	20th c.	Representational, Expressive, Imaginative	Own and others' art, Works by major artists	Art History

Column group headers: Perception (Elements of Design, Principles of Design, Perceive Design Qualities in...) · Creative Expression (Subject/Theme, Forms/Media/Techniques) · Culture and Heritage (Artists, Cultures, Time Periods, Styles/Purposes) · Informed Judgment (Evaluation, Apply Knowledge) · Integrating the Curriculum (Subject Areas)

Subject Areas legend: Language Arts · Social Studies · Mathematics · Science · Music/Drama/Movement

Lesson	Elements of Design	Principles of Design	Perceive Design Qualities in . . .	Subject/Theme	Forms/Media/Techniques	Artists	Cultures	Time Periods	Styles/Purposes	Evaluation	Apply Knowledge	Subject Areas
26	Shape, Line, Texture	Proportion	Own and others' art, Works by major artists, Nature	Portraits, Feelings	Drawing Pencils	Jaramillo Shahn	Mexico U.S.A.	20th c.	Representational Expressive	Own and others' art, Works by major artists, Art of varied cultures	Critical Thinking	
27	Shape, Color, Value, Texture	Emphasis, Proportion	Own and others' art, Works by major artists, Nature	Portraits	Painting Tempera	Henri Johnson	Egypt U.S.A.	2nd c. 20th c.	Representational Expressive	Own and others' art, Works by major artists, Art of varied cultures	Art History	
28	Shape, Color, Texture, Space	Balance, Emphasis, Proportion, Unity/variety	Own and others' art, Works by major artists, Constructed world	Nature, Still life, Cultural symbols	Drawing Drawing media	McCloskey Thiebaud	U.S.A.	19th c. 20th c.	Representational Expressive	Own and others' art, Works by major artists	Art History	
29	Line, Shape, Color, Texture, Value, Form, Space	Movement, Pattern, Unity/variety	Own and others' art, Works by major artists, Constructed world	City, Activities, Feelings, Abstract images	Drawing Drawing media	Amaral Grosz	Brazil U.S.A.	20th c.	Representational Expressive Imaginative	Own and others' art, Works by major artists, Art of varied cultures	Aesthetic Awareness	
30	Color, Line, Shape Texture, Space	Pattern, Emphasis	Own and others' art, Works by major artists, Constructed world	City at night	Painting Tempera Crayon resist	Bacher	U.S.A.	20th c.	Representational Expressive	Own and others' art, Works by major artists		
R2	Line, Shape, Color, Texture, Value, Form, Space	All	Own and others' art, Works by major artists, Constructed world	Places, Objects, Feelings, Abstact ideas	Drawing Crayons or oil pastels	Halpert Marin, Stella Weston	U.S.A.	20th c.	Representational Expressive Imaginative	**Portfolio review** Own and others' art, Works by major artists	Critical Thinking	
U3			Own and others' art, Works by major artists, Constructed world	City, Art careers, Past and present	Drawing Drawing media				Decorative Practical	Own and others' art, Art in everyday life	Community-based Learning	
31	Form, Color, Texture	Unity/variety	Own and others' art, Works by major artists, Constructed world	Industrial design, Art in everyday life	Product design Posters of examples	Beekenkamp Wegner	Canada Denmark	20th c.	Decorative Practical Informative	Own and others' art, Works by major artists, Art in everyday life	Critical Thinking Independent Research	
32	Shape, Color	Emphasis	Own and others' art, Works by major artists, Constructed world	Graphic design	Poster design Colored paper, drawing media	Chermayeff Lang Littlewood and Teixeira Walker Group	U.S.A.	20th c.	Ceremonial Practical Informative	Own and others' art, Works by major artists, Art in everyday life	Cooperative Learning	
33	Line, Shape, Color	Emphasis, Unity	Own and others' art, Constructed world	Cultural symbols, Feelings, Abstract images	Drawing Drawing media Picture writing		Egypt Japan Mexico U.S.A.		Decorative Practical Informative	Own and others' art, Art in everyday life, Art of varied cultures	Community-Based Learning	
34	Shape, Line, Color, Space	Proportion, Unity/variety	Own and others' art, Works by major artists, Constructed world	Lettering, Fantasy, Abstract images	Drawing Drawing media Creative Lettering	Macaulay, Russo	U.S.A.	20th c.	Practical Informative	Own and others' art, Works by major artists, Art in everyday life	Aesthetic Awareness	
35	Shape, Form		Own and others' art, Works by major artists, Constructed world	Bookmaking, Past and present	Folded book or scroll Paper	Rossbach	China England U.S.A.	8th c. 12th c. 20th c.	Practical Informative	Own and others' art, Art in everyday life, Art of varied cultures	Community-Based Learning	
36	Line, Color, Shape, Texture, Space	Emphasis	Own and others' art, Works by major artists, Constructed world	Stories, Illustration	Drawing Drawing media Illustrate story or poem	Domanska Feelings	Poland U.S.A.	20th c.	Practical Informative Realistic Fantasy	Own and others' art, Works by major artists, Art in everyday life	Community-Based Learning	
37	Shape	Balance, Emphasis	Own and others' art, Works by major artists, Constructed world, Nature	People, Objects, Plants, Fantasy	Photography Sun-sensitive paper Sunprint	Atkins	England	19th c.	Representational Expressive	Own and others' art, Works by major artists, Art in everyday life	Community-Based Learning	

Lesson	Elements of Design	Principles of Design	Perceive Design Qualities in . . .	Subject/Theme	Forms/Media/Techniques	Artists	Cultures	Time Periods	Styles/Purposes	Evaluation	Apply Knowledge	Subject Areas
38	Shape, Space	Movement, Proportion	Own and others' art, Works by major artists, Constructed world	Motion pictures, People, Feelings	Collage, Oil pastels or crayons, Animation	Vinton	U.S.A.	20th c.	Imaginative, Practical, Informative	Own and others' art, Art in everyday life, Art of varied cultures	Careers: Animator	
39	Shape	Balance, Pattern, Proportion	Own and others' art, Works by major artists, Constructed world	Architecture	Collage, Drawing media	Alberti	Italy	15th c.	Decorative, Practical, Romanesque	Own and others' art, Art in everyday life	Community-Based Learning, Critical Thinking, Careers: Architect	
40	Color, Shape, Texture	Pattern, Unity/variety	Own and others' art, Constructed world	Past and present	Mosaic, Construction paper		Italy, Iran	6th c., 14th c.	Decorative, Ceremonial	Own and others' art, Art in everyday life	Community-Based Learning	
41	Space, Shape, Color, Form	Emphasis	Own and others' art, Works by major artists, Constructed world, Nature	Architecture at night	Painting, Crayon resist		Canada, U.S.A.	20th	Expressive, Practical	Own and others' art, Art in everyday life	Community-Based Learning, Art History, Careers: Architects	
42	Color	Balance	Own and others' art, Works by major artists, Constructed world	Past and present, Cultural symbols, Stained glass	Collage, Acrylic paint on plastic, Transparent design	Traylor	U.S.A., France	13th c, 20th c.	Expressive, Ceremonial, Practical	Own and others' art, Art in everyday life	Aesthetic Awareness, Cooperative Learning	
43	Shape, Form, Space	Proportion, Balance, Pattern	Own and others' art, Works by major artists, Constructed world	Architecture, Castles, Past and present	Sculpture, Construction paper, Model castle	Reidell and Von Dollman	Germany, France, Netherlands	13th c., 16th c., 19th c.	Expressive, Practical	Own and others' art, Art in everyday life	Cooperative Learning, Art History	
44	Shape, Form, Texture, Space	Balance, Pattern, Proportion	Own and others' art, Works by major artists, Constructed world	Architectural styles, Past and present	Drawing, Drawing media, Imaginary building	Furness, Jefferson, Morgan	U.S.A., Greece, Italy	2nd c., 18th c., 19th c., 20th c.	Expressive, Ceremonial, Practical	Own and others' art, Works by major artists, Art in everyday life, Art of varied cultures	Independent Research, Community-Based Learning	
45	Shape, Form, Color, Texture	Balance, Movement, Proportion	Own and others' art, Constructed world, Nature	Landscape architecture, Objects, People at play, Nature	Mural drawing, Drawing media, Playground design		U.S.A.	20th c.	Expressive, Imaginative, Practical	Own and others' art, Art in everyday life	Cooperative Learning, Careers: Landscape Architect	
R3	Line, Color, Shape, Form, Space	Movement, Pattern	Own and others' art, Constructed world	City planning, Art in everyday life	Drawing, Crayons or oil pastels		Canada, U.S.A.	20th c.	Expressive, Practical	**Portfolio Review** Own and others' art, Art in everyday life	Art Criticism, Careers: City Planner	
U4	Color, Line, Shape, Texture	Pattern, Balance	Own and others' art, Works by major artists, Constructed world, Nature	Traditional arts, Cultural symbols, Sense of past	Drawing, Drawing media, Traditions	Barsa	Australia, Africa, Canada, U.S.A.	19th c., 20th c.	Expressive, Ceremonial, Practical	Own and others' art, Art in everyday life, Art of varied cultures	Critical Thinking, Community Awareness	
46	Form, Shape, Color	Pattern, Balance	Own and others' art, Works by major artists, Constructed world	Containers, Cultural symbols, Past and present	Crafts, Cardboard boxes, Tissue paper decoration	Kimewon, Begay and Muskett	Canada, Korea, U.S.A. (Zuni)	19th c., 20th c.	Decorative, Ceremonial, Practical	Own and others' art, Works by major artists, Art in everyday life, Art of varied cultures	Cooperative Learning, Art History	
47	Shape, Color	Balance, Pattern, Unity/variety	Own and others' art, Works by major artists, Constructed world, Nature	Cultural symbols, Clothing design, Past and present	Clothing design, Colored and white paper		U.S.A., Russia	19th c., 20th c.	Decorative, Ceremonial, Practical	Own and others' art, Works by major artists, Art in everyday life, Art of varied cultures	Cooperative Learning, Cultural Awareness	
48	Color	Balance, Pattern	Own and others' art, Works by major artists, Constructed world, Nature	Traditional arts, Past and present	Crafts, Stencil paper, Decorated fan	Serizama	Japan	20th c.	Decorative, Practical	Own and others' art, Works by major artists, Art in everyday life, Art of varied cultures	Creative Thinking	

Column headings (group bands): Perception | Creative Expression | Culture and Heritage | Informed Judgment | Apply Knowledge

Subject Areas key: Language Arts · Social Studies · Mathematics · Science · Music/Drama/Movement

Lesson	Elements of Design	Principles of Design	Perceive Design Qualities in . . .	Subject/Theme	Forms/Media/Techniques	Artists	Cultures	Time Periods	Styles/Purposes	Evaluation	Apply Knowledge	Subject Areas
49	Shape, Color, Form	Balance, Pattern	Own and others' art, Works by major artists	Animals, Cultural symbols, Past and present	Sculpture, Construction paper, Maskmaking	Davidson	Canada, Africa	19th c., 20th c.	Expressive, Ceremonial	Own and others' art, Works by major artists, Art of varied cultures	Cooperative Learning	[icons]
50	Line, Texture	Pattern, Rhythm	Own and others' art, Constructed world	Fiber arts	Weaving, Yarn, Pulled threadwork				Decorative, Practical	Own and others' art, Art in everday life		[icon]
51	Shape, Color	Balance, Pattern	Own and others' art, Works by major artists, Nature	Fiber arts, Past and present, Cultural symbols	Crafts, Cotton cloth, Batik	Hill	U.S.A., Africa	20th c.	Imaginative, Decorative, Ceremonial, Practical	Own and others' art, Works by major artists, Art in everday life, Art of varied cultures	Cultural Awareness	[icon]
52	Shape, Color, Texture, Space	Unity/variety	Own and others' art, Works by major artists	Personal symbols	Appliqué, Fabric and yarn, Wall hanging	Benglis, Roberts-Antieau	U.S.A.	20th c.	Expressive, Imaginative	Own and others' art, Works by major artists, Art in everday life	Creative Thinking, Cultural Awareness	[icon]
53	Texture, Form	Emphasis, Proportion	Own and others' art, Works by major artists, Nature	Fantasy, Cultural symbols, Animals, Abstract ideas	Sculpture, Oil-based clay, Imaginary animal		China, Cyprus, Mexico	11th c. BC, 4th c., 15th c.	Expressive, Imaginative, Ceremonial	Own and others' art, Art of varied cultures	Cooperative Learning, Cultural Awareness	[icon]
54	Shape, Color, Form	Pattern, Balance, Proportion	Own and others' art, Works by major artists	Fantasy, Animals, People	Sculpture, Found objects and colored paper, Assemblage	Calder, Hudson	U.S.A.	20th c.	Expressive, Imaginative	Own and others' art, Works by major artists	Art History	[icon]
55	Shape, Color, Form	Pattern, Unity/variety	Own and others' art, Works by major artists, Nature	Animals, Fantasy	Sculpture, Craft paper, Soft sculpture	Finn	Egypt, U.S.A. (African American)	14th c. BC, 20th c.	Expressive, Imaginative, Decorative	Own and others' art, Works by major artists, Art of varied cultures	Aesthetic Awareness	[icon]
56	Form, Space	Proportion	Own and others' art, Works by major artists, Nature	People	Sculpture, Ceramic clay, Seated figures	McVey	Mexico, U.S.A.	3rd c., 20th c.	Expressive, Imaginative	Own and others' art, Works by major artists, Art of varied cultures		[icons]
57	Texture, Form, Space	Proportion	Own and others' art, Works by major artists, Nature	Portraits, Work or play, Sense of past	Sculpture, Clay, Relief	Astallia, Pressley	Iran, Italy, U.S.A. (African American)	9th c. BC, 16th c., 20th c.	Expressive, Imaginative, Ceremonial	Own and others' art, Works by major artists, Art of varied cultures		[icon]
58	Texture, Form, Space	Proportion	Own and others' art, Works by major artists, Nature	People, Activities, Past and present	Sculpture, Oil-based clay, Carving	Bullard	U.S.A. (Hopi), Greece	20th c.	Expressive, Imaginative, Ceremonial	Own and others' art, Works by major artists, Art of varied cultures	Independent Research	[icon]
59	Form, Shape, Texture	Balance, Movement, Proportion	Own and others' art, Works by major artists, Constructed world, Nature	Portraits, Feelings, Sense of past, Abstract ideas	Sculpture, Choice of media/techniques	Barthé, Hunt, Saar	U.S.A. (African American)	20th c.	Representational, Expressive, Imaginative	Own and others' art, Works by major artists	Art Criticism, Careers; Sculptor	[icon]
60	Form, Shape	Balance, Movement, Proportion	Own and others' art, Works by major artists, Nature	People, Activities, Feelings, Abstract ideas	Sculpture, Printmaking, Choice of media/ techniques	Catlett	U.S.A. (African American)	20th c.	Expressive, Imaginative	Own and others' art, Works by major artists		[icons]
R4	Shape	Balance, Proportion	Own and others' art, Constructed world	Art Exhibitions	Mount and display artwork	Miles, Wade	U.S.A.	20th c.	Expressive, Informative	**Portfolio Review** Own and others' art, Art in everyday life, Works for class or school artshow		[icon]

Subject Areas key: Language Arts · Social Studies · Mathematics · Science · Music/Drama/Movement

Adventures in Art

Laura H. Chapman

Davis Publications, Inc.

Worcester, Massachusetts

Program Author
Laura H. Chapman, Cincinnati, Ohio

Reading Consultant
Dr. JoAnn Canales, University of North Texas,
Denton, Texas

Extensions
Dr. Lila G. Crespin, California State University,
Long Beach, California

Overhead Transparencies
Bill MacDonald, Art Education Consultant,
Vancouver, British Columbia, Canada

Dr. Connie Newton, University of North Texas,
Denton, Texas

Sandra Noble, Cleveland Public Schools,
Cleveland, Ohio

Large Reproductions
Dr. Cynthia Colbert, University of South Carolina,
Columbia, South Carolina

Unit Planners
Kaye Passmore, Notre Dame Academy,
Worcester, Massachusetts

National Standards correlations
Judith Stross Haynes, Cincinnati, Ohio

John Howell White, Kutztown University,
Kutztown, Pennsylvania

© 1998 Davis Publications, Inc.
Worcester, Massachusetts, U.S.A.

Printed in U.S.A.
ISBN: 0-87192-325-4

10 9 8 7 6 5 4 3 2 1

Publisher: Wyatt Wade
Editorial Director: Claire Mowbray Golding
Production Editors: Nancy Burnett, Carol Harley
Production/Manufacturing: Steven Vogelsang
Design Assistance: Karen Durlach
Editorial Assistance: Robin Banas, Jane DeVore,
Colleen Fitzpatrick, Michelle Johnson, Stacie Moffat,
Mary Ellen Wilson

Design: Douglass Scott, Cathleen Damplo,
Tong-Mei Chan, Ellen Dessloch, WGBH Design
Electronic page makeup: Glassman/Mayerchak
Illustrator: Mary Anne Lloyd

Front cover: Student artwork by Holly Dyer,
Bethel-Tate School, Bethel, Ohio. From the Crayola®
Dream-Makers® Collection, courtesy of Binney &
Smith Inc.

Contents

Page

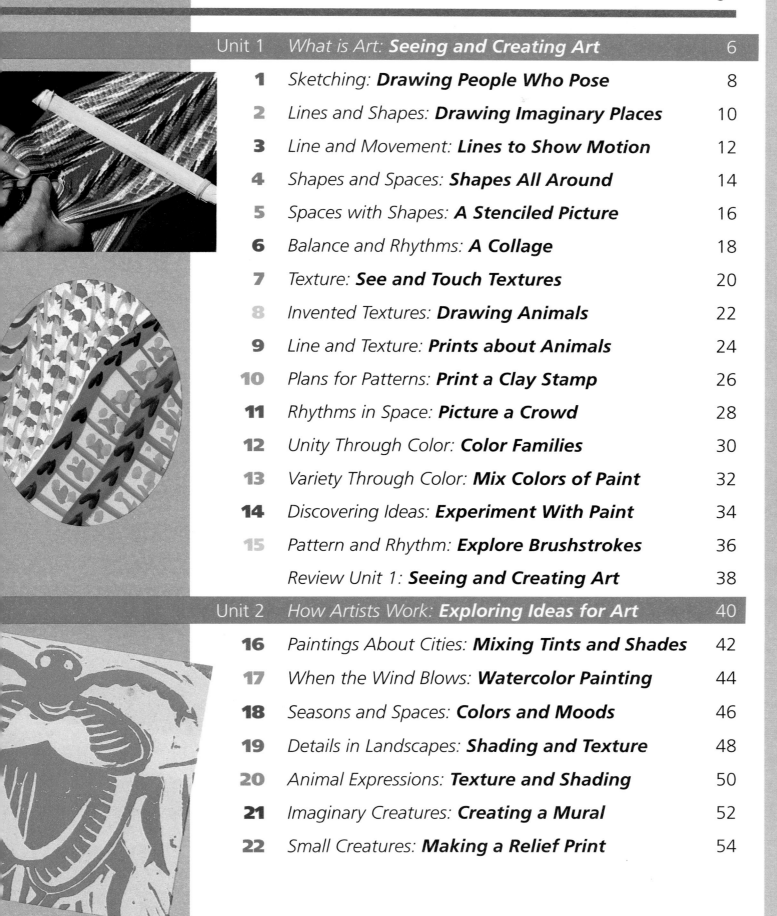

Unit 1 Planner

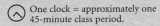

One clock = approximately one 45-minute class period.

Core: *Adventures in Art* provides a balanced sequence of lessons that meet national standards for content and instructional time. If you are unable to teach every lesson, introduce the lessons identified as "core."

Lesson Overview	Objectives	Correlations	Resources	Technology
U1 Core Page 6 **Seeing and Creating Art** *Activity:* **Drawing** *Materials:* **Drawing media, folders** *Concept:* **What is art?** *Related Lessons:* Crafts (fiber art): 17, 50, 51, 52. Design: 34. Photography as Art: 37.	• Discuss nature images and human-made objects in relation to art • Create a planned, humorous drawing of an imaginary bird	*National Standards:* 1a, c, 2a, c, 3a, b, 5a, b	*Large Reproductions:* **9,** Homer, **4** Picasso, **13** Arcimboldo *Overhead Transparencies:* **16** Picasso *Assessment Masters:* **20** Find Out About Art	CD-ROM 2, *Elements of Art,* Lesson 6
1 Core Page 8 **Drawing People Who Pose** *Activity:* **Sketching** *Materials:* **Pencils, assorted props** *Concept:* **Sketching** *Related Lessons:* Animals: 9, 20, 21, 22. Bonheur: 20. People: 23-26. Sketches: 23, U2.	• Understand sketching as a process of seeing, thinking, and exploring ideas • Make sketches of classmates posing in costumes	*National Standards:* 1a, c, d, 2a, b, c, 3a, b, 4a, 5a, b, 6b	*Large Reproductions:* **14** Johnson *Overhead Transparencies:* **1** Shahn *Slide Set:* **1** Degas *Assessment Masters:* **1** What Do You See?, **12** Mix and Match	CD-ROM 5, *People and Animals,* Lessons 1 and 2
2 Core Page 10 **Drawing Imaginary Places** *Activity:* **Drawing** *Materials:* **Viewfinder, Crayons or oil pastels** *Concept:* **Lines/Shapes** *Related Lessons:* Calder: 54. Landscapes (imaginary): 3. Line: 3, 8, 9, 29. Shape: 5, 6, 29, 39.	• Appreciate that lines and shapes can be used imaginatively to create art • Incorporate a variety of lines and shapes into a drawing of an imaginary place	*National Standards:* 1a, b, c, 2a, b, c, 3a, b, 4a, b, c, 5a, c, 6a	*Large Reproductions:* **6** Brown, **10** Kuniyoshi *Overhead Transparencies:* **13** Klee *Slide Set:* **2** Dorazio *Assessment Masters:* **5** An Imaginary Tree, **7** What's For Sale?	CD-ROM 2, *Elements of Design,* Lessons 1 and 2 CD-ROM 4, *Art Adventure,* Lesson 3
3 Core Page 12 **Lines to Show Motion** *Activity:* **Drawing** *Materials:* **Crayons or oil pastels** *Concept:* **Lines imply movement** *Related Lessons:* Landscapes (imaginary): 2. Line: 2, 8, 9, 29. Motion: 17, 38.	• Perceive and discuss line qualities implying movement in both art and environment • Create a drawing with lines that imply specific actions or movements	*National Standards:* 1a, b, c, d, 2a, b, c, 3a, b, 4a, b, c, 5a, c, 6b	*Large Reproductions:* **16** Howell-Sickles, **20** Romero *Overhead Transparencies:* **15** Mandel *Assessment Masters:* **1** What Do You See?	CD-ROM 2, *Elements of Design,* Lesson 1
4 Page 14 **Shapes and Spaces** *Activity:* **Cutting stencils** *Materials:* **Pencils, scissors, stencil paper** *Concept:* **Postitive/negative spaces** *Related Lessons:* Animals: 1, 5, 8, 20. Printmaking: 5, 9, 10, 22. Shape (positive/negative): 37. Space: 5, 11, 18, 42.	• Perceive relationships between positive and negative spaces in familiar contexts and optical illusions • Cut positive and negative shapes for stencils for printing	*National Standards:* 1a, b, c, d, 2a, b, c, 3a, b, 4a, b, 5a, c, 6a, b	*Large Reproductions:* **22** Bearden, **12** *Mask,* **4** Picasso *Overhead Transparencies:* **13** Lichtenstein *Assessment Masters:* **2** A Pattern Puzzle	CD-ROM 2, *Elements of Design,* Lesson 2

■ boxed sidebar information
on lesson pages.

Literature Link codes:
(A) Artwork links to lesson
(S) Story line links to lesson
(I) Information links to lesson

Special Features	**Cultures/History**	**Integrating the Curriculum**	
		Extensions	**Literature Link**
		Language Arts: Poster	*Sky Tree,* Thomas Locker with Candace Christiansen. (A) *Fox Song,* Joseph Bruchac. (A) *Reflections,* Ann Jonas. (A)
■ Meeting Individual Needs ■ Aesthetic Awareness	France: Bonheur Millet	*Language Arts:* Sketching diary	*Miranda's Smile,* Thomas Locker. (S) *My Ballet Class,* Rachel Isadora. (A) *Bill Peet: An Autobiography,* Bill Peet. (I)
■ Meeting Individual Needs ■ Aesthetic Awareness	Spain: Miró United States: Calder ■ *Cultural Awareness:* Picture-writing	*Language Arts:* Cursive letters	*Roxaboxen,* Alice McLerran. (S) *A Day with Wilbur Robinson,* William Joyce. (S) *Free Fall,* David Wiesner. (S)
■ Meeting Individual Needs ■ Aesthetic Awareness	Canada: Macdonald United States: Randall	*Language Arts:* Motion vocabulary	*The Flame of Peace: A Tale of the Aztecs,* Deborah Nourse Lattimore. (A) *Old Black Fly,* Jim Aylesworth. (A)
■ Cooperative Learning	The Netherlands: Escher	*Science:* Identify shadows *Social Studies:* Shadow puppets	*The Trek,* Ann Jonas. (A) *Opt: An Illusionary Tale,* Arline and Joseph Baum. (A,S) *Visual Magic,* David Thomson. (A)

5 ⌃ Page 16

Spaces with Shapes
Activity: **Stencil printing**
Materials: **Lesson 4 stencils, tempera, stencil paper**
Concept: **Stencil printing**
Related Lessons: Animals: 1, 4, 8, 9. Printmaking: 4, 9, 10, 22. Shape: 2, 6, 10, 11. Space: 4, 11, 18, 42.

- Understand the basic principles of stencil printing
- Collaborate with other students to create a picture with stenciled elements

National Standards: 1a, b, c, d, 2a, b, c, 3a, b, 4a, b, c, 5a, c, 6b

Large Reproductions: **10** Kuniyoshi, **17** Matisse
Overhead Transparencies: **16** Picasso
Slide Set: **3** Mungitok
Assessment Masters: **10** City Skylines

CD-ROM 2, *Elements of Design,* Lesson 2

■ Serigraphy

---

6 ⌃ Core Page 18

Balance and Rhythms
Activity: **Collage**
Materials: **Colored paper, scissors, paste**
Concept: **Symmetry, rhythm**
Related Lessons: Balance: 39, 46, 47, 48. Collage: 7, 21. Matisse: 15. Rhythm: 11, 15.

- Be aware that the design principles of balance and rhythm can unify an artwork
- Choose a theme and create a symmetrical collage with visual rhythm

National Standards: 1a, b, c, d, 2a, c, 3a, b, 4a, b, c, 5a, b, c, 6a, b

Large Reproductions: **12** *Mask,* **3** Sioux
Overhead Transparencies: **6** Boulle, **24** Hopper
Slide Set: **2** Dorazio
Assessment Masters: **2** A Pattern Puzzle, **3** Using an Artist's Colors

CD-ROM 2, *Elements of Design,* Lesson 5

■ Efficiency

---

7 ⌃ Page 20

Seeing and Touching Textures
Activity: **Rubbing collage**
Materials: **Oil pastels or crayons, paper, textured flat objects**
Concept: **Texture**
Related Lessons: Collage: 6, 21. Texture: 8, 9, 19, 20.

- Compare and contrast visual and tactile textures and understand that texture rubbings can be art
- Create a collage of crayon rubbings and the textures from which they were made

National Standards: 1a, c, d, , 2a, c, 3a, 4b, 5a, c, 6a, b

Large Reproductions: **29** Romero, **21** Blackwell, **1** Markovitz
Overhead Transparencies: **13** Klee
Assessment Masters: **20** Find Out About Art

CD-ROM 2, *Elements of Design,* Lesson 3

---

8 ⌃ Core Page 22

Invented Textures
Activity: **Drawing**
Materials: **Viewfinders, drawing media**
Concept: **Drawing texture**
Related Lessons: Animals: 1, 4, 5, 9. Line: 2, 3, 9, 29. Pattern: 10, 15, 50, 54. Texture: 7, 9, 19, 20.

- Appreciate that artists use lines in varied media to indicate textures and patterns
- Create a drawing of an animal using lines inventively to suggest textures and patterns

National Standards: 1a, c, 2a, c, 3a, b, 5a, b, c, 6a

Large Reproductions: **20** Romero, **21** Blackwell, **6** Brown, **16** Howell-Sickles
Overhead Transparencies: **9** Toulouse-Lautrec
Assessment Masters: **19** Comparing Two Artworks

CD-ROM 2, *Elements of Design,* Lesson 3

CD-ROM 5, *People and Animals,* Lessons 2 and 3

---

9 ⌃ Page 24

Prints About Animals
Activity: **Monoprinting**
Materials: **Tempera, plastic inking plates, tools to remove ink**
Concept: **Line and texture**
Related Lessons: Animals: 1, 20-22. Line: 2, 3, 8, 29. Printmaking: 5, 10, 22, 60. Texture: 7, 8, 19, 20.

- Understand the special print qualities of monoprints
- Create a monoprint that portrays an animal as a symbol for an idea

National Standards: 1a, c, d, 2a, c, 3a, b, 4b, 5a, c, 6b

Large Reproductions: **6** Brown, **1** Markovitz, **16** Howell-Sickles, **17** Matisse
Overhead Transparencies: **14** Tlingit
Assessment Masters: **12** Mix and Match

CD-ROM 2, *Elements of Design,* Lessons 1 and 3

CD-ROM 5, *People and Animals,* Lessons 2 and 3

---

10 ⌃ Core Page 26

Plans for Patterns
Activity: **Clay stamp printing**
Materials: **Construction paper, oil-based clay, tempera**
Concept: **Printing patterns**
Related Lessons: Pattern: 8, 15, 50, 55. Printmaking: 5, 9, 22, 60. Shape: 2, 6, 11, 39.

- Perceive and describe repeated patterns on printed surfaces
- Create a clay stamp and use it to print a repeated pattern

National Standards: 1a, c, d, 2a, c, 3b, 4a, b, c, 5a

Large Reproductions: **3** Sioux, **12** *Mask,* **17** Matisse
Overhead Transparencies: **8** Lee
Assessment Masters: **2** A Pattern Puzzle, **14** Design a Pot

CD-ROM 2, *Elements of Design,* Lesson 4

Special Features	Cultures/History	Integrating the Curriculum	
		Extensions	**Literature Link**
■ Meeting Individual Needs ■ Community Awareness		*Social Studies:* Historic stencils	*The Amazing Book of Shapes*, Lydia Sharman. (I) *Ed Emberley's Picture Pie 2: A Drawing Book and Stencil*, Ed Emberley. (A, I) *The Animals: Selected Poems*, Michio Mado. (A)
■ Meeting Individual Needs	France: Matisse	*Language Arts:* Reading *Music:* Rhythm	*The Mountain That Loved a Bird*, Alice McLerran. (A) *The Stone-cutter: A Japanese folk tale*, adapted by Gerald McDermott. (A)
■ Aesthetic Awareness	Germany: Ernst United States: Ruiz, Mexican American	*Language Arts:* Vocabulary *Science:* Nature rubbings	*Where the Forest Meets the Sea*, Jeannie Baker. (A) *Red Leaf, Yellow Leaf*, Lois Ehlert. (A) *Snowsong Whistling*, Karen E. Lotz. (A)
■ Cooperative Learning	The Netherlands: Rembrandt Russia United States: Cuban American	*Language Arts:* Writing *Science:* Leaf drawings	*The Eagle's Song: A Tale from the Pacific Northwest*, adapted by Kristina Rodanas. (A) *Animals should definitely not wear clothing*, Judi Barrett. (A) *Animals should definitely not act like people*, Judi Barrett. (A)
■ Meeting Individual Needs ■ Art Criticism	United States: Lomahaftewa, North American Indian, Hopi-Choctaw	*Language Arts:* Animal symbolism *Social Studies:* Dating art	*Dancing Teepees: Poems of American Indian Youth*, selected by Virginia Driving Hawk Sneve. (A) *Star Boy*, retold by Paul Goble. (S) *Moon Song*, Byrd Baylor. (A)
■ Meeting Individual Needs	■ *Cultural Awareness:* Stamp history	*Social Studies:* Patterns	*The Leopard's Drum: An Asante Tale from West Africa*, Jessica Souhami. (A) *The Amazing Book of Shapes*, Lydia Sharman. (I)

6d

Lesson Overview	Objectives	Correlations	Resources	Technology
11 Page 28 **Picture a Crowd** *Activity:* **Drawing** *Materials:* **Crayons or oil pastels** *Concept:* **Rhythms in Space** *Related Lessons:* Crowds: 24, 25. People: 23-26. Rhythm: 6, 15. Space: 4, 5, 18, 41.	• Understand that visual rhythm can be created by repeating and overlapping shapes • Create a drawing using repeated overlapping shapes	*National Standards:* 1a, b, c, 2a, b, c, 3a, b, 4a, b, c, 5a, c, 6a, b	*Large Reproductions:* **10** Kuniyoshi, **6** Brown, **17** Matisse *Overhead Transparencies:* **12** Lawrence *Slide Set:* **4** *Fourth Pennsylvania* *Assessment Masters:* **19** Comparing Two Artworks	CD-ROM 4, *Art Adventure,* Lesson 2
12 Core Page 30 **Color Families** *Activity:* **Drawing** *Materials:* **Crayons or oil pastels, viewfinders** *Concept:* **Color unity** *Related Lessons:* Color: 14, 18, 30, 40. Color schemes: 48. Flowers: 13. Styles of art with similar theme: 17, 18, 26, R1.	• Perceive and describe differences in the mood of art unified by warm and cool colors • Create a drawing dominated by warm and cool colors, including intermediate colors	*National Standards:* 1a, b, c, 2a, b, c, 3a, b, 5a, 6a, b	*Large Reproductions:* **6** Brown, **8** Audubon, **13** Arcimboldo *Overhead Transparencies:* **18** Phillips, **24** Bleumner, **23** Delaunay *Slide Set:* **5** Monet *Assessment Masters:* **3** Using an Artist's Colors, **4** Match That Color	CD-ROM 1 *Color,* Lesson 3
13 Core Page 32 **Mixing Colors of Paint** *Activity:* **Painting** *Materials:* **Tempera** *Concept:* **Primary/secondary colors** *Related Lessons:* Color mixing: 27. Landscape: 17, 18, 24, R1. Monet: 16, 18. Painting: 14-17.	• Identify primary and secondary colors on the color wheel and in artwork • Create a colorful landscape with tempera paint, using primary and secondary colors	*National Standards:* 1a, c, d, 2a, c, 3a, 4a, b, 5a, c, 6a, b	*Large Reproductions:* **6** Brown, **20** Romero, **14** Johnson *Overhead Transparencies:* **24** Bleumner *Slide Set:* **5** Monet *Assessment Masters:* **3** Using an Artist's Colors, **4** Match That Color	CD-ROM 1, *Color,* Lesson 1
14 Page 34 **Experimenting with Paint** *Activity:* **Painting** *Materials:* **Tempera** *Concept:* **Diluted paint** *Related Lessons:* Color: 12, 18, 30, 40. Landscape: 17, 18, 24, R1. Painting 13, 15, 16, 17.	• Perceive and discuss qualities of paintings created with fluid diluted paint • Create paintings using fluid paint to discover and develop an expressive theme	*National Standards:* 1a, b, c, d, 2a, b, c, 4a, b, c, 5a, c, 6b	*Large Reproductions:* **20** Romero, **6** Brown, **19** Courtney-Clarke *Overhead Transparencies:* **21** Vigée-Lebrun, **21** Rivera *Slide Set:* **6** Baber *Assessment Masters:* **3** Using an Artist's Colors, **4** Match That Color	CD-ROM 1, *Color,* Lesson 3
15 Core Page 36 **Exploring Brushstrokes** *Activity:* **Painting** *Materials:* **Students' Lesson 14 paintings, tempera** *Concept:* **Pattern, rhythm** *Related Lessons:* Matisse: 6. Painting: 13, 14, 16, 17. Pattern: 8, 10, 50, 55. Rhythm: 6, 11.	• Understand that artists can plan their brushstrokes to create patterns and rhythms • Complete two paintings from the previous lesson by creating patterns and rhythms with brushstrokes	*National Standards:* 1a, b, c, d, 2a, c, 4a, b, c, 5a, c, 6a	*Large Reproductions:* **20** Romero, **19** Courtney-Clarke, **7** Liberian Mask *Overhead Transparencies:* **13** Klee *Slide Set:* **7** Vlaminck *Assessment Masters:* **5** An Imaginary Tree, **10** City Skylines	CD-ROM 3, *Artists at Work,* Lesson 1
R1 Core Page 38 **Review Unit 1** *Activity:* **Drawing** *Materials:* **Unit 1 student artwork folders, drawing media** *Concept:* **Art analysis/description** *Related Lessons:* Landscape: 17, 18, 24, U2. Marin: R2. Styles of art with similar theme: 17, 18, 25, 26. Van Gogh: 23.	• Demonstrate their knowledge of art terms by describing and analyzing their own and others' art • Independently create a picture of an expressive landscape with light as a center of interest	*National Standards:* 1b, 2a, b, c, 4c, 5a, c, 6a	*Large Reproductions:* **11** Chagall, **10** Kuniyoshi, **9** Homer *Overhead Transparencies:* **16** Picasso *Assessment Masters:* **21** A Vote for Art	CD-ROM 2, *Elements of Design,* Lesson 6

Special Features	Cultures/History	Integrating the Curriculum	
		Extensions	**Literature Link**

■ Meeting Individual Needs
■ Creative Thinking
	Mexico:
	  Orozco
	United States:
	  Doriani
		Language Arts: Reading
		Science: Nature rhythms
			Yankee Doodle, Dr. Richard Shackburg. (A)
			Yankee Doodle, Steven Kellogg. (A)
			The Great Migration: An American Story, Jacob Lawrence. (A)

■ Meeting Individual Needs	Germany:
	  Nolde
	United States:
	  Leone
		Language Arts: Writing
		Language Arts: Phrases
			The Night of the Whippoorwill, Nancy Larrick. (A)
			The Way To Start a Day, Byrd Baylor. (A)

■ Meeting Individual Needs	France: Monet	*Science:* Color mixing *Science:* Overlapping colors	*Claude Monet,* Peter Harrison. (I,A) *Linnea in Monet's Garden,* Christina Bjork. (I, A) *Nate the Great,* Marjorie Weinman Sharmat. (S)

■ Meeting Individual Needs	United States:
	  Frankenthaler
	  Louis
	■ *Art History:* Color Field
		Science: Environment	*Over the Green Hills,* Rachel Isadora.(A)
			Cherries and Cherry Pits, Vera B. Williams. (A)

■ Meeting Individual Needs	Australia:
	  Indji, Aborigine
	France:
	  Matisse
	■ *Cultural Awareness:* Ceremonies
		Music: Rhythm	*Zomo the Rabbit: A Trickster Tale from West Africa,* Gerald McDermott. (A)
			Morgan and the Artist, Donald Carrick. (S)
			The Little Painter of Sabana Grande, Patricia Maloney Markun. (S)

	The Netherlands:
	  van Gogh
	United States:
	  Burchfield
	  Marin
		Evaluation Guide: Outlines	*Painting the Wind,* Michelle Dionetti. (A, S)
			Vincent Van Gogh, Peter Harrison. (A, I)

PREPARE

Objectives

Students will:
- discuss images of the natural world and human-made objects in relation to questions about art.
- create a humorous and consciously planned drawing of an imaginary bird.

Vocabulary

art	*arte*
line	*línea*
color	*color*
shape	*forma*
space	*espacio*
texture	*textura*

Materials

paper for drawing, 12 x 18" (30 x 46 cm), 1 per student

choice of drawing media

folders or portfolios, 1 per student (See Setup)

Setup

Place students' names on folders. Use monitors or another system to collect and distribute folders. Save all two-dimensional art for end-of-unit reviews. Save the best works from each unit for an end-of-year art show.

Write these bird names on the chalkboard: catbird, cowbird, flycatcher, fool duck, horned screamer, mud hen, ricebird, shoebird, yellowhammer, turtledove.

TEACH

Engage

1 Briefly discuss experiences students have had in drawing, painting, and creating art. Have students describe any visits to art museums, galleries, or places where artists work. Explain that art is more than using crayons, clay, and other materials; it is also a special way of seeing and thinking.

2 Introduce the books and help students locate lesson numbers, letters next to each picture, and special sections at the end. Identify the elements of the credit line for **C** in Lesson 2. Emphasize proper care of books. (They should not be written or marked in.)

Explore

1 Ask students to look at photographs **A**, **B**, and **C** and give their impressions.

2 Discuss the questions and explain why there are no right or wrong answers. The image in **A** might be called art because it shows the photographer's thought, skill, and choice. Many people think beauty in nature can be called art. The weavings in **B** and **C** show highly developed skills. In many cultures, these skills are respected, but are not called art. Other definitions of art emphasize expression, imagination, or communication.

3 In **D**, the student is concentrating and developing skills as an artist. Explain that students will learn to think about art and to see and plan their use of design elements. Today they will create imaginative drawings that go with the names of birds.

Create

1 From the list, ask students to choose a bird they have never seen. They should draw an imaginary bird that matches the name and show what the bird likes to do. The drawing can be funny: A secretary bird might be shaped like a typewriter or a pad of paper with pencil-like feathers. The bird's beak might hold a telephone; a wing might use a stapler.

2 Distribute materials, except folders. Ask students to decide on a vertical or horizontal composition. Encourage them to draw large main shapes and gradually add details.

B   Finger weaving. Photograph: Veronique Deplanne.

A   ***Sunset, Newport Beach, California.*** Photograph: Woody Woodworth, Superstock, Inc.

You can think about **art** in many ways. Many people say art is something very beautiful in nature, like a rainbow or a sunset. Do you think the sunset in picture A is art? Why or why not?

Some people say that art is a carefully made object, like a woven cloth. Are the weavings in pictures B and C done with great skill? Are the designs carefully planned? Do you think the weavings are art?

There are other ways to think about art. Art is a way to share what you see and feel. You can create artworks that tell stories. You can draw pictures or model clay to express your ideas.

6

Photograph: Dorothy Johnson.

Finished finger weaving (detail). Photograph: Veronique Deplanne.

In this unit you will learn how artists see their world. The special things artists see are called the **elements of design**. Some of the elements are line, color and shape. Others are texture, form and space.

Artists also plan their artwork. Artists plan the way colors and shapes fit together in a design. In this unit, you will learn how artists make plans by using **principles of design.** A principle is a guide for thinking about an artwork's design.

7

Extensions ▼

Language Arts Students who have had prior levels of *Adventures in Art* will be familiar with some of the terms below. You may wish to develop a poster with the following entries to display throughout the year.

Elements of Design
line
shape (2-D)
form (3-D)
color
value
texture
space

Principles of Design
rhythm
movement
pattern
proportion (size)
balance
emphasis
unity and variety

During the year, help students develop charts or posters for more specific art terms. For example, a diagram can describe lines as thick/thin, dark/light, curved/straight, even/uneven, and so on.

Literature Link
• *Sky Tree*, Thomas Locker with Candace Christiansen. (A)
• *Fox Song*, Joseph Bruchac. (A)
• *Reflections*, Ann Jonas. (A)

CLOSE

Assess

1 Call on volunteers to describe their drawings. Provide a model of thoughtful, positive questioning and encourage students to participate. Guide the conversation to create an awareness of art terms and the unique choice of subject matter, colors, and other ideas.

2 Distribute folders. Establish a routine procedure for collecting and distributing them.

Cleanup

1 Establish and maintain procedures for cleanup. Explain reasons for the procedures.

2 Place names and date on artwork. Collect and put away crayons.

3 Explain why the artwork will be collected into a folder. At the end of each unit, students will select their best work from the folder and take the rest home. This helps everyone see their progress.

3 About ten minutes before the lesson ends, ask questions such as: What might you add to spaces that are empty? Where might you add patterns or textures? Teach students to evaluate their work by viewing it from about the same distance that others will see it from.

RESOURCES

Large Reproductions
  Indian Boy, Homer, 9
  Three Musicians, Picasso, 4
  Summer, Arcimboldo, 13

Overhead Transparencies
  First Steps, Picasso, 16

 CD-ROM
  2, *Elements of Design*, Lesson 6

Assessment Masters
  Find Out About Art, 20

1 Drawing People Who Pose
Sketching

PREPARE

Objectives

Students will:
- understand that sketching is a process of seeing, thinking, and exploring ideas.
- make sketches of classmates who pose in costumes.

Vocabulary

model	*modelo*
pose	*pose*
sketch	*bosquejo*
sketching	*bosquejando*

Setup

Choose two locations in the room where two students can pose at the same time. Rotate the role of model between boys and girls. Each half of the class will draw the model nearest to them.

Materials

soft drawing pencils

newsprint paper, 9 x 12" (23 x 30 cm), 2 per student

assortment of old hats, scarves, and other clothing

assortment of props (umbrella, broom, bat, ball, book, etc.)

A **Rosa Bonheur, *Studies of a Fawn.*** Oil on paper, mounted to canvas, 15 x 20 3/4" (38 x 53 cm). The Snite Museum of Art, University of Notre Dame, Indiana (On extended loan from Mr. & Mrs. Noah L. Butkin).

Have you ever wondered how artists get ideas for their work? One way is by making sketches. **Sketches** are drawings you make to learn things. A sketch can help you remember what you see.

Do you like to make sketches?

What are some of your favorite things to draw?

Look at the sketches in picture A. The artist loved to study animals. She made sketches to learn how animals look and move around. Why do you think she sketched so many views of a fawn?

8

TEACH

Engage

1 Explain that artists often make drawings just for themselves. Define a *sketch* as a drawing that helps you remember what you see or helps you explore ideas for artwork. Often sketches are made to plan artwork.

2 Discuss why sketching can help artists get ideas. (Sketching helps you remember what you see. You can make different sketches and decide which ideas are best.)

Meeting Individual Needs

Simplify Students may draw one pose and then add details.

Challenge Have students sketch members of their families or their friends. Sketches can be made while the models are watching television, reading, or the like.

Explore

1 Explain that **A** is a page from a *sketchbook,* a book with paper for drawing. The artist Rosa Bonheur is remembered as a great painter of animals. She also made sculptures of animals. Guide students to see that this page shows many views of a fawn. She made the sketches quickly to capture the different positions.

2 Focus on **B** and **C**. Explain that this artist, Jean François Millet, often used his sketches to plan the composition of paintings. Guide students to compare the sketch in **B** with the painting in **C**.

3 Refer to **D**. Explain that students will sketch a student who poses for the class. The person who poses is called a *model.*

Create

1 Explain that students will draw several models. Each pose lasts about five minutes. Students can use both sides of their paper.

2 Distribute materials. Call on a boy and a girl to model. Help them select a special item of clothing or a prop. Ask each model to sit, recline, or stand in a comfortable position.

3 Have students:
- observe the pose and decide whether to sketch on a vertical or horizontal page.
- begin by lightly drawing the main shapes and angles of the body and furniture.
- add details.
- carefully observe where hands and feet are placed and other ways parts are related.

(Break the five-minute pose if the model is uncomfortable.)

D Student artwork.

Sometimes artists make sketches to **design**, or plan, an artwork. The sketch in picture B was made with black crayon. The artist made the sketch to plan his painting in picture C. How are the sketch and the painting alike? How are they different?

A student made the sketch in picture D. She drew a classmate who was wearing a costume. Have you ever sketched a model? Have you ever taken a **pose** so someone could sketch you?

9

INTEGRATING THE CURRICULUM

Extensions ▼

Language Arts Compare the process of sketching to the process of keeping a diary or a journal. The ideas are first recorded to remember events, but can later be used to write a story or essay. In a similar way, scientists and inventors often fill notebooks with ideas and observations for an experiment.

Literature Link

• *Miranda's Smile*, Thomas Locker. (S)
• *My Ballet Class*, Rachel Isadora. (A)
• *Bill Peet: An Autobiography*, Bill Peet. (I)

---

4 Proceed with at least two five-minute poses. Extend the activity to match students' interest and concentration. In the second sketch, ask students to look at the edges of shapes and to draw lines slowly, showing bumps and ridges in clothing.

Aesthetic Awareness

Explore other strategies for drawing people. In "gesture" drawing, the drawing is made quickly (in about one minute) to capture only the main angles and paths of movement. A "pressure" drawing is also made quickly. You press hard on the pencil to capture areas of weight or pressure (a hand supporting a chin, the feet supporting the legs). In "continuous energy" drawing, lines are quickly drawn to suggest the form, energy, and muscle tensions in the body. These drawings often start with the head, feet, or torso.

CLOSE

Assess

1 Have students share their best sketches of the first pose, the second pose, and so on.

2 Guide students to see how the sketches reflect careful observation of any of the following: general proportions, bends and angles, important details, edges with grooves or bumps. Have students participate in identifying these strengths in their own drawings and those of their classmates.

Cleanup

1 Have students place their names on each drawing. Have folders ready for students to save their work.

RESOURCES

Large Reproductions
  Jim, Johnson, 14

Overhead Transparencies
  Dr. Oppenheimer, Shahn, 1

 CD-ROM
  5, *People and Animals*, Lessons 1 and 2

Slide Set
  Seated Violinist, Degas, 1

Assessment Masters
  What Do You See?, 1
  Mix and Match, 12

2 Drawing Imaginary Places
Drawing

PREPARE

Objectives

Students will:

- appreciate that lines and shapes can be used imaginatively to create a work of art.
- incorporate a variety of lines and shapes into a drawing that shows an imaginary place.

Vocabulary

lines	*líneas*
shapes	*formas*
media	*medios*

Setup

Prepare viewfinders by folding index cards or stiff paper in half and cutting a window-like opening ½" deep and 1½" long (1 x 4 cm) into the center of the fold. Students will place viewfinders over pictures and view details through the holes. Save for future lessons.

Materials

viewfinders, 1 per student (See Setup)

crayons or oil pastels

drawing paper, 12 x 18" (30 x 46 cm), 1 per student

A **Alexander Calder,** *Autumn Leaves,* 1971. Tapestry, woven by Pinton Freres. By Courtesy of the Trustees of the Crown Copyright. Victoria and Albert Museum, London.

Some kinds of lines

thin   thick

wavy

zigzag

jagged

dashed or dotted

thick to thin

B

light to dark

Look at the lines and shapes in picture A. Alexander Calder created looping **lines** and curved **shapes** in this artwork. Why do the lines and shapes go with the title of his artwork?

Look at the lines in picture B. When might you want to draw thin or thick lines? wavy or zigzag lines? Can you think of other kinds of lines? What ideas or feelings might go with the lines?

What art materials do you like to use for drawing? Do pencil lines look the same as lines made with a marker or crayon? What other **media** can you use to create lines?

10

TEACH

Engage

1 Review the previous lessons. Focus on the idea that art can be based on imaginative ideas or on things you observe and want to remember. Stress that both ways of creating art have fascinated artists. Explain that this lesson will be about imagination in art and ways artists invent lines and shapes.

Meeting Individual Needs

Simplify Have students begin by drawing several arbitrary lines with their eyes closed and then find an idea that includes the lines.

Challenge Have students make a set of cards with lines similar to those in **C**. Use the cards to play "I Spy" in the classroom or on a walk through the school ("I spy a wavy line over there"). Trade cards during the game.

Explore

1 Focus on **A**. Guide students to see how the looping lines create shapes and flowing movement, such as the falling of leaves.

2 Focus on **B**. Have students gesture the lines and propose ways of using lines in artworks. For example:

- Thin lines help show delicate things.
- Thick lines suggest something is bold, strong, or important.
- Wavy lines suggest gentle motions.
- Zigzags and jagged lines suggest sharp changes or edges.

Explain that the quality of a line is also related to the medium (pencil, marker, paintbrush).

3 Guide students to identify types and qualities of lines in **C** using some of the terms in **B**.

4 Have students identify the shapes in **C**, beginning with the four in **D**. Distribute viewfinders. Have students place viewfinders over **C** and find other lines and shapes. Some resemble trees, comets, birds, a woman with a funny hat, a fire, a stream, or a magic lamp.

Aesthetic Awareness

Have students go outside with paper for sketching. Have them draw varieties of linear things such as telephone poles with wires, cracks in concrete or asphalt, fencing, and tree branches. When they return, discuss some of the differences and similarities in the lines. Contrast and compare lines in the human-made environment and lines in nature.

Can you find shapes like these?

C Joan Miró, *The Hermitage,* 1924. Oil and/or aqueous medium, crayon and pencil, 45 x 57 7/8" (114 x 147 cm). Philadelphia Museum of Art (The Louise & Walter Arensberg Collection).

D

Joan Miró liked to create artworks about make-believe places, animals and people. His painting in picture C has dotted lines and wavy lines. Do you see zigzag lines? What other lines do you see?

When lines meet or cross each other they make a shape. What shapes do you see in pictures A and C? Do some shapes remind you of things you know about? Why?

Alexander Calder and Joan Miró created **imaginative** artwork. An imaginative artwork is one you make up. It is not meant to look realistic.

Draw a picture of a make-believe place. Use your imagination. The place you draw could be strange or beautiful. Funny or dream-like things could happen there. What lines and shapes will you use for your artwork?

11

INTEGRATING THE CURRICULUM

Extensions ▼

Language Arts Compare the skill of drawing to the skill of using cursive letters in handwriting. In both, the eye, mind, and hand must work together. Discuss why the two tasks are different and whether one seems more difficult than the other.

Literature Link

• *Roxaboxen,* Alice McLerran. (S)
• *A Day with Wilbur Robinson,* William Joyce. (S)
• *Free Fall,* David Wiesner. (S)

CLOSE

Create

1 Distribute materials and ask students to create a drawing about an imaginary place. Have students think about absurdities: people who live in Cloud Land; a place where all the vehicles look like animals; a place where everyone and everything wiggles and giggles, including the trees and houses!

2 While students are working, encourage them to use a variety of lines—thick, thin, wavy, and so on. Most students will understand that lines create shapes, but you may need to illustrate this concept on the chalkboard.

Assess

1 Discuss the drawings. Guide students to appreciate imaginative elements as well as varieties of lines and shapes. Praise and reinforce the use of terms to describe specific qualities of line.

2 Ask students to describe the difference between drawing lines and shapes for an imaginative artwork and drawing lines and shapes to record what they see in real life. Accept varied, thoughtful answers.

Cultural Awareness

Some of the oldest forms of recording ideas are based on picture writing. In China and Japan, there are picturelike symbols for thousands of words. When children learn to write, they learn to carefully see and draw each part. Ask students how observing and drawing letters of the alphabet are similar to observing and drawing a person or scene.

11

3 Lines to Show Motion
Drawing

PREPARE

Objectives

Students will:
• perceive and discuss qualities of line that imply movement in artworks and in the environment.
• create a drawing in which lines imply specific actions or movements.

Vocabulary

motion	*movimiento*
line	*línea*
space	*espacio*

Materials

white or manila drawing paper, 12 x 18" (30 x 46 cm), 1 per student

crayons or oil pastels

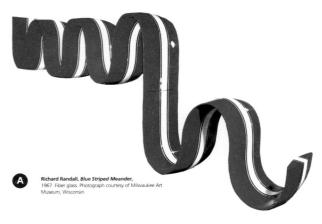

A Richard Randall, *Blue Striped Meander*, 1967. Fiber glass. Photograph courtesy of Milwaukee Art Museum, Wisconsin.

Artists create sculpture, paintings and other kinds of art. Sometimes they use lines to express ideas or feelings about **motion**.

The sculpture in picture A is a ribbon-like line in space. Pretend you can move your hand across the sculpture. What kind of motion do you feel?

The photograph in picture B is a record of motion. The photograph shows cars moving on a highway. Why do the lines help you see the motion?

B **Garden State Parkway, New Jersey.** Photograph: Scott McKiernan. © 1993 Scott McKiernan.

12

TEACH

Engage

1 Ask students to make arm gestures that match the following terms: dart, zoom, flop, skip, swing, sway, jump, hop, creep, wiggle, loop, spiral, zigzag, meander, wander. For each, allow students to try several ways to show the speed of the motion (a fast looping line, a slow looping line, and so on).

2 Ask students how they could make a record of the lines they made in the air. (Draw, photograph, or videotape the lines.) Define a *line* as a visual record of a path of movement. Explain that many works of art are planned with lines to give a feeling of action and movement.

Explore

1 Focus on **A**. Ask students to gesture the rhythmic movement of the sculpture, as if they could touch it with their hands.

2 Focus on **B**. Guide students to see that the photograph is a record that shows the dots and lines of moving car headlights. Ask if they have seen similar effects, when points of moving lights look like lines (fireworks, holiday or store lights that flash in sequence).

3 Focus on **C**. Have students describe some of the lines and shapes using terms from Lesson 2, such as wavy or zigzag, and other terms related to motion (loop, spiral, wander, wiggle). Guide students to see relationships between lines and shapes. For example, have them identify shapes that have wiggly or angular outlines.

Create

1 Distribute materials. Explain that students will record the path of movement made by something. They will draw lines that show how the motion feels and looks, but not the thing that makes the motion (for example, sand after a snake slithers through; a vapor trail from a jet plane that loops or glides through the sky). Invite students to share other examples of moving things and lines that show how they move.

Meeting Individual Needs

Simplify Have students draw action lines on long rolls of calculator paper, creating variations in width, direction, and the like.

Challenge Have students pantomime the action lines in each other's drawings.

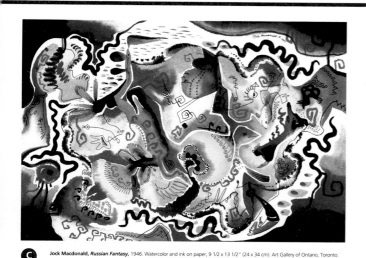

Jock Macdonald, *Russian Fantasy*, 1946. Watercolor and ink on paper, 9 1/2 x 13 1/2" (24 x 34 cm). Art Gallery of Ontario, Toronto.

Look at the colorful lines and shapes in picture C. Some of the lines are wavy or wiggly. Some of the lines loop or zigzag. Why do these lines create a feeling of motion? What else did the artist want you to see?

Practice drawing lines that show motion. What lines might show the motion of a jet plane? a jazzy dance? a grasshopper? a snake?

After you practice, draw a picture filled with "action" lines. You might repeat one action line many times. You might draw a variety of action lines.

13

Extensions ▼

Language Arts Have students find thesaurus entries for line and motion and develop vocabulary lists or web diagrams. Have other students listen to television broadcasts, especially sports reports, and write down the adjectives used to describe motion. Ask the rest of the students to investigate terms used by dancers to describe motion. Have the class apply the terms to describe visual qualities that imply motion.

Literature Link
• *The Flame of Peace: A Tale of the Aztecs,* Deborah Nourse Lattimore. (A)
• *Old Black Fly,* Jim Aylesworth. (A)

CLOSE

Assess

2 As students begin, remind them to draw the action or motion, not the object. After they draw the motion, have them decide whether to fill the page with the same or with different kinds of action lines.

3 Have students finish their drawings by coloring in some of the shapes and spaces. Encourage them to choose colors that go with the action lines.

1 Ask students who have drawings that suggest very fast or very slow motions to stand in two groups and share their work by contrasting the line qualities. Continue with other categories, such as motion shown with curved or straight lines and motion shown with long or short lines.

2 Have students describe what they have learned. Reinforce the lesson concepts as needed. (Lines are records of paths of motion. Lines in an artwork can express action or motion.)

Cleanup

1 Reinforce positive roles and responsibilities for cleanup and the reasons for these procedures.

RESOURCES

Large Reproductions
   Spiral Dance, Howell-Sickles, 16
   Toto, Romero, 20

Overhead Transparencies
   Emptying the Fridge, Mandel, 15

 CD-ROM
   2, *Elements of Design,* Lesson 1

Assessment Masters
   What Do You See?, 1

Aesthetic Awareness

Have students look for pictures that show or imply movement (objects forming a line, telephone lines disappearing in the distance, waves, a flock of birds). Discuss how the lines or linear arrangements give a sense of motion (lead the eye from one place to another).

13

4 Shapes and Spaces
Cutting Stencils

Almost everything you see has one main shape. Look at the trees in picture A. Can you name the main shapes? How are the main shapes in picture B alike? How are they different?

In art, the first shapes you see are called **positive shapes**. The background shapes are called **negative shapes**.

The negative shapes in an artwork can be just as important as the positive shapes. Look at pictures C and D. Find the vase in both of them. Can you also see two faces? Why?

14

PREPARE

Objectives

Students will:
- perceive interactions between positive and negative shapes in familiar contexts and in optical illusions.
- prepare for a printing activity by cutting positive and negative shapes for stencils.

Materials

pencils

scissors

stencil paper, 6 x 9" (15 x 23 cm), 2 per student (See Setup)

Vocabulary

positive shape	*forma positiva*
main shape	*forma más importante*
negative shape	*forma negativa*
background shapes	*formas del fondo*

Setup

Stencil paper is stiff and water resistant. You can substitute a file folder or a large index card. Cut a simple stencil for the class to see. Throughout this lesson, the terms positive and negative can be used to refer to shapes, areas, or spaces.

TEACH

Engage

1 Ask students if they have ever seen a tree that looks like a triangle (some pine trees) or a circle (some maple trees). Explain that many things in nature seem to have one main shape that is easy to see. Artists call these *positive shapes.*

2 Ask students if they have ever looked through the leaves of a tree to see patches of blue sky. Explain that the blue sky is a background, or *negative shape.* Most people see a negative shape (patches of sky) after they see the positive shape (clusters of leaves).

Explore

1 Focus on **A**. Help students see the positive, or main, shape in each treetop. The shapes are triangle, circle, square, oval, and rectangle. Focus on **B**. Guide students to notice the variety of insect shapes and how the white background helps us see each positive shape.

2 Focus on **C** and **D**. Each picture can be seen as a vase or as two faces. Explain that **C** and **D** show that background shapes (white faces in **C**; dark faces in **D**) can be just as important as main shapes.

3 Focus on **E**. Have students identify the birds and fish. Most will discover the white fish shapes between the black bird shapes or the black bird shapes between the white fish shapes (easily seen in center rows).

4 Set the stage for the activity. Hold up your stencil and identify the main shape (cutout piece) and background shape (the rest of the stencil paper). Ask students to preview Lesson 5 to see how the stencil will be used.

M.C. Escher, *Sky and Water I,* 1938. Woodcut, 17 3/8 x 17 3/8" (44 x 44 cm). Collection Haags Gemeentemuseum, the Hague.

Artists plan the positive and negative shapes in their artwork. Sometimes the main and background shapes are like parts of a puzzle. Can you find the positive and negative shapes in picture E?

Cut some positive shapes from paper. Save all of your background or negative shapes. You will use all your shapes in the next lesson.

15

INTEGRATING THE CURRICULUM

Extensions

Science Hang a sheet across the front of the room. Place a strong light behind it (projector lamp) and hold various objects between the lamp and the sheet. Move the objects gradually toward the sheet so students can see the shadows (silhouettes). Have them identify and discuss the objects as positive shapes.

Social Studies Study Javanese shadow puppets. Using the same setup as above, have students put on a shadow-puppet play using paper shapes cut from stiff paper. Tape the shapes to thin sticks or wire. Place a desk or table in front of the sheet to create the effect of a stage.

Literature Link
• *The Trek,* Ann Jonas. (A)
• *Opt: An Illusionary Tale,* Arline and Joseph Baum. (A,S)
• *Visual Magic,* David Thomson. (A)

Create

1 Explain that students will draw the outline of a positive shape in the center of the stencil paper. They will carefully cut it out and save both the positive shape (the cutout) and the negative shape (the rest of the paper). Shapes must be simple and cut from the center.

2 Discuss ideas for positive shapes: fish, birds, insects, cars, planes, boats, flowers, hearts, clouds, and so on. Create simple symmetrical shapes (hearts, flowers, butterflies) by folding the paper, drawing half of the shape, and then cutting it from the center of the fold.

3 Distribute materials, except scissors. Have students draw their shapes. Check that the shapes are simple enough to cut.

4 Distribute scissors. Demonstrate how to press the tip of one blade into a line to start a cut. Make sure the negative shape is saved along with the positive shape and that both remain flat. Save stencils for the next lesson.

CLOSE

Assess

1 Hold up some of the shapes. Ask students to identify positive shapes and negative shapes.

Cooperative Learning

Ask students to find and sketch designs that have positive and negative shapes. Examples are easily found in traffic signs, simple emblems on uniforms or trucks, and TV images that identify channels. Have students discuss some similarities and differences in the designs and their uses.

RESOURCES

Large Reproductions
  Serenade, Bearden, 22
  Sun Mask, Native American, 12
  Three Musicians, Picasso, 4

Overhead Transparencies
  Goldfish Bowl II, Lichtenstein, 13

 CD-ROM
  2, *Elements of Design*, Lesson 2

Assessment Masters
  A Pattern Puzzle, 2

5 Spaces with Shapes
Stencil Printing

PREPARE

Objectives

Students will:
- understand the basic principles of stencil printing.
- collaborate with other students to create a picture with stenciled elements.

Vocabulary

print	*impresión*
printing	*imprimir (imprimiendo)*
positive shape	*forma positiva*
negative shape	*forma negativa*
stencil	*matriz/plantilla*
space	*espacio*
overlap	*sobreponer*
stipple	*punteado*

Setup

Place several spoonfuls of paint of different colors in divided trays or small containers for three or four students to share. Place a sponge brush in each color.

Materials

stencils from Lesson 4

tempera paint (See Setup)

sponge brushes (as shown in student text) or bristle brushes, 1 per color

newsprint paper, 9 x 12" (23 x 30 cm), 1 per student

paper for prints, 18 x 24" (46 x 61 cm), 1 per 2 or 3 students

newspapers

smocks

scissors

stencil paper, 6 x 9" (15 x 23 cm), several per student

You can make a stencil print. A **stencil** is made by cutting a positive shape from stiff paper. The stiff paper with the hole is your stencil. It can be used many times for printing.

Stencils can be used to print on paper or cloth. The traffic arrows on roads are made with large stencils. Where else have you seen stencil printing?

A

C

You can print a stencil with paint and a sponge. Gently press down on the sponge. Do you see how the paint should look?

B

16

TEACH

Engage

1. Hold up two stencil shapes from Lesson 4. Demonstrate how to use each one as a stencil to make a print. Gently dab paint through the stencil with the cutout main shape. Show how to use the second stencil. Place it on paper and dab paint around the edges.

2. Explain that stencils like these are often used to print lettering and simple pictures for signs, posters, or shipping containers. They can also be used to create artwork.

Meeting Individual Needs

Simplify Have students color inside stencil shapes with crayons or oil pastels.

Challenge Set up an area for independent and group work using stencils. Students can cut stencils and use them to print booklet covers.

Explore

1. Call on volunteers to explain **A** and **B**. Ask them to gesture the gentle motion required to print stencil shapes, as shown in **B**.

2. Focus on **C**. Ask students for additional examples of stencil printing (store signs, hobby, signs on trucks).

3. Ask students to point to shapes in **D** that were created with the stencils in **E**. Note how the two shapes of pine trees were cut from a folded paper, making the left and right sides the same (symmetrical).

4. Review how stencil shapes can be used: dabbing paint through the hole or around the outside edge.

5. Guide students to see how some of the stencils used in **D** have been *overlapped* (one printed on top of another) to give a feeling of near and distant space.

Create

1. Have small groups of students think of an idea for a collaborative stencil picture using a theme such as: Deep in the forest we saw . . . ; In the midst of the city we saw . . . ; On a distant planet we discovered . . .

2. Distribute materials for additional stencils; then place the scissors aside.

3. Distribute materials for printing. Use the newsprint paper for practice. Stress that a stencil print should look light and soft.

Community Awareness

Many T-shirts have designs made by silkscreen printing. Ask artists who work for a local company to visit your class and show examples of the screens, stencils, and designs. Students will learn that a different stencil is made for each color.

16

D Student artwork.

Stencils can help you make a picture with repeated shapes. You can make stencil prints with paint, chalk or crayons.

You can combine stencils to make a picture. Four children used stencils to make picture D. What parts of the picture did they print first? Why do you think so? They also printed negative shapes. Do you know how?

E

17

INTEGRATING THE CURRICULUM

Extensions

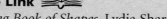

Social Studies Some of the oldest stencil prints are in prehistoric cave paintings in France, created about 15,000 years ago. A human hand was placed on the wall and soot or colored earth applied around it. In countries such as Tibet, stencils are used to print multicolored prayer cards.

In the American colonies, wallpaper was printed with stencils. Students can read *The Pennsylvania Dutch: Craftsmen and Farmers* by Eva Deutsch Costabel (Atheneum Press, 1986), which shows how Dutch settlers used stencils to decorate objects.

Literature Link
• *The Amazing Book of Shapes,* Lydia Sharman. (I)
• *Ed Emberley's Picture Pie 2: A Drawing Book and Stencil,* Ed Emberley. (A,I)
• *The Animals: Selected Poems,* Michio Mado. Translated by the Empress Michiko of Japan. (A)

4 Offer these technique tips:
  • Press the sponge on newspaper several times.
  • Apply paint with a very gentle straight up-and-down motion called *stippling.*
  • If paint runs under the stencil, wipe it off and use less paint.

5 Discuss problems and solutions in the practice prints. (Make sure the stencil is flat. Hold the stencil so it doesn't move.)

6 Have groups begin a final stencil print on the larger paper. Encourage them to print light colors first and dark colors last. Remind them to show how shapes are near or far in space by overlapping them.

CLOSE

Assess

1 Ask students in each group to comment on their choice of subject matter and specific effects, such as the use of repeated or overlapped shapes and the light and airy quality of the edges.

2 Call on students to identify positive shapes in their pictures. Ask any students who printed negative shapes to point out the effect (the outline of the shape is stippled; the interior does not have paint).

Cleanup

1 Make sure names are on artwork. Place prints, unstacked, on a flat surface to dry.

2 Press sponge brushes on newspaper to clean excess paint. Collect paint and brushes.

3 Place stencils inside folded newspaper. Collect newspapers.

RESOURCES

Large Reproductions
  Upstream, Kuniyoshi, 10
  Interior, Matisse, 17

Overhead Transparencies
  First Steps, Picasso, 16

CD-ROM
  2, *Elements of Design,* Lesson 2

Slide Set
  Young Curlew, Mungitok, 3

Assessment Masters
  City Skylines, 10

Technology

A stencil print is related to a professionally made silkscreen print, or serigraph. The stencils in a serigraph are adhered to silk or organdy stretched on a frame. Printer's ink is pressed through the silk, a separate stencil for each color. Artists' prints, fabrics, and decorative papers are often printed by this process.

PREPARE

Objectives

Students will:
- be aware of symmetrical balance and visual rhythm as principles of design that can unify an artwork.
- choose a theme and create a collage with evidence of visual rhythm and symmetry.

Vocabulary

shape	*forma*
similar	*similar/semejante*
identical	*idéntico(a)*
collage	*collage*
rhythm	*ritmo*
balance	*equilibrio*
symmetry	*simetría*

Materials

lightweight colored paper, 9 x 12" (23 x 30 cm), 2 or 3 per student

scraps of colored paper

scissors

pencils

colored paper for background, 12 x 18" (30 x 46 cm), 1 per student

paste

damp paper towels

A Henri Matisse, *Large Composition With Masks*, 1953. Paper on canvas (collage), 139 1/4 x 392 1/2" (354 x 997 cm). © 1992 National Gallery of Art, Washington, DC (Ailsa Mellon Bruce Fund).

Have you ever created a collage? A **collage** is a picture made from paper shapes. Henri Matisse created this large collage.

Henri Matisse liked to cut paper without drawing the shapes first. He cut out many shapes for each collage. He tried different ways to arrange shapes. When he liked a design, he pasted the shapes down.

Many of the shapes in this collage are identical, or exactly alike. Can you find some of them? Can you find shapes that are similar but not identical?

18

TEACH

Engage

1 Allow time for students to look at **A** by Henri Matisse. Explain that students will create a collage today. (Students were introduced to collage at Levels 1 and 2.)

2 Have students locate some identical shapes in **A**. Explain that shapes can be very similar, but have small differences. Have students locate shapes in **A** which are similar, but not identical, to each other.

Meeting Individual Needs

Simplify Guide students step by step through both methods of cutting identical shapes.

Challenge In a second collage, fold and cut shapes from colored tissue paper. Lightly brush diluted white glue on background paper and brush the top of the shape. Compare the effects of the media and techniques used in each collage.

Explore

1 Ask students to speculate on the messages the artist sends through colors and shapes. Encourage personal responses. Explain that Matisse loved to work with bright colors and repeated shapes. Many of the shapes resemble leaves and flowers. Two faces seem to look out at you and smile.

2 Have students identify symmetrically balanced elements. Guide them to point out visual rhythms of repeating colors and shapes. For example, at the top, short angular shapes seem to move in a marching rhythm toward the center. The flowers seem to be dancing together. At the bottom, small "t" shapes create a skipping rhythm.

3 Discuss **B**. Demonstrate the two methods of cutting identical shapes. Show how one of the shapes can be trimmed slightly so it is similar, but no longer identical, to the other shapes.

Create

1 Explain that students will cut and paste shapes for a collage. The shapes should be easy to cut without being drawn first. Have students name shapes they might cut out: leaves, insects, birds, fish, and other shapes. Remind students that Matisse cut simple shapes without drawing them.

2 Distribute materials. Encourage students to vary the size and color of shapes and trim the edges of some so they are similar, but not identical.

This collage has symmetry. **Symmetry** means that the left and right sides of the design are alike, or equally balanced.

This collage also has visual rhythms. **Visual rhythms** are planned by repeating shapes, colors and spaces. How are visual rhythms like rhythms in dance or music?

Make a collage. Plan a design that has symmetry and visual rhythms. Learn to cut identical shapes from thin paper.

B Fold one paper twice.

 Fold two papers once.

19

INTEGRATING THE CURRICULUM

Extensions ▼

Language Arts Read *Meet Matisse* by Nelly Munthe (Little, Brown and Co., 1983) over an extended period of time to allow for discussion. This is a rich source of information about Matisse.

Music Have students listen to music with a strong beat and clap hands to the rhythm. A definition for rhythm in music is a repetition (pattern) of regular or irregular pulses caused by strong and weak beats. A definition for rhythm in art is the repetition of a particular element (e.g., color, line, or shape) at regular or irregular intervals. Ask students to demonstrate how rhythms in dance can be planned.

Literature Link
- *The Mountain That Loved a Bird,* Alice McLerran. (A)
- *The Stone-cutter: A Japanese folk tale* adapted by Gerald McDermott. (A)

CLOSE

3 Have students try several symmetrical arrangements of shapes before they use paste. Arrangements will be easiest to see and change if students stand. Small shapes might be pasted on top of large ones (overlap). Encourage attention to spacing between shapes and location of colors.

4 Check that students have a symmetrical plan and have tried to create visual rhythms by repeating colors, shapes, and spaces. Remind students to use damp paper towels to wipe paste from hands before pressing shapes.

Assess

1 Ask students to describe what they have learned. Ask questions to stimulate recall of the meanings of symmetry and visual rhythms.

2 Call on volunteers to share their work. Provide a model for thoughtful conversation and questioning. Explain that thoughtful conversation helps everyone learn to improve an artwork and solve problems. Ask students to suggest other ideas for thoughtful conversation (listening, asking questions, giving reasons for answers).

Technology

In most settings where technology is important, there is concern for efficiency. In this lesson, students practiced an efficient way to cut identical shapes. Relate the concept of efficiency—doing something accurately and rapidly—to other tasks at home and school.

RESOURCES

Large Reproductions
Sun Mask, Native American, 12
Sioux Vest, 3

Overhead Transparencies
Cabinet, Boulle, 6
Early Sunday Morning, Hopper, 24

CD-ROM
2, *Elements of Design*, Lesson 5

Slide Set
Ambaradam, Dorazio, 2

Assessment Masters
A Pattern Puzzle, 2
Using an Artist's Colors, 3

19

7 Seeing and Touching Textures
Rubbing Collage

Objectives

Students will:
- compare and contrast visual and tactile textures and understand that rubbings of textured surfaces can be artworks.
- create a collage of multicolor crayon rubbings and the textures from which they were made.

Vocabulary

rough	*áspero(a)*
smooth	*liso(a)*
rubbing	*calco*
crayon resist	*crayón indeleble*
visual texture	*textura que se percibe con la vista*
tactile texture	*textura que se percibe con el tacto*

Setup

Cut textured materials into 4" (10 cm) squares so students can glue them to construction paper. Have an ample supply of textured surfaces.

Materials

unwrapped and broken oil pastels or crayons, several dark colors per student

typing or newsprint paper, 6 x 9" (15 x 23 cm), 8 per student

assorted materials with a distinctive texture (pieces of corduroy, burlap, yarn, lace, leaves, feathers, sandpaper, etc.)

colored construction paper, 12 x 18" (30 x 46 cm), 1 per student

scissors

white glue

damp paper towels

Textures can be rough or smooth, bumpy or silky. You can feel textures by touching objects. You can see textures by making a **rubbing**. To make a rubbing, put paper over a surface that has bumps or grooves. Hold the paper still. Rub the paper with the flat side of a pencil point, crayon or oil pastel.

Max Ernst's rubbing, in picture A, shows the texture of pieces of thread. He said the lines looked like lava flowing from a volcano. What other textures do you see in his rubbing?

Artist Eva Ruiz created the artwork in picture B. It is a collage made from rubbings of a floor. She taped paper to the floor. She rubbed the paper with two colors of crayon.

20

Engage

1 Define *texture* as the roughness or smoothness of an object, such as the soft hair of a kitten or stiff bristles of a brush. Explain that there are two ways of identifying texture. One is by touching the surface (*tactile texture*). Have students touch and describe the texture of hair, clothes, skin, and shoes.

2 A second way of identifying texture is by using your eyes (*visual texture*). Give examples such as seeing a fluffy cloud or sharp spikes on a cactus without touching them.

Aesthetic Awareness

Tell students they will make a mystery texture bag. Provide small paper bags for each student. Have them secretly collect items that have varied textures. Have students exchange bags and try to guess the mystery objects by feeling them.

Explore

1 Focus on **A**. Explain that the artist, Max Ernst, put paper over loose threads on a floor and rubbed it with a pencil to make a record of textures. This kind of art is called a *rubbing* (in French, *frottage*). The textures of the threads suggested lava flowing from volcanoes. Ask students where they see the texture of the floor. Ernst liked to experiment with textural qualities of materials. He did not invent frottage, but helped stimulate its use for artwork.

2 The artwork in **B** combines records of textures made by rubbing surfaces of the floor. Explain the additional steps the artist used for assembling the rubbings in a collage. Ask students what the title might mean. Accept a variety of thoughtful answers.

3 Focus on **C**. Ask students to notice that each rubbing has two colors. The best rubbings are arranged in a collage next to the tactile surfaces. Explain that students will make rubbings, choose the best ones, and create a collage with visual and tactile textures.

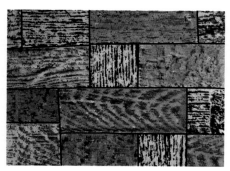

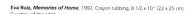
Eva Ruiz, *Memories of Home*, 1992. Crayon rubbing, 8 1/2 x 10" (22 x 25 cm). Courtesy of the artist.

C Student artwork.

Eva Ruiz brushed watery paint on her best rubbings. The paint rolled away from the wax crayon. This process is called **crayon resist**. When the paint dried, she made the collage.

A student created the artwork in picture C. He collected scraps of cloth, string and textured paper.

Then he made rubbings. His rubbings show the visual textures. The objects he glued down have tactile textures. **Tactile** means a texture you know by using your sense of touch.

21

INTEGRATING THE CURRICULUM

Extensions ▼ ▼

Language Arts Have students make and illustrate vocabulary cards for words that describe textures. Have them group related examples (e.g., smooth, silky, slick). Encourage them to use these terms in storytelling and in other activities.

Science Provide students with a variety of leaves, long grasses, and other natural objects. Have them make rubbings using white crayon or oil pastel and black paper. Suggest that students repeat the rubbing until the entire paper is covered. Discuss the results as a record of textures that can be viewed as artwork as well as a display for science.

Literature Link
• *Where the Forest Meets the Sea*, Jeannie Baker. (A)
• *Red Leaf, Yellow Leaf*, Lois Ehlert. (A)
• *Snowsong Whistling*, Karen E. Lotz. (A)

CLOSE

Create

1 Distribute materials. Explain and demonstrate how to make a record of textures.
  • Place paper on top of a flat, textured surface, such as a leaf.
  • Hold paper so it won't slip.
  • Rub the side of a dark crayon over the paper in long, even strokes.
  • Use another color to rub the surface again.

2 Have students make rubbings of textured surfaces. When students have several effective rubbings, have them trim and glue the rubbings down next to the actual material from which the rubbings were made. Make sure heavy materials are firmly attached.

Assess

1 Review the concepts in the lesson. Call on volunteers to show their collages, pointing out the most unusual visual and tactile textures.

2 Have students choose and help to display the clearest and most unusual collages.

RESOURCES

Large Reproductions
  Toto, Romero, 20
  Wolf General, Blackwell, 21
  Bear's Lair, Markovitz, 1

Overhead Transparencies
  The Goldfish, Klee, 13

CD-ROM
  2, *Elements of Design*, Lesson 3

Assessment Masters
  Find Out About Art, 20

8 Invented Textures
Drawing

PREPARE

Objectives

Students will:
- appreciate that artists use lines inventively in varied media to suggest textures and patterns.
- create a drawing of an animal using lines inventively to suggest textures and patterns.

Vocabulary

lines	*líneas*
textures	*texturas*
patterns	*diseños*
media	*medios*

Materials

viewfinders

choice of at least 2 drawing media

white drawing paper, 9 x 12" (23 x 30 cm) or 12 x 18" (30 x 46 cm), 1 per student

(optional) photographs of animals

Have you ever seen or touched the textures of a real hog? Look at picture A. Does the texture of this hog look rough or smooth? silky or prickly? What lines help you see the texture?

Sometimes artists use lines to show textures and **patterns**. Look at the cat in picture B. The striped pattern has many thin lines in rows. The thin lines also remind you of the texture of fur. What animals have you seen with patterns and textures?

22

TEACH

Engage

1 Discuss students' experiences with animals, focusing on textures of fur, feathers, and skin (prickly porcupine quills, rough elephant hide, soft puppy fur). Identify animals that have obvious patterns, such as zebras and tigers (stripes) and leopards (spots). Explain that students will learn how artists show texture and pattern in drawings of animals.

Cooperative Learning

Have students work in small groups to identify textures in some of the artworks in their texts. Ask each group to choose one work, list words that describe the textures, and then share their lists with the class. Encourage everyone to suggest improvements in each list.

Explore

1 Focus on **A**. Explain that a real hog has very thick and bristly hair. Rembrandt has shown the texture by using long and short lines close together. Many of the lines overlap or cross each other to make small patterns. Have students place their viewfinders over **A** to see these variations in line qualities.

2 Discuss **B**. Help students use viewfinders to see the tiny lines in rows that suggest the pattern of stripes. Note how lines also suggest the texture of hair, especially at the edge of ears, head, back, tail, and leg.

3 Focus on **C**. Guide students to see lines that suggest long prickly quills in the drawing of the porcupine by Amanda Larraz. Contrast these lines with the shorter ones that suggest hog bristles in **A**.

The drawing in picture C shows the spiky texture of a porcupine. What lines create the feeling of a rough texture?

Think of a real or imaginary animal to draw. Experiment with different ways to draw the textures and patterns of the animal. Use a pencil, marker or crayon. You might combine some of these drawing **media**. When you make your drawing, use what you learned from your experiments.

23

Extensions ▼ ▼

Language Arts Have students write a story about the animal they drew. Remind them to describe the animal using art terms they have learned. Have students read the stories and show the drawings to a class of younger students.

Science Have students bring in a large leaf. Place viewfinders over one part of the leaf and observe lines, patterns, and textures. Have students create a large drawing of the section seen in the viewfinder. If you have magnifiers available, use them instead of viewfinders.

Literature Link
• *The Eagle's Song: A Tale from the Pacific Northwest* adapted by Kristina Rodanas. (A)
• *Animals should definitely not wear clothing*, Judi Barrett. (A)
• *Animals should definitely not act like people*, Judi Barrett. (A)

CLOSE

Create

1 Discuss animals students might draw and special textures or patterns they might show. Encourage students to choose an animal with a texture they can vividly remember. If students have not had much experience with animals, suggest they draw an imaginary creature of the sea, sky, earth, or another planet. Textures or patterns will be easier to show if the animal is drawn quite large.

2 Distribute materials. Have students use one side of the paper for experiments with drawing media and inventing lines that suggest texture (shaggy, downy, fuzzy, prickly) and patterns (stripes, spots, wavy, zigzag).

3 As students begin drawing on the other side of the paper, encourage them to imagine they could touch or stroke the animal and feel hairs, fur, feathers, etc. Help them remember that lines might be light or dark, thick or thin, wavy or zigzag.

Assess

1 Have students place viewfinders over their drawings and look at the lines. Call on students to describe some of them (thick, thin, curved, straight, etc.).

2 Have volunteers hold up their drawings. Discuss the use of lines to suggest textures and patterns of real or imaginary animals. Contrast and compare the qualities of lines created in different media.

RESOURCES

Large Reproductions
    Toto, Romero, 20
    Wolf General, Blackwell, 21
    Golden Age, Brown, 6
    Spiral Dance, Howell-Sickles, 16

Overhead Transparencies
    Le Jockey, Toulouse-Lautrec, 9

CD-ROM
    2, *Elements of Design*, Lesson 3
    5, *People and Animals*, Lessons 2 and 3

Slide Set
    Young Curlew, Mungitok, 3

Assessment Masters
    Comparing Two Artworks, 19

9 Prints About Animals
Monoprinting

A North American Indian artist created the artwork in picture A. The artist's ancestors are Hopi and Choctaw Indians. Her ancestors taught her to respect nature. The animal-like **symbol** stands for the spirit of many animals. The background suggests the motion of wind and stars in the sky.

This artwork is a **monoprint**. Mono means one. The artist made only one print like this one.

A monoprint is made by following several steps. First you put ink or paint on a smooth sheet of metal or plastic. Then you wipe away some of the ink or paint to create lines and textures.

24

PREPARE

Objectives

Students will:
• understand the special qualities of prints made by the technique of monoprinting.
• create a monoprint that portrays an animal as a symbol for an idea.

Vocabulary

printing	*grabado*
monoprint	*monograbado*
symbol	*símbolo*

Safety Notes

Printing plates must not have sharp edges.

Materials

thick tempera or finger paint in dark colors, 1 container per 2 students (add 1 drop of liquid soap to tempera paint)

plastic inking plates, 1 per student

paintbrushes

newsprint paper, slightly larger than inking plate, 2 per student

newspapers to cover desks

smocks

damp paper towels

scrap paper

tools to remove ink (cotton swabs, pencils with erasers, facial tissues)

TEACH

Engage

1 Review the process of making crayon rubbings from Lesson 7. Explain that rubbings are a simple form of printmaking. The rubbing is a record, or print, of a textured surface.

2 Ask students if they know about monoprinting (introduced at Levels 1 and 2). Tell them you will demonstrate the basic steps. Half the class will observe while the other half discusses the text and images. Then you will switch groups and demonstrate again.

Meeting Individual Needs

Simplify For greater control, use water-based printing ink and a brayer to roll ink on a plate.

Challenge Use colored paper and colored inks to make a series of related prints. Introduce the term *suite* to describe a set of related artworks.

Explore

1 As you demonstrate, talk about your thought process. For example:
  • "It is very important to begin with a solid, even coat of paint."
  • "I've cut this shape for an animal, and I'm putting it over the paint. It will be white in the print."
  • "Now I'm using a tissue to wipe away some of the paint for clouds."
  • "Now I'm suggesting grass with this eraser."

2 Carefully lay paper on top of the paint. Make a fist and gently rub the paper from the center outward to each corner. When you see a faint design on the side you are rubbing, the paper is ready to lift up. This step is called *pulling the print.*

3 Guide students to see the textured background and thick and thin lines in **A**. Ask them to give examples of animals as symbols (sly as a fox, slow as a turtle, strong as an ox, and so on).

4 In **B**, note the use of cut and torn paper for shapes and other areas that suggest textures and details.

Student artwork.

While the ink or paint is wet, put a full sheet of paper over the whole design. Rub the whole paper to press the ink or paint onto it.

A student made the monoprint in picture B. He used a cotton swab to create lines for the fence and grass. He placed the paper shapes on top of the wet ink. What did he do next? Why?

1. Create your design in wet paint or ink.

2. Place paper over the design. Rub it all over.

3. Lift the paper. This is called pulling the print.

25

INTEGRATING THE CURRICULUM

Extensions ▼ ▼

Social Studies Refer to lessons on Native American art in the text. Guide students to determine which works were created before 1900 and which were created more recently. Help them identify dates in the credit lines. Provide additional information about the relationship of the older works to regional influences and ways of life of specific tribes or nations.

Language Arts Have students obtain library books that include stories, poems, myths, or legends in which animals are symbols for ideas or human traits. Guide students to appreciate that many cultural groups use animals as symbols. Have them identify contemporary examples as seen in names for sports teams, automobiles, and other products.

Literature Link
• *Dancing Teepees: Poems of American Indian Youth,* selected by Virginia Driving Hawk Sneve. (A)
• *Star Boy,* retold by Paul Goble. (S)
• *Moon Song,* Byrd Baylor. (A)

CLOSE

Create

1 Discuss and list ideas for monoprinting using animals as a symbol. Encourage students to plan their designs.

2 Distribute materials. Provide technique reminders as needed. Students must begin their prints before paint dries. Emphasize that the printing paper must be thoroughly rubbed before the print is pulled.

Art Criticism

Have students look at the artwork in Lessons 20, 21, and 49. In each work, animals serve as symbols for ideas or traits in human experience. Guide students to contrast and compare meanings of the animals in relation to their own experiences.

Assess

1 Have students describe what they have learned. Discuss some prints in relation to technique and symbolism. Be generous in praise for students' efforts. Have them identify problems they had and explain how they were (or might be) solved.

Cleanup

1 Place artwork, unstacked, on a flat surface to dry.

2 Collect brushes and paints.

3 Have students help each other slip the printing plate inside newspaper to blot up excess paint.

4 Collect inking plates.

RESOURCES

Large Reproductions
  Golden Age, Brown, 6
  Bear's Lair, Markovitz, 1
  Spiral Dance, Howell-Sickles, 16
  Interior, Matisse, 17

Overhead Transparencies
  Salmon Clan Hat, Tlingit Tribe, 14

 CD-ROM
  2, *Elements of Design,* Lessons 1 and 3
  5, *People and Animals,* Lessons 2 and 3

Assessment Masters
  Mix and Match, 12

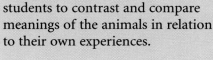

25

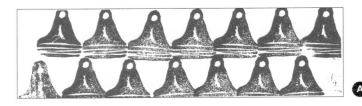

Artists plan patterns for fabrics, wallpaper and other flat **surfaces**. Look around your room for patterns. How can you tell if the designs make a pattern?

Printing is one way to **repeat** a design and create a pattern. The designs in this lesson were made with printing stamps.

An artist printed these designs on paper. She made the printing stamp from clay.

26

PREPARE

Objectives

Students will:
- perceive and describe repeated patterns on printed surfaces.
- create a clay stamp and use it to print a repeated pattern.

Vocabulary

print
printmaking
pattern
surface design

imprima (imprimir)
técnicas de grabado
diseño repetido
diseño sobre una
superficil

Setup

To make stamp pads, place layers of damp paper towels or a thin sponge in a divided frozen-dinner tray or plastic picnic plate. Add a drop of liquid soap to paint. Spread a spoonful on each pad.

Materials

colored construction paper, 12 x 18" (30 x 46 cm), 1 per student

newsprint paper, 9 x 12" (23 x 30 cm), 1 per student

oil-based clay, ⅛ lb. (57 gm) per student

gadgets (toothpicks, paper clips, nuts, twigs, seashells)

stamp pads, 1 per 2 or 4 students (See Setup)

tempera paint

newspapers for desks

damp paper towels

examples of patterned cloth or paper

smocks

TEACH

Engage

1 Discuss and have students identify examples of patterns in their clothing as well as in the classroom. Ask them to point out repeated elements (line, color, shape, etc.), emphasizing rows and even spacing.

2 Show your examples of patterns. Explain that artists plan these and other patterns printed on wrapping paper, wallpaper, and fabric. This artwork is called *surface design*.

3 Review the terms print and printing as used in art. *Printing* means making many copies of a picture or design. The *print* is the finished artwork.

Explore

1 Focus on **A**, **B**, and **D**. Guide students to see that varied patterns are arranged in rows. In **A**, the point of the bell is carefully placed below the bells in the first row. The stamp in **C** is rotated a half turn to create the pattern in **B**. The patterns in **D** are arranged between folds of paper.

2 Explain that each student will make a clay printing stamp similar to the one in **C**. Students will use the printing stamp to create patterns on paper.

3 Call on volunteers to explain the step-by-step illustrations in **D**.

Create

1 Distribute materials. Explain that students will use newsprint to make test prints of their printing stamps and to try out patterns for larger sheets of paper.

2 Provide guidance as students shape clay into a stamp and press objects into the clay. Have them fold the newsprint, then flatten the paper, and try printing various patterns.

Meeting Individual Needs

Simplify Print small pieces of wood, Styrofoam, corks, and the like instead of making clay stamps.

Challenge Review the concept of patterns in music (such as ABAB) or in numbers (such as 1, 2, 2, 1; 1, 2, 2, 1). Have students print visual parallels to fit such patterns.

C

Look at the design in picture B. Imagine you were printing it with the stamp in picture C. How could you print the stamp in even rows? Could you create other patterns from the same stamp? How?

D Student artwork.

Students made printing stamps from clay. They made covers for booklets. You can make and print a clay stamp.

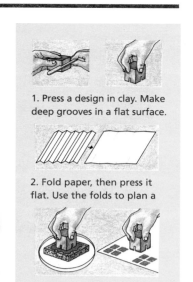

1. Press a design in clay. Make deep grooves in a flat surface.

2. Fold paper, then press it flat. Use the folds to plan a

3. Press your stamp on a pad, then print it.

INTEGRATING THE CURRICULUM

Extensions ▼

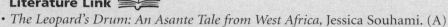

Social Studies Acquaint students with varied historical uses of stamplike designs. For example, in the ancient civilization of Mesopotamia, clay stamps were used to record transactions (like receipts). Asian rulers used stamps carved in wood to identify themselves as authors of written materials or owners of property. Single letters of the alphabet carved in stamplike form were used for printing books in medieval Europe. Modern rubber stamps are a recent version of a very old method of printing.

Literature Link
• *The Leopard's Drum: An Asante Tale from West Africa*, Jessica Souhami. (A)
• *The Amazing Book of Shapes*, Lydia Sharman. (I)

3 When students are ready, have them:
• set aside their test prints and begin printing on the larger paper.
• make folds and then reverse the folds slightly so paper is flat.
• use creases as guidelines for printing even rows.

As students finish, place prints, unstacked, on a flat surface to dry.

CLOSE

Assess

1 Hold up some of the prints. Ask students to identify the plan for printing the pattern. For example, the stamp was printed on (or between) the folds. The stamp was printed in a different position across the row. The color yellow is repeated twice. Then you see blue and then yellow again.

Cleanup

1 Ask everyone to help clean the clay by pressing the printing stamp on newspaper to remove excess paint.

2 Collect reusable gadgets.

3 After the lesson, wash clay and gadgets in soap and water.

4 Collect remaining materials.

RESOURCES

Large Reproductions
  Sioux Vest, 3
  Sun Mask, Native American, 12
  Interior, Matisse, 17

Overhead Transparencies
  Thanksgiving, Lee, 8

 CD-ROM
  2, *Elements of Design*, Lesson 4

Assessment Masters
  A Pattern Puzzle, 2
  Design a Pot, 14

Cultural Awareness

Stamps made of clay or wood are used today in decorating cloth. In Japan, beautiful kimonos are made with a pattern of deep-blue dye printed on white cloth. The patterns are so precisely done that one cannot tell where one single pattern begins or ends. Other traditions of hand-printed textiles are found in Indonesia, Thailand, India, Africa, and many Pacific islands.

11 Picture a Crowd
Drawing

PREPARE

Objectives

Students will:
- understand that a visual rhythm can be created by repeating and overlapping shapes.
- create a drawing using repeated overlapping shapes.

Vocabulary

rhythm	*ritmo*
repeated	*repetido*
overlap	*traslapo*

Materials

crayons or oil pastels

white drawing paper, 12 x 18" (30 x 46 cm), 1 per student

A. **William Doriani**, *Flag Day*, 1935. Oil on canvas, 12 1/4 x 35 5/8" (31 x 98 cm). Collection, The Museum of Modern Art, New York (The Sidney and Harriet Janis Collection).

Can you see the **visual rhythms** in this painting? Look for the repeated lines, colors and shapes. The repeated elements make a pattern. The pattern helps you to see the rhythm of the march.

Do you see how shapes of people in the first row overlap other shapes? **Overlap** means that some shapes are in front of other shapes. How do the shapes create a rhythm?

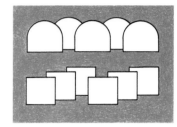

B

28

TEACH

Engage

1 Call on volunteers to demonstrate rhythms in music. Expand demonstration as needed to show different types and variations. Have volunteers demonstrate rhythmic body motions used in sports (e.g., swimming) or dance. Explain that students will learn how to see and create artworks with visual rhythms.

Meeting Individual Needs

Simplify Have students listen to various selections of music, move to the rhythm of the music, and draw lines that echo their movements.

Challenge If you have skills in music or creative movement, use additional improvisational techniques to develop the concepts in this lesson.

Explore

1 Focus on **A**. Have students identify the repeated elements (flags, people marching). Develop kinesthetic awareness by having students pose as a figure in the painting. Clap a rhythm and have them march in place.

2 Help students perceive the overlapping shapes in **A** and **B**. Make sure they see that the shapes behind others have parts hidden from view. Overlapping shapes can create visual rhythms that seem to move from bottom to top.

3 Have students identify some of the repeated and overlapped shapes in **C**. Note visual rhythms created by hats, scarves, and long knives. Explain that the painting by José Clemente Orozco shows a Mexican leader and his followers.

Creative Thinking

List on the chalkboard words that describe rhythmic motions (marching, galloping, skipping, hopping, etc.). Ask students in small groups to create and perform three variations on one of the words. They are to perform or demonstrate that rhythm through:
- body gestures with no sound.
- sounds such as clapping or tapping.
- drawing the rhythm on the chalkboard.

Discuss the performances and how they might be elaborated to create a dance, musical composition, or visual artwork.

An artist created the painting in picture C. Which shapes overlap? Can you find some visual rhythms?

Create a picture of many people, animals, cars or buildings. Overlap some of the shapes. Repeat some lines, colors and shapes to create a visual rhythm.

 José Clemente Orozco, **Zapatistas**, 1931. Oil on canvas, 45 x 55" (114 x 140 cm). Collection, The Museum of Modern Art, New York (Given anonymously).

29

INTEGRATING THE CURRICULUM

Extensions ▼ ▼

Science A nearby hospital or university science department might provide visual records of rhythmic motions of heartbeats (electrocardiographs) or electronic signals of brain waves (electroencephalographs). Collect illustrations of other visual rhythms in nature such as waves, wind-driven sand, animal tracks, etc.

Language Arts Read *Millions of Cats* by Wanda Gag (Putnam, 1977). Have students note how the illustrator used rhythmic patterns to create a visual story.

Literature Link
- *Yankee Doodle*, Dr. Richard Shackburg. (A)
- *Yankee Doodle*, Steven Kellogg. (A)
- *The Great Migration: An American Story*, Jacob Lawrence. (A)

CLOSE

Create

1 Distribute materials. Explain that students are to draw a picture with visual rhythms created by repeating and overlapping shapes. They will first draw large shapes near the bottom of the paper. They will then draw shapes behind the first ones.

2 Have students close their eyes. Ask them to imagine pictures filled with zillions of boats bobbing on waves, people cheering at a ball game, skyscrapers soaring toward the sky, fish swimming, and so on. Allow time for students to think of their own ideas. Stress originality; work should not be copied.

3 Have students begin. Remind them to:
- start near the bottom of the paper.
- fill the paper with the same or similar shapes.
- repeat colors so their picture will have a definite visual rhythm.

Assess

1 Discuss some of the drawings. Encourage students to describe repeated elements and identify overlapped shapes. Guide them to make gestures similar to the visual rhythms or to characterize the visual rhythms by using terms such as swaying, marching, galloping, looping, and bobbing.

RESOURCES

Large Reproductions
 Upstream, Kuniyoshi, 10
 Golden Age, Brown, 6
 Interior, Matisse, 17

Overhead Transparencies
 Parade, Lawrence, 12

 CD-ROM
 4, *Art Adventure*, Lesson 2

Slide Set
 Fourth Pennsylvania, Anonymous, 4

Assessment Masters
 Comparing Two Artworks, 19

PREPARE

Objectives

Students will:
- perceive and describe differences in the mood of artworks unified by warm and cool colors.
- create a drawing dominated by warm colors or cool colors, including warm or cool intermediate colors.

Vocabulary

warm colors	*colores cálidos*
cool colors	*colores fríos*
unity	*unidad*
intermediate colors	*colores intermedios*

Materials

crayons or oil pastels

white or manila drawing paper, 9 x 12" (23 x 30 cm), 1 per student

viewfinders

A **Anne Leone**, ***Water Series XI***, 1988. Oil on linen, 24 x 30" (48 x 76 cm). Private Collection, London, England. Courtesy of the artist.

What **hues**, or colors, do you see in this painting? Artists say hues are related, like members of a family. Most of the hues in this painting are **cool colors**.

Cool colors are blue, green and violet. **Related** cool **colors** are yellow-green, blue-green and blue-violet. Why are these colors called "cool?" How are the colors related?

Why did this artist use cool colors in her painting? Do you think the artist painted exactly what she saw?

30

TEACH

Engage

1 Explain that artworks can give people ideas about warm and cool feelings, objects, or places. Discuss students' experiences with very hot and very cold temperatures. Ask them to name some warm and cool colors (introduced at Levels 1 and 2), including intermediates, using the color wheel in Lesson 13.

2 Explain that warm and cool hues are sometimes called *color families* or *color schemes*. A color family is often chosen to create unity in an artwork. *Unity* means that all the parts are working together, like a team.

Explore

1 Focus on **A**. Help students imagine how it feels near a pond. Guide them to understand why cool colors (blues, greens, and violets) were used. Reasons can be:
- literal (a shaded pond might have these colors).
- expressive (the colors create a feeling of coolness).
- design (cool colors unify the painting so all the parts seem to go together).

2 Focus on **B**. Have students point out the warm colors. Guide them to see that using colors from one family helps unify the artwork and make it glow.

3 Explain that students will make a drawing about natural things. It should be unified by a warm or a cool color scheme. Have the class suggest some appropriate ideas for each color scheme. Examples for warm colors are roses, sunflowers, dandelions; canaries, cardinals; strawberries, oranges, lemons. Examples for cool colors are lilacs, orchids, hyacinths; parrots, peacocks; plums, blueberries.

Meeting Individual Needs

Simplify Have students identify artworks with warm and cool colors. If some students consistently fail to discriminate colors, refer them for color blindness testing.

Challenge Have students use colored paper as a background, choose a cool or warm color scheme, and develop a picture using colors to express a mood.

Most of the colors in this painting are warm hues. Warm colors are red, yellow and orange. Related warm colors are yellow-orange, red-orange and red-violet.

Many artists plan artworks around a "family" of related colors. You have learned about two families of colors: cool and warm.

A color family helps to give unity to an artwork. **Unity** means that things go together. Each painting is unified by using a family of related colors.

31

INTEGRATING THE CURRICULUM

Extensions ▼

Language Arts Have students refer to one of the artworks from this lesson. Using vocabulary they have learned, have students write a description of the work. The descriptions should include an explanation of how the mood of the work is related to the color family. Have them write a separate description of their own work.

Language Arts Explore phrases such as "I'm feeling blue" and "green with envy." Ask students to give examples of color-related words describing moods or feelings. Write the phrases in columns so students can compare and contrast warm and cool colors. Add a third category, called *neutral colors*, for brown, black, white, and gray. Stress the idea that colors are associated with our experiences in many ways.

Literature Link
• *The Night of the Whippoorwill,* Nancy Larrick. (A)
• *The Way To Start a Day,* Byrd Baylor. (A)

CLOSE

Create

1 Distribute materials. Remind students that intermediate colors can be mixed in two ways. Yellow covered with red will be orange. A slightly different orange can be made by coloring with red and then putting yellow on top. Combining colors such as orange with yellow or red creates more subtle colors.

2 While students are drawing, comment on their use of colors to create variations of the basic hues in each color scheme. Encourage them to express a mood or feeling by completing the background. One way is to show the coolness or warmth of the weather, time of day, or location of the scene.

Assess

1 Have students hold up the drawings dominated by warm colors. Call on volunteers to point out warm colors and explain why they chose them. Discuss drawings with cool colors in the same way.

2 Ask students why artists might choose warm or cool colors for their artwork (to give a feeling, to show colors they see, to unify an artwork). Encourage students to think of and discuss other reasons.

Reminder
For the next lesson, be sure to have tempera paint and other supplies.

13 Mixing Colors of Paint
Painting

PREPARE

Objectives

Students will:
- identify primary and secondary colors on the color wheel and in artwork.
- create a tempera painting using primary and secondary colors to portray a colorful landscape.

Vocabulary

primary colors	*colores primarios*
secondary colors	*colores secundarios*
paintbrush	*pincel*
landscape	*paisaje*

Setup

Refer to page Reference 12 for suggestions on preparing the classroom for painting. Before you teach the lesson, read Create. You might want to mix paint just as the students will.

Materials

tempera paint: red, yellow, blue, black, and white, in sets for several students to share

newsprint paper, 9 x 12" (23 x 30 cm), 1 per student

newsprint paper, 12 x 18" (30 x 46 cm), 1 per student

smocks

newspapers for desks

water containers

paintbrushes, 1 per student

sponges, cloths, or paper towels, 1 per student

A Claude Monet, *Poppy Field in a Hollow Near Giverny,* 1885. Oil on canvas, 25 5/8 x 32" (65 x 81 cm). The Museum of Fine Arts, Boston (Juliana Cheney Edwards Collection. Bequest of Robert J. Edwards in memory of his mother).

Many artists love to create paintings of colorful scenes. Claude Monet liked to see color and light outdoors. Why do you think he wanted to paint this scene?

You can create colorful paintings. You can mix many colors from just three colors: red, yellow and blue. These three colors are called **primary colors**.

Orange, green and violet are called **secondary colors**. Look at the color wheel in picture B. What secondary color do you get by mixing yellow and red? How can you mix green? Violet?

32

TEACH

Engage

1 Focus on **A** by Claude Monet. Explain that it is a *landscape*, a scene in which the most important elements are the earth, sky, and natural elements. Monet loved to paint outdoors and quickly record the colors and lighting of scenes. Ask students to describe the colors and speculate on why the artist wanted to paint this scene. Accept varied answers.

2 Read about primary and secondary colors. Check students' knowledge of these concepts.

Meeting Individual Needs

Simplify If students have no prior experience using paint, begin with Lesson 16 (mixing tints and shades). Then teach Lessons 13, 14, and 15.

Challenge If students have extensive prior experience in painting, shorten or omit the practice component.

Explore

1 Focus on the triangular lines in **B**. Ask students what the lines mean (the lines show that yellow and blue make green, yellow and red make orange, and red and blue make violet). Ask students to identify intermediate colors (hues between primary and secondary colors).

2 Discuss the steps in **C**. Have students explain why the "dot" system can help artists mix colors accurately (if the color isn't right, another dot can be added and mixed).

3 Discuss colorful landscapes students have seen. Explain that they will mix secondary colors to paint a colorful landscape.

Create

1 Distribute materials. Structure the period into two blocks of time: (1) practice with color mixing; (2) painting a landscape.

2 Have students:
- paint three solid yellow circles (about the size of a quarter); wash, wipe, and blot brushes.
- add a dot of red to the first circle and brush it around.
- add dots to other circles, brushing each around.

Note that different amounts of red make yellow-orange, orange, and red-orange. Have students wash, wipe, and blot brushes and, beginning with white, mix a light orange by adding dots of yellow and red.

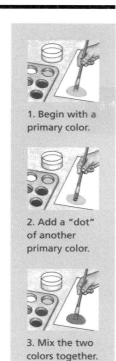

B

Practice mixing secondary colors. Then mix some **intermediate colors** such as yellow-orange and yellow-green. Can you find some intermediate colors in pictures A and B? How can you mix intermediate colors?

After you practice mixing colors, paint a colorful picture. You might show a blazing sunset, a sparkling garden or a glistening rainbow. What other ideas can you think of?

1. Begin with a primary color.

2. Add a "dot" of another primary color.

3. Mix the two colors together.

C

Extensions

▼

Science Set up a station, have students work out other methods for mixing colors, and then share methods with the class. For example, using a paper plate, paint two adjacent circles of red and yellow. Gradually mix and blend them together to create orange.

Science Give each student a swatch of red, yellow, and blue cellophane on white paper. Ask them to predict what color will result from overlapping pieces. Ask students to check their predictions by overlapping colors.

Literature Link
• *Claude Monet,* Peter Harrison. (I,A)
• *Linnea in Monet's Garden,* Christina Bjork. (I, A)
• *Nate the Great,* Marjorie Weinman Sharmat. (S)

3 Guide students to mix green from yellow with a little blue and violet from red with a little blue. Then have them begin with white to mix light greens and light violets.

4 Collect the experiments. Place, unstacked, on a flat surface to dry. As students prepare to create their landscapes, encourage them to begin with very light colors and then add darker colors. Mix browns from red, yellow, and blue. For a bright painting, use brown and black sparingly.

CLOSE

Assess

1 Have students verbally review how to mix varieties of orange, green, and violet. Have them explain why light colors are easiest to mix when beginning with white.

2 When some artworks are dry, discuss the color qualities and ideas.

Cleanup

1 Be sure students understand their specific tasks in cleaning up.

2 Collect supplies in the following order: brushes, paints, water, newspapers, and paper towels.

RESOURCES

Large Reproductions
  Golden Age, Brown, 6
  Toto, Romero, 20
  Jim, Johnson, 14

Overhead Transparencies
  Morning Light, Bleumner, 24

 CD-ROM
  1, *Color*, Lesson 1

Slide Set
  Water Lilies, Monet, 5

Assessment Masters
  Using an Artist's Colors, 3
  Match that Color, 4

Painting

PREPARE

Objectives

Students will:

- perceive and discuss the qualities of paintings created with fluid diluted paint.
- create paintings using the fluid qualities of paint to discover and develop an expressive theme.

Vocabulary

paint	*pintura*
edges	*bordes*
blend	*mezclan (mezclar)*
brushstrokes	*pinceladas*
dilute	*diluir*

Setup

When you distribute the first sheet of paper, dampen it with a clean sponge. In Lesson 15, students will add thicker paint on top of the paintings they create today.

Materials

newsprint paper, 9 x 12" (23 x 30 cm), 2 per student

tempera paints: red, yellow, blue, black, and white, in sets for several students to share

paintbrushes

water containers

sponge (See Setup)

newspapers for desks

smocks

dry paper towels (have extras)

Ⓐ **Helen Frankenthaler, *Mountains and Sea*,** 1952. Oil on canvas, 36 5/8" x 117 1/4" (93 x 298 cm). Collection of the artist, on extended loan to the National Gallery of Art, Washington, DC.

Artists explore many ways of painting. The two paintings in this lesson have very different colors, lines and shapes. You can also see one thing that makes them alike.

Both of these paintings have colors with soft, fuzzy **edges**. The artists diluted their paints. **Dilute** means adding a liquid such as water. A diluted paint flows and lets you blend colors.

Look at both paintings. Where do the colors **blend**? Can you imagine how each artist created the soft, fuzzy edges?

34

TEACH

Engage

1. Explain that artists use paints and brushes in many ways. Sometimes they let the colors run together. They use diluted paint, or paint on a wet background, to make fuzzy, watery effects. Define a *diluted* substance as one to which extra liquid has been added.

2. Briefly discuss why artists might want paint to run together (the runny, watery effect can suggest ideas, be beautiful, or express a mood or feeling).

Meeting Individual Needs

Simplify Have students create one painting rather than two.

Challenge Introduce students to watercolor painting. Make sure students do not use watercolor in the same way they use tempera paints.

Explore

1. Focus on **A**. Ask students how the artist created the shapes. Explain that the artist, Helen Frankenthaler, used very thin watery paint and let the colors run together. The title suggests the artist may want us to see how the mountains and sea interact, or blend together, in the painting.

2. Focus on **B** by Morris Louis. Note how the painted areas blend together. This type of work is called *color stain painting*. The title refers to the letters B and A in the Hebrew alphabet. The painting reminds many people of a colorful waterfall.

3. Explain that students will experiment with diluted paints and begin backgrounds for two paintings. In the next lesson, students will finish their paintings by adding details.

Art History

Helen Frankenthaler (1928–) created paintings with no obvious brushstrokes called *color field painting*. She stained canvas with areas of diluted paint by letting it flow from the end of a stick that she moved across the canvas. Many of her paintings suggest unusual views and forms in landscapes.

Morris Louis (1912–1962) developed color stain painting after seeing Frankenthaler's work. He poured thinned floods of dye or paint onto unstretched canvas. The results were "veils of color" subtly billowing into multicolored shapes. His canvases are large, sometimes more than eight feet wide.

Morris Louis, *Beth Aleph*, 1960. Acrylic on canvas, 95 1/4 x 140" (242 x 357 cm). Indiana University Art Museum (Jane and Roger Wolcott Memorial). Photograph: Michael Cavanagh, Kevin Montague.

You can create paintings with a soft, watery look. Try this. Begin your painting on a damp paper. Then put some water on your brush and dip it in paint.

Try different brushstrokes on the damp paper. Let some of the colors blend. If the paper gets too wet, blot up the water with a tissue. As the paint dries, you can add details to your work.

C

35

Extensions

▼

Science Discuss environmental images that have qualities analogous to the artworks in **A**, **B**, and **C**. Examples are oil-stained puddles with colorful reflections, views through water (still, moving, clear, murky), splash marks on shoes, and sidewalks after a rain.

Literature Link
• *Over the Green Hills,* Rachel Isadora. (A)
• *Cherries and Cherry Pits,* Vera B. Williams. (A)

Create

1 Distribute one sheet of dampened paper and all other materials. Ask students to print their names on the paper.

2 Have students apply small amounts of yellow, white, and red to the dampened sheet. Encourage them to brush colors together gently to mix, blend, and create shapes with fuzzy edges.

3 While students work, comment on colors and shapes they have created. Ask them to think of ways to soak up small puddles of paint (dry paper towel, sponge, dry or blotted brush).

4 Place the first paintings, unstacked, on a flat surface to dry. Distribute the second sheet of paper. Have students rinse brushes and use broad strokes to apply water to the paper. Have them use cool colors to begin this painting and then add a small amount of white or black.

CLOSE

Assess

1 Explain that paintings such as **A** and **B** are enjoyed for their lovely colors and shapes. Hold up several dry paintings and encourage students to point out various shapes and colors. Turn paintings in different positions and ask students to look for colors and shapes that remind them of clouds, trees, animals, etc.

2 Ask students to explain the advantages and disadvantages of using watery paints (answers may vary). Help students understand that experiments with paint are important. They can learn and then use what they have learned.

Cleanup

1 Have students blot any pools of water on their second painting and add their names to the paper. Save paintings for the next lesson.

RESOURCES

Large Reproductions
  Toto, Romero, 20
  Golden Age, Brown, 6
  African Canvas, Courtney-Clarke, 19

Overhead Transparencies
  Self-Portrait, Vigée-Lebrun, 21
  Delfina Flores, Rivera, 21

 CD-ROM
  1, *Color,* Lesson 3

Slide Set
  River Ladder Gold, Baber, 6

Assessment Masters
  Using an Artist's Colors, 3
  Match that Color, 4

15 Exploring Brushstrokes
Painting

PREPARE

Objectives

Students will:
- understand that artists can plan their brushstrokes to create patterns and visual rhythms.
- use brushstrokes selectively to create patterns and visual rhythms and complete two paintings from the previous lesson.

Vocabulary

lines	*líneas*
shapes	*formas*
patterns	*diseños*
visual rhythms	*mitmos visuales*
brushstrokes	*pinceladas*

Setup

Paint should be creamy and thick, not watery.

Materials

students' paintings from Lesson 14

tempera paints: red, yellow, blue, black, and white, in sets for several students to share (See Setup)

paintbrushes

water containers

newspapers for desks

smocks

paper towels

sponges

Artists use paintbrushes in many ways. An artist in Australia made the painting in picture A. His painting is about the "Dreamtime." A Dreamtime story tells about the beginning of life in Australia.

This painting tells about a giant Rainbow snake that went to the desert. It dug holes to bring up water. Then the snake wiggled across the sand, leaving deep grooves. The grooves filled up with water and became rivers. The water changed the desert into a place where people and other living things could survive.

Picture B shows a small part of this painting. Why is the painting filled with tiny dots? What do the patterns and visual rhythms mean?

A Indji, *The Rainbow Snake*, Port Keats Region. 22 1/2 x 10 1/2" (57 x 27 cm). Collection of Louis A. Allen.

B Indji, *The Rainbow Snake* (detail).

36

TEACH

Engage

1 Explain that students will complete their paintings from Lesson 14 by adding lines and shapes to create patterns and visual rhythms.

2 Review that visual rhythms can be set up by repeating lines, shapes, and colors. (See Lessons 6 and 11.)

Meeting Individual Needs

Simplify Have students explore brushstrokes on plain or colored paper.

Challenge Have students create a painting with visual rhythms related to specific themes, such as waves in the sea, leaves of a tree blowing in the wind, or animals with strong patterns of spots or stripes.

Explore

1 Focus on **A**. Guide students to see the rhythmic patterns of dots arranged in wavy and circular lines. Explain that this artist's ancestors were the first people in Australia. The painting tells about ideas from the past. The tiny dots represent the grains of sand in the Australian desert. The circles represent water holes. The long wavy path represents the snake, its trail, and the curved river. Ask students to look at **B** and make gestures to suggest how paint was used.

2 Focus on **C** by Henri Matisse. Guide students to gesture and name some of the lines and shapes that create patterns. Have students identify visual rhythms in the patterns of vase, robe, and background.

3 Focus on **D**. Guide students to see the visual rhythms in the brushstrokes. Point out that **A**, **C**, and **D** show ways to create visual rhythms and patterns by brushing wet paint on top of dry paint. The class will use paint in the same way.

Cultural Awareness

Explain that paintings such as the one in **A** are often used to tell stories about the Dreamtime among the first Australians. While the story is being told, parts of the painting are pointed out. Sometimes the pointing means that all listeners are to chant or say part of the story from memory. Related uses of paintings—in ceremonies and for teaching about a group's beliefs—exist in other cultures (Navajo sand paintings; designs for drumming and dancing in West Africa).

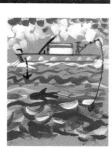

C Henri Matisse, *Purple Robe and Anemones*, 1937. Oil on canvas, 28 3/4 x 23 3/4" (73 x 60 cm). The Baltimore Museum of Art (The Cone Collection, formed by Dr. Claribel Cone and Miss Etta Cone of Baltimore, Maryland).

D Student artwork.

The painting in picture C has many kinds of **brushstrokes**. It is filled with patterns that make visual rhythms. Where do you see wavy lines repeated? Where do you see patterns with straight lines? What other brushstrokes create patterns?

Try different ways to use a paintbrush. Then create a painting with visual rhythms. Make patterns of brushstrokes to create the rhythm. Students created the paintings in picture D. What subjects or themes might you choose?

37

INTEGRATING THE CURRICULUM

Extensions

Music Have students listen to varied styles of instrumental music. As they listen, ask them to gesture how they might use brushstrokes with the music (dots, zigzags, jagged edges, bold straight lines). Encourage them to think about rhythmic patterns. Have them select music they would like to hear again. Ask students to begin painting when the music starts and stop when it ends. Stress that they should create rhythmic patterns as they paint.

Literature Link
• *Zomo the Rabbit: A Trickster Tale from West Africa*, Gerald McDermott. (A)
• *Morgan and the Artist*, Donald Carrick. (S)
• *The Little Painter of Sabana Grande*, Patricia Maloney Markun. (S)

CLOSE

Create

1 Distribute one of the two paintings from Lesson 14. Ask students to look at their paintings from all sides and study the shapes and colors they see. Encourage them to notice how colors or edges of shapes suggest animals, trees, buildings, or other objects. A paintbrush can be used to outline these shapes and add other brushstrokes. If students prefer, they can add lines, textures, and patterns that do not look like real objects.

2 Distribute painting materials. Pace the activity so students can finish both paintings. As students work, comment on ways they are using a brush (point, side, creating dots, stripes, etc.). Place the first paintings, unstacked, on a flat surface to dry.

3 Distribute the second paintings when students are ready. Remind them to explore brushstrokes and develop patterns and rhythms in their work.

Assess

1 Discuss the variety of brushstrokes that students have included in their paintings.

2 Call on students to identify in their own and others' work repeated elements that create patterns and visual rhythms.

Cleanup

1 Ask students to demonstrate their knowledge of proper cleanup procedures.

PREPARE

Objectives

Students will:

- demonstrate their knowledge of art terms by describing and analyzing their own artwork and that of others.
- demonstrate their ability to create art independently by creating a picture in which light is a center of interest in an expressive landscape.

Vocabulary

elements of design	*elementos de diseño*
center of interest	*foco de atención*
source of light	*fuente de luz*

Setup

Structure the review into a studio lesson followed by an evaluation of work from Unit 1. List questions on the chalkboard. (See Evaluation Guide.) If you prefer, make a handout of the questions.

Materials

folders containing artwork completed during this unit

drawing paper, 12 x 18" (30 x 46 cm), 1 per student

choice of drawing media

You have learned that artists use lines, colors and other **elements of design** to express moods or feelings. Use art words to tell what you think about each painting.

These artists have shown light from the sun, moon or stars. The source of light is the **center of interest** in each artwork.

Look at the painting in picture A. What textures do you see? How are they made? What fills up most of the space in the painting? Why? What else do you see? Have you ever seen a sky like this? How do the lines, colors and shapes make you feel?

 **A** Vincent Van Gogh, *The Starry Night*, 1889. Oil on canvas, 29 x 36 1/4" (74 x 92 cm). Collection, The Museum of Modern Art, New York (Acquired through the Lillie P. Bliss Bequest).

Does the painting in picture B show a sunset or sunrise? How do the lines, colors and shapes in this painting help to give you a special feeling? What else did the artist want you to see and feel?

 **B** John Marin, *Sunset, Casco Bay*. Wichita Art Museum, Wichita, Kansas (The Roland P. Murdock Collection). Photograph: Henry Nelson.

38

TEACH

Engage

1 Explain that students will be seeing new examples of artwork and thinking about what they have learned about art.

2 Ask students to identify in **A**, **B**, and **C** the main sources of light. Have them discuss how each light source stands out. Explain that each painting has light as the *center of interest*—the main element noticed.

Explore

1 Discuss **A**. Have students gesture the swirling paths of movement in the sky, the edges of the hills, and the tree. Have them identify the colors Vincent van Gogh used to show the night sky. Ask them to describe the mood— the feelings or messages that come from lines, colors, and shapes. Encourage personal responses.

2 Focus on **B** by John Marin. Help students recall sunsets they have seen. Have them gesture the radial lines from the sun. Discuss the use of blended colors to suggest water, sky, pine trees, and land. To illustrate the relationship between light, color, and mood, ask students to imagine the same scene on a cool, foggy morning.

3 Focus on **C**. Have students gesture the radial lines from the sun, the jagged edges of rocks, and the curves and patterns of leaves. Ask them to identify the very light and very dark colors that Charles Burchfield used. Encourage students to describe the overall feeling or mood.

Does the scene in picture C look like a real or imaginary place? What lines, colors and shapes do you see? What special feelings do you get from the design? Why?

Show what you have learned. Create a picture of a real or imaginary place. Show how light and color can make a place look and feel very special. What design elements will you use? What will your center of interest be?

C Charles Burchfield, *Sun and Rocks,* 1918–50. Gouache and watercolor on paper, 40 x 56" (101 x 142 cm). Albright-Knox Art Gallery, Buffalo, New York (Room of Contemporary Art Fund, 1953).

Evaluation Guide

Students who have had effective art instruction in Grades 1 and 2 should be able to discuss or write about art using a simple outline such as the following:

1 What do you notice first about this artwork? Why?

2 Describe the elements of design:
   • Line
   • Colors
   • Shapes or forms
   • Textures
   • Spaces

3 How is the artwork planned? Why was this plan used?

4 Are there special ways the art materials are used? Why?

5 What else do you see?

6 What ideas or feelings come from seeing the artwork?

7 What did you learn from studying or creating this artwork?

This outline for evaluating art can be compared to an outline a reporter might use to write about artwork for a newspaper or magazine. The role of art critic is introduced at Level 4, and skills in art criticism are developed in Levels 5–8. Because the term *art criticism* tends to have a negative connotation, the outline and activities for Level 3 are introduced as guides for thoughtful conversations about art.

CLOSE

Create

1 Distribute materials. Ask students to close their eyes and concentrate on the mood of the picture they will create. With their eyes closed, ask them to answer these questions silently: What place will your picture show? (It could show a city, mountains, desert, swamp, etc.) What time of day is it? (It might be early morning, midday, sunset, or night.) What is the weather like? (Is it clear, foggy, raining, windy, snowing?) How does the scene make you feel? (Is it quiet, peaceful, full of energy, scared?)

2 Allow students to begin and to demonstrate their ability to work with little supervision. Maintain a quiet atmosphere so they can concentrate. Remind students to make a light source the center of interest. Encourage attention to elements of art and ways to use them for expression. Explain that students will evaluate their artwork from this unit, including today's artwork.

Assess

1 Distribute students' folders. Explain that students are to decide which artworks are the best.

2 Have students put a "1" (for Unit 1) on the back of each artwork they have chosen.

3 Have students gather in small groups to discuss each other's artwork. Have them take turns showing and talking about their art, using the outline as a guide. Stress the idea that good conversations about art are like good conversations about stories and other topics.

4 Evaluate and write comments on students' work. Save the works each student identified as best and others that you judge to be important benchmarks. Allow students to take the rest home.

Cleanup

1 Follow usual procedures for cleanup.

RESOURCES

Large Reproductions
   Time, Chagall, 11
   Upstream, Kuniyoshi, 10
   Indian Boy, Homer, 9

Overhead Transparencies
   First Steps, Picasso, 16

 CD-ROM
   2, *Elements of Design*, Lesson 6

Assessment Masters
   A Vote for Art, 21

Unit 2 Planner

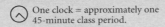
Core: *Adventures in Art* provides a balanced sequence of lessons that meet national standards for content and instructional time. If you are unable to teach every lesson, introduce the lessons identified as "core."

Lesson Overview	Objectives	Correlations	Resources	Technology
U2 Page 40 **How Artists Work** *Activity:* **Drawing** *Materials:* **Viewfinders, pencils** *Concept:* **Sketch, emphasis** *Related Lessons:* Emphasis: 21, R1. Landscape: 17, 18, 19. R1. Sketches: 1, 23.	• Understand that in artwork based on observation, the artist may select, change, or rearrange elements • Use a viewfinder to locate and draw important or interesting lines and shapes in a scene	*National Standards:* 1a, b, d, 2a, c, 3a, b, 4a, c, 5a, c	*Large Reproductions:* **10** Kuniyoshi, **9** Homer, **17** Matisse *Overhead Transparencies:* **23** Delaunay *Assessment Masters:* **6** Create a Community	CD-ROM 3, *Artists at Work,* Lesson 2
16 Core Page 42 **Paintings About Cities** *Activity:* **Painting** *Materials:* **Viewfinders, tempera** *Concept:* **Tints and shades**	• Understand the terms *tint, shade,* and *value* • Create an expressive painting of a real or imaginary city using tints and shades	*National Standards:* 1a, c, d, 2a, c, 3a, b, 4a, c, 5a, c, 6a, b	*Large Reproductions:* **2** Thiebaud, **15** Haas, **14** Johnson, **11** Chagall *Overhead Transparencies:* **15** Wilson *Slide Set:* **7** Vlaminck *Assessment Masters:* **19** Comparing Two Artworks	CD-ROM 1, *Color,* Lesson 4
17 Page 44 **When the Wind Blows** *Activity:* **Painting** *Materials:* **Watercolors** *Concept:* **Landscape painting** *Related Lessons:* Landscape: 13, 14, 18, 19. Motion: 3, 38. Painting: 13-16. Styles of art with similar theme: 12, 18, 29, 30.	• Be aware of art techniques to imply motion in two-dimensional artwork • Create a watercolor painting using tints and shades to portray a windy landscape	*National Standards:* 1a, b, c, d, 2a, c, 3a, b, 5a, 6a, b	*Large Reproductions:* **9** Homer *Overhead Transparencies:* **3** Homer, **10** Peña *Slide Set:* **6** Homer *Assessment Masters:* **19** Comparing Two Artworks	CD-ROM 3, *Artists at Work,* Lesson 1
18 Core Page 46 **Seasons and Spaces** *Activity:* **Drawing** *Materials:* **Colored paper, oil pastels** *Concept:* **Space, colors, and moods** *Related Lessons:* Color: 12, 14, 30, 40. Landscape: 13, 17, 19, 24. Seasons: 2, 19. Space: 4, 5, 11, 41.	• Compare and contrast spaces and color schemes in three seasonal landscape paintings • Create an artwork with planned space and color to portray a season	*National Standards:* 1a, b, c, 2a, b, c, 3a, b, 4a, b, c, 5a, c, 6b	*Large Reproductions:* **6** Brown, **10** Kuniyoshi, **4** Picasso *Overhead Transparencies:* **7** Lewis, **24** Bleumner, **16** Picasso *Slide Set:* **9** Monet *Assessment Masters:* **21** A Vote for Art	CD-ROM 1, *Color,* Lesson 3
19 Page 48 **Details in Landscapes** *Activity:* **Drawing** *Materials:* **Student artwork folders, drawing media, cotton swabs or facial tissues** *Concept:* **Details, shading, texture** *Related Lessons:* Landscape: 4, 13, 14, 17. Light and Shadow: 20, 37. Seasons: 2, 18. Texture: 7, 8, 9, 20.	• Understand that art can be reworked to incorporate details, shading, texture and color changes • Try to improve an artwork by adding details, shading, texture, and colors	*National Standards:* 1a, b, c, d, 2a, b, c, 3b, 4a, b, c, 5a, b, c, 6a, b	*Large Reproductions:* **8** Audubon, **6** Brown, **9** Homer *Overhead Transparencies:* **9** Remington, **2** Miller *Slide Set:* **9** Monet *Assessment Masters:* **11** A Bird's Eye View	CD-ROM 1, *Color,* Lesson 4 CD-ROM 2, *Elements of Design,* Lesson 3

■ boxed sidebar information
on lesson pages.

Literature Link codes:
(A) Artwork links to lesson
(S) Story line links to lesson
(I) Information links to lesson

40b

Special Features	Cultures/History	Integrating the Curriculum	
		Extensions	**Literature Link**

	Canada:
	  Carr
	United States:
	  Davis
	■ *Art History:* Pop art
		Science:
		Magnification
			Knoxville, Tennessee, Nikki Giovanni.
			  (A)
			*Brown Angels: An Album of Pictures
			  and Verse,* Walter Dean Myers. (A)

■ Meeting Individual
  Needs
	France:
	  Bonnard
	  Monet
	■ *Art History:* Impressionism
		Language Arts:
		Write poems
		Science: Cloud
		formations
			Claude Monet, Peter Harrison. (I, A)
			Punch in New York, Alice Provensen. (S)
			My New York, Kathy Jakobsen. (A)

■ Meeting Individual
  Needs
	Canada:
	  Jeffreys
	United States:
	  Homer
		Language Arts:
		Descriptive
		poetry
		Science: Wind
		effects
		Science: Weather
		graphics
			Reflections, Ann Jonas. (A)
			One White Sail, S.T. Garne. (A)
			Mirandy and Brother Wind, Patricia C.
			  McKissack. (S)

■ Art Criticism	Canada:
	  MacDonald
	France:
	  Monet
	United States:
	  Storm
		Social Studies:
		Seasonal adapta-
		tions
			Sky Tree, Thomas Locker with
			  Candace Christiansen. (A)
			Mother Earth, Nancy Luenn. (A)
			In for Winter, Out for Spring, Arnold
			  Adoff. (A)

■ Aesthetic Awareness	France:
	  Pissarro
		Language Arts:
		Writing
		Language Arts:
		Reading
			Where the River Begins, Thomas
			  Locker. (A)
			The Boy Who Held Back the Sea, retold
			  by Lenny Hort. (A)

Lesson Overview	Objectives	Correlations	Resources	Technology

20 Animal Expressions

Core

Page 50

Activity: **Drawing, painting**
Materials: **Homework sketches, tempera**
Concept: **Texture and shading**
Related Lessons: Animal: 1, 8, 21, 22. Bonheur: 1. Light and Shadow: 19, 37. Texture: 7-9, 19.

• Discuss textures, shading, poses, and expressions in artworks showing animals
• Draw and create a painting of an animal emphasizing texture, shading, pose, and expression

National Standards: 1a, b, c, d, 2a, b, c, 3a, b, 4a, b, c, 5c, 6a

Large Reproductions: 20 Romero, 21 Blackwell
Overhead Transparencies: 8 Jones, 2 Miller
Slide Set: 10 Perilli
Assessment Masters: 12 Mix and Match, 9 Imagine That

CD-ROM 1, *Color,* Lesson 4

CD-ROM 2, *Elements of Design,* Lesson 1

21 Imaginary Creatures

Page 52

Activity: **Creating a mural**
Materials: **Drawing media, scissors, paste**
Concept: **Mural, illustration**
Related Lessons: Animals: 1, 8, 9, 20. Asian art: 33, 35, 48, 53. Illustration (story): 15, 36. Mural: 52.

• Perceive and discuss a complex artwork created by a team of artists
• Work in groups to create complex murals about animals

National Standards: 1a, d, 2a, 3a, b, 4a, c, 5a, c

Large Reproductions: 15 Haas, 6 Brown
Overhead Transparencies: 5 Tygart
Assessment Masters: 12 Mix and Match, 9 Imagine That

CD-ROM 5, *People and Animals,* Lesson 3

22 Small Creatures

Core

Page 54

Activity: **Printmaking**
Materials: **Oil-based clay, paper clips, tempera**
Concept: **Relief prints**
Related Lessons: Animals: 1, 4, 8, 20. Printmaking: 4, 5, 9, 10. Relief surfaces: 57.

• Understand procedures used in relief printing
• Create signed and numbered prints

National Standards: 1a, b, d, 2c, 3a, b, 5a, 6a, b

Large Reproductions: 10 Kuniyoshi
Overhead Transparencies: 9 Toulouse-Lautrec
Assessment Masters: 12 Mix and Match

CD-ROM 5, *People and Animals,* Lesson 3

23 Drawing People

Core

Page 56

Activity: **Drawing**
Materials: **Pencils**
Concept: **Figure proportions**
Related Lessons: People: 11, 24, 25, 26. Proportion: 26, 56, 58. Sketches: 1, U2. Van Gogh: R1.

• Understand that some artwork is based on sketches of real people
• Draw pictures of students who pose

National Standards: 1a, c, d, 2c, 3a, 5a, c, 6a, b

Large Reproductions: 13 Arcimboldo, 14 Johnson
Overhead Transparencies: 18 Rockwell, 11 China, 11 Graves
Slide Set: 12 Krans
Assessment Masters: 19 Comparing Two Artworks

CD-ROM 5, *People and Animals,* Lessons 1 and 2

24 People Outdoors

Core

Page 58

Activity: **Drawing**
Materials: **Drawing media, viewfinders**
Concept: **Perspective**
Related Lessons: Crowds: 11, 25. Landscape: R1, 17-19. People: 11, 23, 25, 26. Space (perspective): 25.

• Understand the meaning of perpective as it is used in art
• Draw a picture using perspective to show groups of people outdoors

National Standards: 1a, b, c, d, 2a, b, c, 3a, b, 4a, b, c, 5a, c, 6a, b

Large Reproductions: 15 Haas, 10 Kuniyoshi, 17 Matisse
Overhead Transparencies: 18 Phillips, 8 Lee
Slide Set: 11 Dwight
Assessment Masters: 20 Find Out About Art

CD-ROM 5, *People and Animals,* Lessons 1 and 2

25 A Crowded Scene

Page 60

Activity: **Drawing**
Materials: **Drawing media**
Concept: **Perspective**
Related Lessons: Crowds: 11, 24. People: 11, 13, 24, 26, Space (perspective): 24. Styles of art with similar theme: 12, 26, 27, 30.

• Be aware of size, position, and overlap as ways to suggest perspective
• Create a drawing of themselves in a stage-like space looking out at an audience

National Standards: 1a, c, 2a, c, 3a, b, 4a, b, c, 5a, b, c, 6b

Large Reproductions: 16 Howell-Sickles, 10 Kuniyoshi, 9 Homer
Overhead Transparencies: 18 Rockwell, 18 Phillips
Slide Set: 11 Dwight
Assessment Masters: 19 Comparing Two Artworks, 13 Places to Live

CD-ROM 5, *People and Animals,* Lessons 1 and 2

		Extensions	**Literature Link**

■ Meeting Individual Needs
■ Aesthetic Awareness
■ Critical Thinking
	France:
	  Bonheur
	United States:
	  Audubon
		Language Arts:
		Reading
			Turtle in July, Marilyn Singer. (A)
			The Ice Horse, Candace Christiansen. (A)
			Whale, Judy Allen. (A)

	India ■ *Art History:* Miniatures	*Social Studies:* Community murals	*The Shelf-Paper Jungle,* Diana Engel. (S, A) *Matthew's Dragon,* Susan Cooper. (S) *The Great Ball Game: A Muskogee Story,* retold by Joseph Bruchac. (A)
■ Meeting Individual Needs		*Language Arts:* Reading *Social Studies:* Printing history *Science:* Observation	*My Son John,* Jim Aylesworth. (A) *Tracks in the Wild,* Betsy Bowen. (A)

	The Netherlands:
	  van Gogh
	United States:
	  Bellows
	  Brown
		Science: Human joints
		Mathematics: Proportion
			Vincent Van Gogh, Peter Harrison. (A, I)
			People, Philip Yenawine. (A)
			The Young Artist, Thomas Locker. (S)

	United States:
	  Glackens
	  Shahn
		Social Studies:
		Comparisons
		Mathematics:
		Proportions
			The Green Lion of Zion Street, Julia Fields. (A)
			Market Day, Eve Bunting. (A)
			My Little Island, Frané Lessac. (A)

■ Meeting Individual Needs	United States:
	  Lawrence, African American
	  Shinn
	■ *Art History:* Ashcan School
		Drama: Theater view	*The Great Migration: An American Story,* Jacob Lawrence. (A, I)
			Take Me Out to the Ballgame, Maryann Kovalski. (A)

Lesson Overview	Objectives	Correlations	Resources	Technology
26 Core Page 62 **Faces of People** *Activity:* **Drawing** *Materials:* **Pencils, small mirrors** *Concept:* **Proportion, expression** *Related Lessons:* People: 11, 23-25. Portraits and self-portraits: 27, 57, 59. Proportion: 23, 56, 58. Styles of art with similar theme: 12, 25, 27, 29.	• Perceive and discuss facial expressions and proportions in portraits • Draw an expressive portrait combining basic proportions and observation	*National Standards:* 1a, b, c, d, 2a, b, c, 3a, b, 4a, b, c, 5a, c, 6a, b	*Large Reproductions:* **14** Johnson, **13** Arcimboldo *Overhead Transparencies:* **1** Shahn, **1** Kasebier *Slide Set:* **13** Johnson *Assessment Masters:* **20** Find Out About Art	CD-ROM 6, *Subjects in Art,* Lesson 1
27 Page 64 **Portraits and Self-Portraits** *Activity:* **Painting** *Materials:* **Tempera, mixing tray** *Concept:* **Portrait painting** *Related Lessons:* Color mixing; 13. Painting: 13-16. Portraits and self-portraits: 26, 57, 59. Value: 16, 17, 19.	• Compare and contrast painting styles and expressive details in portraits and self-portraits • Create a painting that portrays a person	*National Standards:* 1a, b, c, d, 2a, b, c, 3a, b, 4a, b, 5a, b, c, 6b	*Large Reproductions:* **14** Johnson *Overhead Transparencies:* **7** Lewis, **21** Vigée-Lebrun, **21** Rivera, **6** Weitz *Slide Set:* **13** Johnson *Assessment Masters:* **19** Comparing Two Artworks	CD-ROM 6, *Subjects in Art,* Lesson 1
28 Page 66 **Still Lifes of Food** *Activity:* **Drawing** *Materials:* **Drawing media** *Concept:* **Symbols, design** *Related Lessons:* Cityscapes: R2. Styles of art with similar theme: 12, 27, 29, 30. Symbols 33, 46, 47, 49.	• Compare and contrast symbols and design in still life paintings of food • Create a still life using favorite foods as symbols and carefully planning the design	*National Standards:* 1a, c, 2a, c, 3a, b, 4a, b, c, 5c, 6b	*Large Reproductions:* **2** Thiebaud *Overhead Transparencies:* **15** Mandel, **15** Wilson *Slide Set:* **14** Coorte *Assessment Masters:* **20** Find Out About Art	CD-ROM 6, *Subjects in Art,* Lesson 2
29 Page 68 **City Spaces** *Activity:* **Drawing** *Materials:* **Drawing media** *Concept:* **Expressive design** *Related Lessons:* Cityscapes: 30, R2. Latin American art: 26, 53. Line: 2, 3, 8, 9. Shape: 2, 5, 6.	• Be aware of how lines and shapes may suggest energetic or calm moods • Create an artwork of either a calm or an active cityscape	*National Standards:* 1a, b, c, 2a, b, c, 3a, b, 4a, c, 5a, c, 6a	*Large Reproductions:* **15** Haas *Overhead Transparencies:* **23** Delaunay, **24** Bleumner, **24** Hopper *Assessment Masters:* **6** Create a Community, **10** City Skylines	CD-ROM 4, *Art Adventure,* Lesson 2
30 Core Page 70 **A City at Night** *Activity:* **Crayon resist** *Materials:* **Oil pastels or wax crayons, dark blue paint** *Concept:* **Color contrasts** *Related Lessons:* Cityscapes: 29, R2. Color; 12, 18, 40, 42. Day and night contrast: 41. Painting: 14-17.	• Be aware of special media and processes for painting • Create a crayon resist painting of a cityscape at night	*National Standards:* 1a, b, c, d, 2a, b, c, 3a, b, 5a, b, c, 6a, b	*Large Reproductions:* **17** Matisse *Overhead Transparencies:* **18** Phillips *Slide Set:* **15** Chase *Assessment Masters:* **13** Places to Live	CD-ROM 4, *Art Adventure,* Lesson 2
R2 Core Page 72 **Review Unit 2** *Activity:* **Drawing** *Materials:* **Student artwork folders, crayons or oil pastels** *Concept:* **Style, originality** *Related Lessons:* Bridge: 16. Cityscape: 29, 30. Marin: R1. Styles: 44.	• Understand originality in art as seen in five works with the same subject • Choose a subject for a picture and create an original drawing about it	*National Standards:* 1a, b, 2a, b, c, 3b, 4a, c, 5a, c, 6a	*Large Reproductions:* **10** Kuniyoshi, **11** Chagall *Overhead Transparencies:* **18** Rockwell, **18** Phillips *Assessment Masters:* **19** Compare Two Artworks, **22** I Like Art	CD-ROM 3, *Artists at Work,* Lesson 2 CD-ROM 4, *Art Adventure,* Lesson 2

Special Features	Cultures/History	Integrating the Curriculum	

■ Critical Thinking	Mexico:
	  Jaramillo
	United States:
	  Shahn
		Extensions
		Social Studies:
		Historical por-
		traits
		Drama: Puppet
		play
			Literature Link
			Miranda's Smile, Thomas Locker. (S, A)
			The Gentleman and the Kitchen Maid,
			  Diane Stanley. (S)

■ Meeting Individual
  Needs
	Egypt
	United States:
	  Henri
	  Johnson, African American
	■ *Art History:* Encaustic
		Language Arts:
		Writing
		Language Arts:
		Biography
			The Young Artist, Thomas Locker. (S)
			The Rough-Face Girl, Rafe Martin. (A)

■ Meeting Individual
  Needs
	United States:
	  McCloskey
	  Thiebaud
	■ *Art History:* Still Life
		Science: Food
		pyramid
			Yum, Yum, Yum, Andy Warhol. (A)
			A Fruit & Vegetable Man, Roni
			  Schotter. (A)

■ Aesthetic Awareness	Brazil:
	  Amaral
	United States:
	  Grosz
		Social Studies:
		City growth
			Street Music: City Poems, Arnold Adoff.
			  (S)
			My New York, Kathy Jakobsen. (A)
			Town and Country, Alice and Martin
			  Provensen. (A)

	United States:
	  Bacher
		Language Arts:
		Reading
		Science: Glow-in-
		the-dark
			Night on Neighborhood Street, Eloise
			Greenfield. (S)
			Citybook, Shelley Rotner and Ken
			  Kreisler. (A)

	United States:
	  Halpert
	  Marin
	  Stella
	  Weston
		Language Arts:
		Writing
			Bridges, Ken Robbins. (I)
			Crossing the New Bridge, Emily Arnold
			  McCully. (S)
			Tar Beach, Faith Ringgold. (S, A)

U2 How Artists Work
Drawing

PREPARE

Objectives

Students will:
- understand that in artwork based on observation the artist may select, change, or rearrange important or interesting elements.
- use a viewfinder to locate and draw important or interesting lines and shapes in a scene.

Vocabulary

scene	*escena*
viewfinder	*visor*
photograph	*fotografía*
sketch	*bosquejo*

Setup

See Lesson 2 or have students make viewfinders out of stiff paper or index cards by folding paper in half and cutting a small rectangle into the fold. Have them use the width of their little finger as a guide for one cut and the width of two center fingers as a guide for the other dimension. Unfolded opening should be about 1 x 1½" (3 x 4 cm).

Materials

viewfinders
(See Setup)

pencils

white drawing paper,
12 x 18" (30 x 46 cm),
1 per student

B *Church, Friendly Cove*, ca. 1930. Courtesy of British Columbia Provincial Museum.

A Emily Carr, *Indian Church*, 1929. Oil on canvas, 42 3/4 x 27 1/8" (109 x 69 cm). Art Gallery of Ontario, Toronto (Bequest of Charles S. Band, 1970).

C Photograph of subject used by Stuart Davis in his *Summer Landscape*, 1930. Collection, The Museum of Modern Art, New York.

Artists get ideas for pictures in many ways. In this unit, you will explore ideas for art. You will create art about people, places and animals. You will explore other ideas too.

Emily Carr, a Canadian artist, created the painting in picture A.

Her idea came from a visit to the place shown in picture B. She chose interesting parts of the scene for her painting. She changed and left out some parts of the actual scene. How is her painting of the church different from the photograph?

40

TEACH

Engage

1 Ask students if they have ever looked through a viewfinder of a camera to compose a picture. Explain that photographers create photographic artworks in this way. The scenes they see in a viewfinder are *compositions*—designs planned so the most important parts stand out.

2 Explain that artists who paint and draw can also look at scenes in this way. Sometimes they use a viewfinder to decide on a composition.

Explore

1 Guide students to find similarities and differences between **A** and **B**. Note how the painting by Canadian artist Emily Carr shows a front view of a church surrounded by a towering forest. Ask students why the artist created her painting around one building rather than the several in the photograph (to make the building the center of interest, to show the tall trees surrounding the small church).

2 Help students compare specific parts of Stuart Davis's painting in **D** with the photograph of the actual scene in **C**. Note similarities and differences in the trees, fences, telephone pole, and smokestack. Help students appreciate that the artist's painting has looping lines, simple shapes, and a livelier mood than the actual scene.

3 Read and discuss the text related to **E**. Stress that students will find a scene within the classroom by looking through viewfinders and then draw it.

Art History

Emily Carr (1871–1945) was one of the first Canadian painters to interpret the special qualities of British Columbian landscapes, including villages of natives. Her paintings have simple forms and dramatize curves, colors, and contrasts in light and dark. In addition to being a well-known painter, she also wrote four autobiographical books.

Stuart Davis (1894–1964), a United States painter, is known for posterlike compositions that contained sharp contrasts in color and precise outlines. He was interested in jazz and tried to find a visual parallel to the "planned improvisation" of jazz. His subjects were often places he considered typical of the United States. He is sometimes viewed as a leader of the later style called Pop art.

Stuart Davis, *Summer Landscape*, 1930. Oil on canvas, 29 x 42" (74 x 107 cm). Collection, The Museum of Modern Art, New York (Purchase).

Compare the photograph in picture C and the painting in picture D. How did the artist make his painting look interesting?

Sketch some scenes near your home or school. Make and use a **viewfinder** to choose the scenes (see picture E). Use your best sketch to create an artwork. In the artwork, show the most important or interesting parts of the scene.

41

Extensions

Science Provide students with magnifying lenses. Have them select an object to observe through the lens and draw the magnified view. The shape of the drawing paper should match the shape of the lens (e.g., for a round lens, cut the paper into a circle).

Literature Link

• *Knoxville, Tennessee*, Nikki Giovanni. (A)
• *Brown Angels: An Album of Pictures and Verse*, Walter Dean Myers. (A)

Create

1 Distribute viewfinders or materials to make viewfinders.

2 Have students rehearse using viewfinders, holding them about 12" (30 cm) from the face with the rectangle vertical (tall). Place the drawing paper in the same vertical position. They should look through the hole in the viewfinder to find a scene. Some may find it easier if they close one eye.

3 Repeat the rehearsal for a horizontal composition.

4 Have students begin. Encourage them to draw main lines and shapes first, very large. The drawing on paper should look like a big version of the scene in the viewfinder.

5 During the last eight to ten minutes, have students put viewfinders aside. Have them look at their drawings and identify the most interesting or important lines and shapes. Encourage them to make these parts stand out (make them darker or wider, add textures, patterns, and so on).

CLOSE

Assess

1 Call on volunteers to hold up their work. Discuss the drawings as well as the use of a viewfinder.

2 Stress that there are many ways to find ideas for artwork. Using the viewfinder is one way. Emphasize that changing, rearranging, and selecting lines and shapes can often help make an artwork more interesting than the real scene.

Cleanup

1 Save viewfinders. Follow usual procedures for cleanup.

RESOURCES

Large Reproductions
 Upstream, Kuniyoshi, 10
 Indian Boy, Homer, 9
 Interior, Matisse, 17

Overhead Transparencies
 Towers of Laon, Delaunay, 23

 CD-ROM
 3, *Artists at Work*, Lesson 2

Assessment Masters
 Create a Community, 6

PREPARE

Objectives

Students will:
• understand the terms *tint, shade,* and *value.*
• create a painting of a real or imaginary city using tints and shades expressively.

Vocabulary

tint   *tono/matiz*
shade   *tono*
value   *valor*

Materials

smocks

newspapers for desktops

viewfinders

tempera paint: sets of black, white, red, yellow, and blue for students to share

water containers

brushes, 1 per student

manila paper, 12 x 18" (30 x 46 cm), 1 per student

sponges

paper towels

---

16 Paintings About Cities
Mix Tints and Shades

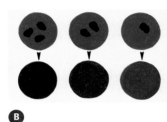

Ⓐ   **Claude Monet,** ***Waterloo Bridge,*** 1903. Oil on canvas, 25 3/4 x 36 5/8" (64 x 93 cm). Worcester Art Museum, Massachusetts.

Artists create paintings with light and dark colors. They mix white or black paint with other colors to create many new colors.

Shades are dark colors. A **shade** is a color with black added to it. Begin with a color. Add dots of black to the color. Mix the paint. What happens when you add more black?

Ⓑ

42

TEACH

Engage

1 Ask students to visualize the brightest, lightest, hottest times in a city. Then have them recall a dull, dark, cold city day. Have them describe what they saw and felt. Tell them that artists often create paintings of scenes showing a time of day or type of weather.

Meeting Individual Needs

Simplify Have students go outside to create drawings of clouds, trees, and other natural forms using crayons, chalk, or oil pastels. Encourage them to observe and record small differences in lightness and darkness.

Challenge Combine this lesson with Lesson 17. Both provide instruction on tints and shades but use different media (tempera and watercolor).

Explore

1 Focus on **A**. Explain that Claude Monet was a French artist who often used sunlight and color as subjects. In this painting, he used light and dark blues to show a bridge, water, and city. Note the reflections on the water, misty air, and smoke.

2 Ask students to place viewfinders on top of **A** to find a section with very light blues. Have them also look for dark blues and middle blues.

3 Focus on **B**. Check for understanding of the term *shade*. Shades of colors should be mixed by beginning with the color and adding a dot of black. A small amount of black will quickly make a color dark.

4 Check for understanding of the term *tint*. Refer to **C** and stress that tints are mixed by beginning with white paint. This is the best way to make a light color without wasting paint.

5 Focus on **D**. Discuss how Pierre Bonnard used light and dark colors to show a hot city day. The colors suggest the glaring light on the street and buildings. Ask students to place viewfinders on **D** and identify tints and shades, inferring how the colors were mixed.

6 Contrast and compare in **A** and **D** the expressive use of warm and cool (and light and dark) colors.

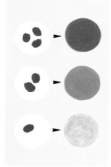

Tints are light colors. A **tint** is a color with white added to it. When you mix a tint, always begin with the white paint. Do you know why?

Artists mix tints and shades so they can express moods and feelings. Why did the artist use many shades for the painting in picture A? What mood comes from the many tints in picture D?

 Pierre Bonnard, *Two Dogs in a Deserted Street*, 1894. Wood, 13 7/8 x 10 5/8" (35 x 27 cm). National Gallery of Art, Washington, DC (Ailsa Mellon Bruce Collection).

Practice mixing tints and shades. When you mix a tint or shade, you are changing the **value** of the color. For example, pink is a light value of red. A dark value of red is often called maroon.

43

INTEGRATING THE CURRICULUM

Extensions ▼   ▼

Language Arts Have students compose poems with two words per line about the city they showed in this lesson. For example:

smoggy sky
tall buildings
busy people
rushing around
my city.

Science Have students draw two pictures of similar cloud formations. Have them color each picture to suggest different times of day. For example, one might have a dark sky and deeply shaded clouds. The other might have a light blue sky with tints in the clouds.

Literature Link
• *Claude Monet,* Peter Harrison. (I, A)
• *Punch in New York,* Alice Provensen. (S)
• *My New York,* Kathy Jakobsen. (A)

CLOSE

Create

1 Have students help you list words on the chalkboard in three columns: seasons, weather, and time of day. Discuss how they might select words in each column and combine them for an idea to paint (e.g., a city on a rainy autumn morning).

2 Distribute materials. Have students begin when they have an idea.

3 Stress the use of light and dark to express a special mood or feeling. Suggest that students begin with tints and gradually mix and add shades. Suggest they emphasize warm or cool colors to unify their work.

4 Help students recall how to mix secondary colors and why they should wash, wipe, and blot the brush.

Assess

1 Have volunteers hold up dry paintings. Encourage students to describe the place, time of day, weather, and season. Ask them to comment on the mood or feeling and how it has been captured.

Cleanup

1 Follow procedures from earlier lessons.

Art History

Claude Monet (Lessons 13 and 18) led the Impressionist painting movement in France in the 1870s. Pierre Bonnard was a follower of the Impressionists during the early 1900s. Both artists painted outdoors and often worked quickly to capture the light, color, and atmosphere of a time of day.

RESOURCES

Large Reproductions
  French Pastries, Thiebaud, 2
  Brotherhood Building, Haas, 15
  Jim, Johnson, 14
  Time, Chagall, 11

Overhead Transparencies
  Mrs. Jenkins, Wilson, 15

CD-ROM
  1, *Color*, Lesson 4

Slide Set
  Blue House, Vlaminck, 7

Assessment Masters
  Comparing Two Artworks, 19

17 When the Wind Blows
Painting

PREPARE

Objectives

Students will:
• be aware of techniques artists use to imply motion in two-dimensional artwork.
• create a watercolor painting using tints and shades to portray a windy landscape.

Vocabulary

watercolor paint	*acuarela*
shadows	*sombras*
tint	*tono/matiz*
brushstrokes	*pincelada*
movement	*movimiento*

Setup

Be prepared to demonstrate the use of watercolors, emphasizing the use of paint with a wet brush and diluting colors so that paper shows through the paint.

Materials

watercolor paints, 1 set per student

white paper, 12 x 18" (30 x 46 cm), 1 per student

watercolor brushes

water containers

sponge

dry paper towels or cloths

newspapers for desks

smocks

white paper, 6 x 9" (15 x 23 cm), 1 per student

A   **C.W. Jefferys, *Wheat Stacks on the Prairies*,** 1907. Oil on canvas, 23 x 35" (58 x 89 cm). Government of Ontario Art Collection, Toronto (Purchase from the artist). Photograph: Tom Moore Photography, Toronto.

How does the wind feel when it is blowing hard? How do the paintings in this lesson capture a feeling of wind blowing?

Look at the painting in picture A. The brushstrokes in the clouds swirl and curve. Find the light and dark colors in the haystacks. How do the **shadows** in the haystacks help to show motion?

Now look at the painting in picture B. The winds of a hurricane are blowing the palm trees. What brushstrokes and colors help to express a windy, stormy feeling?

Students created the paintings in picture C. How did they use brushstrokes and mix colors to capture the feeling of wind?

44

TEACH

Engage

1 Ask students to describe times they experienced extremely windy weather. Have them describe visual clues to the wind's strength and other sensations they recall.

2 Contrast a strong wind on a clear day with a strong wind during a storm. Focus on visual clues. Explain that in artworks such as drawings and paintings artists have to invent ways to suggest motion.

Explore

1 Focus on **A**. Guide students to see and gesture the cloud swirls. Have them identify other visual clues that suggest the direction the wind blows (shadows and shapes of the stacks imply the wind blows left to right).

2 In **B**, guide students to see how the artist shows the palm fronds blowing up, out, and to the right.

3 Have volunteers identify qualities in **C** that student artists have used to suggest wind motion. (At the top, fuzzy shapes suggest motion. At the bottom, strong diagonal lines suggest motion.)

4 Discuss how to use watercolor paints to create tints (much water, a little paint, lighter colors) and shades (less water, more paint, darker colors).

Create

1 Distribute materials. Demonstrate how to wet the brush, lightly pull it across a color, and test the result. Show students the effects of:

• pressing the brush down (a petal or leaflike shape).

• letting two colors run together.

Meeting Individual Needs

Simplify If you do not have watercolor sets, dilute tempera with water, 1:1. Students can further dilute for tints and other effects related to watercolors. (See also Lesson 14.)

Challenge Set up a station for students to create watercolor paintings on their own. Emphasize that the colors in the trays must be diluted with water and not used like tempera paint.

B Winslow Homer, *Hurricane, Bahamas*. Watercolor on paper, 14 1/2 x 21" (35 x 50 cm). The Metropolitan Museum of Art (Amelia B. Lazarus Fund, 1910).

 Student artwork.

The artworks in pictures B and C are painted with **watercolor paint**. Watercolor paints come in small trays. You dip your brush in water. Then you gently rub the brush on the tray of paint.

To make a tint with watercolor paints, use white paper. When you apply the paint, the white paper makes the color look like a tint. Your tempera, or poster paints, can also be used with a lot of water (see Lesson 14).

Think about a time when you saw and felt the wind blowing very hard. Make a painting to share your memory of that time.

45

INTEGRATING THE CURRICULUM

Extensions ▼ ▼

Language Arts Have students discuss the moods shown in their paintings. Encourage descriptive language. Students can write a *tanka* (a form of Japanese poetry) to describe the paintings. A tanka is similar to a haiku. It is based on syllables arranged as follows:

The rain fell like tears (5 syllables)
From the gray sky up above. (7 syllables)
Then the red clouds came (5 syllables)
And the sky lit up with fire. (7 syllables)
We ran in fear of the storm. (7 syllables)

Science Discuss observable effects of wind. Extreme examples include the effects of tornadoes and hurricanes. More subtle examples are seen in cloud movements, birds gliding on currents, whitecap waves, fluttering leaves. Have students identify other examples and draw them.

Science Have students watch a weather report on television for several days. Have them identify ways graphics and special symbols help people know about wind patterns.

Literature Link
• *Reflections*, Ann Jonas. (A)
• *One White Sail*, S.T. Garne. (A)
• *Mirandy and Brother Wind*, Patricia C. McKissack. (S)

• pulling and pressing the brush for thick lines.
• pulling with light pressure for thin lines.
• blotting to create textures and speed up drying time.

2 Have students use the small paper for experiments with brushstrokes, color mixtures, and tints and shades.

3 Before students begin the landscape painting, have them decide whether the composition will be tall or wide. Ask them to consider what areas to paint first (usually the largest ones, such as sky and background).

4 As students work, offer guidance on how to solve problems and suggest motion. Point out that accidental effects, such as blurred edges, can often be incorporated into the design. Remind students to add details in blotted or dry areas.

CLOSE

Assess

1 Ask volunteers who have dry paintings to hold them up. Encourage comments about the use of watercolor techniques, tints, shades, and ways motion has been portrayed.

2 Have students gather in groups to talk about what they have learned from the lesson and each other's work.

Cleanup

1 Teach students to wash paintbrushes and leave the brush tip with a point by bringing the thumb, forefinger, and index finger together and pulling the tip through the fingers.

2 Collect paint, brushes, and water containers. Collect paper towels inside folded newspapers. Put away smocks.

RESOURCES

Large Reproductions
Indian Boy, Homer, 9

Overhead Transparencies
Gulf Stream, Homer, 3
Corn Dance, Peña, 10

 CD-ROM
3, *Artists at Work*, Lesson 1

Slide Set
Blown Away, Homer, 6

Assessment Masters
Comparing Two Artworks, 19

PREPARE

Objectives

Students will:
- compare and contrast spaces and color schemes in three landscape paintings about seasons.
- create an artwork with planned uses of space and color to portray a season.

Vocabulary

space	*espacio*
color scheme	*combinación de*
monochromatic	*colores (plan)*
analogous	*monocromático(a)*
	análogos

Setup

Students should select colored paper to go with their season and color scheme. Trim some paper into squares and non-standard rectangles for a choice of shapes. List on the chalkboard the questions from the Evaluation Guide in Review Unit 1.

Materials

colored drawing paper, 12 x 18" (30 x 46 cm), 1 per student (See Setup)

oil pastels, including white

(optional) videos about seasonal changes, especially important if students live in a climate where seasonal changes are subtle

A   J.E.H. MacDonald, *Leaves in the Brook*, ca.1918. Oil on pressed board, 8 1/4 x 10 5/8" (21 x 27 cm). McMichael Canadian Art Collection (Gift of Mr. A.Y. Jackson, 1966).

Imagine you could walk into the scenes in these paintings. What would you expect to hear or touch? What would you like to do or explore?

Each painting shows a different season. These artists show some of the colors, spaces and moods in nature.

In picture A, Canadian artist J. E. H. MacDonald shows autumn leaves in a brook. The **space** in the picture is filled with autumn-like colors. What else can you see and describe?

What is the **color scheme**, or plan, for this painting? Are most of the colors warm or cool? Why? An artist would say this painting has a warm, dark color scheme. Even the browns look "warm." Many of the browns are mixed from yellow, red and a small amount of blue.

46

TEACH

Engage

1 Discuss the changes seen and felt outdoors during each season. Focus on visible changes as well as changes perceived through other senses.

2 Explain that students will see and discuss ways artists plan works to suggest how seasons look and feel.

Art Criticism

Arrange the class into three groups to describe and record the mood, dominant colors, and other design elements of one painting by Monet (Lessons 13, 16, 18). Ask groups to point out what they have described in the artwork.

Explore

1 Allow time for students to look at **A**. Then guide them to imagine the sound of the brook, the crunching of dry leaves, and the soft texture of damp foliage. Help them see and name dark, warm colors, such as reddish-violet, yellow-brown, and dark red-orange.

2 Explain that students can create a wonderful range of browns by mixing red, yellow, and a small amount of blue. Guide them to see in **A** how the artist used brushstrokes to suggest colors and textures of autumn leaves.

3 Discuss the variety of blues in **B** and reasons snow can be shown with tints of blue and other colors. (The white snow reflects the blue of the sky. At sunset, snow can glow with yellows, reds, and other hues.)

4 Help students understand that a monochromatic color scheme can be based on any hue, such as red with pink and dark reds. Stress that many monochromatic paintings have hints of other colors to create interest.

5 In **C**, guide students to appreciate that a related (or analogous) color scheme contains colors that match only one part of a rainbow.

6 Have students identify—from the color wheel in Lesson 13—analogous colors in Monet's painting (yellow-orange, yellow, yellow-green, blue-green, green).

7 Compare and contrast how each artist composed the picture space:
- **A** is a horizontal close-up view with no sky.
- **B** is square. The viewer looks down a hill. The near trees extend from the bottom to the top. There is no skyline.
- **C** is vertical. The upper fourth of the space has sky. The lower fourth of the space has more shadow than the middle.

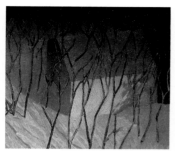

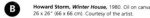
B Howard Storm, *Winter House,* 1980. Oil on canvas, 26 x 26" (66 x 66 cm). Courtesy of the artist.

C Claude Monet, *Meadow at Giverny.* Oil on canvas, 36 1/4 x 32 1/8" (92 x 82 cm). Museum of Fine Arts, Boston (Juliana Cheney Edwards Collection).

In picture B, Howard Storm shows a winter landscape. How has he used the picture space?

This winter landscape has a monochromatic color scheme. **Monochromatic** means one color. Why do you think the artist used many tints and shades of blue?

The landscape in picture C was painted by Claude Monet. This scene was near his home in France. How has he planned spaces to show the sky, trees and sunny meadow?

The main colors in this painting are related, or analogous. Related colors are next to each other on the color wheel (see page 33). Can you identify the related colors in this painting? What mood do the colors help to express?

Think about the season you like best. How will you plan the colors and spaces? What ideas and feelings can your artwork show?

47

INTEGRATING THE CURRICULUM

Extensions ▼

Social Studies Discuss how seasonal changes affect the lives of people in your community. Make students aware of seasonal variations in work and play, the use of energy, availability of foods, clothing, and the like. Then have them conduct research to compare and contrast the cultural adaptations of people who live in arctic, temperate, and tropical regions. Focus on differences in food, clothing, shelter, and activities.

Literature Link
• *Sky Tree,* Thomas Locker with Candace Christiansen. (A)
• *Mother Earth,* Nancy Luenn. (A)
• *In for Winter, Out for Spring,* Arnold Adoff. (A)

CLOSE

Create

1 Ask students to close their eyes and visualize an outdoor scene of a season. Guide them to imagine or recall a special view of the scene (near or far, looking through one space to another).

2 Distribute materials. Have students select paper in a shape and background color to fit their idea.

3 As students work, encourage them to create subtle mixtures of colors and imagine or recall sounds, temperatures, and elements that will help them compose the picture.

Assess

1 Give students the choice of using the outline to write about their work or to discuss their work in small groups. Explain that the outline will help them think about the way an artwork is planned, what it communicates, and what they have learned.

2 Ask students to share any insights they gained by evaluating their work. Praise thoughtful comments.

RESOURCES

Large Reproductions
 Golden Age, Brown, 6
 Upstream, Kuniyoshi, 10
 Three Musicians, Picasso, 4

Overhead Transparencies
 Boy with Flute, Lewis, 7
 Morning Light, Bleumner, 24
 First Steps, Picasso, 16

CD-ROM
 1, *Color,* Lesson 3

Slide Set
 Parc Monceau, Monet, 9

Assessment Masters
 A Vote for Art, 21

PREPARE

Objectives

Students will:
- understand that artworks can be reworked to incorporate details, shading, texture, and color changes.
- try to improve an artwork by adding details, shading, texture, colors, or other design elements.

Vocabulary

subtle colors	*cambios sutiles de color*
shading	*sombreado*
details	*detalles*

Setup

Provide oil pastels, markers, crayons, and soft pencils. Be prepared to demonstrate how swabs or tissues can blend oil pastels and how layers of crayon and oil pastels can be built up and scratched to create details.

Materials

folders with students' artwork

drawing media

newspapers for desks

cotton swabs or facial tissue for oil pastels

paper clips or plastic coffee stirrers

A

When you see your world as an artist, you notice subtle differences in colors. **Subtle** means that you can see small changes or differences. Look at the photograph of clouds in picture A. Where do you see subtle colors?

You can create subtle colors in your artwork. Shading is one way. **Shading** is a gradual change from light to dark. You can also create shading by blending related colors, such as yellow, orange and red. Students created the shaded drawings in picture B.

 B Student artwork.

48

TEACH

Engage

1 Explain that artists often look back at their work and try to improve it. Have students give examples of improvements they achieved by practicing, trying again, or changing an idea.

2 Tell students that they will select one or several previous works to try to improve by adding details, shading, and subtle colors.

Explore

1 In **A**, note that the dramatic colors in the clouds come from a sunset. Guide students to see that the shadows in **A** are not pure black but subtle colors. The colors are related (or analogous) and move from lighter to darker hues.

2 Ask students to explain why the colorful shadows in **A** are on the bottom (the sun is setting but is still above the clouds).

3 In **B**, note how different students have used the variety of light and dark colors and soft, fuzzy edges for the sky.

4 Focus on **C**. Explain that details are small things, but they help you see how one thing is different from another. Ask students to identify some subtle colors, shading, and details.

5 Guide students to see how the artist used details to show differences in each tree. Note where shadows go across the lumpy ground, and how clouds have different shapes.

Camille Pissarro (1830–1903) was a French Impressionist painter. He was influenced by Monet but, unlike other Impressionists, almost always portrayed landscapes with people at work. Like Millet (Lesson 1), Pissarro showed the dignity of farmers and other workers. Ask students to compare and contrast Millet's painting in Lesson 1 with the painting by Pissarro in this lesson. Have them imaginatively enter each scene and describe it from the workers' point of view and then the artist's.

Camille Pissarro, *Orchard in Bloom, Louveciennes*, 1872. Oil on canvas, 17 3/4 x 21 5/8" (45 x 55 cm). The National Gallery of Art, Washington, DC (Ailsa Mellon Bruce Collection).

Artists also learn to see details. **Details** are small shapes that show how one thing is different from another. Look for details in picture C. How do the details help you see the differences in the trees? What other details do you see?

Look at some of the artwork you have made. Study the colors and details. Can you improve your artwork by using subtle colors and more details?

49

Extensions ▼

Language Arts Have students write about the mood they tried to achieve, techniques they used, and how successful they were. Display the artwork with the writing. Have other students read the evaluations and examine the artworks. Discuss the importance of reflecting on your work and learning from others' accomplishments.

Language Arts Read *Giving Tree* by Shel Silverstein (Harper & Row Junior Books, 1964) in its entirety and then reread it slowly. As the story is read the second time, have students make sketches showing how the tree changes in the story. They are to notice and record as many details as possible.

Literature Link

- *Where the River Begins*, Thomas Locker. (A)
- *The Boy Who Held Back the Sea*, retold by Lenny Hort. (A)

CLOSE

Create

1 Distribute folders with students' artwork. Have them choose a work to improve and a medium to use.

2 Have students think about changes or additions. Encourage them to consider shading one side or the bottom edges of shapes, blending colors, and adding details.

3 Demonstrate how to use a swab or tissue to blend oil pastels and how a dark layer of crayon or oil pastel can be put over a lighter color and scratched to create lines and textures.

4 Ask students to think of other ways to use drawing media. Point out that markers are best used on paper, not over crayon or oil pastel. Almost any media can be applied over dry paint.

5 Have students improve a second work if they wish.

Assess

1 Ask students who added shading to hold their works up. Discuss how effects were achieved and other ways students tried to improve their work.

2 Stress that artists often consider ways to revise or improve a work. Sometimes they do improve it; sometimes they prefer to start over. Not every artwork is successful, but something important is learned by creating it.

Cleanup

1 Check the floor. Have students return drawing media and usable supplies. Place tissues and other trash inside folded newspapers for disposal.

Reminder

Preview the next lesson. Have students make sketches at home of several views of a favorite animal and bring in the sketches for the lesson. Students can draw a live animal or use their memories.

RESOURCES

Large Reproductions
 Carolina Parrots, Audubon, 8
 Golden Age, Brown, 6
 Indian Boy, Homer, 9

Overhead Transparencies
 Dash for the Timber, Remington, 9
 The Ark, Miller, 2

 CD-ROM
 1, *Color*, Lesson 4
 2, *Elements of Design*, Lesson 3

Slide Set
 Parc Monceau, Monet, 9

Assessment Masters
 A Bird's Eye View, 11

PREPARE

Objectives

Students will:
• discuss artworks that show animals, noting textures, shading, poses, and expressions.
• draw and create a painting of an animal emphasizing texture, shading, pose, and expression.

Vocabulary

value	*valor*
texture	*textura*
portrait	*retrato*
tint	*tono/matiz*
shade	*sombra*
expression	*expresión*
pose	*pose*

Materials

animal sketches made at home

newspaper or manila paper, 12 x 18" (30 x 46 cm), 1 per student

smocks

newspapers for desks

tempera paints: black, white, red, yellow, and blue

water containers

brushes, 1 per student

sponges

paper towels

Many artists have created artworks about animals. They have shown pets, farm animals and wildlife.

Picture A is a **portrait**, or likeness, of a real dog named Brizo. Rosa Bonheur, an artist from France, painted the picture about 130 years ago.

BRIZO.

 A

Rosa Bonheur, *Brizo, A Shepherd's Dog*, 1864. Oil on canvas, 13 1/4 x 15" (46 x 33 cm). Reproduced by permission of the Trustees, The Wallace Collection, London.

Look at the texture of the dog's hair. If you could pet the real dog, would the hair feel soft or rough? How can you tell? What kind of brushstrokes create the textures?

Now squint your eyes just a little and look at this painting.

Squinting helps you see the **values**, or light and dark areas, in the painting. Where has the artist used shades, or dark values? Where has the artist used tints, or light values? Why did the artist use light and dark colors?

50

TEACH

Engage

1 Discuss sketches of animals made at home, noting views, poses, and expressions.

2 Explain that students will use their best sketch to plan a painting, drawing the most important view and shape of the animal so it fills most of the paper.

Meeting Individual Needs

Simplify Have students create pictures using oil pastels on colored paper.

Challenge Discuss how the work from this lesson might be displayed with titles and brief descriptions of what students learned.

Explore

1 Focus on **A**. Explain that Rosa Bonheur became well known for her animal paintings. She studied animals and carefully observed their differences. Guide students to see how brushstrokes and color changes suggest the texture of fur. The lighter colors are at the top and left of the head. The darker colors are on the right and below the ears and nose. Note that the head fills most of the space and is centered.

2 Focus on **B**. John James Audubon, like Bonheur, combined an interest in animals with art. His paintings show where birds or other animals live, as well as their special motions, poses, or gestures.

3 Guide students to see how Audubon's use of shading helps us see color changes and feathers. Point out the relative size of the animal, and the side view.

4 Focus on **C**. Discuss the special views, poses, expressions, and use of light and dark colors to suggest textures.

Create

1 Distribute materials. Have students adapt their best sketch into a composition for a painting.

2 Ask students to stand while they draw the main shape with pencil, filling most of the picture space. Standing can help them see the whole picture space and judge sizes of shapes. Suggest that students sketch a few other lines so they know where to paint eyes, nose, or background elements.

3 Before students paint, show techniques they might use to suggest hair or fur:

• Put paint on a brush, blot it once, and then spread hairs to "tickle" the paper.

• Mix a slightly darker value of the same hue and use the brush in the same way, painting over the same area.

• Vary the direction of the fine brush lines and change colors to suggest textures and shadows.

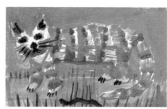

B John James Audubon, *American Flamingo*, Plate
CCCCXXXI, No. 87, from *The Birds of America*, 1838.
Hand-colored engraving with aquatint, 38 x 26"
(97 x 66 cm). National Gallery of Art, Washington, DC
(Gift of Mrs. Water B. James).

C Student artwork.

John James Audubon created the artwork in picture B. He was born in Haiti but he lived in the United States. He created paintings of over 1000 birds. His paintings are in a book called *The Birds of America*.

Where do you see tints and shades in picture B? Why do the changes in light and dark colors help you see textures? What else do you see?

Students created the two paintings in picture C. What did they show? How?

Sketch one of your favorite animals. Give the animal a special pose or expression. Then create a painting of it. Mix tints and shades and show the textures of the animal.

51

Extensions ▼

Language Arts Read the Caldecott Honor book *Swimmy* by Leo Lionni (Knopf/Parthenon, 1963). As the book is read, point out how Lionni uses shapes, textures, tints, and shades in his illustrations. Ask students to find other library books that include drawings created by artists and report on some of the techniques they recognize.

Literature Link
- *Turtle in July,* Marilyn Singer. (A)
- *The Ice Horse,* Candace Christiansen. (A)
- *Whale,* Judy Allen. (A)

---

4 Suggest students begin by painting the background and then mix a basic color for the animal.

5 As students paint the animal, remind them to mix light and dark varieties of the color. For example, a white-furred animal can have textures painted in gray, blue-gray, or pinkish-gray.

Critical Thinking

Have students describe qualities of Rosa Bonheur's paintings in this lesson and Lesson 1. Discuss similarities and then set up two columns labeled Fawns and Dog. Guide students to identify differences in the paintings, such as how quickly they think it was done, how finished the work seems, and the views portrayed.

CLOSE

Assess

1 Call on volunteers to describe what they ll have learned. Guide them to recall the process of looking at artworks by Bonheur and Audubon as well as their own work.

2 Have students gather in groups to discuss textures, poses, and expressions in one another's work using the vocabulary words.

Cleanup

1 Students should be able to follow cleanup procedures with minimal supervision. Discuss why certain procedures are more helpful than others.

RESOURCES

Large Reproductions
  Toto, Romero, 20
  Wolf General, Blackwell, 21

Overhead Transparencies
  Jennie, Jones, 8
  The Ark, Miller, 2

 CD-ROM
  1, *Color*, Lesson 4
  2, *Elements of Design*, Lesson 1

Slide Set
  Doe's Head, Perilli, 10

Assessment Masters
  Mix and Match, 12
  Imagine That, 9

Aesthetic Awareness

Have students look at artworks that portray animals in Lessons 8, 20, 21, and 55. Compare and contrast styles, noting special qualities in each work. Encourage students to use descriptive style names, such as scientific or realistic, fantasy or cartoonlike.

PREPARE

Objectives

Students will:
- perceive and discuss a complex artwork created by a team of artists.
- work in groups to create complex murals about animals.

Vocabulary

illustrate	*ilustran (ilustrar)*
mural	*mural*
background	*fondo*
realistic	*realista*
imaginary	*imaginario*

Setup

Arrange the class into groups of four to six students. Set up painting stations so half paint backgrounds while others draw and cut shapes. As paint dries, students make cutouts for the murals.

Materials

mural or background paper, 18 x 24" (46 x 61 cm), 1 for 4 to 6 students to share

white drawing paper, assorted sizes, 2 per student

markers, crayons, or oil pastels

scissors

paste

sets of tempera paints

newspapers

paper towels

smocks

sponge brushes for each color of paint

A **Unknown,** ***Raven Addressing Assembled Animals,*** ca. 1590, India-Mughul School. Reproduced by Courtesy of the Trustees of The British Museum, London.

TEACH

Engage

1 Explain that students will work in groups to create murals with real or imaginary animals.

2 Have students help you list on the chalkboard real or imaginary land, sea, and air animals. List where each animal lives: swamps, grasslands with trees, mountains, desert.

Explore

1 Read and discuss the text, allowing time for students to answer the questions.

2 Guide students to see how the main character in **A**, the raven, perches on top of a triangular group of rocks. In many parts of Asia, the raven is a symbol for a noisy, bossy character who may or may not have important news to share but is hard to ignore.

3 Guide students to see the mythical firebird on the right, the smaller cranes, and the huge dragon, each seeming to listen or speak to the raven. Continue to look down the right side, noting snakes, otter, and elephant.

4 Encourage pairs of students to identify other animals as familiar, unknown, or imaginary. List all the recognizable animals on the chalkboard.

5 Discuss **B**. Note the very simple background (painted first), overlapping shapes of animals, and lines suggesting grass (added last, on top of dry paint).

Create

1 Arrange the class into groups, distribute materials, and explain procedures. Have groups decide on a background and animals to work on first.

2 Ask students to select a group member to watch you demonstrate a technique for painting the background. These students will then teach others in their group.

3 Demonstrate using a wide brush to paint large areas, such as sky. Press crushed newspaper over the paint. Note how the mottled look can suggest grass, rocks, or water (if other colors are used). Because the paint has been blotted, it dries quickly.

4 Pace the activity so backgrounds are prepared in the first fifteen to twenty minutes.

5 Guide students to think about the relative sizes of the cutout shapes. Remind them that two identical animals can be cut from folded paper. To suggest space or distance, place larger shapes near the bottom.

People in many lands write and **illustrate** stories about animals. The painting in picture A is from India.
It illustrates a story about animals. Many animals have gathered to hear a raven speak.

A raven is a very big bird. It looks like a crow. It is the center of interest in this painting. Where do you see the raven? Why are most of the animals looking toward it?

There are many animals in this painting. Some are imaginary creatures. Can you find them? What other animals do you see? Can you tell if they are listening or speaking?

Several artists created paintings like this. They worked together as a team. One designed the background and largest shapes. Some artists worked on the realistic animals. Others worked on the imaginary animals. Are there other ways artists could work together?

With other students in your class, create a large picture, or **mural**, about real or imaginary

animals. You could make up a story to illustrate.

Plan the background first and paint it. List the animals, trees or other shapes that you need. Draw and cut out these shapes. Try several ways to place the shapes. Then paste the shapes down.

53

Extensions ▼

Social Studies When murals are complete, have students conduct library research or discuss murals in their community. Point out that many murals are created in public places. Some send a message to the public; for this reason, they are painted large and placed where many people can see them.

Literature Link
• *The Shelf-Paper Jungle,* Diana Engel. (S, A)
• *Matthew's Dragon,* Susan Cooper. (S)
• *The Great Ball Game: A Muskogee Story,* retold by Joseph Bruchac. (A)

6 Have students paste shapes and add details using drawing media.

Art History

A is one of many paintings created by artists who worked for Emperor Akbar, ruler of India from 1556 to 1605. He set up large studios, where artists created thousands of miniature paintings to illustrate books. The collaborative process of creating small, detailed works is not unique to this time or culture. For example, comic book studios employ artists who do basic sketches of figures, others who do backgrounds or lettering, and still others who do final drawings in ink and make final decisions about color. Have students discuss advantages and disadvantages of collaborative artwork.

CLOSE

Assess

1 Have students assist in displaying the murals. Discuss the general designs, environments, animals, and details.

2 Discuss the overall effect of seeing the murals together. Explain that most murals created by artists are planned for a specific wall on a building.

Cleanup

1 Follow procedures from earlier lessons.

Reminder
For the next lesson, have students create sketches at home of insects or small animals.

RESOURCES

Large Reproductions
  Brotherhood Building, Haas, 15
  Golden Age, Brown, 6
Overhead Transparencies
  Dogware, Tygart, 5
 CD-ROM
  5, *People and Animals,* Lesson 3
Assessment Masters
  Mix and Match, 12
  Imagine That, 9

PREPARE

Objectives

Students will:
- understand procedures used in relief printing.
- create signed and numbered relief prints.

Vocabulary

print	*grabado*
printing	*ink tinta para grabado*
edition	*edición*
printing block	*plancha/bloque de grabado*

Setup

Paint should be creamy. Add one drop of liquid soap. Make a test print with each color. Place clay in a warm area.

Materials

student sketches from home

newsprint paper, 6 x 9" (15 x 23 cm), 5 per student

oil-based clay, about ¼ lb. (114 gm) per student

paper clips to carve clay

tempera paint, black or dark colors, 1 container per 2 to 4 students

brushes, 1 per paint container

newspapers as a cushion for printing

damp paper towels

pencils

smocks

rubber stamp with lettering

Some artists make **prints** by carving a design in a block of wood. They put ink on the wood and press paper on the ink. The design on the block of wood can be printed again and again. The print of the insect in picture A was made in this way.

You can make prints from a block of clay. Make a thick, smooth block.

Draw an insect on the smooth clay. Use a paper clip to carve into the clay. The lines and shapes must be wide and deep. Follow the steps in pictures B and D.

Bug   3/10   C. Kelly

A   **B**

54

TEACH

Engage

1 Briefly review printing definitions introduced in Lessons 5, 9, and 10.

2 Hand the rubber stamp to a student and ask how it is used. Have the student explain why the lettering on the stamp is backward (so it will look correct when printed). Allow the rest of the class to inspect the stamp.

Meeting Individual Needs

Simplify Use water-based printing ink, an inking slab, and brayers to apply ink. For printing blocks, use pieces of foam plastic from egg cartons or meat trays.

Challenge Have students create a class book that includes their prints and poems or stories about insects. Set up a printing station so students can create an improved print if they wish.

Explore

1 Guide students to see how the insect in **A** was carved into a wooden block and then used to create the print below it.

2 Discuss the steps in **B**:
- Press clay on the desk to make a flat, smooth surface as thick as an index finger.
- Use a paper clip, as shown, to carve grooves.
- Carefully lift away carved clay.

3 Guide students to see that the print in **C** was created by using a clay stamp. The paint is brushed on the flat surface, not inside the grooves.

4 Explain how artists number prints. The first number tells whether the print was made first, second, third, and so on. The second number tells the total number of prints made from one printing block, also called an *edition*.

5 Explain that students will create prints using their insect sketches to plan designs.

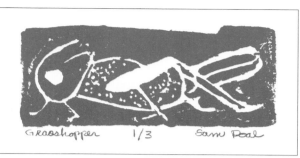

 Student artwork.

A student made this print of a grasshopper. He signed his print as artists do. He gave his print a title.

The print has two numbers. The 1 tells you this was the first print he made. The 3 tells you he made three prints like this one.

1. Brush paint or printing ink on the flat parts of the block.

2. Put paper over the block. Rub the back of the paper.

3. Carefully lift the paper. Let your print dry.

55

Extensions ▼ ▼ ▼

Science Contrast the ways an artist and a scientist might study insects. Point out that scientists and artists are both keen observers. An artist is more likely to study an insect to discover the beauty of its lines, shapes, and colors. A scientist may look at the same features but is likely to analyze how they help the animal with food gathering, protection, or reproduction.

Language Arts Read *Once a Mouse* by Marcia Brown (Scribner, 1961). Point out that the illustrations were done with woodcuts. Explain that a new woodcut was carved and printed each time the artist changed the mouse into a different animal. Allow students to examine the book individually.

Social Studies Have students conduct research on the invention of paper, printing techniques, and the influence of printing on literacy as well as art (especially posters).

Literature Link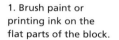
- *My Son John*, Jim Aylesworth. (A)
- *Tracks in the Wild*, Betsy Bowen. (A)

CLOSE

Create

1 Distribute materials, except printing paper. Lead students step by step as they press clay on a smooth newspaper. Have them trim irregular edges of the slab with a paper clip. Note that the shape of the slab can fit the shape of the insect.

2 Students may refer to their insect drawings to create a design on the block. Remind them that designs carved in the block will face the opposite direction on the print.

3 Before students begin printing, have them remove loose crumbs of clay from the slab and save them in a ball. Then have them lightly press the carved side of the block on a smooth surface.

4 Distribute printing paper. Have students lightly number the sheets in one corner and print them in order from one to five. Provide guidance as needed. Have students place each wet print, unstacked, on a flat surface to dry so that desks are clear for making more prints.

Assess

1 Have students determine which prints are best and have volunteers explain the procedures used to create a print. Guide students as they sign, number, and title each print, as shown in **C**.

Cleanup

1 Collect brushes, paint, and paper clips or other tools. Remove excess paint from the clay by pressing the block on newspaper. Collect the clay. Clay can be reused if paint is washed off with soap and water. Make sure hands and desks are clean and dry.

RESOURCES

Large Reproductions
  Upstream, Kuniyoshi, 10

 Overhead Transparencies
  Le Jockey, Toulouse-Lautrec, 9

CD-ROM
  5, *People and Animals*, Lesson 3

Assessment Masters
  Mix and Match, 12

(A) Vincent Van Gogh, *Old Man Grieving*, 1882. 20 x 12 1/4" (50 x 31 cm). Van Gogh Museum, Amsterdam.

(B) J. B. Brown, *Boy Playing Piccolo*, 1885. Etching, 20 x 14" (127 x 36 cm). Butler Institute of American Art, Youngstown, Ohio (Gift of Mrs. M. J. Sampson).

There are many ways to see and think about art. The artworks in this lesson show people in different poses. A **pose** is a special way to stand or sit.

Study the figures, or people, in these artworks. Take the same pose that you see in each picture. Imagine how it feels to be posing for the artist. Tell what each person might think or feel.

Now imagine you are the artist who created each picture. Study the **angles**, or bends, in each figure. Where do you see similar bends in your own body?

56

PREPARE

Objectives

Students will:
- understand that some artwork is based on sketches of real people.
- draw pictures of students who pose.

Vocabulary

pose	*pose*
angle	*ángulo*
proportions	*proporción*
portrait	*retrato*

Setup

Place tape on each student model's clothes and draw arrows on tape, as shown below. Reuse tape for each new model. Help students pose with props such as a broom, bucket, or sports equipment. A wide, strong counter or desk may be the best place for poses.

Materials

pencils

newsprint paper, 9 x 12" (23 x 30 cm), at least 3 per student

wide tape and marker

TEACH

Engage

1 Explain that students will practice drawing each other. Several students will take turns posing while others draw. Stress that many artists practice drawing this way.

Explore

1 Ask each student to assume a position similar to those shown in **A**, **B**, and **C**. As they do so, guide them to mimic the exact positions.

2 Have students look at each drawing as if they were the artist. Have them point out the angles in **A** and **B** where knees and elbows bend. Have them identify other bends (neck, wrist, finger, ankles, hips) in all three artworks.

3 Define *proportion* as the size of one part in relation to another part or the whole. Call on volunteers to stand and help you demonstrate proportions:
- Hips are about halfway between the top of the head and feet.
- Knees are near the midpoint of the leg.
- Elbows can be pressed in near the waist.
- The upper and lower arm are about the same length.
- A hand is about the same length as the face from hairline to chin.

4 Discuss the sketch in **C** and finished painting in **D**. Note that both are portraits: a likeness of a real person.

C George Bellows, *Lady Jean,* 1924. Black lithographic crayon on white paper, 22 x 13" (56 x 35 cm). The Fogg Art Museum, Harvard University, Cambridge, Massachusetts (Bequest of Meta and Paul J. Sachs).

The bends in a figure show proportions. A **proportion** is the size of one part in relation to another. For example, the upper part of an arm is about the same length as the lower part. What other proportions in a figure can you discover?

Compare the sketch in picture C and the painting in picture D. What proportions do you see? Why

D George Bellows, *Lady Jean,* 1924. Oil on canvas, 72 x 36" (183 x 91 cm). Yale University Art Gallery, New Haven, Connecticut (Bequest of Stephen C. Clark).

did the artist make the sketch before the painting?

Make sketches of students who pose for your class. Show the bends in the body and the proportions.

57

INTEGRATING THE CURRICULUM

Extensions ▼ ▼

Science Display diagrams, models, or x-rays that show a human skeleton. Have students identify joints that move and directions in which they move.

Mathematics Tape mural paper on the wall to review proportions as fractional parts of a whole. Choose three students about the same height. Have them stand in front of the paper. Draw lines to show the relative lengths of parts of the body: top of head to chin, shoulder to elbow, waistline, and so on. Discuss the results.

Literature Link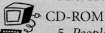
• *Vincent Van Gogh,* Peter Harrison. (A, I)
• *People,* Philip Yenawine. (A)
• *The Young Artist,* Thomas Locker. (S)

Create

1 Distribute materials. Call on a volunteer to pose. Place tape on the volunteer's clothes.

2 Ask the class to observe while the model takes several poses with a prop. Help students see how taped lines on the body change direction with each pose. Suggest that students first quickly draw these action lines and then draw the rest of the figure.

3 Explain that each pose will last about one minute. The model will then move around before resuming the pose for another minute. Everyone must draw quickly. The best sketches can be finished later.

4 Have different students model. Change the action and view for each pose. If interest is high, students may draw on both sides of their paper or on additional paper. Conclude the lesson before students tire.

CLOSE

Assess

1 Ask students which part of the lesson they enjoyed most. Discuss some of the drawings. Note specific parts that are based on careful observation of actions or proportions. Make sure that effort, not just the final result, is praised.

Reminder

Make sure students save their sketches for reference in Lessons 24 and 25.

RESOURCES

Large Reproductions
    Summer, Arcimboldo, 13
    Jim, Johnson, 14

Overhead Transparencies
    Dugout, Rockwell, 18
    Bactrian Camel, China 11
    Camels, Graves, 11

Slide Set
    Mrs. Krans, Krans, 12

CD-ROM
    5, *People and Animals,* Lessons 1 and 2

Assessment Masters
    Comparing Two Artworks, 19

PREPARE

Objectives

Students will:
- understand the meaning of perspective as it is used in art.
- draw a picture that uses perspective to show groups of people outdoors.

Vocabulary

perspective	*perspectiva*
space	*espacio*
illusion	*ilusión*

Materials

drawing paper, 12 x 18" (30 x 46 cm), 1 per student

choice of drawing media

viewfinders

A **Ben Shahn,** ***Handball,*** 1939. Tempera on paper over composition board, 22 3/4 x 31 1/4" (58 x 79 cm). Collection, The Museum of Modern Art, New York (Abby Aldrich Rockefeller Fund).

Where do you play and have fun outside? What games and activities do you enjoy with friends? Have you ever stopped playing and looked at people who are near or far away from you? What did you notice?

Look at the painting in picture A. The artist has shown two players who look near to you. These players are large and close to the bottom of the painting. The other players are small and higher up in the picture. This makes them look far away.

When artists show things that are near or far away, they are using **perspective**.

58

TEACH

Engage

1 Ask students to gather in the hallway with their viewfinders. Ask four students, about the same height, to stand at equal distances along the hall.

2 Have students hold their viewfinders so they focus in turn on each student along the hall. Ask students to describe what they observe (the farther away people are, the smaller they look).

3 Explain that students are seeing the way artists see when they want to show things near and far away. Students will learn more about this way of seeing, called *perspective*.

Explore

1 Focus on **A** and guide students to see two ways this artist uses perspective. Have them use viewfinders to compare the sizes of the figures and then focus on the location of the feet to see that distant figures are higher up in the space.

2 As students view **B**, have them first compare the sizes and locations of the figures that look like adults. Then have them focus on the children.

3 Discuss the action poses in **A** and **B** to reinforce the concepts from Lesson 23 and set the stage for drawing.

B William Glackens, *Bathing at Bellport, Long Island,* 1911. Oil on canvas, 26 1/16 x 32" (66 x 81 cm). The Brooklyn Museum (Bequest of Laura L. Barnes).

Now look at the painting in picture B. The people who look far away are small. The people who look near are larger and closer to the bottom of the picture.

You can use these ideas about perspective. Remember: When you want to show something is near, draw it large and close to the bottom of your picture. When you want to show something is farther away, draw it smaller and higher up in the picture.

Create a picture of a place outdoors where you like to have fun with other people. How can you show things in perspective?

59

INTEGRATING THE CURRICULUM

Extensions ▼ ▼

Social Studies Have students look at both paintings in this lesson and focus on the activities, places, and clothing. Have students identify features that are similar and dissimilar to life today. Have them use the dates of the artworks to help explain why some features are dissimilar.

Mathematics Develop an awareness of proportionate size as a way to show perspective. Make a mural that shows a crowd of people. Provide three pieces of paper for each student. Trim the paper to these sizes:

- 6 x 18" (15 x 46 cm)
- 4 x 12" (10 x 30 cm)
- 2 x 6" (5 x 15 cm)

Have students draw one standing action figure on each paper, cut out the figures, and arrange them on the mural to show a large crowd in perspective. Remind them to place the small figures closer to the top, the large figures toward the bottom, and others between. The figures can overlap to enhance the illusion of perspective.

Literature Link
- *The Green Lion of Zion Street,* Julia Fields. (A)
- *Market Day,* Eve Bunting. (A)
- *My Little Island,* Frané Lessac. (A)

CLOSE

Create

1 Distribute materials. Have students think about a favorite outdoor activity with family or friends and where on their paper they will draw the figures.

2 Suggest that students first draw the figures that will be near, making them large and placing them close to the bottom. Then they can draw people farther away.

3 While students draw, offer guidance on drawing in perspective and portraying action. Many students will have a general grasp of the concepts but may have difficulty representing them. Perspective techniques are reviewed and reinforced in other lessons in this unit as well as at other levels of *Adventures in Art.*

Assess

1 Discuss student works that successfully portray figures in action in an outdoor space and that show perspective through locations or sizes of figures.

2 Explain that students will learn more about perspective in the next lesson.

RESOURCES

Large Reproductions
  Brotherhood Building, Haas, 15
  Upstream, Kuniyoshi, 10
  Interior, Matisse, 17

Overhead Transparencies
  Night Baseball, Phillips, 18
  Thanksgiving, Lee, 8

CD-ROM
  5, *People and Animals,* Lessons 1 and 2

Slide Set
  Trapeze Act, Dwight, 11

Assessment Masters
  Find Out About Art, 20

25 A Crowded Scene
Drawing

PREPARE

Objectives

Students will:
- be aware of size, position, and overlap as ways to suggest perspective.
- create a drawing of themselves in a stage-like space looking out at an audience.

Vocabulary

space	*espacio*
distance	*distancia*
overlap	*traslapo*
perspective	*perspectiva*

Materials

drawing paper, 12 x 18"
(30 x 40 cm),
1 per student

choice of drawing media

 Everett Shinn, *The Monologist,* 1910. Pastel on paper, 8 1/4 x 11 3/4" (21 x 30 cm). Wichita Art Museum, Wichita, Kansas (The Roland P. Murdock Collection). Photograph: Henry Nelson.

Have you ever been on a stage and seen the audience? Have you ever seen crowds of people in other places? How can you show this kind of scene in an artwork?

Imagine you are the artist who is drawing the scene in picture A. Where would the artist be on the stage? Why did the artist draw the actor so large? Why did the artist draw the people in the first rows larger than the people in the back rows?

Now look at picture B. The largest shape is the person on the stage. Why do the people in the audience look smaller?

In both artworks, the artist created a feeling of **space** and

TEACH

Engage

1 Review briefly the definition of *perspective* from Lesson 24 (showing things that are near or far away).

2 Ask students to recall from Lesson 24 two ways of showing perspective (size and location of figures). Explain that they will use these ideas and learn a third way to show figures near or far in a picture.

Meeting Individual Needs

Simplify Begin the lesson with a trip to an auditorium as described in Drama. Then complete the lesson.

Challenge Encourage students to use their knowledge of perspective techniques when they create artworks based on imagination, recall, or observation.

Explore

1 Focus on **A**, a drawing by United States artist Everett Shinn. Ask students to describe why the figure on stage looks near. The on-stage figure that looks near is large, and the figures in the audience are shown smaller to look farther away.

2 In **A**, guide students to see that the figure on stage overlaps part of the floor and the audience space. Define *overlap* as some shapes that look like they are in front of others. (You can't see all of the shapes behind.)

3 In **B**, a painting by African-American artist Jacob Lawrence, guide students to see how the large figure overlaps the stage and part of the audience. In the audience, the figures in the rows in front overlap the figures in rows behind. Have students find similar placements of the figures in **A**.

4 Tell students they will be creating a drawing of themselves in a stagelike space looking out at an audience.

Art History

Everett Shinn (1876–1953) was member of the Ashcan School who, like Glackens and Bellows, worked as an illustrator as well as a painter. Many of Shinn's paintings focus on New York City, especially scenes related to the world of theater and music.

Jacob Lawrence (1917–) is a well-known African-American artist whose work often portrays the history and cultural achievements of African Americans. Many of his works, like the one in **B**, have crisply defined geometric lines or shapes, flat, posterlike colors, and strong contrasts. You may wish to show additional examples of his work. See *Jacob Lawrence, American Painter,* Seattle Art Museum (University of Washington Press, 1986).

Jacob Lawrence, Concert, 1950. Tempera on paper, 22 x 30" (56 x 76 cm). Wichita Art Museum, Wichita, Kansas (The Roland P. Murdock Collection). Photograph: Henry Nelson.

distance. The sizes of the shapes help you to see what is near and far away.

You can also show distance by overlapping shapes. **Overlap** means that one shape looks like it is behind another one. Can you find some of the overlapping shapes in both artworks?

Think about places where you see a crowd of people. You could be at a ball game, a circus or a store with many people. Begin your picture by drawing the people near to you in the scene. Draw them very large on your paper. How can you show the people who are farther away?

61

INTEGRATING THE CURRICULUM

Extensions ▼

Drama Take students to an auditorium where they can experience the approximate relationships portrayed in these drawings. Ask several students to stand on the stage, others to stand at the side or back of the stage, and others to be in the audience. Rotate the groups and have them discuss what they see from each position. After this experience, have them draw the most memorable view.

Literature Link
- *The Great Migration: An American Story,* Jacob Lawrence. (A, I)
- *Take Me Out to the Ballgame,* Maryann Kovalski. (A)

CLOSE

Create

1 Distribute materials. Ask students to recall or imagine a time or place where they are looking out at or leading a crowd. Examples are a ballpark, auditorium, parade, band, or chorus. The scene could include cars on a street, boats in a harbor, or animals at a fair.

2 Have students plan a tall or wide picture. Encourage students to begin by drawing themselves very large as the main figure, showing how they look from the back.

3 Have students add other figures. Remind them to draw the large shapes first and then the smaller shapes behind.

4 Some students may benefit by looking at their drawings from a distance in the room to make the perspective effect more obvious.

Assess

1 Discuss some of the drawings. Have students comment favorably on the overall effect, overlapping shapes, and changes in size or location of shapes.

RESOURCES

Large Reproductions
  Spiral Dance, Howell-Sickles, 16
  Upstream, Kuniyoshi, 10
  Indian Boy, Homer, 9

Overhead Transparencies
  Dugout, Rockwell, 18
  Night Baseball, Phillips, 18

 CD-ROM
  5, *People and Animals,* Lessons 1 and 2

Slide Set
  Trapeze Act, Dwight, 11

Assessment Masters
  Comparing Two Artworks, 19
  Places to Live, 13

PREPARE

Objectives

Students will:
- perceive and discuss facial expressions and proportions in portraits by artists.
- draw an expressive portrait combining basic proportions and observation.

Materials

pencils

erasers

drawing paper, 9 x 12" (23 x 30 cm), 1 per student

Vocabulary

portrait	*retrato*
expression	*expresión*
guidelines	*guías*
proportion	*proporción*

Setup

Arrange desks so students face each other.

Note

This lesson combines direct observation and the use of guidelines for general proportions of facial features. Stress the importance of observation. Avoid leading students to think of drawing as a matter of memorizing a formula.

 Angel Torres Jaramillo (TEBO), *Portrait of My Mother,* 1937. Oil on cardboard, 9 1/8 x 6 1/8" (23 x 16 cm). Collection, The Museum of Modern Art, New York (The Latin American Collection, Gift of Sam A. Lewisohn).

 Ben Shahn, *Dr. J. Robert Oppenheimer,* 1954. Brush and ink, 19 1/2 x 12 1/4" (50 x 31 cm). Collection, The Museum of Modern Art, New York (Purchase).

The artworks in this lesson are portraits. A **portrait** shows a likeness of a person. These portraits also tell about the feelings or moods of people.

What **expressions** do you see on each face? An expression might be happy, sad, angry or tired. What parts of a face help to give it an expression?

A portrait also helps you know if a person is young or old, fat or thin. How do these artworks help you see these differences in people? What other differences do you see in each artwork?

62

TEACH

Engage

1 Discuss differences in faces and how interesting the differences can be: babies with round cheeks, older people with wrinkled skin, people with bushy eyebrows, and so on.

2 Have students give examples to show that physical appearance and personality can be different. (Attractive people may or may not be pleasant. Older people may be young at heart. People may smile even though they are not happy.)

3 Define a *portrait* as an artwork that shows a likeness of a person.

Explore

1 In **A**, the artist painted a portrait of his mother. Point out that the top and bottom halves of the oval-shaped head are about the same size. Have students point out eyebrows, upper eyelids, nostrils, and upper and lower lips. Note how the chin is shown.

2 Discuss **B**. Note the tight lips, wrinkled forehead, and large eyes that suggest intense thinking or worry. This portrait shows a nuclear physicist who helped develop the atomic bomb

3 Refer to **C**, a photographic portrait. Have students identify features that communicate happiness (position of eyebrows, mouth line, and so on).

4 Guide students to see that in **D** the hairline and forehead take up about half of the total oval. The tip of the nose is about halfway between the eyes and the bottom of the chin. The top and bottom of the ears are parallel to the eyes and bottom of the nose.

5 Focus on **E**. Note evidence of careful observation as well as the use of proportion.

Create

1 Distribute materials. Arrange desks so every student can see and draw another student. Guide students as they fold their paper into quarters and then unfold it.

2 Ask students to study the overall shape of the head and hair of the person, including a hairline between the eyes and top of the head.

3 Encourage students to observe and draw the eyes on the horizontal fold. Note that the space between the eyes is often about the same width as the eye itself. Ask them to study the curves along upper and lower lids, the fold line above the eyes, and the size of the pupils.

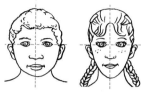

 C

 D

 E Student artwork.

You can draw portraits. Sit across from a classmate. Study the shape of his or her head. Draw this shape very large. Then sketch guidelines similar to the dotted lines in picture D. These lines help you remember some proportions. For example, the eyes are about halfway between the bottom of the chin and the top of the head.

Now ask your classmate to pose with a special expression. Finish your drawing by showing exactly how your classmate looks!

A student your age created the portrait in picture E. Do you think the artwork shows a special expression? Why or why not?

63

INTEGRATING THE CURRICULUM

Extensions ▼ ▼

Social Studies Have students look through their social studies texts for portraits of people (photographs, drawings, paintings, sculpture). Ask them to offer explanations for the use of portraits to illustrate history. Have them analyze the differences between portraits created before and after the invention of photography (about 1835).

Drama Have small groups write and produce a simple puppet play with human characters. Draw faces on the outside of paper folded in half. On one side, draw the character in a certain mood; on the other side, draw the same character in a different mood. Tape the two-faced drawings on a stick for students to use as puppets, turning a different face toward the audience to suggest a change in mood.

Literature Link
• *Miranda's Smile,* Thomas Locker. (S, A)
• *The Gentleman and the Kitchen Maid,* Diane Stanley. (S)

4 Remind students to draw the bottom edge of the nose about midway between the eyes and the bottom of the chin. Note how the length, width, and curves of noses vary.

5 Guide students to observe the shape and location of lips, ears, and neck. As they finish, encourage students to suggest a definite expression by slightly changing lines, especially the eyebrows, pupils of the eyes, and corners of the lips.

CLOSE

Assess

1 Ask volunteers to hold up their work. Lead the class to make positive comments on the use of guidelines as well as the individuality and expression captured in each drawing. Stress the fact that students, like artists, can learn to draw through practice and careful observation.

2 Preview the next lesson. Explain that students will paint portraits or self-portraits. They can paint the drawing they did today or take home paper to draw themselves (using a mirror) or a family member. If they draw at home, be sure they bring their work to school.

RESOURCES

Large Reproductions
    Jim, Johnson, 14
    Summer, Arcimboldo, 13

Overhead Transparencies
    Dr. Oppenheimer, Shahn, 1
    Has-No-Horses, Kasebier, 1

CD-ROM
    6, *Subjects in Art*, Lesson 1

Slide Set
    Self Portrait, Johnson, 13

Assessment Masters
    Find Out About Art, 20

Critical Thinking

Using additional artworks or reproductions that portray people, have the class practice looking at artwork from the vantage point of both model and artist.

27 Portraits and Self-Portraits
Painting

PREPARE

Objectives

Students will:
- compare and contrast painting styles and expressive details in portraits and self-portraits.
- create a painting that portrays a person.

Vocabulary

portrait	*retrato*
self-portrait	*autorretrato*
details	*detalles*
center of interest	*foco de atención*

Setup

Mixing trays should have three or more sections so students can mix flesh-colored paint, then modify it into a tint and a shade.

Materials

drawings from Lesson 26 or prepared at home

tempera paint: red, yellow, blue, black, and white, in sets for several students to share

newsprint paper, 9 x 12" (23 x 30 cm), 1 per student

newsprint paper, 12 x 18" (30 x 46 cm), 1 per student

smocks

newspapers for desks

mixing tray

water containers

paintbrushes, 1 per student

sponges

paper towels

A   Robert Henri, *Eva Green*, 1907. Oil on canvas, 24 1/8 x 20 3/16" (61 x 51 cm). Wichita Art Museum, Wichita, Kansas (The Roland P. Murdock Collection). Photograph: Henry Nelson.

B   *Portrait of a Boy,* Egyptian. Encaustic on wood panel, 7 x 15" (19 x 39 cm). The Metropolitan Museum of Art (Gift of Edward S. Harkness, 1918).

You have learned that a portrait shows how a real person looks. A **self-portrait** is an artwork that shows the person who created it. Have you ever painted a portrait or self-portrait?

Look at the paintings in this lesson. Each artist has made the face the center of interest. How have the artists shown the eyes, nose and other details in the faces? What expressions do you see? How have the artists shown the expression on each face?

64

TEACH

Engage

1 Briefly review drawing faces in Lesson 26. Explain that students will paint a portrait or self-portrait using these drawings or drawings created at home.

2 Briefly review the difference between a portrait and a self-portrait. A *portrait* is a work that shows another person, as in Lesson 26. A *self-portrait* is an artwork that shows the likeness of the artist who made it.

Meeting Individual Needs

Simplify Have students use oil pastels instead of tempera or have them make a painting of a person without making it portraitlike.

Challenge After paintings are dry, students may add more details. They can use markers or oil pastels. Have students help to mount and display the artworks.

Explore

1 Guide students to see how **A** captures the smiling child's expression. The dark hair and background make her face glow with color. Have students identify details that help capture the expression. Note the position of the eyebrows, shading that reveals the upper and lower eyelids, and other details.

2 In **B**, help students see the oval shape of the head and location of the eyes, about midway between the top of the hair and the chin. Note that the tops of the ears are near the same line. Have students point out shading near the eyebrows, upper eyelids, nostrils, upper and lower lips, and chin.

3 Discuss **C**. Guide students to see how the right side of the face is shaded to bring out a feeling of form. In **D**, note the subtle tilt of the eyebrows, mouth, and other expressive features.

4 Discuss the technique tips on the right-hand page. Tell students they will add paint to their drawings.

Create

1 Distribute materials and drawings. Demonstrate how to mix flesh tones in the tray by combining dots of yellow, red, and blue. The more blue is added, the browner the tone.

2 Have each student mix about two tablespoons of one basic flesh color to use for the head, neck, and other areas of flesh.

3 Demonstrate how to:
- use a brush to scoop some basic flesh color into two sections of the tray.
- add some white to one section to create a tint.
- add blue or black to the other section to create a shade.

 William H. Johnson, *Jim*, 1930. Oil on canvas, 21 x 18" (53 x 46 cm). National Museum of American Art, Washington, DC (Gift of the Harmon Foundation). Courtesy Art Resource, New York.

When you paint a portrait, mix one main color for the skin. Paint all the skin areas first. The skin usually shows on the head, neck and shoulders. Then mix other colors for the hair and important details. Can you explain why details are the last parts to paint?

The portraits in pictures A, B and C were created by adult artists. A student created the self-portrait in picture D. She used a mirror to

 Student artwork.

create a drawing. Then she made the painting.

Paint a portrait or a self-portrait. Make the face large and show the neck and shoulders. Remember to paint the skin and other large shapes first. Then paint the details. Why are these steps helpful?

65

INTEGRATING THE CURRICULUM

Extensions ▼

Language Arts Have students select one of the portraits from Lesson 26 or this lesson and imagine they meet the person portrayed. Have them develop five questions for the person. Then have them write answers to the questions as if they are the person.

Language Arts Have students write a biography about the person in their portrait or an autobiography for their self-portrait.

Literature Link
• *The Young Artist*, Thomas Locker. (S)
• *The Rough-Face Girl*, Rafe Martin. (A)

---

4 Have students begin using their basic color for the skin. As they work, they can use the tint and mix lighter colors for parts of the face that stand out. They can use the shade and mix darker colors to show details and shadows.

5 As students work, suggest they blot areas that are too wet. The hair and details are best added last. A painted background completes the portrait.

CLOSE

Assess

1 Call on volunteers to share their work. Guide the discussion to focus on the use of values (tints, shades), development of details, and evidence of shading.

2 Have students gather in groups to discuss their work or use their evaluation guides (from Review Unit 1) individually.

Cleanup

1 Cleanup is easiest if you first place the artwork on a flat surface to dry. Then collect supplies in this order: brushes, paints, water, newspapers, paper towels.

RESOURCES

Large Reproductions
  Jim, Johnson, 14

Overhead Transparencies
  Boy with Flute, Lewis, 7
  Self-Portrait, Vigée-Lebrun, 21
  Delfina Flores, Rivera, 21
  Cabinet, Weitz, 6

CD-ROM
  6, *Subjects in Art*, Lesson 1

Slide Set
  Self Portrait, Johnson, 13

Assessment Masters
  Comparing Two Artworks, 19

Art History

The Egyptian portrait in **B** was probably created for a coffin, a practice common in ancient Egypt. The medium, *encaustic*, is a mixture of pigments (colored minerals ground into a fine powder) and wax. The wax is melted and applied while warm.

PREPARE

Objectives

Students will:
- compare and contrast the symbols and design qualities in still-life paintings of food.
- create a still life in which favorite foods are symbols and the design is carefully planned.

Materials

choice of drawing media

drawing paper, 12 x 18" (30 x 46 cm), 1 per student

Vocabulary

still life	*naturaleza muerta*
symbols	*símbolos*
space	*espacio*

Setup

Display photographs of unpackaged fruits, vegetables, nuts, and so on for reference. Real foods should only be used if they can later be eaten or prepared for meals.

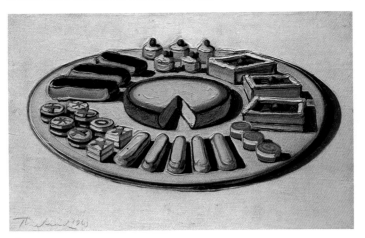

A **Wayne Thiebaud,** *French Pastries,* 1963. Oil on canvas, 16 x 24" (41 x 61cm). Hirshhorn Museum and Sculpture Garden, Smithsonian Institution, Washington, DC (Gift of Joseph H. Hirshhorn, 1966). Photograph: Lee Stalsworth.

The two paintings in this lesson are still lifes. A **still life** shows objects such as food, shoes, books or dishes on a table. The objects in a still life are often things people admire or use.

The objects in a still life can also be **symbols**. For example, a book may be a symbol for wisdom. Food may be a symbol for health or happiness. Look at the foods in both paintings. What ideas might they stand for?

Why do you think each artist wanted a simple, plain background in the paintings?

How did each artist show the textures of the food? Where do you see shadows in each painting?

66

TEACH

Engage

1. Discuss kinds of food and foods students especially like. Explain that artists sometimes create pictures about food. Have students speculate on reasons food might be an interesting subject.

2. Explain that the class will study artworks about food. The artworks are still-life paintings. Define a *still life* as an artwork that shows things that are not alive, such as food, books, and dishes.

Meeting Individual Needs

Simplify Have students draw and cut out shapes for their still life, then arrange them into a collage. After main shapes are pasted on, have students use drawing media to enrich the sense of texture and shadows.

Challenge Have students use the Evaluation Guide from Review Unit 1 to evaluate their work.

Explore

1. In **A**, guide students to see that these pastries are arranged on a large tray in groups around a central cake. Help them see the shadows, careful spacing, and varied colors.

2. Have students offer ideas for what the pastries might symbolize. Encourage interpretations that are not literal. Sweet things might connote good-natured or sweet people, tempting someone by flattery (sweet talk, sugarcoating), self-indulgence, or excess, as well as more conventional ideas of having a special party or celebration.

3. Focus on **B**, showing oranges—some wrapped in paper—neatly laid on a table. Explore their symbolism: They quench thirst, provide energy, are luxuries in places where they do not grow. Wrapped oranges imply the fruits are of high quality, with flavors worthy of being savored.

4. Refer to **C**. Help students see how both artists used most of the picture space to show food. In both works, the space taken up by the food is planned so the background is like a frame around the shapes. The food becomes the center of interest.

Create

1. Ask students to name favorite fruits, vegetables, drinks, and prepared foods. Have them consider their meanings beyond flavor. For example:
   - special foods prepared for holidays or treats, suggesting family warmth and love.
   - scarcity of food in some places: What foods would students want hungry people to have for nutrition and flavor?
   - the colors, textures, and shapes of food in baskets, dishes, or on a counter ready for preparation.

Now look at the **space** in each painting. Most of the space is used to show the food. Why did each artist fill up most of the space with the shapes of food?

Create an artwork about your favorite foods. Think about the reasons you like the food. Are some of the foods symbols for ideas? Are they foods you enjoy or need?

Plan your artwork. Use most of the picture space to show the food. What other ideas should you think about?

C

67

INTEGRATING THE CURRICULUM

Extensions ▼

Science Students can create still-life collages with each student working on one part of the food pyramid. Have students decide on ways to combine the collages in larger displays. Emphasize design concepts students have learned, such as creating a center of interest, overlapping, and planning patterns and colors.

Literature Link

• *Yum, Yum, Yum,* Andy Warhol. (A)
• *A Fruit & Vegetable Man,* Roni Schotter. (A)

CLOSE

2 Distribute materials. Have students sketch the main large shapes for their pictures first.

3 Encourage students to group the foods so their still-life artworks have one food as the center of interest. Help them recall design ideas from earlier lessons, such as overlapping shapes.

4 As students work, remind them to think about adding texture, mixing colors, and introducing tints or shades to create a feeling of roundness.

Assess

1 Have students describe the foods they portrayed and the symbolism of their choices.

2 Discuss the grouping of shapes within the picture space and other design elements students used.

Art History

Artists in ancient Greece and Rome created still-life artworks for homes. In medieval and Renaissance art, still lifes contained symbolic elements. Seventeenth-century Dutch still-life paintings were created primarily for the homes of merchants. Arrangements symbolized social status or moral and religious values. From the eighteenth century to the present, still-life subjects allowed artists to explore new styles of painting and new ways of seeing commonplace objects. Such artwork may cause people to see ordinary things as extraordinary, not only in the painting but in daily life as well.

RESOURCES

Large Reproductions
  French Pastries, Thiebaud, 2

Overhead Transparencies
  Emptying the Fridge, Mandel, 15
  Mrs. Jenkins, Wilson, 15

CD-ROM
  6, *Subjects in Art,* Lesson 2

Slide Set
  Strawberries in Bowl, Coorte, 14

Assessment Masters
  Find Out About Art, 20

PREPARE

Objectives

Students will:
• be aware of artists' uses of lines and shapes to suggest a mood of motion and energy or a calm and quiet mood.
• create an artwork that expresses a calm and quiet cityscape or an active and energetic cityscape.

Vocabulary

elements of design	*elementos de diseño*
geometric	*geométrico*
vertical	*vertical*
horizontal	*horizontal*
diagonal	*diagonal*

Setup

List the following design elements on the chalkboard: line, shape, color, texture, space.

Materials

choice of drawing media

drawing paper, 12 x 18" (30 x 46 cm), 1 per student

There are many ways to express ideas and feelings in art. The paintings in this lesson show two cities. Each artist sends you special messages by using the **elements of design**. Which painting expresses the feeling of a very busy city? Which painting shows a very quiet town? How can you tell?

 Tarsila do Amaral, *Central Railway of Brazil*, 1924. Oil on canvas, 55 7/8 x 50" (142 x 127 cm). Museu de Arte Contemporânea da Universidade de São Paulo, Brazil.

Let's look at picture A. This artist has used many geometric lines and shapes. **Geometric** lines and shapes have smooth, even edges. What geometric lines and shapes do you see in this painting?

Now look at main directions of lines and shapes. Many of the lines and shapes have **vertical** and **horizontal** edges. Some have gentle curves. These design elements help to create the feeling of a quiet place.

What other design elements do you see? How do they help to give you a special feeling?

68

TEACH

Engage

1 Discuss students' experiences in a city or neighborhood. Focus on times and places they recall as very busy and action-packed versus times and places they remember as quiet, calm, or still.

2 Explain that many artists have created paintings with design elements planned to help capture moods of life in a city or neighborhood.

Explore

1 Discuss the lesson so students become aware of the following points about **A**:
• There are no people or activities. The smooth, even outlines and flat colors of paint add to the feeling of a quiet, momentarily deserted scene.
• The bridge, railroad, homes, and trees are simple geometric shapes with little texture. The main lines and shapes are vertical and horizontal.
• The diagonal and curved lines are related to structures, such as the railroad and bridge, not to an action.

2 In **B**, guide students to see:
• Diagonal lines and warm colors create a feeling of a busy city street filled with people and flashing lights.
• The fuzzy, uneven edges of shapes contribute to the feeling of action and energy.
• The textures look blurred, the spaces between shapes tilt, and colors blend together.

Aesthetic Awareness

Have students work in small groups. They will secretly choose either **A** or **B** from this lesson and present an interpretation of its mood using sounds or body movements. They can use their voices or create sounds using instruments, such as desktops or pencils, in the room. After students collaborate, have them present their interpretations. The class will guess the artwork chosen. When presentations are finished, discuss why people often associate what they see with sounds and motions.

Look closely at picture B. Have you ever walked down a busy street like this? Have you ever seen flashing signs or people moving so fast that they look blurred?

B George Grosz, *Dallas Broadway*, 1952. Watercolor on paper, 19 1/2 x 15 1/2" (49 x 39 cm). University Art Collection, Southern Methodist University, Dallas, Texas (Gift of Leon A. Harris, Jr.)

Notice how the main lines and shapes are **diagonal**, or slanting. The edges of many shapes are also fuzzy or uneven. These design elements help you see and feel the motions in a busy place.

What other design elements create the feeling of a busy place? For example, what are the main colors and textures? How are they different from the colors and textures in picture A?

Create a picture about your neighborhood or town. Will you make your picture look very quiet and calm or full of action? What design elements can help you express your ideas?

69

INTEGRATING THE CURRICULUM

Extensions ▼

Social Studies Read *The Changing City* by Jorg Muller (Atheneum, 1977). This book contains eight full-color, foldout pictures of a changing city. After studying the illustrations, have students list ways the city changed. Have them discuss and evaluate the changes before making a final list. Then have them imagine their city's or community's past. Have them draw images showing several stages of growth. Provide time and resources for historical research to enhance the accuracy of their images.

Literature Link

• *Street Music: City Poems*, Arnold Adoff. (S)
• *My New York*, Kathy Jakobsen. (A)
• *Town and Country*, Alice and Martin Provensen. (A)

CLOSE

Create

1 Explain that students will create a picture of a special time and place in their city or neighborhood. List starter ideas on the chalkboard:

   • busy and action-packed: grocery stores, crowded ballparks or theaters, street corners, school buses, and recess.

   • calm and quiet: deserted school playgrounds, city streets at night, an empty room or home.

2 Distribute materials. As students begin, have them decide if they will create a vertical or horizontal picture.

3 Ask students to refer to the design elements on the chalkboard and think about how to apply them.

4 While students work, offer individual guidance on the use of design elements to create expressive qualities. For example, bright, intense colors can add to a feeling of energy and excitement. Dull or light colors often add to a feeling of calm or quiet.

Assess

1 Ask students to gather in groups to discuss their work. Have them discuss themes, places, and times in the works, as well as design elements.

2 Then ask students who portrayed quiet places and busy places to gather on opposite sides of the room and hold up their work. Invite students to comment on some major differences in each set of works.

RESOURCES

Large Reproductions
   Brotherhood Building, Haas, 15

Overhead Transparencies
   Towers of Laon, Delaunay, 23
   Morning Light, Bleumner, 24
   Early Sunday Morning, Hopper, 24

 CD-ROM
   4, *Art Adventure*, Lesson 2

Assessment Masters
   Create a Community, 6
   City Skylines, 10

30 A City at Night
Crayon Resist

A Tom Bacher, *Mount Adams (In the Light)*, 20th century. Phosphorescent acrylic on canvas, 24 x 30" (61 x 76 cm). Cincinnati Art Galleries.

Do you like to see the lights in city buildings at night? At night, you see the **contrast**, or difference, between very dark and very bright colors.

Tom Bacher loves to see the contrasting colors in a city at night. In pictures A and B, you see one of his paintings of a city.

This artwork is created with a special kind of paint. The paint
70

absorbs, or soaks up, light. His paint is similar to "glow in the dark" paints.

Picture A shows how his painting looks in daylight. Picture B shows how the same painting glows in a dark room. Which design has more contrast in the colors? What other differences do you see?

PREPARE

Objectives

Students will:
- be aware of special media and processes for painting and why artists may use them.
- create a crayon-resist painting of a cityscape at night.

Vocabulary

contrast   *contraste*

crayon-resist   *pintura hecha con*
    painting   *crayón indeleble*

Setup

Before teaching, draw several lines on paper with an oil pastel or wax crayon, pressing hard. Brush paint once over a wide area. If paint does not roll away from the oil pastel or wax, add more water until it does. Set up painting stations.

Materials

oil pastels or wax crayons

newsprint or manila paper, 12 x 18" (30 x 46 cm), 1 per student

diluted dark blue paint, 1 container per 2 or 3 students

newspaper for desks

paper towels

(optional) items that glow in the dark

TEACH

Engage

1 Ask students to identify sources of light in the room (sunlight from windows, artificial light from bulbs). Turn the lights off and on. Discuss differences that bright light makes. (Colors become more vivid, shadows change, and everything is easier to see.)

2 Explain that many artists study how light changes the colors that we see. Examples of light changing color include the warm glow of a sunset, the cool gray-blue of a rainy day, colors on a clear day, and colors at night.

Explore

1 If you have a glow-in-the-dark object, demonstrate the effect by showing it in bright light and in the dark. Explain that **A** and **B** are photographs of a painting that has glow-in-the-dark paint.

2 In **A**, you see the qualities of light and color the painting has in daylight. The colors are bright, intense, and suggest a city at twilight. In the foreground, or near the bottom, you see the boards in the buildings.

3 Focus on **B**, which shows how the painting looks in the dark. Guide students to see the contrasts between light and dark areas. In the foreground, the windows seem to be lighted from inside.

4 Have students identify other strong differences between **A** and **B**.

5 Tell students they will create a nighttime scene. Explain that they will use heavy pressure to draw their pictures, with bright colors and patterns of light. They will then change the drawings into night scenes by painting over them with dark paint.

 B Tom Bacher, *Mount Adams (In the Dark)*, 20th century. Phosphorescent acrylic on canvas, 24 x 30" (61 x 76 cm). Cincinnati Art Galleries.

Create an artwork that shows your home, school or neighborhood at night. You can create strong contrasts by drawing on dark paper with bright colors of oil pastel.

You might create a resist painting. Use wax or oil crayons on white paper. Press hard to make a thick layer of each color. When the drawing is finished, brush a dark color of watercolor paint over the whole paper. Use a wide brush. The paint will **resist**, or roll away from, the parts you've colored.

71

INTEGRATING THE CURRICULUM

Extensions ▼ ▼

Language Arts Read *Happy Birthday Moon* by Frank Asch (Prentice-Hall, 1982). As you read, discuss how the illustrator shows moonlight in the book. Have students describe their memories of how things look at night when the moon is full. Encourage imaginative recall about shadows and special differences in snow or rain. Have students draw a picture using techniques learned in this lesson and write a story or poem to go with their work.

Science Have students work in small groups with science books. Have them conduct research on topics such as glow-in-the-dark animal life (firefly, glowworm, electric eel) and glow-in-the-dark visual effects (reflective surfaces on roads, fluorescent colors).

Literature Link
• *Night on Neighborhood Street,* Eloise Greenfield. (S)
• *Citybook,* Shelley Rotner and Ken Kreisler. (A)

CLOSE

Create

1 Distribute materials, except paint. Ask students to close their eyes and picture a night scene in a city.

2 Encourage thoughtful preparation. Much of the space should show lights (in buildings, streetlights, moon, stars). Encourage students to blend colors, show textures, and invent lines and patterns.

3 Before students use paint, demonstrate the steps:
  • Dip the brush in paint and stir lightly.
  • Hold the container steady and wipe brush on the inner edge.
  • Brush across the top of the drawing, edge to edge, using one stroke.
  • Continue down the page, slightly overlapping the strokes.

4 If you have several painting stations, schedule students to use them; explain the need to take turns. Have students take drawings to and from these stations on folded newspaper.

Assess

1 Ask students to explain what they learned. Help them recall special qualities of the artwork in **A** and **B** and reasons for its bright, glowing colors.

2 Discuss some student artworks. Continue to model the conversational steps of listening, asking questions, and suggesting ideas for further consideration.

Cleanup

1 Collect paint and brushes.

2 Have students center their artwork on folded newspaper to dry.

3 Put away other supplies.

RESOURCES

Large Reproductions
  Interior, Matisse, 17

Overhead Transparencies
  Night Baseball, Phillips, 18

 CD-ROM
  4, *Art Adventure,* Lesson 2

Slide Set
  Palmolive Building, Chase, 15

Assessment Masters
  Places to Live, 13

PREPARE

Objectives

Students will:
- understand originality in art as seen in five works that have the same subject.
- choose a subject for a picture and create an original drawing about it.

Vocabulary

subject   *tema*

original photograph   *fotografía original*

Setup

Structure the review into a lesson based on the text with a separate evaluation period of about the same length. Prepare a handout or list evaluation questions on the chalkboard. (See Evaluation Guide in Review Unit 1.)

Materials

folders of students' artwork

drawing paper, 12 x 18" (30 x 46 cm), 1 per student

crayons or oil pastels

A   **Samuel Halpert,** ***Brooklyn Bridge,*** 1913. Oil on canvas, 34 x 42" (86 x 107 cm). Collection of Whitney Museum of American Art, New York (Gift of Mr. and Mrs. Benjamin Halpert). Photograph: Geoffrey Clements.

B   ***Brooklyn Bridge.*** Photograph: Wayne Andrews.

C   Brett Weston, *Brooklyn Bridge.*

All of the artworks in this lesson show the Brooklyn Bridge in New York City. The Brooklyn Bridge was designed by John Roebling more than 100 years ago. Many artists have created pictures about the bridge.

Each artist has seen and thought about the bridge in a special way. Each artist created an **original**, or different, artwork about the same subject.

You are learning to see and discuss art like an expert. Show what you have learned. Take time to look at the pictures in this lesson. Study the different views of the bridge. Which artworks do you like? Why? Make up your own mind.

72

TEACH

Engage

1 Explain that students will see new examples of artwork and think about what they learned in Unit 2.

2 Allow time for students to look at all five artworks. Have them share their first impressions of each work.

Technology

Have students do research on the basic structures used in constructing bridges, such as arches, beams and columns, trusses and suspension systems. Encourage students to work in groups and create model bridges from materials such as tongue depressors, small cartons, cardboard, string, and the like.

Explore

1 Guide students to perceive design qualities that each artist emphasizes. **A** shows the activity on the river, the great arched bridge, and the city in the distance. **B** shows the cable construction. **C** shows the height of the massive bridge tower along with the delicate, yet strong, cables.

2 The painting in **D** suggests the energy and action of people walking across the bridge on a windy or rainy day. The diagonal lines and irregular bridge shapes capture a feeling of motion around the structure and in the bridge itself (which moves slightly in heavy traffic).

3 In **E**, the towering height of the bridge is dominant. We see the city through the towers. The idea of the bridge going into the city is shown in the bottom panel.

4 Emphasize that artists in many times and places create unique pictures about the same subject, each using a different, original style.

5 Ask students to express opinions about which of these artworks they like. Discuss reasons. Note that students may like more than one kind of art and that not everyone may like the same work.

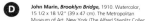
John Marin, *Brooklyn Bridge*, 1910. Watercolor, 15 1/2 x 18 1/2" (39 x 47 cm). The Metropolitan Museum of Art, New York (The Alfred Stieglitz Collection).

Joseph Stella, *Brooklyn Bridge, Variation on an Old Theme*, 1939. Oil on canvas. Collection of Whitney Museum of American Art, New York.

Choose the artwork you like best. Tell what you see in the artwork. Use art words you know. Tell why you chose the work. Then find out which artworks your classmates chose.

You can also create art in your own way. Help to choose a subject that everyone in the class will draw.

After the subject is chosen, create an original picture about it. Original means that your picture will be very different from others.

73

Extensions ▼

Language Arts Help students develop several web-like diagrams to explore their feelings and experiences with bridges. Then have them write a story or poem on the topic, using ideas from the diagrams and others that emerge as they are writing.

Literature Link
• *Bridges*, Ken Robbins. (I)
• *Crossing the New Bridge*, Emily Arnold McCully. (S)
• *Tar Beach*, Faith Ringgold. (S, A)

CLOSE

Create

1 Explain that everyone will draw the same subject today. The first task is to choose a subject everyone has seen. Have students suggest possibilities and list these on the chalkboard. Examples include the classroom, school, playground, streets, and landmarks near school. Vote to choose one topic.

2 Discuss ways students can achieve originality such as showing a detail very large; drawing a worm's-eye or bird's-eye view; showing a subject during a special time of day, season, or kind of weather; or drawing the subject from its own point of view.

3 Distribute materials. While students draw, comment individually on details, viewpoints, or other original features. Encourage students to demonstrate what they have learned about mixing colors, suggesting textures, planning shapes and spaces, and so on.

Assess

1 Distribute students' art folders. Have them place two or three of their best works from Unit 2 on top of their folder and write a "2" (for Unit 2) on the back of each.

2 Refer to the evaluation questions on the chalkboard. Invite students who have selected the same kinds of artwork (such as a painting) to share reasons they chose their paintings. Prompt students to notice specific qualities, such as the subject, brushstrokes, variety of lines, and so on.

3 Evaluate and write comments on students' work. Save the works each student identified as best. Save others that you judge to be important for evaluation at the end of the year. Allow students to take the rest of their work home.

RESOURCES

Large Reproductions
  Upstream, Kuniyoshi, 10
  Time, Chagall, 11

Overhead Transparencies
  Dugout, Rockwell, 18
  Night Baseball, Phillips, 18

CD-ROM
  3, *Artists at Work*, Lesson 2
  4, *Art Adventure*, Lesson 2

Assessment Masters
  Comparing Two Artworks, 19
  I Like Art, 22

Unit 3 Planner

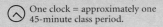

Core: *Adventures in Art* provides a balanced sequence of lessons that meet national standards for content and instructional time. If you are unable to teach every lesson, introduce the lessons identified as "core."

Lesson Overview	Objectives	Correlations	Resources	Technology
U3 ⌃ Core Page 74 **Art in Your World** *Activity:* **Drawing** *Materials:* **Drawing media** *Concept:* **Artists, art careers** *Related Lessons:* Careers: 31, 32, 36, R3. Crafts: 40, 46, 48, U4. Television and motion picture: 32, 38.	• Be aware of art-related careers and places to see art in their community • Draw a picture of a product, labeling the parts planned by an artist	*National Standards:* 1a, c, d, 2c, 3a, b, 4a, b, c, 5a, b, c, 6a	*Large Reproductions:* **19** Courtney-Clarke *Overhead Transparencies:* **5** Tygart *Assessment Masters:* **20** Find Out About Art	CD-ROM 3, *Artists at Work,* Lesson 2
31 ⌃ Core Page 76 **Industrial Design** *Activity:* **Design critique** *Materials:* **Magazines, scissors, paste** *Concept:* **Industrial design** *Related Lessons:* Careers: 32, 39, U3, R3. Design in everyday life: 42.	• Be aware of industrial design as an art form and career • Create a posterlike display of industrial designs that includes their judgments of these designs	*National Standards:* 1a, b, c, d, 2a, b, c, 3b, 4a, b, c, 5a, c, 6b	*Large Reproductions:* **2** Thiebaud *Overhead Transparencies:* **5** Tygart, **4** Brundege *Slide Set:* **16** Bjorn-Bernadotte *Assessment Masters:* **18** Designs for Lamps	CD-ROM 3, *Artists at Work,* Lesson 1
32 ⌃ Page 78 **Graphic Design** *Activity:* **Poster design** *Materials:* **Colored paper, drawing media** *Concept:* **Graphic design** *Related Lessons:* Careers: 35, 36, U3, R3. Graphic design: 33, 34, 36. Lettering: 34. Television and motion pictures: 38, U3.	• Identify examples of graphic design and visual qualities planned by a designer • Create a posterlike design in a basic shape (circle, square, triangle) that communicates a message	*National Standards:* 1a, b, c, 2a, b, c, 3a, b, 5a, c	*Large Reproductions:* **22** Bearden, **2** Thiebaud *Overhead Transparencies:* **15** Mandel *Assessment Masters:* **16** Changes in Style	CD-ROM 3, *Artists at Work,* Lesson 1 ■ Computer graphic design
33 ⌃ Core Page 80 **Picture Writing** *Activity:* **Drawing** *Materials:* **Drawing media** *Concept:* **Visual symbols** *Related Lessons:* Asian art: 21, 35, 46, 48. Graphic design: 32, 34, 36, North American Indian art: 9, 46, 47, 49. Symbols (visual): 9, 28, 46, 47.	• Compare and contrast visual symbols in various cultures, past and present • Create visual symbols to communicate a command or simple sentence	*National Standards:* 1a, b, c, 2a, b, c, 3a, b, 4a, b, c, 5a, b, c, 6a, b	*Large Reproductions:* **3** Sioux, **6** Brown, **21** Blackwell, **13** Arcimboldo *Overhead Transparencies:* **14** Tlingit *Assessment Masters:* **16** Changes in Style	CD-ROM 2, *Elements of Design,* Lesson 2
34 ⌃ Core Page 82 **Picturing an Alphabet** *Activity:* **Drawing** *Materials:* **Drawing media** *Concept:* **Lettering** *Related Lessons:* Graphic design: 32, 33, 36. Lettering: 32	• Understand that graphic design includes creative lettering • Help create a theme-based picture alphabet	*National Standards:* 1a, b, c, d, 2a, c, 3a, b, 5a, c, 6b	*Large Reproductions:* **13** Arcimboldo *Overhead Transparencies:* **21** Rivera *Assessment Masters:* **20** Find Out About Art	CD-ROM 2, *Elements of Design,* Lessons 1 and 2

■ boxed sidebar information
on lesson pages.

Literature Link codes:
(A) Artwork links to lesson
(S) Story line links to lesson
(I) Information links to lesson

74b

Special Features	Cultures/History	Integrating the Curriculum	
		Extensions	**Literature Link**
■ Meeting Individual Needs ■ Community-Based Learning		*Social Studies:* Art-related careers	*Visiting the Art Museum,* Laurene Krasny Brown and Marc Brown. (I) *Disney's Art of Animation: From Mickey Mouse to Beauty and the Beast,* Bob Thomas. (I, A) *Puddle Jumper: How a Toy Is Made,* Ann Morris. (I)

■ Meeting Individual Needs
■ Independent Research
■ Critical Thinking
	Canada:
	    Beekenkam
	Denmark:
	    Wegner
		Social Studies: Local products	*Sneakers: The Shoes We Choose!,* Robert Young. (I)
			How Does Soda Get Into the Bottle?, Oz Charles. (I)

■ Meeting Individual Needs
■ Cooperative Learning
	United States:
	    Chermayeff
	    Lang
	    Littlewood and Teixeira
	    Walker Group
		Social Studies: Traffic signs	*The Sign Painter's Dream,* Roger Roth. (S)
			The Signmaker's Assistant, Tedd Arnold. (S)
			The Sign Painter's Secret: The Story of a Revolutionary Girl, Dorothy and Thomas Hoobler. (S)

■ Meeting Individual Needs ■ Community-Based Learning	Egypt (Africa) Japan Mexico United States, Southwest Indian	*Social Studies:* Alphabet	*Puff . . . Flash. . . Bang! A Book About Signals,* Gail Gibbons. (I) *You Don't Need Words! A Book about Ways People Talk Without Words,* Ruth Belov Gross. (I)

■ Meeting Individual Needs
■ Aesthetic Awareness
	United States:
	    Macaulay
	    Russo
		Language Arts: Reading	*The Z was Zapped,* Chris Van Allsburg. (A)
			The Graphic Alphabet, David Pelletier. (A)
			Alphabetics, Sue MacDonald. (A)

Lesson Overview	Objectives	Correlations	Resources	Technology

35 ⌃
Page 84

Making a Book
Activity: **Folded book/scroll**
Materials: **Shelf paper, tubes or straws, glue**
Concept: **Book arts**
Related Lessons: Asian art: 21, 33, 46, 48. Careers: 32, 6, U3, R3.

• Perceive and discuss different types of handmade books
• Create a scroll or folded book to illustrate in Lesson 36

National Standards: 1a, c, d, 2a, c, 4a, b, 5a, c, 6a, b

Large Reproductions: **6** Brown, **21** Blackwell
Overhead Transparencies: **2** Miller
Assessment Masters: **8** Sketch a Story

CD-ROM 3, *Artists at Work,* Lesson 1

---

36 ⌃ ⌃
Page 86

Illustrating Stories
Activity: **Drawing**
Materials: **Drawing media, students' Lesson 35 artworks, students' written stories or poems**
Concept: **Illustration**
Related Lessons: Careers: 32, 35, U3, R3. Graphic design: 32-34. Illustration: 15, 21.

• Compare and contrast book illustrations, particularly their styles and art media
• Illustrate an original story or poem to complete their handmade scrolls or folded books

National Standards: 1a, c, d, 2a, c, 3a, b, 5a, b, 6b

Large Reproductions: **6** Brown, **21** Blackwell
Overhead Transparencies: **2** Miller
Assessment Masters: **8** Sketch a Story

CD-ROM 3, *Artists at Work,* Lesson 1

---

37 ⌃
Page 88

Photography
Activity: **Creating a sunprint**
Materials: **Sun-sensitive paper, black paper, assorted objects**
Concept: **Photography**
Related Lessons: Careers: 36, 38, U3, R3. Light and shadow: 19, 20. Photography as art: U1. Shape: 4.

• Be aware of photography as an art form and a process of recording light and shadows
• Create a photographic artwork by making a blueprint (sunprint)

National Standards: 1a, c, d, 2a, c, 3a, 4a, c, 5a, 6b

Large Reproductions: **19** Courtney-Clarke
Overhead Transparencies: **19** Gilpin
Slide Set: **17** Talbot

CD-ROM 1, *Color,* Lesson 4

---

38 ⌃
Core
Page 90

Pictures That Move
Activity: **Collage rubbing**
Materials: **Posterboard, oil pastels or wax crayons, scissors**
Concept: **Animation**
Related Lessons: Careers: 36, 37, U3, R3. Motion: 3, 17. People: 23-26, Television: 32, U3.

• Understand that animated films are composed of sequences of pictures
• Create a sequence of pictures of faces with different expressions

National Standards: 1a, c, d, 2a, c, 3a, b, 5a, c, 6b

Large Reproductions: **16** Howell-Sickles, **10** Kuniyoshi
Overhead Transparencies: **9** Muybridge
Assessment Masters: **21** A Vote for Art

CD-ROM 3, *Artists at Work,* Lesson 1

■ Computer animation

---

39 ⌃
Core
Page 92

Shapes in Buildings
Activity: **Collage**
Materials: **Colored paper**
Concept: **Architectural shapes**
Related Lessons: Architecture: 41-44. Balance: 6, 46-48. Careers: 31, 32, U3, R3. Shape: 2, 5, 29, 40.

• Be aware of exterior shapes, patterns, and their arrangement in architectural facades
• Create a symmetrical collage design of a building facade

National Standards: 1a, c, 2a, d, e, 3a, 4a, b, c, 5a, c, 6b

Large Reproductions: **15** Haas, **10** Kuniyoshi
Overhead Transparencies: **24** Hopper
Slide Set: **18** Chartres
Assessment Masters: **7** What's For Sale

CD-ROM 2, *Elements of Design,* Lesson 2

---

40 ⌃
Page 94

Colorful Mosaics
Activity: **Paper mosaics**
Materials: **Magazines, glue, construction paper**
Concept: **Mosaics**
Related Lessons: Architecture: 39, 41-43. Color: 12, 14, 18, 30. Crafts; 46, 48, U3, U4. Shape: 6, 10, 29, 39.

• Be aware of mosaics as an ancient and contemporary art form
• Create a paper mosaic with a planned design

National Standards: 1a, b, c, d, 2a, c, 4a, b, 5a, b, c, 6a

Large Reproductions: **22** Bearden, **13** Arcimboldo
Overhead Transparencies: **17** Egypt
Slide Set: **19** Roman
Assessment Masters: **3** Using an Artist's Colors

CD-ROM 2, *Elements of Design,* Lesson 4

74c

Special Features	Cultures/History	Integrating the Curriculum	
		Extensions	**Literature Link**
■ Community-Based Learning	China England United States: Rossbach	*Social Studies:* Creating books	*Breaking into Print: Before and After the Invention of the Printing Press*, Stephen Krensky. (I) *Go In and Out the Window: An Illustrated Songbook for Young People*, Dan Fox. (A) *A Book Takes Root: The Making of a Picture Book*, Michael Kehoe. (I)

■ Community-Based Learning	Poland:
	  Domanska
	United States:
	  Feelings, African American
		Language Arts:
		Book fair
			Daydreamers, Eloise Greenfield. (A)
			Something on My Mind, Nikki Grimes. (A)

■ Meeting Individual Needs ■ Community-Based Learning	England: Atkins	*Social Studies:* Photography	*Click: A Book about Cameras and Taking Pictures*, Gail Gibbons. (I) *The Science Book of Light*, Neil Ardley. (I) *Light and Shadow*, Myra Cohn Livingston. (S)
■ Meeting Individual Needs	United States: Vinton	*Mathematics:* Numbers	*Disney's Art of Animation: From Mickey Mouse to Beauty and the Beast*, Bob Thomas. (I, A) *That's a Wrap: How Movies Are Made*, Ned Dowd. (I) *Ed Emberley's 3 Science Flip Books*, Ed Emberley. (A)
■ Meeting Individual Needs ■ Community-Based Learning ■ Critical Thinking	Italy: Alberti	*Mathematics:* Geometric shapes	*What It Feels Like To Be a Building*, Forrest Wilson. (A) *Architects Make Zigzags: Looking at Architecture from A to Z*, Diane Maddex. (A)
■ Meeting Individual Needs ■ Community-Based Learning	Italy Iran ■ *Art History:* Byzantine Art	*Mathematics:* Tangram shapes	*Cleopatra*, Diane Stanley and Peter Vennema. (A) *The Romans and Pompeii*, Philip Steele. (A) *Jerusalem*, Saviour Pirotta. (A)

Lesson Overview	Objectives	Correlations	Resources	Technology
41 ⌃ Core Page 86 — **Spaces and Lighting** *Activity:* **Resist painting** *Materials:* **Oil pastels or wax crayons, dark blue paint** *Concept:* **Interior design** *Related Lessons:* Architecture: 39, 40, 42, 44. Day and night contrast: 30. Lighting of spaces: 42. Space: 4, 5, 11, 18.	• Be aware of relationships between interior and exterior spaces and lighting in architecture • Create a resist painting that portrays the exterior or interior lighting of buildings	*National Standards:* 1a, c, d, 2a, c, 3a, 4c, 5a, c	*Large Reproductions:* **15** Haas *Overhead Transparencies:* **15** Wilson *Assessment Masters:* **13** A Place to Live	CD-ROM 4, *Art Adventure,* Lesson 2
42 ⌃ Page 98 — **A Colorful Window** *Activity:* **Transparent collage** *Materials:* **Acrylic paint, clear plastic folders, black paper** *Concept:* **Stained glass, color** *Related Lessons:* Architecture: 39, 40, 43, 44. Color: 12, 14, 30, 40. Lighting of spaces: 41. Space: 4, 5, 11, 41.	• Understand that stained glass is an art form related to architecture • Explore transparent qualities of color	*National Standards:* 1a, c, d, 2a, c, 4b, 5a, b, c, 6b	*Large Reproductions:* **17** Matisse *Overhead Transparencies:* **24** Hopper *Slide Set:* **20** Cathedral *Assessment Masters:* **20** Find Out About Art	CD-ROM 4, *Art Adventure,* Lesson 2
43 ⌃ ⌃ Page 100 — **A Model of a Castle** *Activity:* **Paper construction** *Materials:* **Drawing media, assorted forms, construction paper** *Concept:* **Architectural form** *Related Lessons:* Architecture: 41, 42, 44, 45. Form: 44, 54, 55, 58.	• Identify geometric forms in architectural monuments (castles) and in their environment • Create and assemble forms to make a model of a castle	*National Standards:* 1a, d, 2a, c, 3b, 4a, b, c, 5a, c, 6a	*Large Reproductions:* **15** Haas *Overhead Transparencies:* **6** Boulle *Slide Set:* **21** Castle *Assessment Masters:* **6** Create a Community	CD-ROM 4, *Art Adventure,* Lesson 2
44 ⌃ Core Page 102 — **Styles of Buildings** *Activity:* **Drawing** *Materials:* **Drawing media, architectural photographs** *Concept:* **Architectural styles** *Related Lessons:* Architecture: 39, 41, 42, 43. Form: 43, 54, 55, 56.	• Be aware of cultural and historical influences on architectural styles • Draw a picture of a building using design ideas from art history	*National Standards:* 1a, 2a, c, 3a, 4a, c, 5a, c, 6a	*Large Reproductions:* **15** Haas *Overhead Transparencies:* **23** *San Francisco* *Slide Set:* **22** Thornton, et al. *Assessment Masters:* **15** Changing Chairs	CD-ROM 4, *Art Adventure,* Lesson 2
45 ⌃ ⌃ Page 104 — **Landscape Architecture** *Activity:* **Mural drawing** *Materials:* **Drawing media, butcher or mural paper, colored paper** *Concept:* **Landscape architecture** *Related Lessons:* Architecture: 39, 41, 43, 44. Parks and Gardens: 13, R3, U4. Playground equipment: 31, R3.	• Understand that parks and playgrounds can be designed for safety, beauty, and entertainment • Work together to create a mural of a park or playground design	*National Standards:* 1a, c, d, 2a, c, 3a, b, 4a, 5a, b, c	*Large Reproductions:* **24** Frey *Overhead Transparencies:* **22** *McNay Art Museum* *Assessment Masters:* **11** A Bird's Eye View	CD-ROM 4, *Art Adventure,* Lesson 2
R3 ⌃ Core Page 106 — **Review Unit 3** *Activity:* **Drawing** *Materials:* **Folders with artwork, crayons or oil pastels** *Concept:* **City planning** *Related Lessons:* Careers: 31, 32, 39, U3. City: 16. Parks and gardens: 13, 45, U4. Playground equipment: 31, 45.	• Be aware of the role of citizens and art experts in planning cities • Draw a well-designed part of their city and discuss various opinions of good design	*National Standards:* 1a, c, 2a, b, c, 3a, 4b, c, 5a, b, c, 6a	*Large Reproductions:* **24** Frey, **15** Haas, **19** Courtney-Clarke *Overhead Transparencies:* **23** *San Francisco* *Assessment Masters:* **6** Create a Community, **13** A Place to Live	CD-ROM 4, *Art Adventure,* Lesson 2

Special Features	Cultures/History	Integrating the Curriculum	
		Extensions	**Literature Link**
■ Meeting Individual Needs ■ Community-Based Learning	Canada United States ■ *Art History:* Interior design	*Science:* Light sources	*Night on Neighborhood Street,* Eloise Greenfield. (S) *Night of the Moonjellies,* Mark Shasha. (A) *On a Starry Night,* Natalie Kinsey-Warnock. (A)
■ Meeting Individual Needs ■ Aesthetic Awareness ■ Cooperative Learning	France United States: Traylor	*Language Arts:* Prepare questions	*Light Color, & Lenses,* Pam Robson. (I, A) *Disney's The Hunchback of Notre Dame.* Walt Disney. (S, A) *Disney's The Hunchback of Notre Dame Stained Glass Kit.* (A, I)

■ Independent Research
■ Cooperative Learning
	France:
	   Chambord
	Germany:
	   Riedell and Von Dollman
	
	■ *Art History:* Castles
		Social Studies: Feudal life	*The Truth about Castles,* Gillian Clements. (I, A)
			A Medieval Feast, Aliki. (I, A)
			A Tournament of Knights, Joe Lasker. (A)

■ Meeting Individual Needs
■ Independent Research
■ Community-Based Learning
	Greece
	Italy
	United States:
	   Furness
	   Jefferson
	   Morgan
		Language Arts: Reading	*Thomas Jefferson: A Picture Book Biography,* James Cross Giblin. (S, A)
			Monticello, Catherine Reef. (I, A)

■ Cooperative Learning		*Science:* Landscape architect	*Linnea in Monet's Garden,* Christina Bjork. (S) *Roxaboxen,* Alice McLerran. (S) *Miss Rumphius,* Barbara Cooney. (S)
■ Art Criticism	Canada United States	*Social Studies:* Maps	*The Little House,* Virginia Lee Burton. (S) *Town and Country,* Alice and Martin Provensen. (S)

U3 Art in Your World
Drawing

PREPARE

Objectives

Students will:
- be aware of art-related careers and places to see art in their community.
- draw a picture of a product with labels that show the parts planned by an artist.

Materials

drawing paper, 12 x 18"
(30 x 46 cm),
1 per student

choice of drawing
media

Vocabulary

craftsworkers	*artifices*
easel	*caballete*
palette	*paleta*
career	*carrera*
authentic	*auténtico*
storyboard	*guión y dibujos preliminares para una pelicula*

Setup

List these design elements on the chalkboard: line, color, shape, texture, space (spacing). Also list these design principles: pattern, balance, center of interest (emphasis), proportion, unity, variety.

B   Photograph of Francisco Mora. Photograph: Juan Mora.

A   Photograph: Ann Hawthorne for the Penland School.

Do you know people who draw, paint or create other kinds of art? Where do they create art?

The man and woman in picture A create metal trays, cups and jewelry. They use hammers, saws and other tools to create the metal forms. Artists who use a material skillfully are **craftsworkers**.

Artists use different tools and materials for their work. The artist in picture B is creating a painting. An **easel** holds the painting so it is easy to see and work on. The artist holds a **palette**, a tray for mixing paint. He will display his best artwork in an art gallery or museum.

The students in picture C are in an art museum. A museum has authentic artworks. An **authentic**

74

TEACH

Engage

1. Ask students to describe meeting artists or visiting places where art is created. Ask about the kind of artists students have met, materials they use, and where they work.

2. Discuss kinds of art that many people see or use. To make students aware of possibilities, have them look at some of the images in this unit.

Meeting Individual Needs

Simplify Have students look through old magazines for products such as cars, furniture, appliances, or clothing. Have them cut out pictures, paste them on paper, and label the parts designed by an artist.

Explore

1. In **A**, guide students to see that these craftsworkers shape flat sheets of metal (and wire) into a variety of art forms. *Craftsworkers* are artists who create original designs and are skilled in using certain materials, tools, and processes. Discuss crafts such as leatherworking, glassmaking, metalsmithing, and weaving.

2. In **B**, guide students to see the artist's workspace, called a *studio*, as well as his special tools and equipment. Francisco Mora is one of Mexico's most respected artists. He is a painter and printmaker.

3. In **C**, help students become aware of the role of art museums in exhibiting authentic artwork from many lands. In this picture, students see and discuss fabric designs from West Africa.

4. In **D**, the artist's sketches show the kind of picture he wants for scenes in a story for a television show.

5. Ask students to think about things artists have designed, focusing on products that many people see (cars, buses, furniture, clothing, containers, toys).

74

artwork is one the artist makes. It is not a copy made by someone else. Where else can you see authentic artworks in your community?

Many artists work on designs for toys, cars and other things people need or buy. Artists also design motion pictures and television shows.

The artist in picture D is making a storyboard. A **storyboard** has drawings of each scene in a motion picture. The storyboard includes words that actors will speak. The words are under each drawing. A storyboard helps everyone plan a motion picture.

The world of art includes many people who have a job, or career, in art. In this unit, you will learn more about art in your world and the people who create it.

75

INTEGRATING THE CURRICULUM

Extensions ▼

Social Studies Have students research and report on art-related careers of people they know. Provide a definition of art that includes crafts, design, and architecture. Students can help to construct weblike diagrams of careers by looking over the images in this unit and Unit 4. Guide students to identify careers that involve basic human needs such as architecture (shelter), graphic design (communication), industrial design (tools, transportation), etc.

Literature Link
- *Visiting the Art Museum*, Laurene Krasny Brown and Marc Brown. (I)
- *Disney's Art of Animation: From Mickey Mouse to Beauty and the Beast*, Bob Thomas. (I, A)
- *Puddle Jumper: How a Toy Is Made*, Ann Morris. (I)

Create

1 Distribute materials. Have students draw an object from memory, a product they like to use. Their drawing will look like a diagram with labels. After they draw the object, they will write phrases about the parts of the object that an artist planned. The words should be near an arrow that points to the part described.

2 Tell students to draw very light guidelines, about four fingers wide, to create a border.

3 Have students draw the object inside the border. In the top border, have them write, "An artist planned this to be:"

4 Guide students as they write the first phrase. For example, have them point to a color in the drawing. In the real object, an artist would have helped decide on that color. If the object is a yellow raincoat, a complete statement might be, "An artist planned this to be: a bright and safe color for a rainy day."

CLOSE

Assess

1 Call on students to share their work. Have them give reasons for their choice of an object. Discuss the labels and planned elements of design; point out additional elements.

2 Continue the discussion to help students see the variety of objects and their design qualities.

RESOURCES

Large Reproductions
African Canvas, Courtney-Clarke, 19

Overhead Transparencies
Dogware, Tygart, 5

 CD-ROM
3, *Artists at Work*, Lesson 2

Assessment Masters
Find Out About Art, 20

PREPARE

Objectives

Students will:
- be aware of industrial design as an art form and career.
- create a posterlike display of industrial designs that includes their judgments of these designs.

Vocabulary

industrial design	*diseño industrial*
factory-made objects	*objecto producido industrialmente*

Materials

picture magazines and advertising sections of newspapers

pencils

scissors

paste

background paper, 12 x 18" (30 x 46 cm), 1 per 2 students

lined notebook paper, 1 per student

damp paper towels

A *Melamine Dinnerware, Sticks and Bricks pattern.* Courtesy of Copco ® division of Wilton Enterprises.

B Hans J. Wegner, *The Peacock Chair* and *The Chair,* 1949. Courtesy of the artist.

Artists design many of the factory-made objects that you see and use. Artists plan the textures you touch. They design the forms you hold. They plan the colors and shapes.

Artists who plan factory-made objects are called **industrial designers**. After an object is designed, the object can be made in a factory. Many people can have objects that have the same design.

Industrial designers planned the objects shown in this lesson. They chose the materials and planned the forms you see, touch or hold.

Look at each picture. What parts of the objects were carefully designed? What makes you think so?

76

TEACH

Engage

1 Ask students if they see anything in the classroom that artists have helped to create or plan. Select one example, such as a chair, and discuss the parts an artist designed (contour of seat, back, height of legs, etc.). Have students discuss the best and worst designs of chairs they have seen. Build an awareness of criteria for judgment related to safety, ease of use or comfort, and appearance.

Meeting Individual Needs

Challenge Have students select a specific product, such as furniture, and cut out pictures from newspapers and magazines. Have them mount each example to use for matching games based on general types, styles, or purposes.

Explore

1 Guide students toward an understanding of mass production as a process involving many steps, including decisions about product design. The industrial designer plans the parts of a product that people see, touch, hold, or manipulate.

2 Discuss the design qualities in **A–D**. Encourage students to add to the points outlined here. The dinnerware in **A** is made of unbreakable plastic for everyday use. The designs can be combined in different ways, adding variety to a table. Forms are smooth, making them safe and pleasing to hold.

3 The chairs in **B** were designed by Hans Wegner as "sculpture to fit the body." Each piece of the chair has subtle curves that make it attractive to see and touch and comfortable to sit in.

4 In **C**, the designer planned the airfoil on the truck cab, front grill, shapes and forms of the fenders, cab, and so on. The slide in **D**, designed by Canadian Gerald Beekenkamp, is another international product. The parts are colorful rustproof Fiberglas™.

Independent Research

Have students research whether the function of a product is improved by modernizing its design. Have them ask their parents about the oldest furniture or appliance at home or look through old catalogs such as a reprint of a 1901 Sears catalog. Have students record the year an object was made and how it works. Then have them find a newly designed version of the same object. They can determine whether the new object functions better or merely looks better and share their findings with the class.

Duraglide Spiral Slide. Designer: Gerald Beekenkamp. Courtesy of Paris Slides, Inc.

Industrial designers plan radios, bicycles, cars and many other objects. The designer helps to make sure that factory-made objects are safe, attractive and easy to use.

Look for examples of industrial design in newspapers or old magazines. Cut out the pictures and display them. Which designs are the best? How can you decide?

77

INTEGRATING THE CURRICULUM

Extensions ▼

Social Studies Introduce students to products designed and manufactured locally. Check to see if an association of industrial designers has an educational program. Invite a designer who works for a manufacturer to speak to your students or arrange a field trip that allows students to see the design process as well as the manufacturing process.

Literature Link
• *Sneakers: The Shoes We Choose!*, Robert Young. (I)
• *How Does Soda Get Into the Bottle?*, Oz Charles. (I)

Create

1 Explain that students will work in pairs to create posterlike displays of well-designed and poorly designed products. Assign each pair a category. They will look for three or four examples of products in one category. The products should be of the same type so students can, for example, compare several designs for radios.

2 Distribute materials. Instruct students to look through magazines and fold down the corner of a page where they see a product design for their category. Carefully tear out these pages and put the magazines aside.

3 Have students fold their display paper in half. After they decide which design is best and why, have them cut it out. Have them write down several reasons why the design is effective, trim the statement, and paste it on the top half of the paper with the design. Have them complete the bottom part of the display so that it shows the least effective design and written reasons.

CLOSE

Assess

1 Arrange some of the displays on a bulletin board. Have students discuss their examples and give reasons for their judgments.

2 Guide students toward an awareness of the criteria they are using to judge the best examples, such as safety, ease of use, durability, comfort, and appearance.

3 Discuss other criteria students may use: cost, popularity (often established through advertising), and personal preference.

RESOURCES

Large Reproductions
  French Pastries, Thiebaud, 2

Overhead Transparencies
  Dogware, Tygart, 5
  Swan Bed, Brundege, 4

CD-ROM
  3, *Artists at Work*, Lesson 1

Slide Set
  Bowls, Bjorn/Bernadotte, 16

Assessment Masters
  Designs for Lamps, 18

Critical Thinking

Have students look at handmade products in Lessons 46, 47, and 48, contrasting their design with that of mass-produced versions.

32 Graphic Design
Poster Design

PREPARE

Objectives

Students will:
- identify examples of graphic design and visual qualities planned by a designer.
- create a posterlike design that fits within a basic shape (circle, square, triangle) and communicates an important message.

Vocabulary

graphic designer	*diseñador gráfico*
lettering	*caracteres*
poster	*cartel*
design	*diseño*

Materials

pencils

colored paper, bright hues, choice of cut squares, rectangles, triangles, all at least 9" (23 cm) wide, and strips, about 6 x 18" (15 x 46 cm), 1 per student

newsprint paper, 9 x 12" (23 x 30 cm), 1 per student

oil pastels or crayons

markers

reference chart for proper manuscript lettering

scissors

(optional) additional examples of graphic design

A *Brookview Plaza roadside sign.* Designer: Richard Lang. Photograph from *Successful Sign Design.* Reprinted by permission of Retail Reporting Corporation.

B *Lucky Stores, San Francisco.* Design: Walker Group/CNI, New York. Photograph: Toshi Yoshimi, from *Successful Food Merchandising and Display.* Reprinted by permission of Retail Reporting Corporation.

Some artists are graphic designers. A **graphic designer** plans the lettering and artwork for signs, books and many other things people read. Graphic is an ancient Greek word. It means you share ideas by writing and drawing. The outdoor sign in picture A is a graphic design. An artist planned the sign and the lettering.

A grocery store has many graphic designs. The designer plans the lettering and pictures on displays and packages. What other graphic designs can you find in picture B?

78

TEACH

Engage

1 Help students recall from Lesson 31 that industrial designers plan forms of factory-made objects. Explain that some artists, called *graphic designers*, design things such as signs, posters, and packages.

2 Call students' attention to examples of graphic design in the room. Guide them to identify planned elements such as size, color, and kinds of letters; placement of letters; and spacing of these elements to attract attention.

Meeting Individual Needs

Simplify Have students select a theme for a stamp design and then create original designs related to the theme.

Challenge Help students identify examples of products in which the skills of industrial and graphic designers are combined (such as the truck in Lesson 31).

Explore

1 Guide a discussion of **A** and **B**. In **A**, help students see how simple lettering is designed to show up day or night. Discuss similar signs students have seen. In **B**, develop an awareness of the variety of graphic designs: bannerlike signs, numerals for checkout lanes, magazine covers, labels on packages. Discuss why designs on packages and in stores are planned. (For contrast, ask students to describe a store with poor planning and packages with unidentifiable contents.)

2 Discuss how the graphic design in **C** identifies the television station and kind of program. Have students give other examples of graphic design they have seen on television. Guide them to see how **D** reminds people they can see dinosaurs at the museum.

3 Explain that students will create posters to send an important message to everyone in their school. Set up starter ideas on the chalkboard and have students add words or phrases. Examples include Say Yes to (Courtesy, Good Health); Say No to (Litter, Drugs); Think (Safety, Before You Speak).

Cooperative Learning

Put special issue postage stamps on index cards. Center one stamp on each card. Give these to small groups of students to discuss. Groups must decide whether or not the design of the stamp sends a clear message about the subject. A recorder can list reasons the graphic design of the stamp is effective or not. Then a spokesperson can share results with the class.

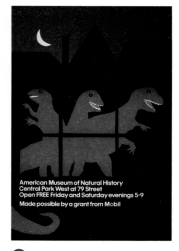

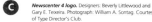

C *Newscenter 4 logo.* Designers: Beverly Littlewood and Gary E. Texeira. Photograph: William A. Sontag. Courtesy of Type Director's Club.

American Museum of Natural History
Central Park West at 79 Street
Open FREE Friday and Saturday evenings 5-9
Made possible by a grant from Mobil

 D Ivan Chermayeff, *Poster for American Museum of Natural History,* 1982. Courtesy of Chermayeff and Geismar, Inc.

You see many graphic designs on television. The design in picture C is for a news program on television. What parts of the design did an artist plan? What other graphic designs do you see on television or at home?

Look at the poster in picture D. What parts of the poster did a graphic designer plan? What messages do you get from the poster?

Look for examples of graphic design in your school, home and neighborhood. Create a graphic design that sends an important message to people. Describe how your design helps people understand the message.

79

INTEGRATING THE CURRICULUM

Extensions ▼

Social Studies Discuss graphic designs that students see in their neighborhoods which are often overlooked. For example, traffic signs have carefully planned shapes and colors that give different messages. Some also include words, but others use simple pictures without words. (See Lesson 33.) Ask students to sketch traffic signs in their neighborhoods. Make a class chart of the kinds of signs they identify and discuss why the signs are needed.

Literature Link
• *The Sign Painter's Dream,* Roger Roth. (S)
• *The Signmaker's Assistant,* Tedd Arnold. (S)
• *The Sign Painter's Secret: The Story of a Revolutionary Girl,* Dorothy and Thomas Hoobler. (S)

CLOSE

Create

1 Distribute materials. Explain that students are to create a graphic design for a sign or poster. The message will begin with a simple statement. They can choose an idea from those listed or come up with another message.

2 Show them how to fold the newsprint in quarters to create four spaces for sketches.

3 Guide students to see how design skills from earlier lessons can be used:

• A simple shape or symbol can be the center of interest.
• Lettering can be spaced carefully.
• Contrasting colors will show up from a distance.

4 Ask students to choose their best sketch. Have them complete their work, keeping in mind that signs and posters must have simple shapes, well-planned lettering, and colors that contrast to attract attention.

Assess

1 Call on volunteers to show and discuss relationships between their sketches and their posters. Discuss the value of sketches as a way to try out ideas. Guide students to consider why sketches may not be the same as finished artwork (you make changes to fit the final size, shape, materials; you get ideas as you work on the final version).

2 Discuss some artworks in relation to categories of messages, shapes of posters, color choices, etc.

3 Have students participate in deciding where to display their posters.

Technology

Have students create graphic designs on a computer. Have them add picture elements by drawing on the computer or leaving a space on the printout that will allow them to add a drawing.

RESOURCES

Large Reproductions
Serenade, Bearden, 22
French Pastries, Thiebaud, 2

Overhead Transparencies
Emptying the Fridge, Mandel, 15

 CD-ROM
3, *Artists at Work,* Lesson 1

Assessment Masters
Changes in Style, 16

PREPARE

Objectives

Students will:
• compare and contrast visual symbols used to communicate ideas in various cultures, past and present.
• create visual symbols to communicate a command or simple sentence.

Vocabulary
visual symbols
picture writing

símbolos visuales
pictografía

Materials
choice of drawing media

choice of calculator paper, about 3 x 18" (8 x 46 cm), or drawing paper, 9 x 12" (23 x 30 cm), 1 per student (See Create 1)

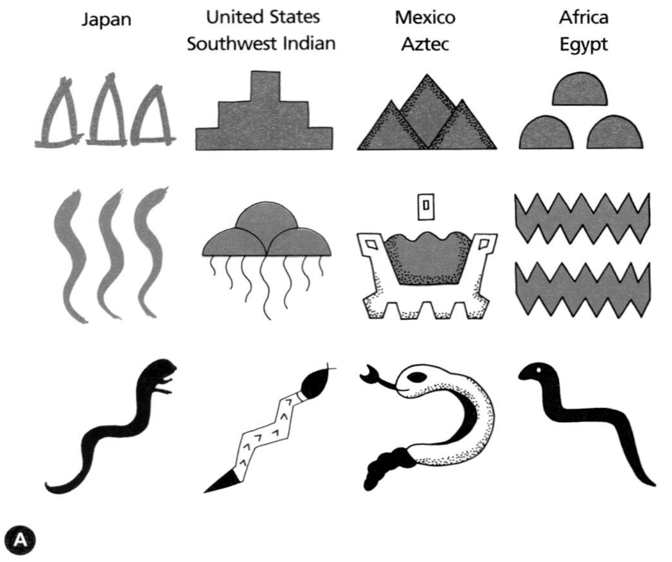

| Japan | United States Southwest Indian | Mexico Aztec | Africa Egypt |

A

Long ago, people began to draw pictures to share ideas. Picture writing became a way for people to tell about things without using words.

People in many lands invented pictures for ideas. Look at the simple pictures in A. Each picture is a visual **symbol** for an idea. What ideas in picture A can you name? How are the visual symbols alike? How are they different?

80

TEACH

Engage

1 Discuss ways people communicate without speaking or writing words. Develop responses that focus on sounds (laughing), hand signals (pointing), and body motion (pantomime).

2 Explain that artists have invented visual symbols to communicate ideas. Explain that a *symbol* stands for something else. For example, a stoplight and its colors are symbols for stop, go, and caution. Explain that students will learn more about visual symbols.

Explore

1 Have students examine **A**. Point out that each column shows symbols from picture writing in different cultures. Symbols such as these were invented in many different cultures.

2 Focus on the top row in **A**, symbols for mountains. Have students identify and offer explanations for similarities and differences in the symbols. In the center row, the symbols stand for water. (In the Aztec culture of Mexico, large stone cisterns were used to collect water.) In the bottom row, the symbols stand for snakes. Help students see that these and other visual symbols are simple shapes related to experiences.

3 Have students identify the message each sign communicates in **B**. The circle with a diagonal line means "not permitted." Symbols in the center column warn motorists. On the right are signs that help highway travelers.

4 List some starter ideas on the chalkboard for messages students could communicate through visual symbols: I'm thirsty. Laundry facilities. Caution, road ends. Quiet, please. Ducks cross here.

Meeting Individual Needs

Simplify Instead of calculator paper, provide large unlined index cards for each drawing. Then arrange the cards in a sequence.

Challenge Encourage students to sketch picture symbols they have seen in more than one part of town (chain or franchise signs) or on more than one kind of product (brand identity symbols such as different cereals from one company). Have them explain why picture symbols are used in this way.

B

You see picture writing every day. Picture B has symbols that help people understand ideas. Can you tell what these visual symbols mean?

You can share ideas without using words. You can use picture writing. You can invent simple

pictures to tell what you mean.

Think of a sentence or command that sends a message. Draw one or more pictures to share your message. Make each picture very simple. Simple means you show only the most important lines and shapes.

81

Extensions ▼

Social Studies Have students research the evolution of the alphabet, varieties of alphabets, and picture-writing systems (ancient Egypt, Greece, Rome; China, Maya, Cherokee nation). Read the story *A, B, C's The American Indian Way* by Richard Red Hawk (Sierra Oaks, 1988) and show the accompanying illustrations. This book has an alphabet that contains cultural symbols of Native Americans.

Literature Link
• *Puff . . .Flash. . . Bang! A Book About Signals*, Gail Gibbons. (I)
• *You Don't Need Words! A Book about Ways People Talk Without Words*, Ruth Belov Gross. (I)

Create

1 Have students select a rectangular sheet of paper if they wish to draw a sign or a strip of calculator paper if they wish to create a sentence with picture writing. Stress that artwork will have no written words and no letters from the alphabet. The message they send will be shown by the drawing. Lines, shapes, and colors should be simple and easy to understand. Each student is to create original symbols for an original message.

2 As students work, lead them to create easy-to-see shapes with carefully planned spacing. Encourage them to imagine how other people—those who see the symbols—might interpret them. Remind them that colors can be symbols, as in traffic lights.

CLOSE

Assess

1 Call on volunteers who designed symbols on rectangular paper to show them. Invite the class to guess the messages. Have the designers tell the message they intended to communicate. If symbols seem to send more than one message, discuss why this happens and what changes might be made to clarify the message.

2 Discuss some messages developed on calculator paper in the same way.

RESOURCES

Large Reproductions
  Sioux Vest, 3
  Golden Age, Brown, 6
  Wolf General, Blackwell, 21
  Summer, Arcimboldo, 13

Overhead Transparencies
  Salmon Clan Hat, Tlingit Tribe, 14

CD-ROM
  2, *Elements of Design*, Lesson 2

Assessment Masters
  Changes in Style, 16

Community-Based Learning

Ask students and school resource specialists to identify people in the community who can demonstrate differences between the alphabet for English and the writing system for another language such as Hebrew, Arabic, Chinese, Japanese, or the language of the Cherokee nation. Have students select several universal images (sun, moon, water, fire) and develop a chart that shows how each image or word is represented in different systems of writing.

(A) *Alphabet vegetables*, 1985. © 1991 David Anson Russo.

Graphic designers use letters of the alphabet in many of their artworks. Some graphic designers create **picture alphabets**.

In a picture alphabet, the shape of each letter is also a picture. The designer makes each picture fit the shape of a letter.

Picture alphabets often have related shapes and ideas. For example, in picture A, the picture alphabet is made up of things you can eat.

Look carefully. Do you see ears of corn and carrots? Both of these vegetables have long narrow shapes. Where has the artist used these shapes to create part of a letter? What round shapes did he use to make letters? How are they used?

82

PREPARE

Objectives

Students will:
- understand that graphic design includes creative lettering.
- help create a theme-based picture alphabet as a class project.

Vocabulary

theme   *tema*
shape   *forma*
picture alphabet   *alfabeto formado*
                        con dibujos

Materials

white drawing paper, 6 x 9" (15 x 23 cm), 1 per student

pencils and soft erasers

oil pastels or crayons

examples of highly creative alphabet books or alphabet cards

standard reference chart for manuscript lettering

white drawing paper, 8 x 9" (20 x 23 cm), for students assigned the letters M and W

TEACH

Engage

1 Explain that some artists design letters of the alphabet. Sometimes they design alphabets with unusual elements, such as extra wide or extra tall letters.

2 Explain that students will be learning about picture alphabets.

Meeting Individual Needs

Challenge Have students write a sentence, using their letter more than once. Have them neatly transcribe the sentence, using the manuscript writing guide, on paper that can be mounted under their artwork.

Explore

1 Focus on **A**. Guide students to see how the alphabet is made up of small shapes that resemble vegetables. Have students identify some vegetables. Guide them to appreciate how inventive the artist has been. Vegetables with long shapes tend to be used for straight lines. Curved letters are often composed of vegetables with smaller shapes.

2 In **B**, have students note how some letters (S, W, O, K) illustrate a path of movement. In **C**, the artist has created a whole alphabet around shapes of birds.

3 Show some alphabet books or cards. Discuss similarities and differences in design qualities and parallels, if any, with the alphabets in this lesson.

4 Explain the studio activity. Discuss themes and select one for the class project. The theme should be broad and differ from illustrations in students' books. Possibilities include clothing, transportation, toys, people, and animals. Stress that everyone's alphabet letter will have picture elements related to the chosen theme.

Create

1 Distribute materials. Refer to capital letters of the alphabet as shown on your chart for manuscript writing (not cursive). Assign each student one letter of the alphabet. You may need to add symbols such as an exclamation point or numerals so each student has a unique assignment.

Joseph Volpicelli, *Alphabet.* Courtesy of Werner Pfeffer.

Cover illustration from *The Way Things Work* by David Macaulay. Illustration © 1988 by David Macaulay. Text © 1988 by David Macaulay and Neil Ardley. Reprinted by permission of Houghton Mifflin Company. All Rights Reserved.

Look at the letters on the book cover in picture B. This book is about machines, tools and inventions. Each letter has some shapes from a machine, tool or invention.

Can you find the letter that looks like an open zipper? Where do you see the point of a pen? What other shapes are used to make picture letters?

Your class can make a picture alphabet. Choose a theme everyone can work on. Each student can make one letter for the picture alphabet. When all the artwork is finished, your class can display the whole alphabet. What theme did the artist use for the alphabet in picture C?

INTEGRATING THE CURRICULUM

Extensions ▼

Language Arts Read and show illustrations for *On Market Street* by Arnold Lobel (Greenwillow, 1981). Have students note and discuss different ways the author/illustrator has incorporated the object of the story into his illustrations.

Literature Link
• *The Z was Zapped*, Chris Van Allsburg. (A)
• *The Graphic Alphabet*, David Pelletier. (A)
• *Alphabetics*, Sue MacDonald. (A)

2 Have students:
  • place paper in a tall orientation.
  • draw the general shape of the letter very lightly; these guidelines can be erased later.
  • lightly draw the letter, fitting it into height and width of paper.

3 Explain that the basic letter each student has drawn can now be changed to create a picture letter. If picture shapes are drawn near guidelines, the letter can be read from a distance.

4 As students work, encourage them to apply their design skills. For example, symmetrical letters might have symmetrical picture elements. Colors might be selected to go with the letter. Contrasting colors and wide lines might make the picture letter stand out.

CLOSE

Assess

1 Have students stand in a circle with their letters in alphabetical order. Discuss artwork in relation to overall effectiveness and specific qualities that make letters stand out from backgrounds.

2 Invite students to improve their work, as needed, so the whole alphabet is visually effective and related to the theme.

Reminder

If students are to create scrolls in Lesson 35, have them bring in two cardboard tubes from paper towels or bathroom tissue—or use plastic soda straws or dowels.

RESOURCES

Large Reproductions
  Summer, Arcimboldo, 13

Overhead Transparencies
  Delfina Flores, Rivera, 21

CD-ROM
  2, *Elements of Design*, Lessons 1 and 2

Assessment Masters
  Find Out About Art, 20

Aesthetic Awareness

Ask students to look through newspapers or old magazines for examples of picture lettering. Have them cut out examples and assemble them for display. Discuss some reasons for the use of picture lettering instead of a more common style of lettering.

PREPARE

Objectives

Students will:
• perceive and discuss examples of handmade books of different types.
• create a scroll or folded book and, in Lesson 36, illustrate it.

Vocabulary

scroll	*rollo*
folded book	*libro plegable*

Setup

Long paper can be used for scrolls or a continuous fanfolded book. If possible, provide materials so students can choose which type of book to make. Set up two stations, one for each type. If only one type is made in this lesson, encourage students to make others on their own.

Materials

For scrolls:

shelf paper, in 2'
(61 cm) lengths, 1 per
student (See Setup)

tubes, plastic straws, or
dowels, 2 per student

removable tape

glue

For books:

white drawing paper
or light-colored
construction paper,
9 x 12" (23 x 30 cm),
3 per student

notebook paper,
1 per student

rulers

pencils

(optional) examples
of handmade books
or scrolls

Have you ever seen books like these? Long ago, people in many lands made their own books by hand. They did not have printed books like you have.

The very old book in picture A is a **scroll**. You unroll the ends to read it. This kind of book was made for thousands of years in many lands.

This scroll is made so you roll the left and right sides. Some scrolls are made so you roll them from the top and bottom.

Picture B shows a book with pages that fold back and forth. This folded book was made in China many years ago. The lettering was printed. Artists carved letters into a block of wood. Then the woodblock was covered with ink and pressed down on the page.

84

TEACH

Engage

1 Ask students if they have ever made a booklet. Explain that some artists make books and that they can be made for different reasons.

2 Have students share their knowledge of types of handmade books. Encourage them to speculate on reasons people might make a book by hand. Explain that students will learn more about handmade books.

If your community has a crafts organization, check on the possibility of in-school programs or field trips to see artists who create paper and/or produce books with handmade paper. Some public libraries and art museums have collections of handmade books. Plan a field trip to a local printing plant that binds books.

Explore

1 Explain that the scroll in **A**:
• is about ten feet long (305 cm).
• was made over 1000 years ago in England.
• has drawings that illustrate the life of a religious leader.
• is made on parchment, a very thin leather.
• shows one of the first ways to make a book that could be easily carried.

2 **B** is made from long sheets of paper. Explain that:
• the paper is carefully folded back and forth (often called a fanfold) and joined together.
• Chinese people invented ways to make paper and print letters on it using blocks.
• this book, over 600 years old, was made and used by Buddhist monks.

Have students imagine the time, effort, and care taken to create and to preserve **A** and **B**.

3 Explain that the artist who made **C** has been a weaver for more than forty years. In this book, he shares some ideas about weaving. He made five copies of his book by hand.

4 Focus on **D** and **E**. Ask students to study the types of books and choose one type to create. Explain that they will illustrate their books in the next lesson.

Create

1 Ask students who will make scrolls to gather their materials and sit near each other so you can give them pointers. Give similar instructions to students making fanfolded books.

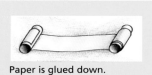

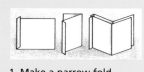

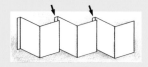

C   Ed Rossbach, *The Weaver's Secret Book,* 1977. Mixed print media, accordion-folded, 5 x 5 1/2 x 3/4" (13 x 14 x 2 cm). Courtesy of the Textile Museum.

Some artists still make books by hand. An artist who likes to weave made the book in picture C.

Make a scroll or a folded book. Write and draw in it. What ideas will you include?

A scroll

Paper is glued down. Use tubes or sticks.

D

A folded book

1. Make a narrow fold.
2. Fold in half.
3. Make others.
4. Put glue here.

E

85

Extensions   ▼

Social Studies Have students research topics related to creating books. A starter list might include bookbinding, illuminated manuscript, printing press (invention), paper (invention), woodcut prints, colophon (a printer's mark similar to a trademark), Sumerian or Mesopotamian clay tablets, and cylinder seals.

Literature Link
• *Breaking into Print: Before and After the Invention of the Printing Press,* Stephen Krensky. (I)
• *Go In and Out the Window: An Illustrated Songbook for Young People,* Dan Fox. (A)
• *A Book Takes Root: The Making of a Picture Book,* Michael Kehoe. (I)

RESOURCES

Large Reproductions
   Golden Age, Brown, 6
   Wolf General, Blackwell, 21

Overhead Transparencies
   The Ark, Miller, 2

 CD-ROM
   3, *Artists at Work,* Lesson 1

Assessment Masters
   Sketch a Story, 8

CLOSE

Assess

1 Discuss students' work. Guide students to see and appreciate that their handmade books are part of a tradition of bookmaking that goes back thousands of years.

2 Have students use notebook paper to write down ideas for an original story or poem so they can complete books next time. Have them think of ideas they would like people to know about 1000 years from now.

Cleanup

1 Collect materials.

2 Ask students to print their names lightly in pencil on the scrolls and books.

2 For scroll books, have students:
   • roll up paper lightly from one end and then the other.
   • glue one edge of the inward curve and place the tube, straw, or stick on the glue.
   • repeat at opposite end (removable tape can be used to hold paper in place until glue dries).

3 To make a fanfolded book, have students:
   • score and fold the narrow edge of each paper.
   • hold the ruler parallel to one edge of paper.
   • use a hard object with a thin edge (paper clip, coin, etc.) to trace along the edge of the ruler, creasing the paper; then fold along the crease.
   • fold paper in half, lifting the creased edge of the paper so it matches the other edge.
   • apply glue as shown in **E**.

PREPARE

Objectives

Students will:
- compare and contrast book illustrations in relation to styles and art media.
- illustrate an original story or poem to complete their handmade scrolls or folded books.

Vocabulary

illustrator	*ilustrador(a)*
illustration	*ilustración*
art media	*medios artísticos*
style	*estilo*
realistic	*realista*
fantasy	*fantasía*

Setup

Have short poems on hand that can be illustrated by students who did not prepare a poem or story.

Materials

- students' scrolls or books from Lesson 35
- markers
- pencils
- erasers
- wax crayons
- notebook paper, 1 per student
- stories or poems students have written
- children's books with award-winning illustrations
- standard reference chart for manuscript lettering (not cursive)
- scissors
- paste
- damp paper towels
- rulers

A   Photograph of Thomas Feelings.

B   Cover illustration from *Black Pilgrimage*. © 1972 Thomas Feelings.

Meet Thomas Feelings. He is an illustrator of books for children. An **illustrator** creates pictures that explain ideas.

    Mr. Feelings began to illustrate children's books after a trip to Africa. He works on books that teach people about Africa and African Americans. His illustrations have won prizes.

C   Cover illustration from *Tommy Traveler in the World of Black History*. © 1991 Thomas Feelings.

86

TEACH

Engage

1 Discuss your examples of illustrated books. Ask students to comment on the design of pages (pictures and words), media used for illustrations, and reasons they like some more than others.

2 Explain that students will learn more about illustration and complete their books over the next two periods.

Note

The visual art components of this project reinforce skills in manuscript lettering, which often decline as students concentrate on cursive writing.

Explore

1 Guide students to make observations about **B**–**E**: how the subject matter is portrayed and design qualities such as spacing, color, balance, and so on.

2 Compare and contrast the styles of **B** and **C** with **D** and **E**. Develop additional comparisons or contrasts with styles and media used in other books. Encourage students to identify with and describe thought processes each illustrator may have used.

Create

1 Before distributing materials, explain how students might plan the written text and illustrations. In a scroll, text can flow across the bottom or top of the long paper. As a guide for lettering, align a ruler with the long edges and draw parallel lines. Use the lines on notebook paper to set up spacing of lines on the scroll. For a folded book, cut and paste notebook paper to fit book pages.

2 Have students begin lettering, including a title page. Encourage them to:
- divide key sentences or paragraphs to fit with illustrations (light pencil lettering is best for this stage).
- apply knowledge of design elements and principles (for example, each illustration should have a center of interest that fits the content).
- make characters or events stand out through color choices, sizes, outlines, etc.

D Cover illustration from *King Krakus and the Dragon,* © 1979 by Janina Domanska. By permission of Greenwillow Books, a division of William Morrow & Co., Inc.

E Interior illustration from *King Krakus and the Dragon,* © 1979 by Janina Domanska. By permission of Greenwillow Books, a division of William Morrow & Co., Inc.

Pictures for books can be done in different **art media**, or art materials. Some illustrators like to use one material, such as markers, for their work. Others like to use different media together, such as paint and chalk.

Illustrations can also be done in different **styles**. Mr. Feelings' pictures have a realistic style. The illustrations in Ms. Domanska's book are done in the style of fantasy. Why do you think these books have different styles?

Find an illustrated book with pictures you like. Tell why you like the illustrations. Can you write and illustrate a story?

INTEGRATING THE CURRICULUM

Extensions ▼

Language Arts Many schools sponsor book fairs that feature students' creative writing. Have students plan and write invitations to parents and give a synopsis of each book they have written and illustrated. For your book fair, display all students' books, organized into "authors' corners." As adults come in, ask them to stay together in groups and to move from one "authors' corner" to another so small groups of students can show and discuss their books.

Literature Link
• *Daydreamers,* Eloise Greenfield. (A)
• *Something on My Mind,* Nikki Grimes. (A)

CLOSE

Assess

3 At the end of the first period, follow usual cleanup procedures. Open the second period with a brief discussion of progress, problems and possible solutions, and reminders about knowledge from previous lessons.

1 Have students circulate and look at each other's work.

2 Assemble the class for a conversation about the project. Discuss how students might apply their knowledge of design to related projects, such as reports for science or social studies. Ask if students might like to become illustrators.

3 Discuss how and where students can display books.

Reminder
Be sure to have supplies and a source of running water for the next lesson. Have students bring in small, nearly flat objects with interesting lines and shapes. Objects can be natural or manufactured.

RESOURCES

Large Reproductions
   Golden Age, Brown, 6
   Wolf General, Blackwell, 21

Overhead Transparencies
   The Ark, Miller, 2

 CD-ROM
   3, *Artists at Work,* Lesson 1

Assessment Masters
   Sketch a Story, 8

Community-Based Learning

If your community has an art school or college that offers a program in illustration, see if instructors or advanced students can show and discuss examples of artwork designed for children. Similar programs might be arranged with a librarian or a publishing company that employs illustrators.

A

Anna Atkins, *Lycopodium Flagellatum (Algae),* 1840-50. Blueprint, 11 1/8 x 8 3/16" (28 x 21 cm). Gernsheim Collection, Harry Ransom Humanities Research Center, The University of Texas at Austin.

Picture A is a photogram. A **photogram** is like a photograph. It is a record, or print, of light and shadow made on special paper. Photograms like this one are called sunprints or blueprints.

For this photogram, the artist arranged a plant on special paper. She put the paper in bright light.

The paper made a record of the plant's shadow. Then the artist put the paper in a special liquid. The liquid made the paper turn blue and the shadow turn white.

Photograms are one kind of **photograph**. What kinds of photographs do you know about? Can you explain why a camera is used for many photographs?

PREPARE

Objectives

Students will:
- be aware of photography as a process of recording light and shadows.
- create a photographic artwork by making a blueprint (sunprint).

Vocabulary

photogram	*fotograma*
photograph	*fotografía*
light	*luz*
shadow	*sombra*
camera	*cámara*

Setup

Activity must be done on a sunny day with little wind.

Safety Notes

Use sun-sensitive paper marked safe for children. Water used in developing may irritate eyes, especially those of contact lens wearers.

Materials

sun-sensitive paper, 6 x 9" (15 x 23 cm), 1 per student (See Safety Notes)

running water/sink

black paper, 6 x 9" (15 x 23 cm) or larger, 1 per student

pencils

newsprint folders, 1 per student

stiff notebooks or cardboard, 1 per student

objects to arrange on paper, several per student

safety glasses (See Safety Notes)

removable tape

black-and-white photo and negative

TEACH

Engage

1 Ask students to describe their photography experiences. Have them explain in their own words how a photograph is made. Build on correct answers. Use your film negative and the print made from it to explain the basic steps in photography.

2 Explain that students will learn about *photograms*, one of the first types of photographs, made about 150 years ago.

Meeting Individual Needs

Challenge If your school can provide cameras, film, and fees for developing, teach students to use a camera. Students at this level should not handle or be exposed to photographic chemicals.

Explore

1 Focus on **A**. The image is a record of a delicate plant made by a special photographic process that is now called *blueprinting* or *sunprinting*. This process makes a record of a shadow on paper.

2 Point out that photograms do not require a camera or film, just special paper. The paper contains chemicals that change when light strikes them. An adult must be present when the paper is used.

3 Guide students to identify some design qualities in **B** and **C**. Explain that all of the white shapes are shadows of objects placed on the paper. When the print was developed, the shadows turned white.

Create

1 Explain that the room lights will be turned off until prints are finished. Have students:
- write names lightly on white side of blueprint paper, near the edge.
- put paper on a notebook or stiff background.
- arrange objects on blue side of paper, creating a well-balanced design or picture-like composition.
- cover the design with black paper so it is not exposed to light.
- go outside, lift black paper, expose blueprint paper to sunlight until paper is almost white, and then return to classroom. (Keep room lights off.)

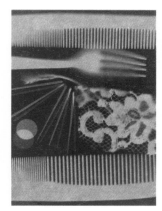

B Student artwork.

C Student artwork.

Photograms can be artworks. Look again at picture A. This photogram is not just a record of a plant's shadow. The artist carefully arranged the plant to show the delicate outlines and tiny leaves.

Look at the photograms in pictures B and C. Students made them. Do you think they are artworks? Why or why not?

You can create a photographic artwork. Your teacher will explain

how. First, collect objects with interesting edges. The objects must be nearly flat. Some examples are leaves, coins, buttons or yarn.

Arrange the objects on top of stiff paper. Move the objects around. Do the objects suggest ideas? Can you plan a center of interest? What kind of balance will your design have? How else can you plan your artwork?

89

INTEGRATING THE CURRICULUM

Extensions ▼

Social Studies Discuss and have students do research on photography as an invention. Assist them in developing a timeline showing related developments, such as color film, motion pictures, color motion pictures, television, and satellite photography. An almanac is one source for dates.

Literature Link

• *Click: A Book about Cameras and Taking Pictures,* Gail Gibbons. (I)
• *The Science Book of Light,* Neil Ardley. (I)
• *Light and Shadow,* Myra Cohn Livingston. (S)

CLOSE

2 Have students remove objects. Collect these and black paper. Turn blueprint paper over to avoid additional exposure. Ask volunteers to distribute several newspapers to each desk.

3 Assist groups of students in developing prints until they are dark blue. (They can be exposed to light.) Place on newspapers to blot water. Have students discuss each other's prints.

Assess

1 View prints in groups that show differences between picturelike compositions and abstract designs.

2 Ask students to summarize what they have learned.

Cleanup

1 Collect everything, except artwork.

2 Distribute newspaper folders. Have students put names on folders.

3 Place damp prints inside newspaper folders and stack with books on top so prints will dry flat.

Community-Based Learning

Ask a local newspaper for a staff photographer to visit and discuss her or his photographs, typical and unusual assignments, and related aspects of this career. Other presentations might be arranged with the help of an art museum, galleries specializing in photographic art, or freelance photographers.

RESOURCES

Large Reproductions
    African Canvas, Courtney-Clarke, 19

Overhead Transparencies
    Navaho Wagon, Gilpin, 19

 CD-ROM
    1, *Color,* Lesson 4

Slide Set
    Untitled (leaves), Talbot, 17

Assessment Masters
    Find Out About Art, 20

PREPARE

Objectives

Students will:
- understand that animated films are composed from sequences of pictures.
- create a sequence of pictures of faces with different expressions.

Vocabulary

camera	*cámara*
motion pictures	*películas*
characters	*personaje*
television	*televisión*
movie	*película*
animated pictures	*películas de dibujos animados*

Setup

Stick tape lengthwise along edge of desks. Students can tear off the amount they need. Removable tape (correction tape) is sold in office-supply stores. Masking tape or contact paper can be substituted.

Materials

white removable tape, 1 x 18" (3 x 46 cm), 1 per student (See Setup)

posterboard or manila folder, trim to about 6 x 9" (15 x 23 cm), 1 per student

oil pastels or wax crayons, dark colors unwrapped

newsprint paper or typing bond, 6 x 9" (15 x 23 cm), at least 3 per student

scissors

(MUSIC UP)

(SFX: Finger snaps)

SINGERS: *Ooo, Ooo*

I heard it through the grapevine.

Raised in the California sunshine.

ANNCR (VO): *California Raisins from the California Vineyards.*

SINGERS: *Don't ya know*

I heard it through the grapevine.

California raisins from the California vineyards.
ANNCR (VO): *Sounds grape, doesn't it?*
(MUSIC OUT)

 A Will Vinton, *Late Show*. Courtesy of California Raisin Advisory Board.

Motion pictures and television are two kinds of art that many people see. In both kinds of art, you see action and movement.

Look at the artwork in picture A. Each scene is part of a movie. Do you know why each picture is slightly different from the next?

90

TEACH

Engage

1 Discuss students' experiences watching animated motion pictures. Define *animated films* as cartoons and stories in which the motion pictures seem to be drawings.

2 Explain that animated images for motion pictures and television can be made in many ways. Some animations combine sculptures, puppets, and drawings. Advertisements sometimes combine photographs of people with cartoon characters. Explain that students will learn how artists make animated pictures showing motion and change.

Meeting Individual Needs

Challenge Have students go beyond basic shapes and cut several related shapes to increase the effect of animation. For example, cut two sets of arms (straight, bent) or two sets of mouths (open, closed) to use in different rubbings.

Explore

1 Focus on **A**. Ask students to identify some similarities and differences in the images. Explain that the main characters in this animated commercial are small sculptures made of claylike material, flexible tubes, and plastic parts. Artists created the figures. To make the film, the sculptures were arranged in front of a motion picture camera. The artists made slight changes in the position of the sculptures so the camera could record the scene again. The same steps were repeated many times, recording separate images on the film. When the film is shown rapidly, the figures seem to move. Each scene and the sculptures needed for it were carefully planned to fit script and music. (Note: SFX means sound effects; VO means voice-over.)

2 Guide students to understand relationships between pictures designed for animation and the student art in **B** and **C**. For example:
- Experiments with animation techniques are often made with collagelike elements.
- Slight changes in one or many elements can be made quickly and recorded as a picture.
- Elements can be rearranged many times to create other pictures.

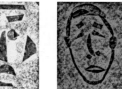

B Student artwork.

C Student artwork.

Many artists work together to create a movie or television show. There are writers and actors. Some shows have dancers and musicians. Artists design costumes and the sets, or backgrounds, for many shows.

Some movies and television shows have cartoons. The cartoon pictures are drawings but the characters move and speak like people or animals.

Movies and television shows with cartoons are created from many separate pictures. A camera is used to record each picture on a long piece of film or tape. When the film or tape is shown very quickly, you see motion. This kind of art is called an **animation**.

Students created the pictures in B and C. They learned how to create animated pictures with a collage. You can explore this idea.

Cut some eyes and other parts of a face from removable tape. Stick the tape to a background paper. You have made a **collage**. Now make a crayon **rubbing** of the collage.

To make a second picture, carefully remove pieces of the tape, such as an eye and eyebrow. Tape the same shapes on the paper again. Put them in a slightly different place. Make a crayon rubbing of the collage.

Make several faces with different expressions. Then give a name to your animated character.

91

Extensions

Mathematics Show students a short animated film or video. Freeze consecutive frames to demonstrate how movement is achieved in separate pictures (called *frames*). Discuss the large number of drawings required to create the illusion of smooth motion. For one second of animation, artists prepare between six and twenty-four pictures. This means that one minute of an animated film can have 360 to 1440 pictures. Ask students to offer reasons why, with fewer pictures, the action appears jumpier.

Literature Link

• *Disney's Art of Animation: From Mickey Mouse to Beauty and the Beast,* Bob Thomas. (I, A)
• *That's a Wrap: How Movies Are Made,* Ned Dowd. (I)
• *Ed Emberley's 3 Science Flip Books,* Ed Emberley. (A)

CLOSE

Create

1 Distribute materials. Demonstrate how to cut out shapes for a face, place them on a flat surface, and create a rubbing similar to those in Lesson 7.

2 Have students:
   • cut out main shapes to rearrange in each picture.
   • arrange shapes for their first rubbings.
   • plan where shapes overlap and the spacing around the main shapes.

3 Have students place paper over shapes and rub the flat side of a crayon from top to bottom, side to side, and from the center to each corner. Discuss the first rubbings and how others can be improved. Allow students to work at their own pace, completing at least three rubbings to make a sequence.

Assess

1 Have students place their rubbings in order and place a number on the back of each to show the sequence. Have students circulate to see each other's work.

2 Call on students to describe motions they have shown, discussing differences in method. For example, shapes of the same size are in different positions, or some shapes vary in size and position.

3 Ask students to explain how cartoons for television and motion pictures are similar to those they have made.

RESOURCES

Large Reproductions
   Spiral Dance, Howell-Sickles, 16
   Upstream, Kuniyoshi, 10

Overhead Transparencies
   Mohammed Running, Muybridge, 9

 CD-ROM
   3, *Artists at Work,* Lesson 1

Assessment Masters
   A Vote for Art, 21

Technology

If your school has computers, ask the resource specialist to purchase software for students to explore animation. The software allows students (and professionals) to create drawings that show the beginning and end of an action. The software produces additional images with slight changes to create the illusion of motion between beginning and end. These intermediate images are called *tweens.*

PREPARE

Objectives

Students will:
- be aware of exterior shapes, patterns, and their arrangement in architectural facades.
- create a symmetrical design of a building facade using the medium of collage.

Vocabulary

architect	*arquitecto(a)*
facade	*fachada*
arch	*arco*
Romanesque	*Románico*
symmetry	*simetría*

Setup

Before the lesson, have students look at exterior shapes, patterns, and placements of details in the architecture of their school and nearby buildings.

Materials

colored paper, 12 x 18" (30 x 46 cm), 1 per student

scraps of colored paper

paste

scissors

damp paper towels

water-based markers or crayons

 Alberti, Facade for the Church of Santa Maria Novella, Florence, 1456–1470.

An **architect** is an artist who designs buildings. Many parts of the building must be planned. The exterior, or outside, walls of the building are one part of a plan. The front or main entrance is often the center of interest. The front of a building is called the **facade**.

The facade in picture A was designed over 300 years ago in Italy. The architect's name was Alberti. This facade has a symmetrical design. The left side is just like the right side.

92

TEACH

Engage

1. Ask students if they know the meaning of the terms *architect* and *architecture*. Explain that architects are artists who plan buildings. Discuss some parts of a building that must be planned and why.

2. Discuss students' observations of buildings they have seen. Focus on shapes, patterns, and details of exteriors. Explain that students will learn more about how exteriors of buildings are planned.

Meeting Individual Needs

Simplify Have students observe and draw the front of the school or a nearby building.

Challenge Have students research other styles of architecture. Have them create collages of architectural facades based on a specific style, culture, or period and then create a mural-like display.

Explore

1. Focus on **A**, which shows the facade, or main face, of a church in Italy. The architect, Leon Battista Alberti, is known as the leader of an elegant style of building with symmetry. Guide students to see how the left and right sides of the building mirror each other.

2. Have students point out in **A** the details shown in **B**. Encourage them to identify other basic shapes and placements of shapes that create patterns or a symmetrical design.

3. The detail in **C** shows the Roman arch that Alberti often included in buildings. Guide students to appreciate that architectural ideas can be borrowed from one period or culture and used in a new way.

4. Discuss **D**, pointing out symmetrical features. Show or ask students to demonstrate:
   - how to fold paper in half, trim edge to create a large shape, and then unfold.
   - how to fold paper and cut smaller symmetrical shapes such as a triangle, circle, and oval.

Community-Based Learning

The remaining lessons in this unit relate to architecture and environmental design. Have students and a resource specialist help assemble a variety of materials for individual and collaborative research. Preview lessons for additional ideas. See if parents who are specialists in architecture, historical preservation, and landscape architecture (or related crafts and trades) can assist by speaking, providing plans or models of projects, demonstrating skills, and the like. You may wish to set up a major project integrating knowledge from science, language arts, and social studies.

B **Alberti,** Detail of facade for the Church of Santa Maria Novella, Florence.

Look at the shapes in picture B. Can you find them in Alberti's building? Where else do you see shapes inside of other shapes?

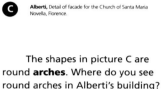

C **Alberti,** Detail of facade for the Church of Santa Maria Novella, Florence.

D Student artwork

The shapes in picture C are round **arches**. Where do you see round arches in Alberti's building? Round arches were invented about 2,000 years ago by Roman architects. Architecture with many round arches is called **Romanesque**.

Design a symmetrical facade for a building. Fold your paper in half. Cut a large symmetrical shape for the building from paper. Unfold the paper. Then add the details. Details are the shapes of windows, doors and decorations. You can draw or cut shapes for the details.

93

INTEGRATING THE CURRICULUM

Extensions

▼

Mathematics Discuss and have students point out geometric shapes they see in the classroom. Ask students to explain why geometric shapes are often seen in architecture. Guide them to see how standard sizes and shapes of building materials influence the geometry of many buildings.

Literature Link

- *What It Feels Like To Be a Building,* Forrest Wilson. (A)
- *Architects Make Zigzags: Looking at Architecture from A to Z,* Diane Maddex. Illustrated by Roxie Munro. (A)

CLOSE

Create

1 Distribute materials. Explain that students' designs for facades can be planned so the building looks tall or wide. Guide them to consider types of buildings that might be designed, such as a house, fire station, courthouse, place of worship, or store.

2 While students work, guide them to use symmetry. Encourage them to use efficient procedures for cutting and pasting. Remind them to paste small shapes on top of large ones for borderlike effects around windows, doors, and other details.

3 As students finish the collage, have them suggest small patterns and finer details using markers or crayons.

Assess

1 Ask students to describe what they have learned about architecture. Encourage them to make statements that reinforce understanding of art vocabulary.

2 Discuss some designs for facades in relation to their orientation (tall or wide), type of building, symmetry, and overall effectiveness. Encourage students to make up a style name for the designs.

Critical Thinking

Show and discuss the book *Then and Now* by Stefania and Dominic Perring (Macmillan, 1991). This book shows students how the ruins of buildings look now and, using transparencies, how the buildings probably looked when they were first constructed. Lead students to predict which fragments were once arches or other details of buildings.

RESOURCES

Large Reproductions
  Brotherhood Building, Haas, 15
  Upstream, Kuniyoshi, 10

Overhead Transparencies
  Early Sunday Morning, Hopper, 24

 CD-ROM
  2, *Elements of Design,* Lesson 2

Slide Set
  Cathedral, Chartres, 18

Assessment Masters
  What's for Sale?, 7

93

PREPARE

Objectives

Students will:
- be aware of mosaics as an ancient and contemporary art form.
- create a paper mosaic with evidence of a planned design.

Vocabulary

mosaic	*mosaico*
mosque	*mezquita*
design elements	*elementos de diseño*

Setup

For safety and efficiency, remove staples from magazines. Use a paper cutter to cut ¾" (2 cm) wide strips from colorful pages. Students can then cut across the strips to make smaller shapes. Dilute three parts glue with one part water. Wash brushes in soapy water before glue dries.

Materials

strips cut from picture magazines (See Setup)

scissors

diluted white glue, 1 container for several students (See Setup)

damp paper towels

dark colors of construction paper, about 7" (18 cm) square, 1 per student

paintbrushes, 1 per student

newspapers for desks

pencils

bucket of soapy water (See Setup)

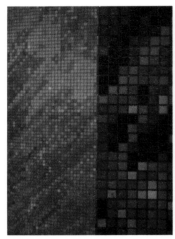

B   *Empress Theodora and Her Attendants* (detail), 547. Mosaic, San Vitale, Ravenna, Italy. Courtesy of Scala/Art Resource, New York.

Have you ever seen stones placed side-by-side in cement? Have you ever seen a wall with small colorful tiles next to each other? This kind of artwork is called **mosaic**. The mosaic in picture A is on a large fountain in Paris, France.

Hundreds of years ago artists created mosaics for churches in Europe. The mosaic in picture B is made from pieces of glass, marble and gold. These sparkling pictures helped people to remember their beliefs and Bible stories.

94

TEACH

Engage

1 Ask students if they have seen a mosaic. Guide them to understand that mosaics are made from pieces laid next to each other to create patterns. Mosaic tiles are used for floors, walls, and other surfaces that need to withstand water or heavy traffic. Some of the oldest mosaics were pictures created for homes or public buildings in Greece and Rome over 2000 years ago.

2 Explain that students will learn about mosaics and then create a paper mosaic.

Meeting Individual Needs

Challenge Have students collect natural materials (stones, nuts, shells) and sort them by size, color, and texture. Use full strength white glue to make small mosaics on thick cardboard or wood.

Explore

1 Focus on **A**. The small mosaic pieces are called *tesserae*. Guide students to notice how colors change and how pieces fit side by side with cement between.

2 Contrast the regular pattern of tiles in **A** with the irregular shapes and varied sizes of tiles in **B**. Help students see how smaller shapes are placed in curves to create lines and suggest the forms of a face. This detail from a much larger mosaic is nearly 1500 years old. It is an example of Byzantine art. (See Art History.)

3 Guide students to see how designs in **C** create delicate lacelike patterns that include graceful curves and geometric shapes. Designs for Islamic mosques, or places of worship, often include curves from Arabic writing along with geometric patterns.

4 Focus on **D**. The shiny look of this mosaic comes from colored areas of magazine paper. Have students help you list starter ideas for mosaics on the chalkboard. Then list design choices (color schemes, placement of shapes and lines, patterns, centers of interest).

Create

1 Distribute materials. Have students fold background paper in quarters and then unfold. Explain that the creases can help them plan a design. Instruct students to:
- lightly sketch a mosaic idea.
- collect several strips with colors and textures.
- cut across the strips to make smaller tilelike pieces.

 Student artwork.

 Mihrab (mosque niche), from the Madrasa Imami, Isfahan, Iran, ca. 1354. Glazed ceramic tiles, 11' 3" (343 cm) high. The Metropolitan Museum of Art, New York (Harris Brisbane Dick Fund).

The mosaic in picture C was created over 600 years ago in Iran. It was made by Islamic artists for their mosque, or place of worship. The designs combine lines from plants and beautiful handwriting.

You can create a collage that looks like a mosaic. Find some old magazines with colorful pages. Neatly tear out some of these pages.

Cut the colored parts of each page into strips about as wide as your thumb. Stack several strips neatly and cut across them to make squares. You can cut other shapes, too.

Sketch several ideas for a mosaic. Your design might show your name, a plant or animal. What other ideas can you try out? What is the best way to glue down your pieces of paper? What design elements should you remember?

95

INTEGRATING THE CURRICULUM

Extensions

▼

Mathematics Have students make simple pictures of animals and objects using tangram shapes. Compare this process to the process of making a mosaic.

Literature Link
- *Cleopatra*, Diane Stanley and Peter Vennema. (A)
- *The Romans and Pompeii*, Philip Steele. (A)
- *Jerusalem*, Saviour Pirotta. (A)

2 Have students:
- brush glue onto paper.
- use the brush to pick up a paper tile and set it into place.
- build a mosaic by placing the shapes side by side, letting some background paper show.
- develop an orderly pattern by working from edges to center or from center to edges.

Remind students that squares can be cut diagonally to make triangles or trimmed to create circles and octagons.

3 As students finish, have them carefully brush glue over the whole mosaic, taking care that no puddles of glue remain.

CLOSE

Assess

1 Ask students to describe the kind of art they have created. Have them identify differences between a mosaic made of paper and one made of clay tile or glass (the thicker materials would be placed in cement that shows between each piece. It would probably be part of a wall, ceiling, or other architectural form).

2 Discuss ideas and design qualities in students' mosaics. Encourage them to use art terms.

Cleanup

1 While collecting supplies, have some students clean brushes in soapy water.

2 Collect glue and reusable scraps of paper.

3 Use damp paper towels to wipe glue from hands and desks.

RESOURCES

Large Reproductions
Serenade, Bearden, 22
Summer, Arcimboldo, 13

Overhead Transparencies
Glass Fish, Egypt, 17

 CD-ROM
2, *Elements of Design*, Lesson 4

Slide Set
Bird Mosaic, Roman, 19

Assessment Masters
Using an Artist's Colors, 3

Art History

Byzantine art is named for the Byzantine Empire, which was the capital of the Eastern Roman Empire, in the region of Constantinople (present-day Istanbul, Turkey) in 330 AD. The stiff, rigid figures in this work combine artistic influences from the Middle East (see **C**) with a legacy of naturalism from ancient Greek and Roman art.

41 Spaces and Lighting
Resist Painting

PREPARE

Objectives

Students will:
- be aware of relationships between interior and exterior spaces and lighting in architecture.
- create a resist painting that portrays the exterior or interior lighting of buildings at night.

Vocabulary

interior space	*espacio interior*
exterior space	*espacio exterior*
lighting	*iluminación*

Setup

Set up several painting stations. Have students take drawings to and from these stations on folded newspaper slightly larger than drawing paper.

Materials

oil pastels or wax crayons

newsprint or manila paper, 12 x 18" (30 x 46 cm)

diluted dark blue paint, 1 container for 2 or 3 students to share

newspapers for desks, folded to serve as a traylike support for wet paintings

paper towels

A Atrium interior. Courtesy of Allward + Gouinlock, Inc., Ontario, Canada.

B Courtesy of Roger Brooks & Associates.

Architects plan buildings so the light inside is beautiful during the day. They design the shapes and sizes of windows so daylight comes into many rooms. Most people like to see daylight and look out of a window. The building in picture A has a glass roof that allows daylight to come into the space.

Architects also try to plan buildings that are beautiful at night. Do you like to see buildings with lights glowing at night? The light you see often comes from the **interior**, or inside, of the building. In picture B, the light flows through the glass in the windows or doors. You can see the bright shapes glowing at night.

96

TEACH

Engage

1 Explain that architects must plan interior spaces so people can have light during the day. They often plan buildings so the inside and outside are also lighted at night.

2 Discuss students' experiences seeing lights inside buildings at night. Help them recall how brilliant the lights are and their relationship to spaces inside the building (lights are seen from outside because rooms or interior spaces have windows).

Meeting Individual Needs

Challenge Have students do color sketches at home of lighting they see inside a room or outside lights they see through a window at night.

Explore

1 Focus on **A**. Guide students to see how glass has been used for roof and walls, providing daylight. Explain that this kind of space, called an *atrium*, also lets people who are inside see out to the sky and garden.

2 Discuss **B**. Guide students to see how lighting from inside makes the window shapes glow. Have them point out exterior lights.

3 In **C**, guide students to see how the shapes of windows, doors, and other glass surfaces show up by lighting the interior space. Have them identify exterior lighting and explain why it shows up.

4 Focus on **D**. Develop a starter list of ideas for drawings of buildings where lights from inside show up at night. Discuss ideas for showing other kinds of exterior lights.

Create

1 Distribute materials. Students should be familiar with the process of resist painting from Lesson 30. Remind them to:
- use light colors and press down firmly.
- draw shapes, lines, and textures to show sources of light at night.
- color over white and yellow with other hues to create bright, sparkling hues.

2 Have students develop their drawings, reminding them to consider the placement of windows and doors and how to show sources of lighting.

Community-Based Learning

Ask an architectural firm to identify interior designers or specialists in lighting who might serve as resource persons for the class.

 C *Rivercenter*, San Antonio, Texas. Photograph from *Successful Sign Design*. Reprinted by permission of Retail Reporting Corporation.

Some buildings have colorful lights on the **exterior**, or outside. Picture C shows a building at night. You can see lights on the exterior of the building. Where do you see light from the interior spaces?

You can think like an architect. Draw a building. Plan the shapes of the windows and doors carefully. You might add some lampposts or signs.

D Student artwork.

After your drawing is done, color the windows and other places where the light would be glowing at night. Use wax crayons or oil pastels. Press hard so the color is thick.

Then make your drawing a night scene. Brush dark blue or black watercolor over the whole paper. The watercolor will roll away from, or resist, the parts you have colored. Your drawing will glow with light.

97

INTEGRATING THE CURRICULUM

Extensions

▼

Science Develop students' understanding of types of light sources, natural and artificial, and how the human eye perceives light and color. Prisms and colored filters for flashlights can be used for simple experiments.

Literature Link

• *Night on Neighborhood Street,* Eloise Greenfield. (S)
• *Night of the Moonjellies,* Mark Shasha. (A)
• *On a Starry Night,* Natalie Kinsey-Warnock. (A)

---

3 Before students add paint, review the following steps:

• Dip brush in paint and stir lightly.
• Hold container steady and wipe brush on edge, leaving extra paint in the container.
• Brush across the top edge of the drawing, edge to edge, using one stroke.
• Continue down page with slightly overlapping strokes, adding paint to brush as needed.

4 If you have several painting stations, schedule their use, explaining the need to take turns.

CLOSE

Assess

1 Discuss some students' artworks. Encourage students to identify light sources they have portrayed and whether the light comes from interior or exterior spaces.

Cleanup

1 Collect paint and brushes. If artworks have puddles of paint, have students blot with the torn edge of a paper towel or newspaper.

2 Have students center their artwork on folded newspaper and place them, unstacked, on a flat surface to dry.

RESOURCES

Large Reproductions
  Brotherhood Building, Haas, 15

Overhead Transparencies
  Mrs. Jenkins, Wilson, 15

 CD-ROM
  4, *Art Adventure,* Lesson 2

Assessment Masters
  A Place to Live, 13

Art History

Acquaint students with the difference between an *interior decorator* (person with a special interest in choosing and arranging elements of an interior space) and an *interior designer*. An interior designer has training in architecture and knows how to plan a space that fits the client's needs for beauty, use, and other purposes. The origin of the profession is usually traced to the Industrial Revolution, especially from the 1850s, when large international trade shows provided surveys of mass-produced furnishings and other items for interiors.

42 A Colorful Window
Transparent Collage

PREPARE

Objectives

Students will:
- understand that stained glass is a form of art related to architecture.
- explore transparent qualities of colors.

Vocabulary

stained glass	*vitral*
transparent	*transparente*
glowing colors	*colores resplandecientes*
light	*luz*

Setup

Several students can share a set of paints. Put one brush in each color of each set. Before teaching, make an example. For smaller panels, cut folders to make single sheets of plastic.

Materials

pencils

nontoxic red, yellow, and blue acrylic paint, or tempera paint with 1 or 2 drops of liquid detergent added

paintbrushes (See Setup)

clear plastic folders, notebook size, 1 per student

scissors

cellophane tape

black paper to fit size of plastic, 1 per student

A *Episodes From the Life of St. Catherine of Alexandria*, 1290. Stained and painted glass, oak, 29 x 81" (74 x 216 cm). The Nelson-Atkins Museum of Art, Kansas City, Missouri.

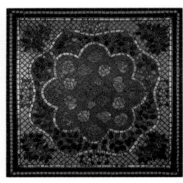

B Angelika Traylor, *Magic Carpet No. IX*. Stained glass, 33 x 33" (84 x 84 cm). © Angelika Traylor.

Artists work with color and light in many ways. Long ago in Europe, artists made **stained glass** windows for large churches. When people are inside the church, they see the glowing colors.

Picture A shows one of these windows. It is made from pieces of colored glass. The glass is held together with strips of metal. Colored glass is transparent. **Transparent** means the light shines through it. 98

You may have seen stained glass in homes, restaurants or libraries. Picture B is an example of present-day stained glass. Today, some artists use transparent plastic instead of glass. Have you seen artwork made from transparent materials? Where?

You can experiment with transparent colors. One way is shown on the next page. Can you think of other experiments?

TEACH

Engage

1 Ask students if they have ever seen a stained glass window. Discuss where they have seen such windows (religious settings, restaurants). Explore reasons why windows with colored glass might appeal to people.

2 Explain that students will learn more about stained glass and its special colors.

Meeting Individual Needs

Simplify Have students use colored cellophane or tissue paper and glue it on one side of the open folder. Place black paper over colored paper and close the folder.

Explore

1 Explain that **A** was saved from an old church in France. The window is made up of many small pieces of glass held together with strips of metal. Over time, the metal turned black. The thick straight lines are heavier metal supports. When light shines through the glass, the colors glow like jewels. Designs inside the circles portray St. Catherine, patroness of learning, wisdom, and beauty (a third-century Christian counterpart of the ancient Greek goddess, Athena).

2 **B** is one of many window designs that the artist creates for buildings. Guide students to see large and small flowers, carefully planned borders, clusters of flowers in each corner, and glowing colors. Have them point out some shapes surrounded by black lines. The lines are really metal strips with grooves that help clamp the pieces of glass together.

3 Focus on student artworks in **C**. Hold up your example to show how colors glow when held near a window.

4 Discuss the steps that describe how students will explore colors that glow.

Aesthetic Awareness

Have students take turns displaying their work on an overhead projector. Experiment with the projected images by changing size and focus.

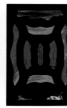

1. Cut a piece of dark paper and a clear plastic folder the same size.

2. Fold the paper twice. Cut shapes from the folded edges. Open the paper. Put paste on one side of the paper. Put the paper inside the folder.

3. Put the folder on newspaper so the pasted side of the paper is facing you. Brush paint on the plastic. Repeat some colors to unify the design. When the paint dries, the design shows from the front.

Display your work in a window. How is it like stained glass? How is it different?

99

INTEGRATING THE CURRICULUM

Extensions ▼

Language Arts Invite a local craftsperson who works in stained glass to bring in a small completed work and discuss the process. Have students prepare by compiling questions. Afterwards, have students write about the difference between authentic stained glass and the artwork they created.

Literature Link

• *Light Color, & Lenses,* Pam Robson. (I, A)
• *Disney's The Hunchback of Notre Dame,* Walt Disney. (S, A)
• *Disney's The Hunchback of Notre Dame Stained Glass Kit.* (A, I)

CLOSE

Create

1 Distribute supplies, except paint. Guide students to:
   • fold black paper twice and cut shapes into folded edges (without cutting away the folds).
   • unfold paper, check design, and refold to make additional cuts.
   • paste paper to plastic.
   • write names on paper.

2 Distribute paint. Make sure students place the design so plastic and pasted side of paper face them. (The finished design will be seen on the opposite side from where they apply paint.) Explain procedures for sharing brush and paint. Remind students to brush out the paint so light will show through plastic and paint. Colors can be repeated to create symmetrical or radial designs.

Assess

1 Have a small group of students temporarily tape their panels to windows. Help students to observe the effect of several panels side by side. Remove panels and have other students hold their panels near windows.

2 Have students describe differences between their color panels and real stained glass. Discuss similarities (primarily color) and reinforce the meaning of transparent. *Transparent* means you can see details through the surface (for example, as when wearing eyeglasses or sunglasses).

Reminder

For the next lesson, ask students to bring in small clean boxes and/or tubes from paper rolls. Ask them to rinse and save small cardboard milk cartons.

RESOURCES

Large Reproductions
   Interior, Matisse, 17

Overhead Transparencies
   Early Sunday Morning, Hopper, 24

 CD-ROM
   4, *Art Adventure,* Lesson 2

Slide Set
   Bourges Cathedral, 20

Assessment Masters
   Find Out About Art, 20

Cooperative Learning

Have students work together to create a window display of their panels. Explore ways to group the work, using some design principles to plan the display. For example, panels with similar colors or shapes might be placed in rows or used in a pattern to contrast with other panels.

99

43 A Model of a Castle
Paper Construction

A *Chateau Chambord,* Loire-et-Char, France, 1519.

The large house in picture A is a castle in France. Castles were built long ago in many lands. People lived in the castles so they could be safe. Sometimes castles were near villages. Many castles had towers. The towers let people see the land around the castle.

Castles and other buildings have **forms**. Forms are thick. You can see them from the top, bottom and many sides. Forms like cones and cylinders make the towers of castles. What forms can you see in pictures A, B and D?

cone   pyramid   sphere

cylinder   slab   cube

B *Castle of Muiden,* The Netherlands, 13th century. Courtesy of Benelux Press.

C

100

PREPARE

Objectives

Students will:
- identify geometric forms in architectural monuments (castles) and in their environment.
- create and assemble forms to make a model of a castle.

Vocabulary

forms	*formas*
tower	*torre*
cone	*cono*
cylinder	*cilindro*
pyramid	*pirámide*
slab	*loza/bloque/tabla*
sphere	*esfera*

Setup

Stick tape lengthwise along edges of desks. Students can cut or tear off the amount needed.

Materials

drawing media

white glue

removable tape, about 18" (46 cm) per student (See Setup)

scissors

forms (tubes, boxes, bottle tops, cups, etc.), 2 or 3 per student

colored construction paper, 12 x 18" (30 x 46 cm), 2 per student

cardboard or extra construction paper for model base, 1 per student

damp paper towels

TEACH

Engage

1 Provide background information about the function of castles as villages or communities surrounded by walls to protect people. Provide a historical context for the building of castles in Europe, Asia, and Africa during times of danger.

2 Explain that some old castles are museums now. Some castles gave architects ideas for new homes, courthouses, and fantasy castles for amusement parks.

Art History

Read and show illustrations from *Castle* by David Macaulay (Houghton Mifflin Company, 1972). This book has excellent drawings of castle architecture and illustrates how castles were actually constructed.

Explore

1 Help students to imagine themselves standing in front of the castles in **A** or **B**. Have them imagine interior spaces with tall, wide halls and many rooms to explore.

2 Guide students to see relationships between the geometric forms in **C** and structures in **A**, **B**, and **D**. Explain that basic forms are combined in buildings. For example, many houses have a cubelike or slablike base with a pyramid roof.

3 Point out that some forms in **D** were used to plan castles in Disney's amusement parks.

4 Guide students to see how details such as windows, doors, and patterns can be created by drawing or by using cut paper as shown in **F**, **G**, and **H**.

5 Focus on **E**. Have students explain how the basic forms were made.

Create

1 Distribute materials. Make sure students understand that textures, patterns, and other details should be drawn while paper is flat. Students can temporarily curl or fold paper to visualize where to draw elements such as windows or doors. After details are drawn, the three-dimensional form can be assembled with glue.

2 Encourage students to use materials inventively. Provide guidance in joining materials, reminding students that white glue takes time to dry. Removable tape can help hold parts together until glue dries

Cooperative Learning

Develop a plan with students for displaying the models. For example, some might remain in the room. Others might be placed in the library or main office.

You can make a model of a castle or a tower. Find some tubes or small boxes. Make other forms from paper. Use tape and glue to join your forms. Do you see how?

 Neuschwanstein, Germany, 1869–1881. Architects: Eduard Riedell and Georg Von Dollman. Photograph: Mike Horwell/ International Stock Photography.

You can glue and tape forms together.

You can make forms from paper.

Can you make a cone?

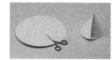

F **G** **H**

INTEGRATING THE CURRICULUM

Extensions ▼

Social Studies Have students research the role of castles in feudal life. Have them use this knowledge to create their models. Other details can be added to complete the models. Clay can be used to support twigs (for trees) or cut-paper figures; animals can be made from clay.

Literature Link
• *The Truth about Castles,* Gillian Clements. (I, A)
• *A Medieval Feast,* Aliki. (I, A)
• *A Tournament of Knights,* Joe Lasker. (A)

RESOURCES

Large Reproductions
  Brotherhood Building, Haas, 15

Overhead Transparencies
  Cabinet, Boulle, 6

CD-ROM
  4, *Art Adventure,* Lesson 2

Slide Set
  Bodiam Castle, 21

Assessment Masters
  Create a Community, 6

---

3 While students work, promote skills in critical thinking and problem solving. Ask such questions as:
  • Are there other ways to combine the forms?
  • Have you thought about details and how to show them?
  • What else might you include?

4 If you wish to extend to another class period, have students proceed with cleanup. Make sure names are on artwork.

CLOSE

Assess

1 Have students look at each other's models. Encourage them to make positive comments about the work, noting specific forms (cones, cylinders, etc.) and strengths (combination of forms, excellent detail, etc.).

2 Have students offer their own descriptions of what they learned. Ask questions to help them recall art vocabulary terms and the context in which real castles were built.

Independent Research

Have students identify and draw examples of castlelike forms that may be evident in nearby architecture. Examples can be found in fast-food restaurants, Victorian homes, large public buildings, and the like. Have students display their sketches and offer theories (tentative explanations) for the use of castlelike forms in buildings that are not castles.

PREPARE

Objectives

Students will:
- be aware of cultural and historical influences on styles of architecture.
- draw a picture of a real or imaginary building using design ideas from art history.

Vocabulary

style	*estilo*
Parthenon	*Partenón*
Pantheon	*Panteón*

Setup

Bring in library books and audiovisual resources to acquaint students with varied styles of architecture. List on the chalkboard some features of architecture: columns, sculpture, wide steps, domes, bell towers, balconies.

Materials

choice of drawing media

white drawing paper, 12 x 18" (30 x 46 cm)

resource materials: architecture of different periods and cultures (See Setup)

photographs of historically important local buildings

world map or globe

A   **Parthenon,** model. The Metropolitan Museum of Art, New York.

The people who settled in North America brought ideas from many lands. Some of their ideas about art came from ancient Greece and Rome.

Many buildings in Europe and North America have forms like buildings in ancient Greece and Rome. Picture A is a model of the Parthenon, a building constructed about 2,400 years ago in Athens, Greece.

B   **Frank Furness, *East pediment of the exterior of the Philadelphia Museum of Art,*** 1839–1912. Philadelphia Museum of Art, Pennsylvania. Photograph: Eric Mitchell, 1980.

The building in picture B is in the United States. It is part of the Philadelphia Museum of Art. How is it like the Parthenon? How is it different? There are similar buildings in many large cities in North America. Can you explain why?

Do some research on styles of **architecture** in your community. Draw a picture of a building with design ideas that go back to another country and time.

102

TEACH

Engage

1 Explain that students will be learning about important architecture from the past. They will see how architectural ideas from other lands and times have been used in North American buildings. Discuss features of buildings in the resource materials.

Meeting Individual Needs

Challenge Have students identify one of the oldest or most unusual buildings in their neighborhood. Have them observe and draw it, giving special attention to details. Discuss drawings in relation to concepts in this lesson.

Explore

1 Explain that colonists from Europe who settled along the east coast of North America used many design ideas from their homelands. **B**, an art museum in Philadelphia, looks much like the ancient Greek building in **A**. Have students compare and contrast **A** and **B**, noting columns, sculptured area in the triangle, and proportions. Discuss buildings in your community with related design ideas. Explain why North American architects borrowed ideas from **A** (it was thought to be beautiful and symbolic of a great culture).

2 Compare **C** and **D**. Guide students to see domes, columns, and porchlike areas. The columns and sculptured triangle in **C** are ideas that Romans borrowed from Greeks (see **A**). The Romans invented a way to make domes that many architects borrowed, as in **D**.

3 Focus on **E**. Provide information on the role of Spanish colonists in setting up churches and schools in much of Central America, southwestern United States, and California. Explain that the design of this Spanish-style mansion in California uses ideas from homes, castles, and churches in Spain. The architect, Julia Morgan, included two tall towers with bells. Parts of the towers are decorated with mosaics. There are several balconies so people can look out and down at the garden and entry steps. The main entrance, towers, and balconies have lacelike carvings.

4 Ask students to imagine they are architects. Explain that they will draw a building with these or other design ideas.

Independent Research

Many communities have buildings that feature the neoclassical style of architecture (**B** and **D**). Have students sketch and discuss examples.

Picture C is a model of the Pantheon, a building constructed over 1,800 years ago in Rome, Italy.

C *Pantheon,* model. The Metropolitan Museum of Art, New York.

D **Thomas Jefferson,** *Monticello,* west garden facade, 1768-1809. Charlottesville, Virginia.

E **Julia Morgan,** *La Casa Grande,* 1920–1937. Courtesy of Hearst Monument. Photograph: John Blades.

Thomas Jefferson, a United States president, was also an architect. He designed the building in picture D. How is it like the Pantheon? How is it different?

Julia Morgan was one of the first women in North America to become an architect. She designed the Spanish-style mansion in picture E. The mansion is now used as an art museum. It is in California. Why do you think she used ideas from buildings in Spain?

INTEGRATING THE CURRICULUM

Extensions ▼

Language Arts Introduce students to some of the meanings of *classical* and *classic* as they are used today in fine arts, design, and advertising. Then have them research root and historical meanings of the terms, especially in art.

Literature Link
• *Thomas Jefferson: A Picture Book Biography,* James Cross Giblin. (S, A)
• *Monticello,* Catherine Reef. (I, A)

Create

1 Distribute supplies. Ask students to think of a real or imaginary building they could draw. They might, for example, draw a design for a house or school that includes fancy columns, wide steps, a large dome, or towers with bells. Some students may prefer to draw an old building they have seen and can recall vividly.

2 Before students draw, encourage them to plan their picture:

• Will it be tall or wide? Why?

• What shapes will be drawn first? Why? (The large shapes are drawn first so everything will fit in the picture space.)

• What else can be planned? (Spaces, lines, colors, etc. can all be planned.)

3 Have students begin. While they work, ask questions about the relative sizes and shapes of windows and doors, the location of important edges or rows of windows, the materials from which the building is constructed, and the like.

CLOSE

Assess

1 Discuss students' drawings. Encourage them to identify specific features using terms from the lesson. Guide students to offer explanations for the type of building they drew and why they included specific features.

2 Briefly discuss architecture as a career. Encourage students to create architectural drawings on their own.

Community-Based Learning

Many communities have special groups or architectural specialists engaged in historical preservation. Ask them for an in-school program or for help in arranging a field trip to historically important buildings or districts. Have students prepare questions to ask.

RESOURCES

Large Reproductions
Brotherhood Building, Haas, 15

Overhead Transparencies
San Francisco, 23

 CD-ROM
4, *Art Adventure,* Lesson 2

Slide Set
US Capitol, Thornton et al., 22

Assessment Masters
Changing Chairs, 15

PREPARE

Objectives

Students will:
- understand that designs for parks and playgrounds can be planned for safety, beauty, and entertainment.
- work together to create a mural of a park or playground design.

Vocabulary

mural	*mural*
landscape design	*diseño de ambientes exteriores*
landscape architect	*arquitecto diseñador de ambiente exteriores*

Setup

Paintings can be done in a hall. To mix colors, fill ⅓ of a small milk carton with white paint and a little blue. Shake well. Pour into additional cartons. Mix other colors in the same way. Protect floor with newspapers. Have students take turns painting and work one arm's length apart.

Materials

- white butcher paper or light green mural paper
- scissors
- paste
- removable tape
- drawing media
- colored paper, large scraps
- manila paper, 9 x 12" (23 x 30 cm), 2 per student
- (optional) tempera paint in mixed colors for background (See Setup)
- (optional) sponge brushes, 1 for each paint container

A Sculpture garden of Patsy and Raymond Nasher. Photograph: © Hickey-Robertson Photography, Houston.

Some architects plan parks, gardens and other outdoor spaces. These artists are **landscape architects**.

The lovely garden in picture A was carefully planned. What parts do you think the landscape architect designed?

104

TEACH

Engage

1 Discuss parks and playgrounds that students are familiar with. Ask them why people want to enjoy the natural environment and have special places to play, hold picnics, etc.

2 Explain that some artists, called *landscape architects*, plan spaces in parks and playgrounds. They create designs that include elements of the natural environment (trees, grassy areas, gardens, ponds, etc.) and outdoor spaces that people want or need (hiking trails, play areas, shelters, etc.). Explain that students will learn more about landscape architecture.

Explore

1 Focus on **A** and discuss planned elements in the garden. Guide students to see how the pathway with steppingstones and well-trimmed grass leads through a space with flowers and trees. Note how the sculpture can be seen from the path or from the terraced area beyond. Encourage comments about the design and how it might feel to visit the garden.

2 Focus on **B**. Guide students to see that the park area is bordered by trees and a fence. Ask them why this arrangement helps make the playground safe and attractive.

3 List ideas on the chalkboard for a park or playground design that the class will show in a mural. Guide students to consider areas where people might:
   - enjoy beauty alone or in small groups.
   - play in groups.
   - find shelter from bad weather.

- use facilities such as bathrooms and drinking fountains.
- enjoy fields or woodland, water or gardens.

Encourage students to develop other ideas.

4 Ask the class to decide what kind of place or activities can be planned for the park's center and assign a group to work on this. Determine other places or activities to include, where they will be placed in the mural, and who will be in the groups. Use chalk to mark the sections.

Create

1 If the background will be painted, make sure students understand that they will take turns in small groups. After the groups paint what is needed for the background of the mural, they draw and cut out paper shapes to add to the background.

 B *Castle Climber IV.* Courtesy of Rainbow Playground Mfg. Co.

Some landscape architects design playgrounds. They decide where to put the lawns and places to play. They plan the places for trees, fences and shelters. Can you think of other things to plan for a fun, safe and attractive playground?

Your class can design a park or playground. You can show your design in a mural, or large picture.

Plan the ideas for your park. Will it have trees and gardens? Will it have a pond and trails to walk? Will it have places to play or have picnics?

Paint or color a background on mural paper. Draw and cut out the shapes for your design. Plan where you will paste the shapes for your landscape design.

105

Extensions

Science Ask a landscape architect or a representative of an architecture firm to explain some examples of landscape architectural projects. A large nursery may also have experts. To utilize the visitor's time efficiently, have students prepare questions in advance. Topics for questions might focus on types of plants, seasonal changes, planned areas for water or wildlife, and the like.

Literature Link
- *Linnea in Monet's Garden,* Christina Bjork. (S)
- *Roxaboxen,* Alice McLerran. (S)
- *Miss Rumphius,* Barbara Cooney. (S)

CLOSE

Assess

1 Have students view the mural from a distance. Ask them to share overall impressions of the landscape design in relation to the human activities it was designed for (active/quiet; large/small group, individual; sports, eating, etc.).

2 Discuss the design in relation to types of natural features students have included.

2 Distribute materials. Pace the activity so students meet in small groups first and then work individually. Make sure members of each group focus on the largest shapes needed for their section.

3 As students complete shapes, have them temporarily tape them to the mural. Conclude the first period by discussing ideas for the next steps.

4 Open the second period by asking students to point out the best parts of their park design (use and type of area) and ways that less successful areas can be improved. Continue the discussion with a greater emphasis on the appearance of the mural (do shapes stand out? How could they be improved so they are easier to see?).

5 Distribute materials. Ask students to gather in small groups to plan what to change. Have them continue pasting all the shapes down.

RESOURCES

Large Reproductions
  Double Grandmothers, Frey, 24

Overhead Transparencies
  Courtyard, McNay Art Museum, 22
  Front Entrance, McNay Art Museum, 22

 CD-ROM
  4, *Art Adventure,* Lesson 2

Assessment Masters
  A Bird's Eye View, 11

Cooperative Learning

Have students meet in small groups and decide how to improve an area on the school grounds. They should make two drawings: one showing the area as it presently exists and the other showing the area as it might exist. Have students compile some of the best ideas and present them to other classes for additional opinions. Continue until students present an actual proposal and find support for creating it.

PREPARE

Objectives

Students will:
• be aware of the role of citizens and art experts in planning well-designed facets of a city.
• draw a well-designed part of their city and discuss why people may have different ideas about good design.

Vocabulary

city planner	*urbanista*
well-designed	*bien diseñado(a)*

Setup

Structure the review into a studio lesson based on the text with an evaluation period of about the same length. Prepare a hand-out or write the evaluation list on the chalkboard. (See Art Criticism.)

Materials

folders with artwork

drawing paper, 12 x 18" (30 x 46 cm), 1 per student

crayons or oil pastels

Many artists help plan parts of a community or city. **City planners** are artists who help people make choices about the design of a city. Good choices help make a city a nice place to live.

Look at the pictures on this page and discuss the questions. This will help you think like a city planner.

 Photograph: Robert Burley, Robert Burley Design Archives.

What makes a business district nice to visit?

What are some ways to arrange houses and apartments?

Ⓐ

106

TEACH

Engage

1 Define a *city planner* as an artist, usually an architect, who helps other people design large sections of a city. Some city planners work with projects in many parts of one city. They help people decide how to improve places for living, working, and playing. For example, they may help decide where to put new streets and buildings.

2 Explain that students will learn more about city planners in this lesson.

Explore

1 Focus on **A**. Guide students to see how planning benefits the downtown business area in Worcester, Massachusetts. The city hall and many stores and businesses look out on a grassy area with beautiful trees. There are many benches where people can rest and look at the reflecting pool. These elements help make this city beautiful.

2 Refer to **B** as an apartment building—a kind of building that offers a place for people to live. Discuss other types of housing and ways of arranging them (with courtyards, on streets in rows, in curved streets, or in culs-de-sac).

3 Refer to **C** and discuss advantages and disadvantages of factories or industrial buildings near homes. Have students make inferences about the location of these grain elevators (near the edge of town) and why they are colorful (for beauty).

4 Refer to **D** and **E**. Ask students to reason why a city might be planned with many parks or playgrounds. Help them realize the importance of open spaces. People enjoy nature and are refreshed by green spaces. Discuss the importance of other city services and activities such as health, safety, education, museums, etc.

 C Grain elevator. Superstock, Inc.

Where should big factories be located?

D Photograph courtesy of the San Antonio Parks & Recreation Department, Texas.

Where should parks and playgrounds be located?

E Courtesy of CN Real Estate, Canada.

A good design for a city includes places for people to live and work. It has places for people to play and shop. It has streets and walks so people can travel. These and other parts of a city should be safe, attractive and work together.

Think about parts of your city that are well-designed. Discuss why. Then create an artwork that shows the good design in your city. Display your artworks. Invite other students to agree or disagree with your ideas about good design.

INTEGRATING THE CURRICULUM

Extensions ▼

Social Studies There are many ways to analyze and plan a city. Categories used by professionals in architecture and environmental planning may be used by students. They can look for and map areas such as a neighborhood boundary, a street for shopping, places to play, industrial areas, highways, open land, housing, etc. Have students choose several categories or add their own. Have them identify a neighborhood nearby and analyze it by drawing a simple map and developing visual symbols (map codes) for each category.

Literature Link
• *The Little House*, Virginia Lee Burton. (S)
• *Town and Country*, Alice and Martin Provensen. (S)

CLOSE

Create

1 Ask students to recall a part of their city that is well designed (pleasing or attractive). It should also be safe and meet the needs of people who use the space. They should keep their choice a secret until everyone has finished drawing.

2 Distribute materials. Encourage students to draw a well-designed part of the city. Ask them to apply what they have learned. (Will the picture be tall or wide? Why is it best to draw the large shapes first?)

3 While students draw, circulate and ask questions that stimulate visual recall of details. At the same time, make notes about the subjects students have chosen (central city, neighborhood, special tourist attractions, parks, etc.).

Assess

1 Have students who have chosen similar subjects show their work in groups. Call on them to point out features they chose and why they regard them as well designed.

2 Stress that ideas about good design for cities may vary for many reasons. For example, some places are nice to visit for a short time, but may be difficult to use every day.

3 Open an evaluation of all the work from Unit 3 by distributing folders. Have students place two or three of their best artworks from Unit 3 on top. Ask them to put a 3 (for Unit 3) on the back of each they have chosen. Have them gather in groups of three or four, use the list under Art Criticism, and take turns talking about their art.

4 Save the works each student identified as best. Write comments on all work you judge to be important for evaluation.

RESOURCES

Large Reproductions
 Double Grandmothers, Frey, 24
 Brotherhood Building, Haas, 15
 African Canvas, Courtney-Clarke, 19

Overhead Transparencies
 San Francisco, 23

Assessment Masters
 Create a Community, 6
 A Place to Live, 13

Art Criticism

Students should be able to discuss or write about art using these concepts:

1 What kind of artwork or design is this? (This unit includes terms such as *architecture* and *graphic design*.)

2 Describe the elements of design: lines, colors, shapes or forms, textures, spaces.

3 How was the artwork planned? Why was this plan used?

4 Are there special ways the art materials are used? Why?

5 What ideas or feelings come from seeing the artwork?

6 What did you learn from studying or creating this artwork?

Unit 4 Planner

Core: *Adventures in Art* provides a balanced sequence of lessons that meet national standards for content and instructional time. If you are unable to teach every lesson, introduce the lessons identified as "core."

Lesson Overview	Objectives	Correlations	Resources	Technology
U4 Core Page 108 **Kinds of Art, Past and Present** *Activity:* **Drawing** *Materials:* **Drawing media** *Concept:* **Cultural art traditons** *Related Lessons:* African art: 27, 49, 51, 55. Body adornment: 47, 50, 51. Crafts: 40, 46, 48, U3. Parks and gardens: 13, 45, R3.	• Appreciate that people of many cultures create art as part of a tradition • Create a drawing about a family or community tradition, including special colors	*National Standards:* 1a, b, c, 2a, c, 3a, b, 4a, b, c, 5a, b, c, 6a	*Large Reproductions:* **19** Courtney-Clarke, **3** Sioux, **24** Frey *Overhead Transparencies:* **10** Peña *Assessment Masters:* **15** Changing Chairs, **22** I Like Art	CD-ROM 3 *Artists at Work,* Lessons 1 and 2
46 Page 110 **Art in Containers** *Activity:* **Box decoration** *Materials:* **Cardboard boxes, colored paper** *Concept:* **Cultural containers** *Related Lessons:* Balance: 6, 39, 47, 48. Crafts: 40, 48, U3, U4. North American Indian art: 33, 47, 49, 58. Symbols (visual): 9, 33, 47, 49.	• Understand that containers can be useful, decorative, and have symbolic meaning • Carefully plan, craft, and decorate a box with personal symbols	*National Standards:* 1a, b, c, d, 2a, c, 3b, 4a, b, c, 5a, b, 6a	*Large Reproductions:* **12** *Mask,* **3** Sioux *Overhead Transparencies:* **5** Tygart *Assessment Masters:* **14** Design a Pot	CD-ROM 3, *Artists at Work,* Lessons 1 and 2
47 Page 112 **Art in Clothing** *Activity:* **Clothing design** *Materials:* **Colored and white paper, crayons or oil pastels** *Concept:* **Clothing design** *Related Lessons:* Balance: 6, 39, 46, 48. Adornment: 50, 51, U4. North American Indian art: 9, 33, 46, 49. Symbols (visual): 28, 33, 46, 49.	• Understand symmetrical balance in the human body and clothing design • Create an original design for clothing	*National Standards:* 1a, c, d, 2a, c, 3a, b, 4a, b, c, 5a, b, c, 6a, b	*Large Reproductions:* **3** Sioux, **19** Courtney-Clarke *Overhead Transparencies:* **10** Peña *Slide Set:* **23** Guatemalan *Assessment Masters:* **18** Designs for Lamps	CD-ROM 3, *Artists at Work,* Lesson 3
48 Core Page 114 **Art for Comfort** *Activity:* **Stenciled fan** *Materials:* **Index cards or stencil paper, scissors, tempera** *Concept:* **Craftsmanship** *Related Lessons:* Asian art: 21, 33, 35, 46. Balance: 6, 39, 46, 47. Crafts: 40, 46, U3, U4. Color schemes: 12.	• Be aware of cultural traditions that lead artists to create beautiful crafts • Create a well-crafted stenciled fan using a related color scheme	*National Standards:* 1a, b, c, d, 2a, b, c, 4a, b, 5a, 6a	*Large Reproductions:* **8** Audubon, **6** Brown *Overhead Transparencies:* **4** Brundege, **4** Zaire *Assessment Masters:* **18** Designs for Lamps	CD-ROM 3, *Artists at Work,* Lesson 1
49 Page 116 **Art for Special Times** *Activity:* **Maskmaking** *Materials:* **Paper bags, colored construction paper, crayons** *Concept:* **Cultural masks** *Related Lessons:* African art: 27, 51, 55, U4. North American Indian art: 9, 46, 47, 58. Symbols (visual): 9, 33, 46, 47.	• Understand that people in various cultures create symbolic animal masks • Create a mask of an animal character from a paper bag	*National Standards:* 1a, b, c, d, 2a, b, c, 3a, b, 4a, c, 5a, c, 6a, b	*Large Reproductions:* **7** *Liberian Mask,* **12** *Mask,* **1** Markovitz *Overhead Transparencies:* **14** *Headdress,* **14** Tlingit *Slide Set:* **24** Mexico *Assessment Masters:* **21** A Vote for Art	CD-ROM 5, *People and Animals,* Lesson 4

■ boxed sidebar information
on lesson pages.

Literature Link codes:
(A) Artwork links to lesson
(S) Story line links to lesson
(I) Information links to lesson

Special Features	Cultures/History	Integrating the Curriculum	

		Extensions	**Literature Link**

■ Critical Thinking
■ Community Awareness
	Africa:
	  Ashanti
	Australia:
	  Barsa
	Canada
	United States
		Mathematics:
		Radial/symmet-
		rical
			Kenté Colors, Debbi Chocolate. (A)
			Tonight Is Carnival, Arthur Dorros.
			  (A)
			*Lion Dancer: Ernie Wan's Chinese New
			  Year,* Kate Waters and Madeline
			  Slovenz-Low. (I)

■ Meeting Individual
  Needs
■ Cooperative Learning
	Canada:
	  North American Indian,
	  Ottawa
	Korea
	United States:
	  North American Indian,
	  Zuni
	
	■ *Art History:* Symbols
		Science: Natural
		materials
			How Raven Brought Light to People,
			  retold by Ann Dixon. (S)
			The Piñata Maker/El Piñatero, George
			  Ancona. (I)
			Hannah's Fancy Notions, Pat Ross. (S)
			*Go In and Out the Window: An
			  Illustrated Songbook for Young
			  People,* Dan Fox. (A)

■ Cooperative Learning	United States:
	  North American Indian,
	  Sioux
	
	■ *Cultural Awareness:* Clothing
		Language Arts:
		Writing
		Social Studies:
		Ceremonial
		clothing
			Powwow, George Ancona. (A)
			Her Seven Brothers, Paul Goble. (S, A)
			Powwow: Festivals and Holidays, June
			  Behrens. (A)

■ Meeting Individual
  Needs
■ Creative Thinking
	Japan:
	  Serizama
		Language Arts:
		Poems
			*The Badger and the Magic Fan:
			  A Japanese Folktale,* adapted by
			  Tony Johnston. (S)
			The Boy of the Three-Year Nap, Dianne
			  Snyder. (A, S)
			The Tale of the Mandarin Ducks,
			  Katherine Paterson. (A, S)

■ Meeting Individual
  Needs
■ Cooperative Learning
	Canada:
	  Davidson, North American
	  Indian, Haida
	Africa:
	  Mali-Dogon
		Language Arts:
		Reading
		Social Studies:
		Jobs
		Social Studies:
		Mask traditions
			Masks, Meryl Doney. (I, A)
			*Raven's Light: A Myth from the People
			  of the Northwest Coast* retold by
			  Susan Hand Shetterly. (S, A)

Lesson Overview	Objectives	Correlations	Resources	Technology

50 ⌄ ⌄
Core
Page 118

Weaving and Unweaving
Activity: **Fabric design**
Materials: **Crayons, burlap, yarn**
Concept: **Weaving fiber arts**
Related Lessons: Body adornment: 47, 51, U4. Crafts (fiber art): U1, 50, 52. Pattern: 10, 15, 54, 55 .

• Understand the terms fiber, fiber artist, weaving, and pulled threadwork
• Create a fabric design in burlap using the pulled threadwork technique

National Standards: 1a, c, d, 2a, c, 4a, b, c, 5a, 6a

Large Reproductions: **19** Courtney-Clarke, **3** Sioux
Overhead Transparencies: **1** Kasebier
Slide Set: **25** Hammerstrom
Assessment Masters: **22** I Like Art

CD-ROM 2, *Elements of Design,* Lesson 4

---

51 ⌄ ⌄
Page 120

Batik Designs on Cloth
Activity: **Fabric resist**
Materials: **Cotton cloth, resist medium, index card or stencil paper**
Concept: **Batik fiber arts**
Related Lessons: African art: 27, 33, 49, 55. Body adornment: 47, 50, U4. Crafts (fiber art): U1, 50, 52.

• Be aware of batik and related resist processes for creating fabric designs
• Create a batik-like design on cloth using a stencil

National Standards: 1a, b, c, d, 2a, b, c, 3a, b, 4b, 5a, b, 6a

Large Reproductions: **6** Brown, **17** Matisse
Overhead Transparencies: **8** Lee, **10** Peña
Slide Set: **26** Indonesian
Assessment Masters: **22** I Like Art

CD-ROM 3 *Artists at Work,* Lesson 1

---

52 ⌄ ⌄
Page 122

Fiber Arts
Activity: **Appliqué/stitching**
Materials: **Craft needs, fabric scraps, yarn, burlap**
Concept: **Stitching and appliqué**
Related Lessons: Crafts (fiber art): U1, 50, 51. Mural: 21. Unity and variety: 12, 13.

• Understand that fabric, yarn, and thread can be used to create artwork
• Create an appliqué and add stitching

National Standards: 1a, c, 2a, c, 3a, b, 4a, b, 5a, 6a

Large Reproductions: **3** Sioux
Overhead Transparencies: **21** Rivera
Slide Set: **27** Fon people
Assessment Masters: **22** I Like Art

CD-ROM 2, *Elements of Design,* Lessons 3 and 4

---

53 ⌄
Core
Page 122

An Imaginary Animal
Activity: **Clay sculpture**
Materials: **Oil or water-based clay, cardboard, tools**
Concept: **Imaginary sculpture**
Related Lessons: Animals (imaginary): 54. Asian art: 21, 33, 35, 46. Latin American art: 26, 29. Sculpture: 54, 56, 58, 59.

• Understand that people in many cultures have created unusual or imaginary animal sculptures
• Create a clay sculpture of an imaginary animal

National Standards: 1a, b, c, d, 2a, b, c, 3a, b, 4a, c, 5a, c, 6a

Large Reproductions: **5** Picasso
Overhead Transparencies: **20** Nadelman, **20** Marisol
Slide Set: **28** Persian
Assessment Masters: **9** Imagine That, **12** Mix and Match

CD-ROM 5, *People and Animals,* Lesson 4

---

54 ⌄
Core
Page 126

Found Object Sculpture
Activity: **Assemblage**
Materials: **Containers, colored paper**
Concept: **Creative assemblage**
Related Lessons: Animals (imaginary): U1, 53. Calder: 2. Form: 43, 55, 56, 58. Sculpture; 53, 56, 59, 60.

• Understand that sculpture can be made by assembling and joining materials
• Create an imaginative sculpture by assembling and joining materials

National Standards: 1a, b, c, d, 2a, b, c, 3b, 4b, c, 5b, c, 6b

Large Reproductions: **5** Picasso, **1** Markovitz
Overhead Transparencies: **20** Marisol
Assessment Masters: **18** Designs for Lamps

CD-ROM 5, *People and Animals,* Lesson 4

---

55 ⌄
Page 128

Creating a Form
Activity: **Soft sculpture**
Materials: **Kraft paper, markers or crayons**
Concept: **Form and pattern**
Related Lessons: African art: 33, 49, 51, U4. Animals: 1, 8, 20, 21. Form: 43, 54, 56, 58. Pattern: 8, 10, 15, 50.

• Be aware of forms and patterns that can give unity and variety to sculpture
• Create a soft sculpture of a bird or fish with unity and variety in the design

National Standards: 1a, b, c, d, 2a, c, 3a, b, 4a, 5a, 6a, b

Large Reproductions: **12** *Mask,* **1** Markovitz
Overhead Transparencies: **17** Egypt, **11** China, **11** Graves
Slide Set: **29** Chinese
Assessment Masters: **19** Comparing Two Artworks

CD-ROM 5, *People and Animals,* Lesson 4

Special Features	Cultures/History	Integrating the Curriculum	
		Extensions	**Literature Link**
■ Meeting Individual Needs		*Science:* Natural materials	*Annie and the Old One,* Miska Miles. (S) *Unraveling Fibers,* Patricia A. Keeler and Francis X. McCall, Jr. (I, A)
	Africa: Nigeria United States: Hill ■ *Cultural Awareness:* Textile techniques	*Language Arts:* Titling artwork	*Dia's Story Cloth: The Hmong People's Journey of Freedom,* Dia Cha. (A) *Som See and the Magic Elephant,* Jamie Oliviero. (A) *Kenté Colors,* Debbi Chocolate. (A)
■ Meeting Individual Needs ■ Creative Thinking	United States: Benglis Roberts-Antieau ■ *Cultural Awareness:* Banners	*Language Arts:* Writing	*Dia's Story Cloth: The Hmong People's Journey of Freedom,* Dia Cha. (A) *Tonight Is Carnival,* Arthur Dorros. (A) *Life Around the Lake,* Maricel E. Presilla and Gloria Soto. (A, I)
■ Cooperative Learning	Chinese Cyprus Mexico, Aztec ■ *Cultural Awareness:* Aztec symbols	*Language Arts:* Stories *Movement:* Cooperative decision-making	*Animals That Ought To Be: Poems About Imaginary Pets,* Richard Michelson. (S) *Animals in Art,* Louisa Somerville. (A) *Totem Pole,* Diane Hoyt-Goldsmith. (A)
■ Meeting Individual Needs	United States: Calder Hudson	*Language Arts:* Writing	*Stay Away from the Junkyard,* Tricia Tusa. (S) *The Sweet and Sour Animal Book,* Langston Hughes. (A)
■ Meeting Individual Needs ■ Aesthetic Awareness	Egypt (Africa) United States: Finn	*Science:* Theories	*Toys,* Meryl Doney. (A, I)

|---|---|---|---|---|
56 Core Page 130 **People in Action** *Activity:* **Clay modeling** *Materials:* **Ceramic clay** *Concept:* **Figurative sculpture** *Related Lessons:* Form: 43, 54, 55, 58. People: 23, 26, 58, 60. Proportion: 23, 26, 58. Sculpture: 53, 58, 59, 60.	• Know basic procedures for using ceramic clay • Use a planned procedure to create a clay sculpture of the human figure	*National Standards:* 1a, c, d, 2a, c, 5a, c, 6a, b	*Large Reproductions:* **24** Frey *Overhead Transparencies:* **7** Nigeria *Assessment Masters:* **14** Design a Pot	CD-ROM 3, *Artists at Work,* Lesson 3
57 Page 132 **A Relief Sculpture** *Activity:* **Clay carving** *Materials:* **Clay, rolling pins** *Concept:* **Relief sculpture** *Related Lessons:* People: 26, 56, 58, 60. Portraits and self-portraits: 26, 27. Relief Surfaces: 22. Sculpture: 53, 56, 58, 59.	• Be aware of carving and modeling procedures to create relief sculptures • Carve and model clay to make a relief sculpture with a profile view of a face	*National Standards:* 1a, b, c, d, 2a, c, 3b, 4a, c, 5a, b, c	*Large Reproductions:* **18** Marisol *Overhead Transparencies:* **14** Tlingit *Slide Set:* **29** Chinese *Assessment Masters:* **14** Design a Pot	CD-ROM 3, *Artists at Work,* Lesson 3
58 Page 134 **A Standing Figure** *Activity:* **Carved clay sculpture** *Materials:* **Oil-based clay, paper clips** *Concept:* **Carved figure, form** *Related Lessons:* Form: 43, 54, 55, 56. People: 26, 56, 57, 60. Proportion: 23, 26, 56. Sculpture: 53, 56, 59, 60.	• Be aware of carving as a process of subtracting material from a solid form • Create a carved sculpture in clay of a standing figure	*National Standards:* 1a, b, c, d, 2a, b, c, 4a, b, 5a, c, 6a	*Large Reproductions:* **24** Frey *Overhead Transparencies:* **6** Weitz, **19** Moore *Assessment Masters:* **20** Find Out About Art	CD-ROM 3, *Artists at Work,* Lesson 3
59 Core Page 136 **African-American Sculptors** *Activity:* **Working independently** *Materials:* **Drawing media, oil-based clay** *Concept:* **African American art heritage** *Related Lessons:* Portraits and self-portraits: 26, 27, 57. Sculpture: 56, 57, 58, 60.	• Be aware of twentieth-century African American art styles • Independently plan and create an artwork using media and a theme of their choice	*National Standards:* 1a, c, d, 2a, c, 3a, b, 4b, c, 5a, c	*Large Reproductions:* **18** Marisol, **1** Markovitz, **5** Picasso *Overhead Transparencies:* **7** Nigeria, **14** *Headdress* *Assessment Masters:* **17** My Own Museum	CD-ROM 3, *Artists at Work,* Lesson 3
60 Page 138 **Meet the Artist** *Activity:* **Completing artwork** *Materials:* **Drawing media, oil-based clay** *Concept:* **Artists as people** *Related Lessons:* People: 26, 56, 57, 58. Printmaking: 5, 9, 10, 22. Sculpture: 46, 57, 58, 59.	• Understand that some artists express their basic values through their art and life • Express their interests and demonstrate their skills in art	*National Standards:* 1a, c, d, 2a, c, 3b, 4a, b, 5a, b, c	*Large Reproductions:* **24** Frey *Overhead Transparencies:* **12** Lawrence *Slide Set:* **30** Catlett *Assessment Masters:* **17** My Own Museum	CD-ROM 3, *Artists at Work,* Lesson 3
R4 Core Page 140 **Review Unit 4** *Activity:* **Judging and displaying art** *Materials:* **Folders, pencil** *Concept:* **Art exhibitions**	• Understand that artists exhibit their best work for many people to see • Discuss their reasons for selecting a particular artwork for an art show	*National Standards:* 1b, d, 2b, 4a, 5a, b, c	*Large Reproductions:* **12** *Mask,* **18** Marisol, **13** Arcimboldo *Overhead Transparencies:* **11** Graves, **11** Chinese *Assessment Masters:* **17** My Own Museum, **22** I Like Art, **23** Labels for Artworks	CD-ROM 3, *Artists at Work,* Lesson 2

Special Features	Cultures/History	Integrating the Curriculum	
		Extensions	**Literature Link**
■ Meeting Individual Needs	Mexico United States: McVey	*Mathematics:* Proportions *Science:* Evaporation *Movement:* Imaginative Description	*Marie in Fourth Position: The Story of Degas' "The Little Dancer,"* Amy Littlesugar. (A, S) *Henry Moore: From Bones and Stones to Sketches and Sculptures,* Jane Mylum Gardner. (I)

■ Meeting Individual Needs	Iran:
	  Assyrian
	Italy:
	  Astallia
	United States:
	  Pressely, African American
		Social Studies: Prehistoric carvings	*The Story of Money,* Betsy Maestro. (A)

■ Meeting Individual Needs ■ Independent Research	United States: Bullard North American Indian, Hopi	*Language Arts:* Writing	*The Storyteller,* Joan Weisman. (S) *Pueblo Storyteller,* Diane Hoyt-Goldsmith. (A, I) *Pueblo Boy: Growing Up in Two Worlds,* Marcia Keegan. (I)

	United States:
	  Barthé, African American
	  Hunt, African American
	  Saar, African American
	
	Emphasis: African American
		Social Studies: Research	*African American Art For Young People: Volume 1,* Samella Lewis. (A, I)

■ Meeting Individual Needs	Mexico: Catlett, African American	*Social Studies:* Careers *Movement:* Mirror imaging	*Walt Disney: His Life in Pictures,* Russell Schroeder. (I) *Bill Peet: An Autobiography,* Bill Peet. (I) *Self-Portrait: Trina Schart Hyman,* Trina Schart Hyman. (I)

■ Meeting Individual Needs	United States:
	  Miles
	  Wade
		Language Arts: Writing labels	*Visiting the Art Museum,* Laurene Krasny Brown and Marc Brown. (I)
			Aunt Lilly's Laundromat, Melanie Hope Greenberg. (S)
			Jamaica Louise James, Amy Hest. (S)

U4 Kinds of Art, Past and Present
Drawing

PREPARE

Objectives

Students will:
- appreciate that people in many lands create art as part of a tradition.
- create a drawing about a family or community tradition, including special colors, symbols, or artwork.

Vocabulary

tradition	*tradición*
traditional art	*arte tradicional*

Materials

manila paper, 12 x 18" (30 x 46 cm), 1 per student

choice of drawing media

(optional) world map or globe

(optional) additional examples of handcrafted arts from various cultures

---

Around the world, people create art. Some art is part of a tradition. A **tradition** is something people have remembered for a long time.

A *Kente Cloth* (detail). Ashanti tribe, Ghana.
Photograph: Jacqueline Robinson.

B *Nitobe Memorial Garden*, Vancouver, British Columbia.

In some African villages, men weave strips of cloth with beautiful designs. Strips are stitched together to make clothing. This kind of weaving is a tradition.

In Japan, people have a tradition of keeping beautiful gardens. Some of the plants are carefully trimmed to look like sculpture. A gardener from Japan designed the traditional garden in picture B. This garden is in Canada.

108

TEACH

Engage

1 Discuss traditions unique to your city or community. Traditions are preserved and expressed in a variety of art forms: preservation of historic buildings; special fairs; parades and festivals; city emblems or flags; parks, buildings, plazas, memorial sculptures that honor citizens, and so on.

2 Explain that students will be learning more about traditions and traditional art forms in different lands.

Explore

1 Focus on **A**. Have students note the colors and patterns. Clothes made from West African kente cloth are worn as symbols of pride and for special occasions such as birthdays and weddings. The colors and designs have special meanings.

2 In **B**, stress that the photograph shows part of a Japanese garden where people walk slowly or sit on benches to enjoy the beauty of nature.

3 An Australian aboriginal artist who lives near the Great Barrier Reef created the painting in **C**. It shows some of the sea life of the reef and a giant kangaroo, important subjects in the legends of his people, who were the first to inhabit Australia (analogous to Native Americans).

4 In **D**, help students see the radial design of a star and the repeated colors and shapes in the border. Briefly explain how traditional quilts are made. Note that **A** and **D** are examples of fiber art.

5 Explain that students will use symbols and colors to create a drawing to celebrate a family or community tradition.

Create

1 Ask students to think about special traditions in their own family, neighborhood, or city. Focus on the kinds of art that help make the tradition special. For example, people may:
- wear special costumes or clothes for ceremonies and celebrations.
- carry banners or flags.
- prepare special foods or table decorations.
- gather to sing special songs, have a parade, or dance.
- hear traditional stories.

Tell students to think of one of the most important traditions they could show in a drawing.

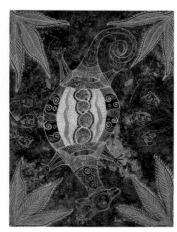

C Tatipai Barsa, *Ringtail Possum*, 1991. Acrylic on paper, 22 x 30" (56 x 76 cm). Courtesy of Derek Simpkins Gallery of Tribal Art.

D Unknown, *Star of Bethlehem Quilt*, ca. 1830. Cotton. New York State Historical Association, Cooperstown.

A native artist from Australia created the painting in picture C. His artwork shows plants and animals from traditional stories. Some native artists create similar paintings on tree bark. They make paints from colored clay.

The quilt in picture D was created over 150 years ago. Quilts are made from scraps of cloth. Quiltmaking is a tradition in some families. Sometimes the designs honor important people or events.

Does your family have special traditions? Do you create or use special artwork to keep the tradition? Why?

In this unit, you will learn about art made from different materials. You will learn about art created to celebrate special times and to express ideas. You will learn how artists work with traditional ideas and new ideas about art.

109

INTEGRATING THE CURRICULUM

Extensions

▼

Mathematics Have students analyze the designs in D along with A, B, and C in Lesson 46. Provide grid paper and encourage them to create radial and symmetrical designs using the lines of the grid as a guide.

Literature Link
• *Kente Colors*, Debbi Chocolate. (A)
• *Tonight Is Carnival*, Arthur Dorros. (A)
• *Lion Dancer: Ernie Wan's Chinese New Year*, Kate Waters and Madeline Slovenz-Low. (I)

RESOURCES

Large Reproductions
  African Canvas, Courtney-Clarke, 19
  Sioux Vest, 3
  Double Grandmothers, Frey, 24

Overhead Transparencies
  Corn Dance, Peña, 10

CD-ROM
  3, *Artists at Work*, Lessons 1 and 2

Assessment Masters
  Changing Chairs, 15
  I Like Art, 22

2 Distribute materials. If students need an idea, suggest they think of a national tradition or holiday and special kinds of art that go with it. They might also draw a picture of a tradition they would like to start.

3 While students work, circulate and ask questions to stimulate attention to the visual qualities of the tradition such as dominant colors or symbols, arrangements of people or objects, and details of any surrounding interior or exterior spaces.

Community Awareness

Invite members of different cultural groups to present traditional arts to the class and explain their meaning. Have students research and prepare questions before the visits.

CLOSE

Assess

1 Ask volunteers to show their artwork, describe the tradition, and tell the special meaning of the colors, symbols, or art forms they have shown.

2 Explain that students will be learning more about traditional and new kinds of art in this unit.

Reminder
Explain that students will make treasure boxes in the next lesson. Ask everyone to bring in a clean empty cardboard box to decorate (no larger than a shoebox). Cardboard cylinders with straight sides can be used. Encourage students to bring in extra boxes for students who are absent today. (Save any containers from your own household that students might use.)

Critical Thinking

Have small groups compare and contrast the following artworks:
A in this lesson and B in Lesson 51;
B in this lesson and A in Lesson 45;
C in this lesson and A in Lesson 15;
D in this lesson and B in Lesson 52.
Have the students make notes on the design qualities, themes, and purposes of the artworks.

109

PREPARE

Objectives

Students will:

- understand that containers can be useful, decorative, and have symbolic meaning.
- decorate a box so it has personal symbols, is carefully planned, and well-crafted.

Vocabulary

culture	*cultura*
papier-mâché	*papel maché*
symbol	*símbolo*
materials	*materiales*
design	*diseño*

Setup

Dilute three parts white glue with one part water. Brushes must be washed in soapy water before glue dries.

Safety Notes

Make sure all containers are sanitary and free of sharp edges.

Materials

clean cardboard boxes, 1 per student

scraps of colored paper, various textures and weights

scraps of colored tissue paper

diluted white glue, 1 container per 2 or 3 students (See Setup)

brushes for glue, 1 per student

scissors

newspapers for desks

container of soapy water

waxed paper

lightweight colored paper, 9 x 12" (23 x 30 cm), 1 per student (have extras)

damp paper towels

(A) Rose Kimewon (Williams), *Tufted, quilled, lidded box,* 1979-81. Birchbark, quills, sweetgrass, dye, thread, 3 1/8 x 6 1/4" (8 x 16 cm). Photograph: Bobby Hansson.

(B) Calvin Begay and Wilbert Muskett, Jr., *Jewel Case, Canyon Collection.* Courtesy of B.G. Mudd Limited and Dick Ruddy Commercial Photography, Albuquerque, New Mexico.

Artists in many lands create fancy boxes and other containers. These artworks often express ideas about the artist's **culture**.

A North American Indian of the Ottawa tribe created the box in picture A. She used natural materials from the woodlands near her home in Canada.

The lid of her box has shapes from a star and a flower. The lid has a radial design that moves out from the center. The star and flower shapes express her respect for nature. What other parts of the design help to express this idea?

110

The Zuni Indians have a tradition of making art from silver and colorful stones. These materials are mined in New Mexico, where many Zuni people live.

Zuni artists created the box in picture B. The symbol in the center of the lid represents "Father Sun." The pattern around the top three edges symbolizes feathers. The feathers lift prayers to Father Sun. Can you guess why the artist's design has cool colors?

TEACH

Engage

1 Ask students if they have any special containers at home such as baskets, vases, bowls, boxes, or cups.

2 Explain that people of every time and culture have created special boxes, vases, bowls, and other containers.

Meeting Individual Needs

Simplify Have students decorate a paper cup with a lid, a clean plastic box, or a tray (from carryout or microwave food).

Explore

1 Define *culture* as a people's way of life—how they think, act, and live as a group. The containers in **A** and **B** were made by Native American artists using traditional materials and ideas.

2 In **A**, guide students to see the radial design and repeated pattern. The materials and visual symbols reflect the culture of the artist's tribe and neighboring Great Lakes tribes (Ottawa, Ojibwa, Micmac).

3 In **B**, artists created a mosaic-like design on the top and sides of a handmade metal box. The symbols represent mountains (triangles), rivers (pattern on top three edges), and the sun (center of lid).

4 The colors, pattern, and shapes in **C** have symbolic meanings in Korea and China. Point out that the center circles are made up of three comma-like shapes that seem to be interlocked and swirling (a symbol for movement and change).

5 Explain that students will use colored paper and white glue, as in Lesson 40, to decorate their own box. They will choose two or three colors and create shapes to make it personal and special.

Create

1 Distribute materials. Have students study their boxes to determine what they might hold and what colors or symbols to use.

Cooperative Learning

Have students develop a chart of the types of containers they use in a single day, with categories that describe materials, contents, and symbols used. Have students make inferences from the information such as whether most containers are reusable or disposable and why.

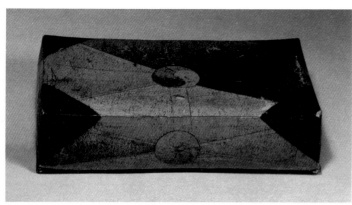

The box in picture C was made in Korea. It is used to hold things for writing letters. These boxes are made by gluing layers of paper together. This process, or technique, is called **papier-mâché**.

The boxes are finished with colored paper. Sometimes the box has a painted or stenciled design.

The triangles in this box move toward a circle, creating a **radial** design. This circle design is a symbol for unity in all living things. Red and yellow are traditional colors for the rising and setting sun.

Find an empty box and decorate it in a special way. Think about the way you can use the box. What symbols could you use in your design? How can you arrange all the parts of your design?

111

INTEGRATING THE CURRICULUM

Extensions

Science Ask students to think of natural materials people might use to create containers, depending on the climate and resources where they live. For example, in the deserts of Africa and Australia, people have made water containers from large ostrich eggshells. Animal hides (leather), banana leaves, baskets woven from long grass or vines, and clay pottery are examples of materials from other regions.

Literature Link

- *How Raven Brought Light to People,* retold by Ann Dixon. (S)
- *The Piñata Maker/El Piñatero,* George Ancona. (I)
- *Hannah's Fancy Notions,* Pat Ross. (S)
- *Go In and Out the Window: An Illustrated Songbook for Young People,* Dan Fox. (A)

CLOSE

Assess

1 Discuss design qualities and symbolism in the students' artwork. Encourage them to use their knowledge of art terms such as radial or symmetrical balance, pattern, and color scheme (warm, cool).

Cleanup

1 While supplies are being collected, assign students to rinse brushes in running water.

2 Collect glue and reusable scraps of paper.

3 Use damp paper towels to wipe glue from hands and desks.

4 Place boxes on waxed paper until glue dries.

2 Have students:
- apply the larger background paper to the box.
- brush glue on the box.
- place the paper on top.
- cut any additional shapes from paper.

Remind students that they can create patterns and radial or symmetrical designs. They can cut small, similar shapes of the same height by cutting a strip of paper and crosscutting it, as in Lesson 40. These procedures should be used on all sides except the bottom.

3 While students work, remind them that glue on the hairs of the brush will pick up a small piece of tissue paper so it can be placed without having to touch the paper.

4 As students finish, have them carefully brush glue over the outside of the box, except the bottom, taking care no puddles of glue remain. Have them clean the brush in a container of soapy water.

RESOURCES

Large Reproductions
   Sun Mask, Native American, 12
   Sioux Vest, 3

Overhead Transparencies
   Dogware, Tygart, 5

CD-ROM
   3, *Artists at Work,* Lessons 1 and 2

Assessment Masters
   Design a Pot, 14

Art History

Discuss symbols used in artworks in varied times and cultures. Share definitions for these symbols as you draw them on the chalkboard: vertical line = life, health, stability; horizontal line = earth, rest; cross = Christianity; Star of David = Judaism; S-line dividing a circle = Buddhism, yin and yang (opposites forming perfection); figure 8 = endlessness; etc. Encourage students to identify other symbols, including those used in advertising and by students or their families.

111

A *Vest*, front view, 19th century. Courtesy of Hogan Gallery, Inc., Florida. Photograph: Ed Chappell, Inca.

B *Vest*, back view, 19th century. Courtesy of Hogan Gallery, Inc., Florida. Photograph: Ed Chappell, Inca.

For thousands of years, people have designed and made their own clothing. About one hundred years ago, a Sioux Indian created the vest in pictures A and B. It was worn for special ceremonies.

Long ago, the Sioux Indians made clothing and tents from the hides of animals. The vest has symbols for their way of life in the plains. What symbols can you identify?

The design on the front of the vest in picture A has **symmetrical balance**. Symmetry means that the left side looks like the right side. Each side of the design is like a mirror image of the other.

The back of the vest, in picture B, is nearly symmetrical. Two buffalo are facing each other. A large bird is centered near the top, inside of flowers on vines.

112

---

47 Art in Clothing
Clothing Design

PREPARE

Objectives

Students will:
- understand the principle of symmetrical balance in the human body and its application in clothing design.
- create an original design for clothing.

Vocabulary

symmetrical   *simétrico(a)*
clothing design   *diseño de ropa*

Materials

colored and white paper, 12 x 18" (30 x 46 cm), 2 per student

scissors

crayons or oil pastels

paste

scraps of colored paper

damp paper towels

TEACH

Engage

1 Discuss the concept that clothing is worn for practical reasons, such as keeping warm or cool, and as a form of expression. Have students identify clothing designs that show someone is part of a group (uniforms for clubs, occupations, sports). Discuss how people may dress to express their individuality (unique combinations of clothes, making one's own, or modifying ready-made clothes with decorations).

2 Explain that clothing design is a form of art in many cultures and a possible art career.

Cooperative Learning

Have students work in small groups to create clothing designs for a specific purpose, such as sports uniforms, costumes for a play, or comfortable clothing for people who use wheelchairs.

Explore

1 Focus on **A**. Discuss the life of North American Plains tribes so students can appreciate the symbols for nature, especially the horses in **A** and the buffalo in **B**.

2 Guide students to see the symmetrical designs in **A**, the nearly symmetrical designs in **B**, and the nearly symmetrical designs of the front and back of the vest.

3 Focus on **C**. Guide students to see how shapes and colors are arranged to create bold, symmetrical patterns. Explain that Varvara Stepanova's designs were extremely modern, practical, and bold for their day.

4 To preview the activity, explain that the overall shapes in **D** are cut from a paper folded lengthwise as shown in **E**. Many of the smaller shapes were cut from smaller sheets of folded paper.

Create

1 Distribute materials. Ask students to fold their paper lengthwise. Then discuss ways students might begin:

- Cut one shape for a shirt, blouse, vest, or sweater. Use a second folded paper to make a pair of shorts, slacks, or skirt to go with the top.

- Draw a waistline slightly above the midpoint of the paper. Trim the paper to show a dress, jumpsuit, or top and bottom of clothing as one unit, as in **C**.

2 Have students begin. After the paper is cut and unfolded, students can draw decorations, cut out smaller pieces of colored paper, and paste them down.

 Student artwork.

C Designs for sports clothing, 1923. © Varvara Stepanova.

Many people today buy their clothing in stores. Artists create the designs for manufactured clothing. These artists are called **clothing designers** or fashion designers.

An artist from Russia created the designs for sports clothes in picture C. She designed the clothes over seventy years ago. Do you think these are still good designs?

Why or why not?

Students created the clothing designs in picture D. They sketched ideas first. They cut a large symmetrical shape for their clothing. Then they cut smaller shapes and added decorations. Which designs are symmetrical? Which designs are nearly symmetrical?

113

INTEGRATING THE CURRICULUM

Extensions ▼ ▼

Language Arts Have students pretend that the clothing they designed will be used by a special person. Ask them to write a creative story about that person, including where the clothing will be worn. Make a display of the clothing designs and stories.

Social Studies Have students research the ceremonial uses, symbols, and designs on clothing among various Native American groups; then develop a chart of the results. Students should be able to identify similarities and differences related to geographic regions, traditions, age, and gender.

Literature Link
• *Powwow,* George Ancona. (A)
• *Her Seven Brothers,* Paul Goble. (S, A)
• *Powwow: Festivals and Holidays,* June Behrens. (A)

---

3 While students work, suggest creating a design using:
• planned patterns of lines, shapes, and colors.
• a color scheme.
• symmetry and special symbols.
• buttons and the like or borders for cuffs and collars.

Students who have created separate two-piece outfits may wish to paste them together.

CLOSE

Assess

1 Have students look at and discuss some of the designs for clothing. Focus on overall shape and design qualities.

2 Discuss the relationship between paper designs or drawings and the way real clothes look when worn. Guide students to appreciate clothing as soft, with constantly changing forms as the body moves. Briefly discuss clothing design as one of many careers in art.

RESOURCES

Large Reproductions
Sioux Vest, 3
African Canvas, Courtney-Clarke, 19

Overhead Transparencies
Corn Dance, Peña, 10

 CD-ROM
3, *Artists at Work,* Lesson 3

Slide Set
Tourist Shirt, Guatemala, 23

Assessment Masters
Designs for Lamps, 18

Cultural Awareness

Discuss why students may prefer to wear plain or fancy clothing designs and the occasions on which they prefer each. Stress that choice of proper clothing can be related to cultural or religious beliefs. For example, plain clothes may be preferred by people who believe that how you behave (being kind, helpful) is more important than how you look (appearance).

113

PREPARE

Objectives

Students will:
- be aware of cultural traditions that lead artists to create subtle beauty in crafts.
- create a well-crafted stenciled fan using a related color scheme.

Vocabulary

subtle	*sutil*
stencil	*stencil/matriz*
symmetry	*simetría*
asymmetry	*asimetría*
related color scheme	*esquema de colores relacionados*

Setup

Place several spoonfuls of paint in divided trays or small containers for three or four students. Stick the tape lengthwise on the desk (not on the newspaper). The tape is used to assemble the fan.

Materials

index cards or stencil paper, 4 x 6" (10 x 15 cm), 1 per student

scissors

white or pastel colors of paper, 12 x 18" (30 x 46 cm), 1 per student

tempera paints: red, yellow, blue, and white, in sets for students to share (See Setup)

sponge brushes, 1 per color of paint

mixing trays

smocks

newspapers for desks

cellophane tape, 8" (20 cm) per student

A   **Keisuka Serizama,** *Fan,* Japan, 20th century. Dyed stencil design. Collection of Mingei International.

Useful artworks can be beautiful. For thousands of years people have made useful objects that are beautiful to see.

An artist in Japan created the fan in picture A. The artist was known as a "living treasure." The title "living treasure" is the highest honor for an artist in Japan. It means that people cherish and respect the artist's skill.

114

TEACH

Engage

1 Discuss the difference between a well-made object and a poorly made object using familiar examples such as toys or clothing.

2 Explain that artists in many cultures are taught to create beautiful objects by hand with great care and skill. Students will learn more about these ideas.

Meeting Individual Needs

Simplify Have students create a fan using crayons for a carefully planned design.

Challenge Have students look for examples of beauty in nature, or finely crafted objects people use or wear, and describe why these have subtle beauty or superior crafting.

Explore

1 Explain that Japanese artists designated as "living treasures" have learned more than any other person about a traditional art form, such as ceramics, dyeing fabrics, or working with paper. They create beautifully designed and superbly made objects. Each living treasure has students who hope to achieve the same title.

2 Guide students to see the color scheme in **A**. Several values of blue dominate the work. The thin reeds covered with paper give the fan a delicate structure and radial balance. The printed design shows a water hyacinth bending to the left. The design is not symmetrical, but is visually balanced. Review the term *asymmetrical balance*.

3 Discuss **B** and **C**. Make sure students see how the flat designs are related to the fans below. Call on students to identify the colors and placements of the stencil shapes. Have them turn to the color wheel in Lesson 13 and identify sets of related colors.

4 Briefly review steps in making and printing a stencil, as presented in Lesson 5.

Create

1 Distribute materials, except paint.

2 Have students cut a simple stencil shape from the center of a folded index card and then unfold the card. The stencil must have a solid border at least 1" (3 cm) wide all around.

3 Distribute paint and sponge brushes. Remind students to apply paint with a very gentle, straight up-and-down motion called *stippling*. If the sponge has too much paint, press it on newspaper several times.

4 Discuss problems and solutions in practice prints. (Make sure stencil is flat. Hold it so it doesn't move. Use less paint. Wipe off paint that may get under the stencil.)

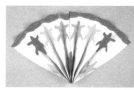

 B Student artwork.

 C Student artwork.

Many artists from Japan have a tradition of creating artworks with subtle beauty. **Subtle** means that you must look closely to notice details.

Look again at the fan in picture A. What color scheme did the artist use? What kind of balance do you see in the design? What details give the fan subtle beauty?

Students your age created the fans in pictures B and C. They used related colors. **Related colors** are next to each other on the color wheel. Related colors have subtle similarities and differences.

Create a fan with subtle beauty. Find a related color scheme by looking at the color wheel on page 33. Cut one or several stencils. Print your stencil carefully. When the paint is dry, carefully fan-fold your paper. Then fold the paper in half and tape the center.

115

Extensions ▼

Language Arts Have students write a haiku poem to go with their fans. A *haiku* is a Japanese poem written in three lines. The first line has five syllables, the second line has seven syllables, and the third line has five syllables.

The pattern I make
quietly touches the edge
with color that sings

Literature Link
• *The Badger and the Magic Fan: A Japanese Folktale,* adapted by Tony Johnston. (S)
• *The Boy of the Three-Year Nap,* Dianne Snyder. (A, S)
• *The Tale of the Mandarin Ducks,* Katherine Paterson. (A, S)

CLOSE

Assess

5 Have students make finished prints. Ask them to help put supplies away, except for scissors and tape. Explain that paint must be dry before completing the fan.

6 Demonstrate how to make the fan. Place paper on desk horizontally. Fanfold it neatly, gathering all the folds into a strip. Fold this strip in half and tape center folds together.

1 Have students hold up their fans. Discuss design qualities and crafting of the printed patterns. *Crafting* is the careful placement of the stencil and printing with a crisp edge and delicate stipple. Ask students whether their skill in stencil printing is better than in Lesson 5. Discuss why practice is important.

2 Ask students to describe other ideas they have learned. Guide their recall of art terms.

Creative Thinking

Have students create rubbings of leaves, as in Lesson 7. Suggest that their leaf arrangement allow space for a haiku poem. Have them draft the poem on separate paper and lightly draw guidelines for the writing space of the artwork. The poem should then be written with a felt-tipped pen in their best handwriting. Explain that combining beautiful handwriting with an original poem and picture is a tradition in Japan and other Asian countries.

RESOURCES

Large Reproductions
  Carolina Parrots, Audubon, 8
  Golden Age, Brown, 6

Overhead Transparencies
  Swan Bed, Brundege, 4
  Headrest, Zaire, 4

 CD-ROM
  3, *Artists at Work,* Lesson 1

Assessment Masters
  Designs for Lamps, 18

49 Art for Special Times
Maskmaking

PREPARE

Objectives

Students will:
- understand that people in different cultures create masks about animals that have symbolic meanings.
- create a mask of an animal character from a paper bag.

Vocabulary

mask	*máscara*
symbol	*símbolo*

Setup

Check the bag size. It may be best to have students trim sides before they cut holes for the eyes. (See step 3 in student text.)

Safety Notes

Make sure students create large eye openings. Have them follow steps 1 and 2 in their textbooks for safety in cutting the holes.

Materials

paper bags to fit comfortably over the head, 1 per student (See Setup)

scissors

paste

colored construction paper, large scraps

damp paper towels

crayons

newspapers for desks

(optional) strips of colored paper or yarn

 Robert Davidson, *After He Has Seen the Spirit.* 1980. Wood, paint, feathers, operculum shell, 9 1/2 x 8 1/3 x 4 1/2" (24 x 21 x 12 cm). University of British Columbia Museum of Anthropology (Gift of the Anthropology Shop Volunteers). Photograph: W. McLennan.

 Rabbit Mask, Africa, Mali-Dogon, 19th/20th century. Wood, paint, 5 1/2 x 15 3/4 x 6 3/4" (14 x 40 x 17 cm). The Metropolitan Museum of Art (Gift of Mr. and Mrs. J. Gordon Douglas III, 1982).

People in many cultures create **masks** to keep traditions. Masks are often worn in plays. The masks in pictures A and B help people remember stories about animals and nature.

A Haida Indian artist from Canada created the mask in picture A for a celebration.

The mask has many curved lines. The curves are **symbols** for whales, birds and other animals in Haida stories.

The African mask in picture B shows an imaginary animal who helps farmers. The person who wears the mask dances and pretends to till the soil and pull up weeds. The dance is part of a good luck ceremony.

116

TEACH

Engage

1 Discuss reasons people might wear masks: for fun, disguise, protection (firefighter, hospital masks).

2 Explain that some masks are created because people believe that masks can bring good luck, keep bad things from happening, or help sick people. The masks are often worn with costumes in special celebrations or ceremonies.

Meeting Individual Needs

Simplify Have students make masks from construction paper using skills introduced in Lessons 43 and 47.

Explore

1 Guide students to see how **A** combines elegant curved lines and shapes. Haida artist Robert Davidson has perfected the use of symbols for the animal life in British Columbia, Canada, especially the Queen Charlotte Islands where the Haida live. The wide mouth with teeth is a symbol for the whale. Important Haida stories often include animals of the sea, earth, and sky.

2 Discuss the African mask in **B**, created by an unknown Mali artist from Dogon. Explain that the mask was probably worn during ceremonies for crop planting. Many of the Mali ceremonial masks are based on animals.

3 Discuss reasons for stories and performances in which animals are symbols, or speak and behave like humans. Accept answers that link animal characteristics to human traits or experiences. For example, eagles are often symbols of strength or power; owls may be symbols of wisdom.

4 Work through the step-by-step illustrations and discuss **C** to set the stage for the activity. Call on students to explain each step.

The masks in pictures A and B help people remember important stories about animals. People in many lands have stories about animals who can speak or act like people. Why do you think stories like this are found in many lands?

Think about stories with animals who act like people. Create a mask of one of your favorite characters. Pictures 1-4 show one way to make a mask.

1. Ask a student to help mark the eyes.

3. Do you need to trim the sides like this?

2. Cut out holes for the eyes. What shape do you want them to be?

4. How can you add colors and forms to your mask?

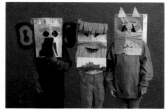
C Students created these masks.

117

INTEGRATING THE CURRICULUM

Extensions ▼ ▼

Language Arts Read *Lord of the Dance: An African Retelling* by Veronique Tadjo (Lippincott, 1989). After reading the poetry, point out the illustrations. The Senufo-style illustrations help to retell this story.

Social Studies Discuss how masks are used in various jobs and for different purposes such as firefighting, medicine, factory work, sports, and entertainment. Have students identify and draw examples.

Social Studies If any students are from ethnic groups that use masks and costumes in rituals and celebrations, ask them and/or their parents to share those traditions with the class. Show films or set up a special book corner for students.

Literature Link
• *Masks,* Meryl Doney. (I, A)
• *Raven's Light: A Myth from the People of the Northwest Coast,* retold by Susan Hand Shetterly. (S, A)

CLOSE

Create

1 Have students think about an animal character for their mask. The character they choose should have traits they admire or would like to mimic when they wear their masks.

2 Distribute materials. Ask students to help each other mark the eyes on their bag. Demonstrate how to snip and cut the opening safely. Assist as needed. Make sure every student has cut large eye openings.

3 Encourage students to make an original design. Remind them that they can cut symmetrical shapes by folding paper and cutting it on the fold. Two (or four) identical shapes can also be cut by folding paper first. Encourage students to decorate their masks.

4 Remind students that pasted paper holds best if it is held in place for about twenty seconds.

Assess

1 Provide time for students to see each other wearing masks. Have each student identify their animal character, the traits that led them to select it, and some of the features of the design.

2 If possible, arrange a short parade so students can show their masks in other classrooms, to the cafeteria staff, or to the principal.

RESOURCES

Large Reproductions
    Cow Mask, Liberia and Ivory Coast, 7
    Sun Mask, Native American, 12
    Bear's Lair, Markovitz, 1

Overhead Transparencies
    Nimba Headdress, West Africa, 14
    Salmon Clan Hat, Tlingit Tribe, 14

 CD-ROM
    5, *People and Animals,* Lesson 4

Slide Set
    Armadillo Mask, Mexico, 24

Assessment Masters
    A Vote for Art, 21

Cooperative Learning

Have students write and produce a play and wear these or specially made masks. They may also create costumes, props, and scenery for a complete production.

Some artists use thread, yarn and fabrics for their artwork. These artists are called **fiber artists**. A **fiber** is a long, thin material such as thread or yarn. Can you name some other fibers?

The fabrics in your clothes are made from threads. In some fabrics, the threads go over and under each other. They are woven together.

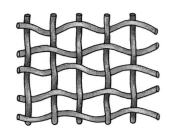

Some threads in your clothes are very thick. Some are thin. Are threads different in other ways?

Some fabrics are woven very tightly. The threads are very close together. Some fabrics are woven very loosely. You can see open space between the threads.

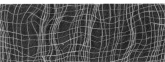

118

PREPARE

Objectives

Students will:

- understand the meaning of the terms fiber, fiber artist, weaving, and pulled thread-work.
- create a fabric design in burlap using the pulled threadwork technique.

Vocabulary

fiber	*fibra*
woven	*tejidas*
pulled threadwork	*tejido calado*
fiber artist	*artista que utiliza fibra*

Setup

To cut burlap straight, pull out one thread every 12" (30 cm). Follow the line where thread was removed. Cut an extra piece for demonstration. Supply the class with small 2 x 2" (5 x 5 cm) samples for practice. Preview the steps in the activity.

Materials

masking or cellophane tape, about 4" (10 cm) per student

crayon that will show on burlap

ruler

burlap, about 12 x 12" (30 x 30 cm), 1 per student (See Setup)

scissors

scraps of colored yarn

TEACH

Engage

1 Discuss students' prior experiences in weaving paper, yarn, and other materials.

2 Explain that weaving is one of the oldest kinds of art and that students will learn more about artistry with yarn.

Meeting Individual Needs

Challenge Combine the reverse weaving process with stitching. Have students use larger fabric and pull fewer threads. Stitch designs in areas of solid fabric. Weave thick yarn or ribbon into open spaces. Make sure burlap is well-starched and stiff.

Explore

1 Most students should understand the concept and terms. In **A**, be sure students see the over/under pattern.

2 Help students understand that the threads woven or knitted into cloth are fibers. Other examples of fibers are string, rope, vines, and long grass (e.g., raffia).

3 Focus on **B**. Have students look closely for thick and thin threads in their clothing. Have them identify tight and loose weaves or knits.

4 Focus on **C**. Explain that threads in burlap have been carefully pulled out to form an open design. Then yarns of different weights were woven into some of the open areas.

5 Explain that students will be working with burlap to create a special design. If you have burlap for practice, distribute it and have students pull threads to form a crosslike open space in the center.

Create

1 Distribute materials. Guide students to mark the border of the fabric. With a crayon, draw a line on the four edges of burlap using the width of a ruler as a guide. Pull out one thread nearest to each of these marked lines. Keep fabric flat on desk with the palm of the hand and forearm and pull threads with the other hand.

2 Discuss ideas for pulling threads:

- simple gridlike design (pull four, leave six, pull four, leave six)
- repeated gridlike pattern (pull four, leave four, and so on)
- stripes (pull threads at regular intervals)
- progressive pattern (pull one, leave three; pull two, leave three; pull three, and so on).

The fiber art in picture C is called **pulled threadwork**. A student created this design in burlap by gently pulling threads out of the cloth. The open spaces create a pattern. Other yarns and stitches also create textures and patterns.

Thousands of years ago, artists in North Africa created clothing with pulled threads. Artists in Europe, Russia and other lands create veils, scarfs or table mats. Some artists create designs for wall hangings.

C Student artwork.

Create your own design in burlap. Gently pull out some threads.

What else can you do to create a new design in the cloth?

119

INTEGRATING THE CURRICULUM

Extensions

Science Acquaint students with some natural fiberlike materials used for weaving, such as long grass, vines, and pine needles. With the help of a local botanist or weaver, identify local materials and sources that are safe for students to use.

Literature Link
• *Annie and the Old One,* Miska Miles. (S)
• *Unraveling Fibers,* Patricia A. Keeler and Francis X. McCall, Jr. (I, A)

Art History

Inform students that humans have been weaving different fibers for thousands of years. The earliest examples of woven cloth may be 10,000-year-old linen fragments unearthed in Switzerland. While the Egyptians were creating fine linen for use in religious garments about 3500 BC, the Chinese were guarding the secrets of the silkworm and inventing the satin weave. Exquisite textiles have come to us from Egypt, Peru, China, India, Africa, and the Middle East. Have students research weaving in different cultures.

RESOURCES

Large Reproductions
 African Canvas, Courtney-Clarke, 19
 Sioux Vest, 3

Overhead Transparencies
 Has-No-Horses, Kasebier, 1

 CD-ROM
 2, *Elements of Design,* Lesson 4

Slide Set
 Upholstery Fabric, Hammerstrom, 25

Assessment Masters
 I Like Art, 22

3 After threads are pulled, discuss uses of colored yarn:

• Group threads together with a regular or shoelace knot; tie gently so the fabric remains flat.

• For tassels, tie several threads next to each other and trim to desired length.

• To stitch, wrap a small piece of tape around one end of yarn. Press the tape into a stiff point. Use the taped end as a needle.

4 Explain ways to finish edges:

• Pull a few threads at edges and corner to make a short, even-fringed border.

• Tie any long, loose border threads together in pairs.

CLOSE

Assess

1 Discuss some artworks, noting patterns, evidence of careful crafting, etc. Point out that most fiber arts take time, patience, and practice.

2 Discuss possible uses of students' fiber art: wall hangings, place mats, vase or planter mats, gifts, etc.

Cleanup

1 Have students check the floor for threads.

2 Ask them to stack pulled threads; then tie in a bundle so they can be collected and saved.

3 Collect other supplies.

Batik Designs on Cloth
Fabric Resist

 Julia Hill, *Africa* (detail), 1985. Silk crepe de chine, resist-painted, 150 x 45″ (381 x 114 cm). Photograph: George Erml.

Do you like to see colorful fabrics? Some artists create dyed fabrics. Dye is a colored liquid that stains the threads in a fabric.

The artwork in picture A is a batik. This **batik** was made by using dyes and wax. The artist brushed warm wax on white cloth. Then she dipped the cloth in dye. The dye resisted, or rolled away from, the areas with wax. She waxed and dyed the cloth many times to create the design.

120

PREPARE

Objectives

Students will:
- be aware of batik and related resist processes for creating designs on cloth.
- create a batik-like design on cloth using a stencil.

Vocabulary

batik	*batik*
stain	*teñir*
dye	*tintura*
resist medium	*medio repelente*
stencil	*stencil/matriz*

Setup

Blend one part aloe-based hand lotion and one part toothpaste to make resist medium, 1 tbsp. per student. Make a sample before the lesson. For the second period, you will need a sink or source of running water and supply of newspapers for desks.

Materials

First period:

washed, pressed white cotton or unsized muslin, 9 x 12" (23 x 30 cm), 1 per student

resist medium, 1 container with bristle brush per 2 students (See Setup)

scissors

index card or stencil paper, 4 x 6" (10 x 15 cm), 1 per student

waxed paper

paper towels

Second period:

tempera paint: violet, red, or orange with sponge brush, 1 container per 2 students

smocks

TEACH

Engage

1 Discuss colored designs on students' clothing. Explain that colors in cloth are created by weaving dyed yarn or by printing on fabric with special inks.

2 Explain that students will learn about a third way to create designs in cloth using dyes, which are colors that stain threads of a cloth.

Cultural Awareness

Almost every culture has a technique of dyeing and decorating cloth. Parents, local crafts organizations, or the textile department of a museum or art school might provide demonstrations and other examples.

Explore

1 Guide students to see similarities between the crayon-resist process in Lesson 30 and the batik process. To create the design in **A**, the artist blocked out lines and shapes with wax, then dyed the cloth, and repeated these steps. In the final work, all wax is removed.

2 The design in **B**, like **A**, is created by a resist process. Instead of wax, a thick, starchy paste is painted or stamped onto a white cloth. The paste is allowed to dry, the cloth is dyed, and then washed to remove the starch (the cloth's white areas appear).

3 Explain that the student art in **C** was made by brushing a resist medium inside a stencil placed in different locations on the cloth.

4 Explain that students will first make a stencil and apply the resist medium to cloth. In the second session, they will stain the cloth and then remove the resist medium.

Create

1 Distribute materials for stencils and preparing the design on cloth. Discuss ideas for stencils that have a simple shape (butterfly, grasshopper, turtle, bird, or fish).

2 After stencils are cut, explain these steps:
- Put the cloth on the waxed paper and position the stencil.
- Brush the resist medium from the cut edge of the stencil toward the center of the hole so it penetrates the cloth.
- Make sure the underside of the stencil is clean. (Wipe with a paper towel.)
- Repeat these steps using a definite plan for the design.

3 Place the work, unstacked, on a counter to dry overnight, with waxed paper under the cloth.

 B *Adire Eleko Cloth* (detail). Oshogbo, Nigeria, 20th century. Cassava starch, indigo dye. From the collection of Mrs. Cyril Miles.

 C Student artwork.

In Africa, the Yoruba people of Nigeria create batik designs in another way. They apply starch to create designs, then they dye the cloth. This dye is called adire. Adire means indigo, or dark violet, the color of the dye.

You can make a batik design. Make a simple stencil. Your **resist medium** can be a paste-like mixture of hand lotion and toothpaste. Place the stencil on the cloth. Brush this paste-like mixture on the cloth.

When the paste is dry, brush tempera paint over the whole cloth. Then put the cloth under running water. When the paste washes away, you will see a stained design.

121

Extensions ▼

Language Arts The Ashanti *adire eleko* designs are applied to cloth with a feather. Although there are traditional designs, two cloths are seldom identical. The designs have names such as "Life is sweet," "All the birds are here," and "Four friends who should know what to do." The name is expected to start a pleasant train of thought for those who see it. After students complete this project, have them title their work in the tradition of the Ashanti. Display the title with each work and ask the artist to explain the title.

Literature Link

• *Dia's Story Cloth: The Hmong People's Journey of Freedom,* Dia Cha. (A)
• *Som See and the Magic Elephant,* Jamie Oliviero. (A)
• *Kente Colors,* Debbi Chocolate. (A)

4 During the second period, supervise students as they apply paint to the cloth. They should:
  • pull the sponge brush across the cloth in broad strokes that slightly overlap.
  • avoid scrubbing the paint and softening the resist.

5 Call two or three students at a time to rinse and drain the cloth. Monitor this step closely. Place wet cloths neatly inside folded newspapers to blot them.

CLOSE

Assess

1 Have students hold up the cloth. Discuss the design qualities, problems encountered, and ways to improve results.

2 Have students describe the basic steps and concepts using art terms.

3 Suggest that students complete the border at home so the work can be hung up or placed on a table. Inform them that the stain is not likely to withstand laundering.

Cleanup

1 Students who are waiting to rinse their cloth can collect paint and blot sponge brushes on newspaper.

2 Soak brushes in soapy water.

Reminder

Ask students to bring scraps of lightweight cloth, buttons, fabric trim, etc. for the next lesson.

RESOURCES

Large Reproductions
  Golden Age, Brown, 6
  Interior, Matisse, 17

Overhead Transparencies
  Thanksgiving, Lee, 8
  Corn Dance, Peña, 10

CD-ROM
  3, *Artists at Work,* Lesson 1

Slide Set
  Batik, Indonesia, 26

Assessment Masters
  I Like Art, 22

A **Linda Benglis, *Patang*,** 1980. Satin appliqué on canvas, 15 x 90' (4.5 x 27.4 m). Atlanta Airport Commission. Photograph: Gary Lee Super.

Some artists create pictures from pieces of cloth or fabric. When the cloth is stitched down, the artwork is called **appliqué**.

Look at the appliqué mural in picture A. The artist used a needle and thread to sew satin fabric on a large piece of canvas. Her abstract design has many shapes based on nature. The shapes seem to dance with a jazzy rhythm.

Unity and variety are important in this design. **Unity** means that all the parts are planned. They look like they belong together. Can you tell how the artist unified the design?

Variety means that parts are different from each other. Variety helps to keep you interested in looking at the work. How has the artist planned for variety?

122

PREPARE

Objectives

Students will:
- understand that fabric, yarn, and thread can be used to create artwork.
- create an appliqué and add stitching.

Vocabulary

appliqué	*apliqué*
stitchery	*labor de aguja*
unity	*unidad*
variety	*variedad*

Setup

Press the end of yarn on a small piece of tape. Fold and press tape to fit into eye of needle. To cut lengths of yarn or thread, wrap thread neatly around the back of a chair. Press tape firmly across threads on one side of chair. Cut near tape. Free ends can be pulled out as needed.

Materials

large craft needles with slightly rounded ends

lightweight fabric scraps, trims, buttons, yarn, thread, in boxes for 3 or 4 students to share

burlap or other cloth background, 9 x 12" (22 x 30 cm), 1 per student

white glue

damp paper towel

school scissors

cellophane tape (See Setup)

examples of appliqué, embroidery, or related fiber art

TEACH

Engage

1 Determine how much experience students have using needle and thread.

2 Show original fiber artworks you have brought in and identify them as weaving, embroidery, needlework, braiding, knotting macramé, quilting, or soft sculpture.

Meeting Individual Needs

Challenge Briefly review the varieties of fiber art in Lessons 50, 51, and this lesson. Have students select one technique and create another artwork with improved design and technique.

Explore

1 Focus on **A**. Have students identify shapes cut from cloth, decorative trim, stitched areas, colors, and textures. Stress that a work of art as complex as **A** takes time and patience.

2 Discuss ways the artist unified this design (larger shapes, repeated colors, balance in light and dark areas). Have students identify visual elements that add variety (combinations of curved and angular shapes, color accents).

3 In **B**, have students note how the artist has added stitches around the appliqué and in the background. The work is unified by the solid background color and large shapes. Stitched details add variety.

4 Focus on **C**. Stress that the student's appliqué shows careful work, patience, and inventive stitches. Explain that design ideas for an appliqué can be imaginative and often come from available materials with odd shapes, colors, textures, and patterns. Note that an appliqué can be designed as a gift, hung on a wall, placed on a table, or stitched on clothing.

5 Explain that students will begin their own appliqué and add stitching. They may need to complete their work at home.

Cultural Awareness

Appliqué is used for a variety of purposes. For example, the Fon artists of Benin, Africa, created appliqué history banners that served as "living picture stories" for ceremonies. They were made of dark cloth with brightly colored appliqué pictures showing symbols of the lineage, bravery, or wealth of the tribe's king. Only men whose families were retained by the king created these banners. Women spun threads and wove them into cloth for the men to use.

Chris Roberts-Antieau, *Shooting Star,* 1989. Fiber appliqué, 24 x 30"
(61 x 76 cm). Courtesy of the artist.

C   Student artwork.

The appliqué in picture B has different kinds of cloth. The stitches are made with a needle and thread or yarn.

The large shapes of the animals fill much of the space. The large shapes help to unify the design. What adds variety to the appliqué?

A student created the appliqué in picture C. You can create your own designs for an appliqué. Collect different kinds of cloth. The textures and patterns in the cloth may give you an idea for a design. Cut out some shapes of cloth. Arrange them on a larger background cloth. Plan your design so it has unity and variety. Then glue the shapes down and add stitches.

123

Extensions   ▼

Language Arts Have students select one of their works from Lesson 50, 51, or this lesson and write down the sequence of steps used to create it. Have students who chose the same art technique to work in groups and edit the steps. Have each group make a poster of the steps and display it with examples of their work.

Literature Link
• *Dia's Story Cloth: The Hmong People's Journey of Freedom,* Dia Cha. (A)
• *Tonight Is Carnival,* Arthur Dorros. (A)
• *Life Around the Lake,* Maricel E. Presilla and Gloria Soto. (A, I)

CLOSE

Create

1 Distribute materials, except needles.

2 Explore design ideas based on the expected use of the project or themes such as nature, family activities, sports, or initials to which fancy stitching can be added.

3 Have students cut shapes and then glue the center and edges of all their shapes to the background. This holds the shapes in place until stitching is completed.

4 Demonstrate how to thread a needle, tie a knot, and begin with a stitch under the cloth. To avoid tangles, slowly pull the thread and always keep a neat U-shaped loop behind the needle. Pull the thread gently so fabric remains flat. Make the last stitch on the back. Stitch or loop through other threads on the back before cutting.

5 Encourage students to make practice stitches on a scrap of cloth. Offer a second demonstration to small groups. Have students work at their own pace.

Assess

1 Discuss some of the artwork. Encourage thoughtful comments about ideas or subjects, unity and variety, and skill in sewing.

Cleanup

1 Have students check the floor for scraps and fold or stack all materials neatly for collection.

2 If needles were distributed, collect them, scissors, and other supplies.

Reminder
Have students begin to save and bring in small containers for Lesson 54.

RESOURCES

Large Reproductions
   Sioux Vest, 3

Overhead Transparencies
   Delfina Flores, Rivera, 21

CD-ROM
   2, *Elements of Design,* Lessons 3 and 4

Slide Set
   Cloth, Fon people, Benin, 27

Assessment Masters
   I Like Art, 22

Creative Thinking

Discuss how Fon banners show pride in a group, especially the family. Help students identify symbols that represent the strengths of each family member or a group to which they belong. Have students design symbols, cut them from construction paper, and glue them onto mural paper. Suggest they make the symbols large and represent each family or group member with a different color.

123

53 An Imaginary Animal
Clay Sculpture

PREPARE

Objectives

Students will:
- understand that people in many cultures have created sculptures of unusual or imaginary animals.
- create a clay sculpture of an imaginary animal.

Vocabulary

sculpture	*escultura*
mosaic	*mosaico*
imaginary	*imaginario*

Setup

Establish a procedure for distributing clay. Cut bulky clay with a thin wire. Grasp both ends and press down through the clay. To protect desks, cut some cloth or burlap mats for water-based clay or heavy plastic for oil-based clay.

Safety Notes

If students have skin abrasions or sores on their hands, have them use clay after skin has healed.

Materials

oil- or water-based clay, about ½ lb. (227 gm) per student (oil-based is recommended for this lesson)

cardboard, 6 x 6" (15 x 15 cm), 1 per student

small tools for clay

smocks

newspapers or mats

damp paper towels

display area

(optional) world map

A *Two-Headed Horse*, Early Iron Age, ca. 1000 B.C. Cypriote, terra-cotta, 11 x 5 1/4" (28 x 15 cm). The Metropolitan Museum of Art, New York (The Cesnola Collection).

B *Two-Headed Serpent*, 15th century. Aztec. 17 1/2" (44 cm) long. Reproduced by Courtesy of the Trustees of the British Museum, London.

Have you ever seen animals like these? Look carefully. Do these **sculptures** show real or imaginary animals?

The sculpture in picture A is very old. Do the animals look like imaginary horses? Why or why not?

The Mexican sculpture in picture B was made long ago. It is covered with a **mosaic** of tiny shells and colorful stones. The serpent was once a symbol for royalty among the Aztec Indians.

124

TEACH

Engage

1 Discuss students' prior experience with modeling clay or related materials. Hold up a sample of clay. Explain whether clay is oil- or water-based.

2 Review that animals are a subject in artworks of many lands. In this lesson, students will learn about sculptures of imaginary animals from different times and cultures.

Explore

1 Allow time for students to look at **A**, **B**, and **C** and answer the questions. As you focus on each sculpture, refer to the Cultural Awareness section.

2 In **A**, guide students to see the two long necks and heads, the pattern on the neck, and body. There are four legs attached to one body. In **B**, review the definition of *mosaic,* a surface made from many small pieces of materials. Note the tension or energy in repeated curves and the opposite pull of the two heads. Have several students stand and invent a body position or movement similar to the two-headed snake. In **C**, point out the curves in the back, spines, and tail, the tension of stiff legs, and the lowered head. Have students assume a pose similar to the dragon.

3 Ask students to begin thinking of an imaginary animal to make in clay.

Cultural Awareness

The exact symbolism of **A** is unknown, but some experts believe these figures were made for tombs and represented two horses (not a two-headed animal) trained to work together to pull a chariot. The two-headed serpent in **B** is an Aztec symbol for the rain god, a sky serpent whose belly is filled with all the waters of the heavens. In China, dragonlike sculptures are associated with the emperor and also with a god who brought rain and controlled all the water on earth.

Dragon. Chinese. Rietburg Museum, Zurich, Switzerland. Photograph: Wettstein & Kauf.

The clay dog in picture C looks like a dragon. The sculpture was made in China. It probably shows Fu, an imaginary creature who guards a home with great courage. How did the artist make it look scary?

These are make-believe animals. Find the surprising parts of each sculpture. People in many lands have made sculptures of imaginary animals. Do you know why?

Think of a strange animal that you could make from clay. Make it surprising or scary. Use your imagination!

125

Extensions

Language Arts Have students tell or write imaginative stories to go with the sculptures. Encourage the use of art vocabulary. Display the stories and sculptures or have students present their work to other classrooms.

Movement Read *Dr. Dolittle* by Hugh Lofting (Dell, 1986). Talk about the adventures of Pushme-pullyu. Discuss how this two-headed animal made decisions about how to move. Allow pairs of students to make up a slow Pushme-pullyu dance. Have students discuss their decisions about movements and how it felt to be "two heads with one body."

Literature Link
- *Animals That Ought To Be: Poems About Imaginary Pets,* Richard Michelson. (S)
- *Animals in Art,* Louisa Somerville. (A)
- *Totem Pole,* Diane Hoyt-Goldsmith. (A)

CLOSE

Create

1 Distribute materials. Remind the class of procedures to follow when using clay. Encourage students to work independently. Some may need ideas such as a strange creature, a monster, an alien, or an absurd animal.

2 As needed, review and demonstrate how to roll out coils, press clay together, and create firm joints by blending the clay across the joints with X strokes. Encourage students to use small tools and to make clay pellets or small coils for textures and details.

3 As students work, make sure they turn their sculpture and view it from each side, front and back, and top. Stress that most sculpture is meant to be seen from all angles.

Assess

1 Ask several students to describe how they have made their sculpture look strange, powerful, scary, and so on.

2 Discuss some of the imaginary creatures and specific techniques students have used to join clay and decorate the surfaces.

Cleanup

1 Students' names should be on the cardboard.

2 Have students clean excess clay from tools, return usable pieces, and check the floor.

Reminder
Preview the next lesson. Ask students to bring several small, clean, empty cardboard or plastic (not glass or metal) containers from home: boxes, tubes, bottle tops, empty eggor milk cartons, and so on. Save clean paper or Styrofoam cups and empty milk cartons from school.

RESOURCES

Large Reproductions
  Baboon, Picasso, 5

Overhead Transparencies
  Horse, Nadelman, 20
  The Generals, Marisol, 20

 CD-ROM
  5, *People and Animals,* Lesson 4

Slide Set
  Winged Bull, Persia, 28

Assessment Masters
  Imagine That, 9
  Mix and Match, 12

Cooperative Learning

Have students assist in creating a display of their work. Cover boxes with colored paper and place animals on the boxes in a multilevel arrangement. Title the display.

Some artists create sculpture from materials they find, such as scraps of wood or metal. The metal rooster in picture A was created by a United States sculptor, Alexander Calder. His artwork is a **found object** sculpture.

Sculpture has form. A **form** has height, width and thickness. Forms are **three-dimensional**. Forms are not flat. What forms did Calder create for his sculpture?

B You can change flat paper into three-dimensional forms.

126

PREPARE

Objectives

Students will:
- understand that sculpture can be made by assembling and joining materials together.
- create an imaginative sculpture by assembling and joining materials.

Vocabulary

form	*forma*
found object	*objeto encontrado*
three-dimensional	*tridimensional*
imagination	*imaginación*

Setup

Stick tape lengthwise along edge of desks. Students can cut or tear off the amount they need. Paint will cover plastic or wax boxes if you add a drop of liquid soap to each color. Painting should be done at three or four stations.

Materials

an assortment of cardboard or plastic containers per student

scraps of colored paper

white glue

scissors

masking tape, 18" (45 cm) per student (See Setup)

newspapers for desks

damp paper towels

(optional) several stations for painting (See Setup)

TEACH

Engage

1 Briefly review that imagination—the ability to make pictures in the mind—is important in artwork.

2 Hold up several cardboard containers and place them in different positions. Ask students to think of ideas for a sculpture that can be made by joining the containers together and adding other parts. Explain that students will use materials at hand to create sculpture.

Challenge If students are capable of doing independent work, set up stations so they can choose between the activities in this lesson and Lesson 55. Introduce each lesson and demonstrate the basic processes.

Explore

1 Focus on **A**. Help students identify the parts of coffee cans, wire, and other materials in Alexander Calder's found object sculpture. Hold up a box and indicate the three dimensions it has: height, width, and depth.

2 Focus on **B**. Review how colored paper can be cut, bent, and pasted into a cone or cylinder and attached to the flat side of a box. Stress that slitting the end of the paper form and folding it back provides a surface for the glue.

3 Focus on **C** and note pieces of metal welded together and then painted. Some pieces are thin, bent, and shaped in the same way that students might use paper. Have students point out patterns of stripes and circles. (The title, *Charm*, implies that the sculpture— awkward, yet decorated and reaching out in many directions—is like a person who may be awkward, but tries to be attractive and reach out to people.)

4 Discuss **D**. Stress that students should try several arrangements of boxes and other forms to get ideas for their sculptures. In a second session, they will paint their sculptures and add details.

126

C **Robert Hudson**, *Charm*, 1964. Polychrome metal sculpture, 45 1/2" (114 cm). Los Angeles County Museum of Art (Museum Purchase, Contemporary Art Council Funds).

D

An artist created the sculpture in picture C. He joined many different materials together. Sculpture can be painted, too. What colors and patterns did the artist create?

What can you create from empty boxes, tubes and other materials you find? How can you join the materials together? Can you use your imagination as artists do?

127

Extensions ▼

Language Arts Using the art vocabulary from this lesson, have students write fantasy stories about the sculptures they have created. Display sculptures and stories together.

Literature Link
• *Stay Away from the Junkyard,* Tricia Tusa. (S)
• *The Sweet and Sour Animal Book,* Langston Hughes. (A)

Create

1 Distribute materials for making the sculptures. (Distribute tape while students are trying arrangements of their forms.) Encourage students to imagine their forms as imaginary creatures, robots, or combinations of both.

2 Have students assemble their forms carefully. Put glue on flat surfaces that touch each other and apply to narrow edges and curved forms; then tape forms together to assure a tight bond until glue dries. Use damp paper towels to wipe away glue drips. Check that forms will have secure joints when glue dries. Follow step 1 under Cleanup.

3 In the second session, discuss ways to complete the sculpture. Stress that lettering or colors on the original containers can be part of the design, as in Calder's work. Caution students that too much paint or water will soften glue.

4 Encourage imaginative additions of paper (fringes, curls, etc.) for enhanced color and detail.

CLOSE

Assess

1 Allow time for students to enjoy seeing the temporary arrangement of their sculptures. Discuss the work in a manner that emphasizes the accomplishments of the total class: use of imagination, problem solving, and so on.

Cleanup

1 Make sure names are on artworks and place them on counter or display area.

2 Collect glue and scissors.

3 Have students check the floor for scrap paper.

4 Have students assist in cleaning brushes and storing other supplies.

RESOURCES

Large Reproductions
  Baboon, Picasso, 5
  Bear's Lair, Markovitz, 1

Overhead Transparencies
  The Generals, Marisol, 20

CD-ROM
  5, *People and Animals*, Lesson 4

Assessment Masters
  Designs for Lamps, 18

55 Creating a Form
Soft Sculpture

PREPARE

Objectives

Students will:
- be aware of forms and patterns that can give unity and variety to sculpture.
- create a soft sculpture of a bird or fish with evidence of unity and variety in the design.

Vocabulary

unity	*unidad*
variety	*variedad*
form	*forma*
pattern	*diseño*
media	*medios*

Setup

Make a sample before the lesson.

Safety Notes

Teach students to pull tape across the sharp edge of the dispenser and then down without fingers touching the edge.

Materials

scissors

white butcher paper or brown kraft paper, 18 x 24" (46 x 60 cm), folded to 12 x 18" (30 x 46 cm), 1 per student

cellophane or masking tape, ¾" (2 cm) wide, 1 dispenser for 3 or 4 students

markers and crayons

strips of newspaper, about 2" (5 cm) wide

stapler (teacher's use)

A Marvin Finn, *Bird with tall patterned tail.* Painted wood. Photograph: © Dan Dry.

Sculpture can be made from many materials. The bird in picture A is made from wood. An African-American artist created it.

Where do you see repeated curves? What patterns do you see? What elements unify this work? What elements add variety?

128

TEACH

Engage

1 Explain that artists throughout history and in many cultures have created sculpture with forms and decorative designs based on nature.

2 Have students look back at the sculptures in Lessons 53 and 54 and discuss them in relation to the two examples in this lesson. Guide them to see that the sculptures vary in style, materials, and surface treatment. Explain that students will learn more about sculpture with animals as a theme.

Meeting Individual Needs

Simplify Some students may wish to draw a large geometric shape—circle, oval, rectangle, square, triangle—and then draw a fish or bird so it fits into and fills the space.

Challenge Have students choose one of the sculptures in Lessons 53, 54, or this lesson and prepare a report about the sculpture without naming the animals. Have the class try to identify the sculpture based only on the references to the sculpture's materials, design qualities, and mood.

Explore

1 Focus on **A**. Help students see the board is cut into a fanciful bird and mounted on a base. The repeated curves of the bird and long tail feathers unify the work. The distinct patterns covering the body and tail add variety. The sculpture is also unified by the use of a few colors.

2 Focus on **B** and guide students to see that the overall shape is simple and unified. Discuss the use of wavy lines and color shifts to create variety. Reinforce the concepts of unity and variety in art by an analogy with team sports. All the different members of a team should work together as a whole unit, just as the various elements in an artwork should be unified. Have students offer other analogies.

3 Discuss steps **C**, **D**, and **E** to preview the activity.

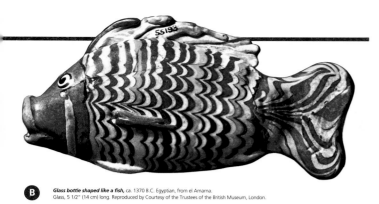

 Glass bottle shaped like a fish, ca. 1370 B.C. Egyptian, from el Amarna. Glass, 5 1/2" (14 cm) long. Reproduced by Courtesy of the Trustees of the British Museum, London.

The sculpture in picture B was made in Africa over 3,000 years ago. The form was used as a bottle. The sculpture is unified by the wavy pattern of lines and a simple shape.

Both sculptures are thick shapes. A thick shape is a form. You can create a form from paper. Your form will be a sculpture.

Fold paper. Draw a big, simple shape. Color it.

Cut the folded paper. Color the other side.

Tape some edges. Stuff paper inside. Add tape.

C **D** **E**

129

Extensions ▼

Science Have students develop one or more theories (hypotheses) that might explain why birds and fish are a common theme in the art of many cultures. Guide them to prepare written or oral reports in which they support their theories with facts and visual art examples.

Literature Link
• *Toys,* Meryl Doney. (A, I)

Create

1 Distribute materials. Explain:
   • Draw a bird or fish, making the parts of the body very simple and smooth.
   • The top of your drawing must bump the folded edge of the paper.
   • Other lines should reach out so they touch each edge of the paper.

2 When drawing is done, have students cut through the two sheets together so front and back will match. Then have them complete the drawing with color, patterns, and details on both sides. Remind them to use other design concepts (color schemes, larger elements for unity/smaller parts for variety, etc.).

3 As students finish, teach them to use short pieces of tape for sharp inside and outside curves and then add other pieces, locking front and back together. Leave a hand-size opening. Stuff the form with crushed newspaper and seal the opening.

CLOSE

Assess

1 Ask students to describe the most interesting and difficult parts of this method of sculpture. Have them speculate on ways to solve problems for a similar sculpture in the future. Ask them to identify unity and variety in the sculptures.

2 Discuss ways to display the work. Check with a custodian on ways to suspend work from the ceiling.

Aesthetic Awareness

Introduce students to optical illusions that illustrate how the human mind must work together with the eyes. Moiré patterns are especially useful to demonstrate this and are available in many science kits. The patterns are printed on acetate and can be used on an overhead projector.

RESOURCES

Large Reproductions
   Sun Mask, Native American, 12
   Bear's Lair, Markovitz, 1

Overhead Transparencies
   Glass Fish, Egypt, 17
   Bactrian Camel, China, 11
   Camels, Graves, 11

 CD-ROM
   5, *People and Animals*, Lesson 4

Slide Set
   Standing Camel, China, 29

Assessment Masters
   Comparing Two Artworks, 19

Many artworks have people as a theme. Look at the sculptures in pictures A and D. How are these sculptures of people alike? How are they different? Why do you think many artworks show people?

These sculptures are made from clay. Clay sculptures must be strong. These artists have created thick arms and legs. The clay joints are strong and smooth.

Make a strong sculpture of one person or a group of people. Create the main forms and join them together. Try different positions for the arms, legs and body. Then add details like the nose, ears and mouth.

A   **William McVey, *Visions*.** Stoneware. Wichita Art Association, Inc. Permanent Collection. Purchase Award, Sixth National Decorative Ceramics Exhibition, 1951. Photograph: Mike Fizer. Courtesy of the artist.

B   **C**

PREPARE

Objectives

Students will:

- know basic procedures for using ceramic or oil-based clay.
- use a planned procedure to create a clay sculpture of the human figure.

Vocabulary

sculpture	*escultura*
form	*forma*
proportion	*proporción*
ceramic	*cerámica*

Setup

Ceramic clay has the right consistency if a pencil-thin coil does not break when wrapped around the thumb. Surface cracks are normal.

Materials

ceramic or oil-based clay, ½ lb. (227 gm) per student (See Setup)

cardboard squares, about 6" (15 cm), 1 per student

small tools for clay

table knife, 1 per 3 or 4 students

smocks

newspapers or mats

water containers

damp paper towels or small cloths

sponges

Safety Notes

Students who have dust allergies should use oil-based clay. Students with sores should not use clay until skin heals.

TEACH

Engage

1 Ask students to report on prior experience using ceramic clay to make permanent artwork.

2 Explain the steps that produce a permanent sculpture in ceramic clay:

- The artist makes a sculpture and allows it to dry out.
- The sculpture is heated in a special oven called a *kiln* (pronounced KILL) to make the clay very hard.
- Because the kiln becomes as hot as fire, this process is called *firing the clay*. Firing also refers to the first kilns, which were pits in the ground into which claywork was put. A fire was then built above (like an earth oven).

Meeting Individual Needs

Simplify Have students use oil-based clay to create a sculpture. Students might assume the pose they are trying to show in order to understand how arms, legs, and neck bend.

Challenge Have students create sculptures of figures in more gymnastic poses, with at least three parts of the body serving as a support for the sculpture.

Explore

1 Focus on **A**. Guide students to see the thick legs and arms and how they touch in the seated figure. Have students take a similar pose, noting bends in parts of the body.

2 Focus on **B** and **C**. Demonstrate how parts of the body might be proportioned.

- Legs: coils as thick as an index finger, about 5" (13 cm) long; bend in center for knee; pinched end for foot.
- Arms: slightly smaller coils than legs; bend in center for elbow; pinched end for hand.
- Body: half the size of one's fist.
- Head: egglike, about 1" (3 cm) long.

3 Help students perceive the details and action of the figures in **D**. Demonstrate the relative size of the original sculpture (height 6½"; width 6½"; depth 3½"; 16 x 16 x 9 cm). Note hats, flute, drum, and cymbals. Have students visualize and gesture how parts might have been pinched, pressed, rolled, and joined.

Three Musicians Seated on a Bench ("Jam Session"), West Mexico, Nayarit, Ixtlan del Rio style, about 100 B.C.–A.D. 250. Buff clay with white and red painted decoration, 6 1/2 x 6 1/2 3 1/8" (17 x 17 x 9 cm). Los Angeles County Museum of Art (The Proctor Stafford Collection, Museum Purchase with Balch Funds).

An artist from Mexico created this sculpture. What are the people doing? What makes this clay sculpture strong?

INTEGRATING THE CURRICULUM

Extensions

Mathematics Have students create charts or oral descriptions of proportions and angles in the human body. For example: The upper leg is about the same length as the lower leg. The arm is bent at a right angle.

Science Explain that water evaporation dries out water-based, but not oil-based, clay. Point out that any pockets of air trapped inside dry water-based clay will expand when the clay is heated. As the air pocket expands (like the air in a balloon), the air presses against the clay around it. The pressure can be so great that the clay breaks or explodes.

Movement Have students use dance movement terms such as darting, gliding, bouncing, and resting to describe the "frozen" movements of sculpture.

Literature Link

• *Marie in Fourth Position: The Story of Degas' "The Little Dancer,"* Amy Littlesugar. (A, S)
• *Henry Moore: From Bones and Stones to Sketches and Sculptures,* Jane Mylum Gardner. (I)

Create

1 Explain that students will create a clay sculpture of a sitting or reclining person.

2 Distribute materials. If students are using water-based clay for the first time, teach them to:

• press clay parts together firmly and blend parts together with X-like strokes.

• keep the clay moist (not wet or slippery) so it will be strong and stable.

• have each part of the body touch or press against another part to make the whole sculpture very strong.

3 Provide guidance as students create parts. The proportions (See Explore 2) will help them create a recognizable human figure.

CLOSE

Assess

1 Review ceramics procedures and vocabulary.

2 Call on students who have created particularly well-made sculptures to describe their artwork. Encourage them to comment on the procedures they used, the proportions in their work, what they thought about, and so on.

Cleanup

1 Make sure names are on artwork.

2 Place pieces of a damp paper towel over the top of the head, hands, and feet so they dry as slowly as thicker parts of the figure.

3 Rub hands together over the mat or newspaper to remove excess dry clay.

4 Return usable pieces of clay and wash hands.

Reminder

Make arrangements to have artwork fired.

RESOURCES

Extensions

Large Reproductions
Double Grandmothers, Frey, 24

Overhead Transparencies
Flute Player, Nigeria, 7

CD-ROM
3, *Artists at Work*, Lesson 3

Assessment Masters
Design a Pot, 14

PREPARE

Objectives

Students will:
- be aware of carving and modeling as procedures for creating relief sculpture.
- carve and model clay to make a relief sculpture with a profile view of a face.

Vocabulary

relief sculpture	*altorrelieve*
carving	*talla*
modeling	*modelado*
profile view	*vista de perfil*

Setup

Self-hardening water-based clay will enable students to keep their sculpture.

Safety Notes

See Lesson 56.

Materials

oil- or water-based clay, ½ lb. (227 gm) per student (See Setup)

cardboard squares, about 6" (15 cm), 1 per student

small tools for clay

smocks

newspapers or mats

damp paper towels

rolling pins or smooth plastic bottles

large tin cans or plastic lids

coins

The lively group of musicians in picture A is a carving in wood by African-American artist, Daniel Pressley. The artwork is a relief sculpture. A **relief sculpture** has parts that stand out from a background.

This sculpture is carved from a piece of lumber. The wood is flat and thick. Some shapes stand out from the background. For example, the hands stand out in front of the guitar. Where do you see shapes that stand out?

You can create a relief sculpture. Make a slab of clay. Carve and build up the clay. Create parts that stand up from a background.

B

A **Daniel Pressley,** *Down By the Riverside,* 1966. Pine relief, 50 x 19" (127 x 48 cm). Schomburg Center for Research in Black Culture, Art & Artifacts Division, The New York Public Library (Astor, Lenox and Tilden Foundations). Photograph: Tom Jenkins.

132

TEACH

Engage

1 Distribute coins to examine or have students examine their own coins. Introduce the term *relief sculpture* to describe the raised images (and lettering) on coins. Have students close their eyes and touch the raised surfaces.

2 Discuss any portraits on the coins. Ask students why the people might have been selected for portraits. Explain that students will learn more about relief sculptures.

Explore

1 Focus on **A**. Guide students to see how the lines, textures, and shadows in this sculpture indicate that the surface is carved, or cut back, from the flat surface. Many of this artist's carvings are inspired by his memories of people and events in rural communities.

2 Discuss the relief sculpture in **B**. Explain that students will begin a relief sculpture similar to a large coin or medallion. The sculpture will have a profile, or side view, of a face. Guide them to see how the clay is carved away, leaving a relief surface.

3 The relief sculpture in **C** shows a mythical god of the ancient Assyrian people. It is part of a long wall of similar sculptures honoring a king. This figure is fertilizing a date palm, a major source of food in the Middle East.

4 Discuss **D**, created to honor the memory of a young woman. Coins such as these, called *medallions*, were made for family and friends as keepsakes.

D *Giulia Astallia* (Style of L'Antico), ca.1490-1520. Bronze, 2 7/16" (6 cm) diameter. National Gallery of Art, Washington, DC (Samuel H. Kress Collection).

C *Winged Deity Relief Sculpture,* Assyria, Nimrud, 9th century B.C. Limestone, 91 1/4 x 71 3/4" (232 x 181 cm). The Nelson-Atkins Museum of Art, Kansas City, Missouri.

The relief sculpture in picture C was created about 2,800 years ago in Assyria. Assyrian rulers lived in the region of present-day Iran and Iraq.

This sculpture was carved on the walls of an ancient palace. It shows an Assyrian god. He wears a beard and has wings. He is taking care of a palm tree that grows food. This food is still important to people who live in the desert lands of Iran and Iraq.

The relief sculpture in picture D was created about 400 years ago in Italy. It was made to remember a person who died. The writing on the border is the name of the girl.

This relief sculpture is similar to a coin. If you look at a coin, you can see the raised parts and background. You can also close your eyes and feel the relief design.

133

INTEGRATING THE CURRICULUM

Extensions ▼

Social Studies Explain that the earliest known relief carvings are of a bison carved in a cave wall in the Dordogne Valley, France, and an antelope engraved in a rock from the Kalahari Desert, Africa. Art historians have dated these relief carvings between 21,000 to 12,000 BC. Both carvings reveal well-developed observational skills. Ask students to research prehistoric art and/or archaeological discoveries.

Literature Link
• *The Story of Money,* Betsy Maestro. (A)

CLOSE

Create

1 Distribute materials. Have students:
  • roll out a slab about the thickness of an index finger.
  • trim the slab into a shape. For a circle, press the open end of a tin can or plastic lid (used like a cookie cutter) through the slab. For other shapes use the point of a paper clip to trim the clay.

2 After the slab is ready, have students draw a profile of a face and then carve away some of the background so the face stands out. The larger the head and profile, the easier it will be to carve and model.

3 After the background is carved, have students build up cheeks, ears, and hair. Then carve into these built-up areas to refine the form and add details.

Assess

1 Discuss the clarity of the profile, development of form (not just lines), and other features that stand out (textures, smooth areas, etc.) in the sculptures.

2 Explain that clay will need to dry for several days. When the top feels very firm, turn the sculpture over carefully so the back can dry. If one side dries at a much faster rate than the other, the form may warp or curl.

Cleanup

1 Place names on the back of the artwork and cardboard.

2 Clean tools and check the floor for clay. Roll usable clay into a ball.

3 Wipe hands with a towel. Wash hands after the assessment.

RESOURCES

Large Reproductions
  Self-Portrait, Marisol, 18

Overhead Transparencies
  Salmon Clan Hat, Tlingit Tribe, 14

CD-ROM
  3, *Artists at Work,* Lesson 3

Slide Set
  Standing Camel, China, 29

Assessment Masters
  Design a Pot, 14

58 A Standing Figure
Carved Clay Sculpture

Helen Bullard carved pieces of very old wood to create the sculpture of a large family in picture A. She wanted to express the idea of many family members living together for a long time. This family lives in the mountains near forests. The wood for the artist's sculpture came from the same forests.

In **carving**, you cut and take away pieces from a solid material like wood or stone. Carving is called a **subtractive** process. If the artist carves very thin parts, they may break off. This is one reason why carving is done slowly and carefully. Each cut is planned first.

134

PREPARE

Objectives

Students will:
• be aware of carving as a process of sub-tracting material from a solid form.
• create a carved sculpture in clay of a standing figure.

Vocabulary

carving	*tallado*
cylinder	*cilindro*
guidelines	*guías*
kachina	*"kachina"*
subtractive process	*proceso por substracción*

Materials

oil-based clay, ½ lb. (227 gm) per student (See Setup)

paper clips (opened flat) or wire sculpture tools

mats for claywork

smocks

damp paper towels

cardboard squares, about 3" (8 cm), 1 per student (for base)

Setup

Oil-based clay is often packaged in boxes with four wrapped sticks or thick coils. Each student should work with the equivalent of two sticks or coils pressed together.

Safety Notes

See Lesson 56. Students should not use knives to carve any materials without adult permission and supervision.

TEACH

Engage

1 Review the kinds of sculpture students studied and created in Lessons 53–57. Explain the basic sculpture processes:
• additive process: materials are joined or assembled.
• modeling process: soft materials are pressed, pulled, stretched, and rearranged.
• subtractive process: materials are carved or removed from a solid form.

2 Tell students they will learn about carving, a subtractive process for creating sculpture.

Explore

1 Discuss **A**. Explain that this artist carved seventeen figures from old chestnut logs to express the idea of families living in the mountains for many generations. Encourage students to identify differences in the carvings, such as the position of hands and types of hair and clothes. Have them select a large figure and imagine how the artist carved the head.

2 Discuss **B**. Explain that *kachina* is a general term for an ancestral spirit of the Hopi people. The sculptures are one way the Hopi honor and remember the spirits. The Hopi also create and wear masks for dance cere-monies in honor of kachinas. The exact meanings of the symbols on this kachina are unknown. The zigzag lines may be symbols for lightning, rain, or flowing water.

3 Guide students to see how **A** and **B** are carved from cylinders. The sculptures look different from the front, back, and sides. Refer to **C** to help students visualize how they will make a cylinder from oil-based clay and then carve it into a person.

Create

1 Distribute materials. Have students roll, tap, and press clay into a cylinder about 5" (13 cm) tall with a diameter of at least 1¼" (3 cm).

Meeting Individual Needs

Simplify Students may not have the forethought to carve clay without wanting to restore it.

Challenge Encourage students to continue developing their skills by carving simple forms. If students work on their own, they should carve soft materials and use wire clay tools only. At home, students might obtain permission to carve a bar of soap using a paper clip, ruler, or tongue depressor.

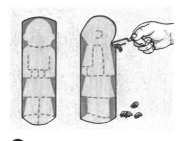

The sculpture in picture B was carved by a North American Indian artist. It is a Kachina doll given to a Hopi child. A Kachina doll is a symbol for a spirit in nature that can teach a lesson. For example, a Kachina doll may have a design that stands for the beauty of flowers or the strength of a bear.

You can practice carving a person. Make a thick **cylinder** of clay. Keep all of the forms close to the body. Plan where you will carve away the clay by drawing guidelines. Carve slowly. Remove just a small amount of clay to show a person.

B **Unknown, *Hopi Kachina Doll,*** ca. 1900. Courtesy of Arrowsmith's, Prescott, Arizona.

C

135

Extensions ▼

Language Arts Suggest that students write about being a carver. Have them describe the tools, materials, and steps they took to complete their sculpture. Have them conclude with a paragraph about how it felt to carve a sculpture.

Literature Link
• *The Storyteller,* Joan Weisman. (S)
• *Pueblo Storyteller,* Diane Hoyt-Goldsmith. (A, I)
• *Pueblo Boy: Growing Up in Two Worlds,* Marcia Keegan. (I)

RESOURCES

Large Reproductions
   Double Grandmothers, Frey, 24

Overhead Transparencies
   Cabinet, Weitz, 6
   Family Group, Moore, 19

 CD-ROM
   3, *Artists at Work,* Lesson 3

Assessment Masters
   Find Out About Art, 20

CLOSE

Assess

2 Guide students to:
   • lightly mark clay to suggest a waistline (about midpoint) and a head on opposite sides of the cylinder (front and back views).
   • lightly mark lines for carving arms, hands, legs, and feet, keeping forms thick and close to the body.

3 Have students begin carving clay in an upright position using the wire loop of the paper clip like a cheese cutter. Encourage them to remove (subtract) clay to develop the form on all sides. Remind them to make the feet broad and flat so the sculpture will stand up.

4 As students work, stress that it is not easy to correct a mistake when carving wood or stone. Gluing or putting the carved parts back on a form is difficult; the parts usually break off again. This is one reason carving must be planned and done slowly.

1 Place the artwork on cardboard squares. Discuss it in relation to development of forms from all views and evidence of thoughtfulness in carving. Have students describe differences between carving clay and a very hard material.

2 Review concepts and vocabulary terms. Stress that students should never carve materials with any sharp tool (in or out of school) unless they are taught by an adult.

Independent Research

Have students look for examples of carved sculpture in their community, including elements in architecture. Others might research sculpture by Native Americans or folk artists. Museums of natural history, art museums, and art schools might acquaint students with varied media, processes, and types of sculpture.

PREPARE

Objectives

Students will:
- be aware of styles of artwork (sculpture) created by twentieth-century African-American artists.
- demonstrate their ability to plan and create an artwork independently using media and a theme of their choice.

Vocabulary

sculpture	*escultura*
portrait	*retrato*
environment	*medio ambiente*
assemblage	*ensamblage*

Setup

Arrange materials and supplies cafeteria-style. During this lesson and the next, students should work as artists do in a studio, getting and returning materials with a minimum of supervision, working thoughtfully, and resolving problems.

Materials

oil-based clay

several sizes and colors of paper

scissors

paste

several drawing media (crayons, markers, oil pastels)

newspapers and paper towels

A Richard Howard Hunt, *Construction*, 1958. Bronze and steel, 20 1/2 x 18 x 12" (52 x 46 x 30 cm). Hirshhorn Museum and Sculpture Garden, Smithsonian Institution, Washington, DC (Gift of Joseph H. Hirshhorn, 1966).

B Richmond Barthé, *Paul Robeson as Othello*, 1975. Bronze, 20" (51 cm) tall. Photograph: Armando Solis.

Every person who creates art has special ideas to explore and express. In this lesson, you see sculptures by African-American artists. Each artist works in his or her own way.

Richard Hunt created the sculpture in picture A. He creates many large sculptures for parks and outdoor areas. Richard Hunt says his 136

sculpture combines ideas from nature and from the environment of big cities.

Richmond Barthé created many sculptures about people. He loved the theater and opera. He often created portraits of actors and singers. The portrait in picture B shows a well-known singer of opera.

TEACH

Engage

1 Discuss the concept that many artists develop special interests. Sometimes they explore one subject or theme, such as family memories, in a variety of art media. Or they become interested in one kind of art, such as sculpture or printmaking, and explore different subjects and themes.

2 In this lesson and the next, students will choose their own ideas and materials for a project and show they can work on their own, as artists do.

Explore

1 Discuss the lesson, emphasizing that artists develop an individual style. **A** has form qualities that lift and move out into space like birds rising from the ground. The metal is welded from rods and pitted shapes of metal that have a strange bonelike quality. The artist, who lives and works in Chicago, says his ideas come from seeing old or weathered materials in scrap yards, streets, and vacant lots. He also looks for beauty in natural forms such as birds in flight and plants growing.

2 In **B**, artist Richmond Barthé demonstrates his skills in portrait sculpture. He also created sculptures of human figures in poses that express loneliness, weariness, or energy. He loved the theater and created sculptured portraits of famous actors. Paul Robeson, shown here, was one of the first African Americans to achieve international fame as both a Shakespearean actor and a singer for musicals and opera.

3 Guide students to see and discuss **C** by Betye Saar. Her found object sculpture grew from her interest in collecting materials that remind her of her childhood or of people and past events. She and her daughter Alison have worked together on special projects and exhibited their sculpture together.

4 Explain that all of these artists learned to plan their own projects and create original art.

Create

1 Set the stage for students to work on a project of their choice. Explain how they will obtain and return materials (for example, by rows or tables) or have them make their own rules to follow.

Extensions ▼

Social Studies Have students do library research on the art of a particular ethnic or cultural group. You might have them focus on North American artists.

Literature Link
• *African American Art For Young People: Volume 1*, Samella Lewis. (A, I)

(C) **Betye Saar, *Bittersweet (Bessie Smith Box)*,** 1974. Assemblage, 14 3/4 x 20 x 2 1/2" (37 x 52 x 6 cm) open. Courtesy of the artist.

The sculpture in picture C is an assemblage by Betye Saar. An assemblage is made from objects or materials the artist finds. This sculpture is inside a box that you can open or close.

Betye Saar likes to collect and save very old objects for her sculpture. Her ideas come from memories of her own life. When she creates a sculpture, she chooses objects that have a similar meaning.

When you look at artworks, you can think about the artists who made them. You can imagine why the artist made them. Why do you think these artists work in different ways?

137

RESOURCES

Large Reproductions
Self-Portrait, Marisol, 18
Bear's Lair, Markovitz, 1
Baboon, Picasso, 5

Overhead Transparencies
Flute Player, Nigeria, 7
Nimba Headdress, West Africa, 14

 CD-ROM
3, *Artists at Work*, Lesson 3

Assessment Masters
My Own Museum, 17

---

2 Make sure the class is quiet. Have them imagine they are working independently in their own studios as artists do and think of their own idea for the artwork, using their imagination, memories, or special interests. They might create sketches if they wish. While they work, they should thoughtfully plan the use of lines, textures, and other design qualities.

3 Ask students to obtain their materials. Circulate during the work period. Enhance the studiolike atmosphere by playing the role of a visitor to the student's studio. Ask for permission to visit for a moment. Then ask open-ended questions such as, "I see you are a sculptor. What can you tell me about your artwork?"

4 Remind students they can continue work during the next lesson.

CLOSE

Assess

1 Ask students to look at their work and consider what they wish to change or add during the next class. If they would like opinions about their progress, have them gather for brief conversations. Compare this process to an artist who might ask other artists for opinions. Stress the idea that opinions may differ, and artists decide for themselves whether an opinion is helpful.

Cleanup

1 Ask students to demonstrate their knowledge of cleanup procedures by returning tools and unused materials in an orderly, efficient manner.

PREPARE

Objectives

Students will:
• understand that some artists express their basic values through their art and their lif
• express their interests and demonstrate their skills in art.

Vocabulary

sculptor   *escultor(a)*
studio   *estudio*
print   *grabado*

Setup

See Lesson 59. Before students begin, discuss and refine procedures for distributing and collecting materials.

Materials

oil-based clay

several sizes and colors of paper

scissors

paste

several drawing media (crayons, markers, oil pastels)

newspapers and paper towels

A Elizabeth Catlett in her studio.

B Elizabeth Catlett, *Homage to My Young Black Sisters,* 1969. Cedar, 71 x 14" (180 x 36 cm). Courtesy of the artist.

Elizabeth Catlett, shown in picture A, is a sculptor. She carves wood and stone. She works with metal too.

Elizabeth Catlett made her first carving when she was ten years old. She carved a bar of soap. Her parents thought she should do more artwork. They encouraged her interest in art.

Elizabeth Catlett studied art in college. Later, she became a teacher of art. She creates art in her **studio**, or workplace, at home in Cuernavaca, Mexico. Her husband,

138

Francisco Mora, is one of Mexico's well-known printmakers.

In picture B, you see two views of a sculpture Elizabeth Catlett carved from wood. Many of her artworks show women and children. Her art expresses the struggles of African Americans for freedom.

TEACH

Engage

1 Discuss students' experiences in getting to know artists, their individual interests, and where and how they work. Using what they have learned during the year, discuss students' individual interests in art.

2 Explain that many artists discover their own interests in subjects or types of work when they are in school or creating art at home. Students will learn about one of these artists today.

Explore

1 In **A**, guide students to see the studio in which Elizabeth Catlett is working. The sculpture she is working on is placed on a sculpture stand with a turntable so she can work on and see all sides of the work. Amplify on the idea that the artist's early love for sculpture led her to study art and a career teaching art in college.

Meeting Individual Needs

Simplify Some students may be unable to sustain work on the project started in Lesson 59. Have these students work on a second artwork using the same media but a different idea or the same basic idea but a different medium.

Challenge Suggest that students develop a title and short paragraph about their work describing why they chose their project.

2 Guide students to see that **B** shows two views of a sculpture by Elizabeth Catlett. One arm is raised to express the idea of young women striving to reach their goals. The curved forms suggest the graceful beauty and strength of the human form.

3 The artwork in **C** reflects the artist's love for children and the freedom of expression all children should enjoy. Help students appreciate that this print and others were created by carving into a flat, thick piece of linoleum. This process is related to carving and to the art of printing learned from her husband, Francisco Mora.

C Elizabeth Catlett, *Baile (Dance)*, 1970. Linocut, 18 x 30" (45 x 76 cm). Courtesy of the artist.

There is one main idea in Elizabeth Catlett's art and in her life. She says that "artists should work for peace, love and equal opportunity for everyone."

Elizabeth Catlett also creates prints. One of her prints is shown in picture C. She creates her prints by carving lines and shapes in blocks of wood or linoleum. This print shows children dancing.

Have you ever seen an artist at work in a studio? An artist's studio has art tools, materials and a place to store artwork.

What kind of art do you like to create? What ideas do you like to express in your artwork?

139

INTEGRATING THE CURRICULUM

Extensions ▼ ▼

Social Studies Discuss the importance of interest, skill, and study in every career, using Elizabeth Catlett's achievements as one example of a career. Ask students to develop a report that tells about something they love to do, do well, and how (with study) it might become a career.

Movement Have students work in pairs, with one serving as a coach and the other serving as the model. Ask each model to choose one of the figures in **C** and assume the same pose. The coach must help the model, checking details such as the tilt of the head, position of arms and fingers, and overall gesture of the body. Complete the activity by having students reverse roles as coaches and models. For variation, have students use dance or pantomime techniques known as mirror imaging. One student initiates movements or gestures and the other tries to duplicate these with little or no delay.

Literature Link 📖
- *Walt Disney: His Life in Pictures,* Russell Schroeder. (I)
- *Bill Peet: An Autobiography,* Bill Peet. (I)
- *Self-Portrait: Trina Schart Hyman,* Trina Schart Hyman. (I)

CLOSE

Create

1 Explain that students will continue working on their projects from the last lesson and should begin by deciding how to improve or complete the artwork. Suggest ways to continue independent work (described under Meeting Individual Needs).

2 Have students gather materials in an orderly, thoughtful manner. While students work, encourage them to reflect on their ideas, uses of materials, and decisions about design. Circulate and respond to questions in a way that contributes to a studio environment, offering unobtrusive guidance as needed.

3 As students finish, have them return materials and tools.

Assess

1 Discuss some of the artwork. Ask volunteers to share reasons for their choices of ideas and subject or theme. Encourage comments about design and special uses of media. Guide students toward an awareness of individual styles and approaches to creating art (imaginative, expressive, realistic).

Reminder

Preview the next lesson. Have supplies on hand to mount two-dimensional work, or encourage students to bring in any three-dimensional art that might be considered for the end-of-year art show.

RESOURCES

Large Reproductions
Double Grandmothers, Frey, 24

Overhead Transparencies
Parade, Lawrence, 12

 CD-ROM
3, *Artists at Work,* Lesson 3

Slide Set
Singing Head, Catlett, 30

Assessment Masters
My Own Museum, 17

PREPARE

Objectives

Students will:
• understand that artists exhibit their best work for many people to see.
• discuss their reasons for selecting a particular artwork for a class or schoolwide art show.

Vocabulary

art gallery	*galería de arte*
mount	*paspartú*
art show	*exposición de obras de arte*

Setup

Plan an exhibit and have students invite parents and friends. Determine how many works can be accommodated to ensure that each student is included. Use the chalkboard to print an example of a completed label. Two forms are presented.

Materials

folders of work and three-dimensional work from previous lessons

pencils

rulers

lined index cards, writing paper, or duplicated forms for labels (See Setup)

paste

damp paper towels

colored paper, larger than artwork, 1 per student

B   Erika Wade. Photograph: Christophe Tcheng.

A   Scott Miles, MFA Student. Courtesy of Savannah College of Art and Design, Georgia.

The artists in these two photographs are getting ready for an **art show**. The artist in picture A has selected some of his best work for a show. The artist in picture B is deciding where to hang her sculpture in an **art gallery**.

How do you think these artists choose their work for an art show? Why do you think artists have shows of their works? Have you seen art shows? Where? What kind of art did you see?

140

TEACH

Meeting Individual Needs

Discuss the kind of art students might create during the summer using inexpensive items such as grocery bags, socks, empty boxes, and paste made from flour and water. Discuss places where students can see artworks such as parks, shopping centers, art festivals, museums, and galleries. You might prepare a list of suggested art activities and the names and telephone numbers of museums or community centers. Have students take the list home or enclose it with the last report card.

Engage

1 Focus on **A** and **B**. Ask students to notice how these artists have gathered their artwork together. One artist is deciding what to include in an art show. Guide students to describe how the artwork in **B** is displayed.

2 Discuss art shows in which students have been exhibitors or observers and why the shows were presented.

Explore

1 Focus on **C**. Explain that the students will select one example of their best work for a show. Discuss specific reasons (or criteria) for students to think about as they select their work: originality, creativity, imagination, and care in planning or using materials.

2 Distribute art folders. Have students select the artwork to be mounted and gather in small groups to discuss reasons for their choices. Collect the folders when decisions are made.

3 Using **D**, introduce the concept of mounting and labeling artwork. Demonstrate how students will be centering their work on top of a piece of paper. The border of the background paper will look like a frame around the picture.

4 Explain that students will be using this technique to prepare their own work for an art show.

Courtesy of Worcester Art Museum School, Worcester, Massachusetts.

 C

Your class can have an art show. Everyone will have some artwork in the show. Choose your best artwork. How will you decide which is your best?

Learn to put your best pictures on a mount. A **mount** is a large sheet of paper. Paste your picture on top of the mount so the picture has a border. Follow the steps shown in picture D and listed here.

1. Center the picture on the mount. Be sure the borders are even. Trace around the corners of your picture.

2. Put paste on the back of your picture. Wipe your hands. Then paste the picture down.

3. Make a label for your artwork. Write neatly.

My name is _____.
My work is _____.
It is titled _____.
I learned _____.

D

141

INTEGRATING THE CURRICULUM

Extensions ▼

Language Arts Examples of labels for artwork.

Name: _____
Kind of art: _____
Title:_____
I learned: _____

My name is: _____
I made: _____
The title is: _____
I learned: _____

Literature Link

- *Visiting the Art Museum,* Laurene Krasny Brown and Marc Brown. (I)
- *Aunt Lilly's Laundromat,* Melanie Hope Greenberg. (S)
- *Jamaica Louise James,* Amy Hest. (S)

Create

1 Distribute materials for mounting the artwork, except labels. Have students center their artwork on top of the mount, or background paper. The top and bottom edges of the mount may be the same width, or ideally, the top and side edges are about the same width and the bottom edge is wider.

2 Ask students to take turns helping each other center and mount their work. They can check alignment by using a ruler or a strip of paper with tick marks. As one student holds the artwork on the mount, the other lightly traces around it to make guidelines for pasting down the artwork. After the lines are drawn, turn the mount face down on newspaper to keep it clean.

3 Have students apply paste on the back of the artwork near the edges and in the center like an X. They should wipe their fingers clean and then help each other turn the mount face up and paste the work inside guidelines.

CLOSE

Assess

1 Distribute cards or paper for labels (or duplicated forms). Remind students these should be neat and legible. Assist with spelling as needed. If the label is pasted below the artwork on the mount, guide students in this step. If students have three-dimensional art to display, place the label near the work.

2 Ask students to hold up their mounted work to preview the art show. Have them give reasons for their choices.

3 Explain when and where you will display the work. Ask for volunteers to help cover boxes with paper so sculpture can be arranged in a multilevel display. Discuss arrangements for parents to see the show.

Reminder

Make sure all art supplies and tools are checked, cleaned, and ready for use next year. Order supplies early so they will be ready when school begins.

RESOURCES

Large Reproductions
 Sun Mask, Native American, 12
 Self-Portrait, Marisol, 18
 Summer, Arcimboldo, 13

Overhead Transparencies
 Camels, Graves, 11
 Bactrian Camel, China, 11

CD-ROM
 3, *Artists at Work,* Lesson 2

Assessment Masters
 My Own Museum, 17
 I Like Art, 22
 Labels for Artworks, 23

Art Safety

Study these safety points. Follow other safety points your teacher tells you about.

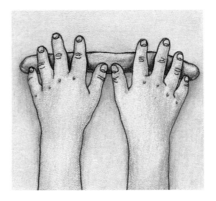

1. If you feel sick or have a health problem, tell your teacher. For example, if you have a rash or scratches on your hands, you should not use clay until your skin heals.

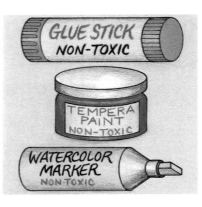

2. Make sure your art materials have a label that says nontoxic. Nontoxic means the materials are safe to use. Read any words that say "Caution." Find out what the words mean.

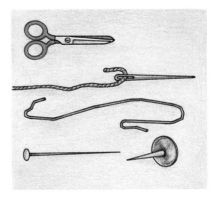

3. Some tools and materials have sharp points or edges. Use these very carefully. Make sure the sharp objects are pointing away from your body.

4. Use all art tools and materials with care. Keep the tools and materials away from your eyes, mouth and face.

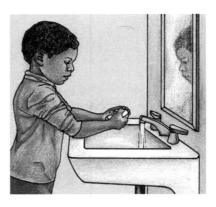

5. Learn to use art materials neatly. After art lessons, wash your hands to remove paint, clay or other materials. Always wash your hands before you eat food.

6. If you drop or spill something, quietly help to clean it up. A wet floor or a floor with pieces of art materials on it can be unsafe to walk on.

Ways to Help in Art

Study these examples of ways to help in the artroom. What else can you do to help?

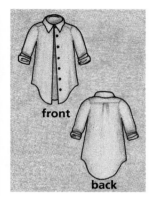

1. Help everyone get ready for art. For some lessons, wear an apron or an old shirt. Button the shirt in the back and roll up the sleeves.

2. Help to clean up. Stack and put art materials away neatly. Wash brushes and store them with the hairs pointing up.

3. Share art tools and materials. Save materials you can use again. You can recycle some materials to create art.

4. Save your artwork in a portfolio. Write your name and the date on all of your sketches and other work. This will help you see and know what you are learning.

5. When you discuss art, listen carefully. Think about what people say. Ask thoughtful questions. In art, there is usually more than one answer to questions.

6. Learn to use art words. Use a dictionary or the glossary on pages 148-154 to find the meaning of art words. Why should you learn art words?

143

Artists and Artworks

145

Glossary

angle (ANG-gul). A bend in a line or shape.

animation (an-ah-MAY-shun). Cartoon-like movies with separate pictures drawn by artists. A camera is used to record each picture on a long piece of film or tape. When the film or tape is shown very quickly, you see motion.

appliqué (ah-plee-KAY). Artwork that is made by sewing pieces of cloth onto a cloth background.

arch. A curved or pointed shape in a building; makes an opening in the wall or holds up the roof.

architect (AR-ki-tekt). An artist who designs buildings.

architecture (AR-ki-tek-chur). The art and science of planning buildings and environments for people.

art. A form of visual communication and expression.

art gallery (art GAL-uh-ree). A building, or a space in a building, where artworks are shown.

art media (art MEE-dee-uh). Art materials and their special qualities.

art museum (art myoo-ZEE-um). A building where artwork is shown and carefully saved.

art show. A display of artwork that people are invited to see.

asymmetrical (AY-suh-met-rick-ul). Artwork that looks balanced when the parts are arranged differently on each side.

authentic (ah-THEN-tik). An artwork that is real and not a copy or fake.

balance (BAL-ens). Arrangement in which the parts seem to be equally important or interesting.

batik (bah-TEEK). A process of using wax and dye to make pictures or patterns on cloth.

blend. To mix things together smoothly.

brushstroke. A definite mark or textured area made by using a paintbrush.

canvas (KAN-vus). A strong cloth on which artists create paintings.

carving (KARV-ing). A way to make sculpture by cutting away or subtracting a material such as clay, wood or stone.

center of interest (SEN-ter of IN-trist). The main, or first, thing you notice in an artwork.

ceramics (sir-AM-iks). The art of making objects of fired clay.

city planner (SIT-ee PLAN-er). An artist who helps people design parts of a community or city.

cityscape (SIT-ee-skayp). Artwork that shows a city.

clothing designer (KLOH-thing de-ZI-nuhr). An artist who creates the designs for handmade or manufactured clothing. Often called a fashion designer.

collage (koh-LAHZH). Artwork made by pasting pieces of paper or other materials to a flat surface.

color scheme (KOL-er skeem). A plan for using colors (see **warm colors, cool colors**). The color wheel can help you understand some ways of planning colors.

construct (kon-STRUKT). To create an artwork by putting materials together.

contrast (KON-trast). A great difference between two things. A light color contrasts with a dark color.

cool colors. Colors that remind people of cool things. Varieties of blue, green and violet.

craft. Skill in creating things by hand. Artwork created carefully by hand.

craftsworker. A highly skilled person who creates artwork by hand.

crayon etching (KRAY-on ECH-ing). A process of scratching through one layer of crayon to let another layer of crayon show.

crayon resist (KRAY-on re-ZIST). An artwork created with wax crayons or oil pastels, then covered with watercolor paint. The paint resists, or rolls away from, the wax or oil.

creative (kree-A-tiv). Able to make things in a new or different way.

culture (KUL-chuhr). The special beliefs, customs and way of life of a group of people.

cylinder (SIL-in-dur). A tall round form.

design (de-ZIGN). A plan for arranging the parts or elements of an artwork. An artwork which has a planned arrangement of visual elements.

detail (de-TAYL or DEE-tayl). A small part.

diagonal (di-AG-uh-nul). A line or edge that slants or tilts.

dilute (di-LOOT). Adding a liquid, such as water, to another liquid to make it thinner or flow more easily. A diluted paint flows and lets you blend colors.

distance. (see **perspective**)

dye. A colored liquid that stains the threads in a fabric.

easel (EEZ-uhl). A piece of furniture that is used to hold a painting so it is easy to see and work on.

edge (edj). A line that helps you see a shape, ridge or groove.

elements of design (EL-uh-ments of de-ZIGN). Parts of an artwork that an artist plans, regardless of the subject matter. These elements are line, color, texture, value, space and shape.

enlargement (en-LAHRJ-ment). A picture that has been made larger.

expression (ex-SPRESH-uhn). A special look that communicates a feeling. An expression might be happy, sad, angry or tired.

exterior (ex-STEER-ee-ur). Outside, or the outside of a form.

facade (fah-SAHD). The whole front wall of a main entrance to a building.

fiber (FI-bur). A long, thin material such as thread, yarn or string.

fiber art (FI-bur art). Artwork created from long, thin, thread-like materials.

fiber artist (FI-bur AR-tist). An artist who uses long, thin, thread-like materials to create artwork.

fired (FI-erd). Made hard by great heat (such as a clay object).

149

form. An element of design. Forms are three-dimensional, such as a cube, sphere or cylinder. They have height, width and thickness. Forms are not flat.

formal design (FOR-mal de-ZIGN). Artwork that has parts arranged the same way on both sides. Also called symmetrical design.

found object (found OB-jekt). Materials that artists find and use for artwork, like scraps of wood, metal or ready-made objects.

geometric (jee-oh-MEH-trik). A shape or form that has smooth, even edges.

graphic designer (GRAF-ik de-ZIGN-er). An artist who plans the lettering and artwork for books, posters and other printed materials.

historical landmark (his-STOR-i-kul LAND-mark). A building or place of importance in history.

horizontal (hor-i-ZON-tal). A straight line that lies flat.

hues (hyooz). The common names for colors, such as red, yellow, blue, orange, green, violet.

illustrate (IL-uh-strayt). The act of drawing a picture to explain something.

illustrator (IL-uh-stray-ter). An artist who creates pictures for books, magazines and the like.

imaginative (ih-MAJ-in-a-tiv). Creating a mental picture of something that is unlike things one has seen.

industrial designer (in-DUS-tree-al de-ZIGN-er). An artist who designs cars, dishes, toys and other products that are made in factories.

informal design (in-FOR-mal de-ZIGN). Artwork that looks balanced when parts are arranged differently on each side. Also called asymmetrical design.

interior (in-TEER-ee-ur). The inner part of something.
interior designer (in-TEER-ee-ur de-ZYN-er). An artist who plans the inner spaces of a building.

intermediate colors (in-ter-MEE-dee-it KOL-ers). Colors that are made from a primary and a secondary color (red-orange, yellow-orange and so on).

kiln (kill). A special oven or furnace that can be heated to a high temperature.

landmark (LAND-mark). Something (a building, a statue, a park) that is easy to see and important to people in a community.

landscape (LAND-skayp). Artwork that shows an outdoor scene.

landscape architect (LAND-skayp AR-ki-tekt). An artists who plans parks, gardens and other outdoor spaces.

line. The path created by a moving point (as one drawn by a pencil point).

mask. An artwork used to cover and disguise a face.

media (see **art media**)

model (MOD-el). A person who poses for an artist. Also, small artwork that shows how a larger artwork might look.

monochromatic (mon-oh-kroh-MAT-ik). A color scheme that uses several values of one color, such as light blue, blue and dark blue.

monoprint (MON-oh-print). A print that is usually limited to one copy.

mosaic (moh-ZAY-ik). Artwork made with small pieces of colored stone, glass or the like.

motion (MOH-shun). Movement, either real or visual.

mount. Paper or cardboard on which a picture is pasted to make a border.

movement (MOOV-ment). Going from one place to another or a feeling of action in an artwork.

mural (MYOOR-uhl). A large painting or artwork, usually designed for a wall.

negative shape or **space** (NEG-eh-tiv shape or space). Shapes or spaces surrounding a line, shape or form. (see **background**)

neutral colors (NEW-tral KOL-ers). In artwork, neutral colors are brown, black, white and gray.

oil paint. A greasy paint that does not mix with water.

original (oh-RIJ-en-al). Artwork that looks very different from other artwork, not copied.

overlap (o-ver-LAP). Overlap means that one shape looks like it is behind another one.

palette (PAL-it). A tray-like surface for mixing colors.

papier-mâché (PA-per MA-shay). A process of making forms by using paper and a diluted paste.

patterns (PAT-terns). Designs that have repeated elements such as lines, colors or shapes.

perspective (pur-SPEK-tiv). Artwork in which the spaces and distances between objects look familiar or "real."

photogram (FOH-toh-gram). A record of shadows that is made on a special photographic paper. The paper is manufactured so that it changes when light strikes the surface.

photograph (foh-TOH-graf). A picture made by using a camera. (see **photography**)

photography (foh-TOG-ruh-fee). The art and science of making a picture by using a camera and film that records the light from a scene.

picture alphabet (PIK-chur AL-fah-bet). In a picture alphabet, the shape of each letter is also a picture.

portrait (POR-trait). Artwork that shows the likeness of a real person.

pose (pohz). A special way to stand or sit.

positive shape or **space** (POZ-ih-tiv shape or space). Shapes or spaces that you see first because they contrast, or stand out from, the background.

primary colors (PRI-meh-ree KOL-ers). Colors from which other colors can be made: red, yellow and blue. (In light, the primary colors are red, green and blue.)

principles of design (PRIN-suh-puhlz of de-ZIGN). Guides for planning relationships among visual elements in artworks. Principles of design are balance, rhythm, proportion, pattern, unity and variety.

prints. Artworks created by pressing sheets of paper on top of an inked design to make copies, or prints, of the design.

151

product designer (PROD-ukt de-ZYN-er). An artist who plans the appearance of factory-made products, such as cars, furniture, kitchen ware.

proportion (pro-POR-shun). The size, location or amount of something as compared to that of another thing (a hand is about the same length as a face).

pulled threadwork (puld thred-work). Creating open patterns in cloth by pulling out threads.

radial (RAY-dee-al). Lines or shapes that spread out from a center point.

related colors (ree-LATE-ed KOL-ers). Colors that are next to each other on a color wheel, such as yellow, yellow-green and yellow-orange. Also called analogous colors.

relief sculpture (ree-LEEF SKULP-chur). Sculpture that stands out from a flat background.

repeat (ree-PEET). Using the same design element over and over again to create a pattern.

resist (ree-ZIST). A material, like wax, used to cover or protect a surface from liquids.

Romanesque (roh-man-NESK). An architectural style used for early Christian churches. These buildings have thick walls and small windows with round arches.

rubbing. The process of moving a tool, such as a crayon, across a surface. An artwork made by putting paper over a textured surface and rubbing a crayon on the paper.

scroll (skrohl). A long roll of paper or cloth illustrated with pictures or lettering. Scrolls were used before the invention of books.

sculpture (SKULP-chur). Three-dimensional artwork made by carving, modeling or joining materials.

seascape (SEE-scape). Artwork that shows a scene of the sea or ocean.

secondary colors (sek-on-dayr-ee KOL-ers). Colors that can be mixed from two primary colors; orange, green, violet.

self-portrait (self-POR-tret). A self-portrait is an artwork that shows the likeness of the person who created it.

shade. A color mixed by adding black. A dark value of hue (dark blue).

shading. Slight or gradual changes in the lightness or darkness of a color or value.

shadow (SHAD-oh). A dark area where there is little light.

shape. The outline, edge or flat surface of a form (a circle or square).

similar designs (SIM-uh-lar de-ZYNZ). Designs that have something in common, but are not exactly alike.

sketch (skech). A drawing that is made to record what you see, explore an idea or to plan another artwork.

space. An empty place or surface, or a three-dimensional area in which something exists.

spirit mask (SPIR-it mask). A mask that is created for use in spiritual ceremonies, not just for fun.

stained glass (staynd glass). Pieces of colored glass that are fitted together like parts of a puzzle, then framed to make a window.

stencil (STEN-sell). A paper or other flat material with a cut-out design that is used for printing. Ink or paint is pressed through the cut-out design onto the surface to be printed.

still life. An artwork that shows nonliving things, such as books, candles or the like.

stitchery (STICH-er-ree). Artwork which is made by using a needle and thread or yarn to create stitches on cloth. A stitch is one in-and-out movement of a threaded needle.

storyboard. A set of words and sketches that are made to plan a motion picture or television program. Each sketch shows a scene in the story.

streamlines (STREEM-linz). Graceful, curved lines and edges. The lines look as if they would help something move easily through air or water.

studio (STOO-dee-oh). The place where an artist creates artwork.

style (stile). An artist's special way of creating art. The style of an artwork helps you to know how it is like or different from other artworks.

subtle (SUH-tle). Very slight changes in color, form or other visual elements.

subtractive (sub-TRAK-tiv). Cutting or taking away the surface to create the form, as in carving wood.

surface (SUR-fiss). The outermost, or exposed, layer of any form or material.

symbol (SIM-bul). Lines, shapes or colors that have a special meaning. A red heart shape is a symbol for love.

symmetrical (sim-MET-ri-cal). Artwork that looks balanced because parts are arranged in the same way on both sides.

symmetry (SIM-et-ree). Parts arranged the same way on both sides.

technique (tek-NEEK). A special way to create artwork, often by following a special procedure.

tactile (TAK-til). The way something feels when you touch it, such as rough or smooth. (see **texture**)

tempera paint (TEM-per-uh paint). A kind of chalky paint that has water in it. Often called poster paint.

texture (TEKS-chur). The way an object feels when it is touched. Also, the way an object looks like it feels, such as rough or smooth.

three-dimensional (THREE-di-men-chen-al). Artwork that can be measured three ways: height, width, depth (or thickness). Artwork that is not flat.

tint. A light value of a color such as pink. A color mixed with white.

tradition (tra-DISH-en). The handing down of information, beliefs or activities from one generation to another.

transparent (trans-PAR-ent). Possible to see through clearly, such as a clear piece of glass.

two-dimensional (TWO-di-MEN-chen-al). Artwork that is flat and measured in only two ways: height and width.

unity (U-ni-tee). The quality of having all the parts look as if they belong together or work together like a team.

value (VAL-yu). The lightness or darkness of a color (pink is a light value of red).

variety (vah-RI-it-ee). A principle of design. Using different visual elements, such as colors, shapes or lines to create interest in an artwork.

vertical (VUR-ti-kul). Lines that go straight up and down.

viewfinder (VIEW-find-er). A sheet of paper with a hole in it. You look through the hole to "frame" a scene. On a camera, the lens that lets you see what you will photograph.

visual rhythm (VIS-yu-al RITH-um). Visual rhythms are planned by repeating shapes, colors and other visual elements so that they remind you of rhythms in music or dance.

visual symbol (VIS-yu-al SIM-bul). Lines, colors and shapes that stand for something else, as a red heart may stand for love.

warm colors (warm KOL-ers). Colors that remind people of warm things. Varieties of red, yellow and orange.

warm hue. (see **warm colors**)

watercolor paint (WA-ter-KOL-er paint). Special paints that are mixed with water and look like a watery, transparent ink or stain.

weaving (WEEV-ing). Artwork created by locking together separate strands of material (as yarn or thread).

Index

Reference

Contents

Philosophy and Features of the Program

Aims and Content

The content of *Adventures in Art* is related to the major aims of contemporary art education: developing an informed appreciation of art and life-long interest in learning more about art. Content is also based on four interrelated disciplines in art.

Perception

Perceptual awareness is a major emphasis throughout *Adventures in Art*. Aesthetic perception means that students are **using their senses, knowledge and feelings** to find meaning in their environment and in works of art. (The opposite term, anesthetic, refers to anything that blocks sensory experience, or disconnects thoughts, feelings and sensations.)

Lessons and activities at each level **heighten students' abilities to see** subtle variations in lines, colors, textures and other visual elements. Students are also taught to look for underlying structures in what they see, such as patterns, proportions, and types of balance.

Aesthetic perception and vocabulary development are emphasized at every level of *Adventures in Art*.

Creative Expression

Within each level of the program, students are encouraged to **develop their own ideas** for artwork, to refine them and to **use media expressively.** Art activities are appropriate to students' levels of development.

At every level, students explore a **variety of media** and two-and three-dimensional art forms. Lessons in *Adventures in Art* show students how to **apply design concepts** to expressive and imaginative themes and to everyday life.

Culture and Heritage

Adventures in Art introduces students to **artistic traditions from around the world—**Europe, the Americas, Africa, and Asia. The artistic achievements of **women and ethnic groups** are well-represented, along with important international influences and trends.

Beginning at Levels 1-3, *Adventures in Art* acquaints students with **diverse styles** and interpretations of **common themes** in art such as animals, people, and the environment.

At Levels 4-6, contrasts and comparisons of art are continued, with greater emphasis on the **cultural, personal, and practical functions of art**, past and present.

The role of **art in contemporary life** is examined at every grade through lessons that focus on art in the community, careers in art, and the uses of art in business.

Informed Judgment

Within *Adventures in Art,* students are introduced to the processes of perceiving, analyzing, interpreting, and judging their own and others' art. The ability to make informed judgments about art requires **critical thinking skills** as well as knowledge about art.

At Levels 1-4, students are introduced to a **"conversational model"** for discussing art with a focus on contrasts and comparisons of design qualities, media, subjects, and other features of their own and others' artwork.

At Levels 5 and 6, students are formally introduced to the **steps in art criticism**, including the use of criteria for judgment. In each lesson, students evaluate what they have learned. **Evaluations at the end of each unit reinforce these skills.**

Structure of the Program

The four content areas of the program are interrelated. Learning in each content area supports and improves learning in another, as suggested in the diagram on the facing page.

This innovative structure, unique to *Adventures in Art,* not only incorporates content for a sound, discipline-based program but helps you (and students) grasp the interdependence of ideas and skills in art.

Continuity and Variety Within Each Level

The sequence of lessons within each level has been carefully planned to accommodate the interests, skills, and abilities of students.

Lessons are **varied** to sustain curiosity, yet **organized in units** so that concepts and skills introduced in one lesson can be reinforced and expanded upon in other lessons.

Each year of the program is organized around four units. In the first unit, perceptual awareness, design and the artistic process are emphasized so that students are prepared to apply these concepts and skills during the year.

The lessons are varied at each level so that students expand their understanding and apply their knowledge in new ways. The lessons also provide **background information** for students who have not had previous levels of the program.

Concepts and skills acquired during the first unit are explored in greater depth and complexity in the second unit. In the same way, content from the first part of the year is applied to new contexts in the remaining units.

Sets of lessons within each unit are also **grouped by topic**—such as color, animals in art, or sculpture—allowing students to examine a particular topic or theme in depth. For example, a series of lessons may have a common theme such as landscape paintings. Specific lessons might focus on subtopics—ways artists portray times of day, seasons, and weather. Teachers and students might choose among the suggested studio experiences for the general theme in the series of lessons.

Continuity and Variety Across the Years

Learning is also reinforced and developed across the years. *Adventures in Art* challenges students to make **new connections among concepts** and **refine their skills** as they progress from one grade to the next.

Major topics introduced in early grades are reintroduced in later grades, but the topics are studied in greater depth or in new contexts and relationships.

Among the topics studied in this spiral-like structure are **design elements and principles**, specific **art forms** (drawing, painting, printmaking, graphic design, sculpture, architecture, crafts, and product design) and **subjects** in art (such as the human figure, landscapes, the city, and animals). Other topics in the spiral-like structure are identified in the titles of lessons and in the Scope and Sequence charts on pages Introduction 20–24.

Student-Centered Teaching Strategies

Throughout the program, teaching methods are designed so students who have **different styles of learning** are challenged to excel in art. In addition to the emphasis on visual perception, students experience art through hands-on activities with materials and by using other sensory channels—tactile, kinesthetic, and spatial.

Critical and creative thinking are also an integral part of each lesson. **Cooperative learning and problem-solving** are encouraged. Students learn to be part of "a community of learners." Evaluations of learning are varied to fit the objectives for the lesson as well as the overall progress of each student.

Relating and Integrating Aims and Content

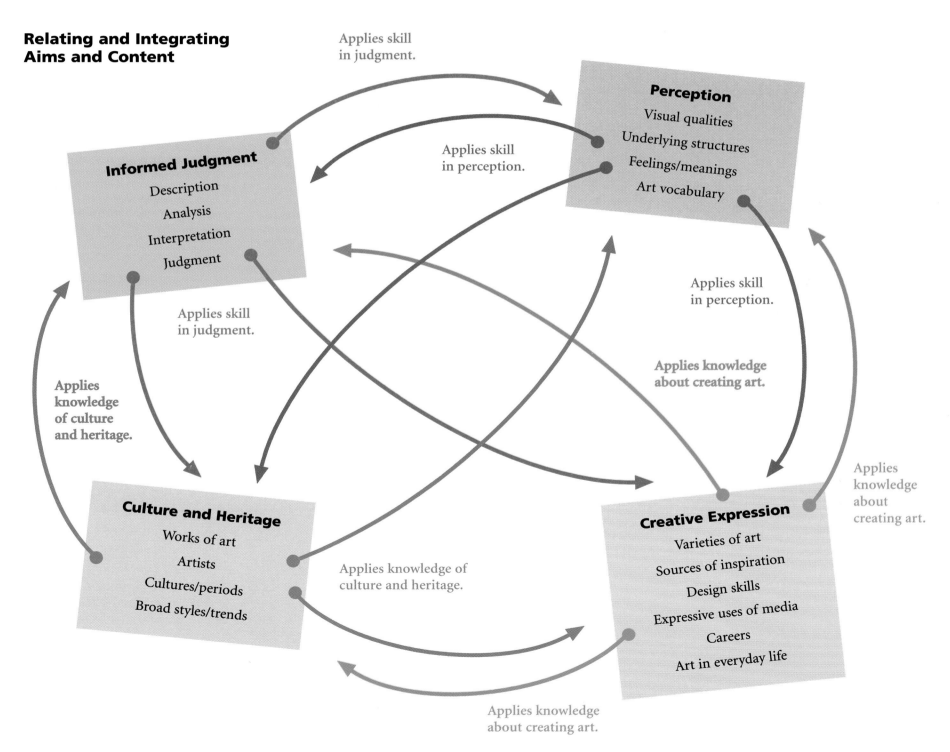

Applies skill in judgment.

Perception
Visual qualities
Underlying structures
Feelings/meanings
Art vocabulary

Applies skill in perception.

Informed Judgment
Description
Analysis
Interpretation
Judgment

Applies skill in perception.

Applies skill in judgment.

Applies knowledge about creating art.

Applies knowledge of culture and heritage.

Culture and Heritage
Works of art
Artists
Cultures/periods
Broad styles/trends

Applies knowledge of culture and heritage.

Creative Expression
Varieties of art
Sources of inspiration
Design skills
Expressive uses of media
Careers
Art in everyday life

Applies knowledge about creating art.

Applies knowledge about creating art.

Scope and Sequence K-6

	Kindergarten	Level 1	Level 2
Perception Identify and respond to: • sensory qualities and design elements in the environment and artworks • underlying structures and design principles in the environment and artworks • aesthetic qualities in the environment and artworks	Introductory lessons focus on multi-sensory experiences so that students develop associations between what they see and sensations of touch, motion, sound, and the like. Students learn to perceive and begin to name visual elements such as colors, textures, and shapes.	Students learn to identify visual elements such as lines, colors, shapes, textures and their sensory qualities. Perceptual skills and a vocabulary for art are developed through role-playing, physical movement, visual searches, and game-like activities.	Students learn that observations of the environment—changes in weather, animals, the city by day and night—have inspired adult artists and can be sources of inspiration for their own art. Perceptual skills and a meaningful art vocabulary are developed with an emphasis on imagination, sensory awareness, and visual recall.
Creative Expression Acquire skills to: • develop ideas for art based on varied sources • refine and extend ideas for visual expression • apply design elements and principles • use two- and three-dimensional media for expression	Students create art based on their personal experiences as well as imagination. Some ideas are developed by exploring media. Basic skills in cutting, pasting, and using clay are introduced through activities that encourage experimentation and growth in skills.	Students create art based on imagination, personal interpretations of nature, familiar places, and activities with family or friends. They learn to plan their use of visual elements to create original artworks. They acquire basic skills in using media for drawing, painting, collage, printmaking, sculpture, and other three-dimensional art.	Students continue to create art based on imagination and personal interpretations of varied themes related to their environment, activities, and events. They learn to make intentional choices of lines, colors, and other visual elements. They use familiar media in new ways and combinations to create two- and three-dimensional art.
Culture and Heritage Know about: • artworks and artistic traditions in different cultures and times • varied influences on styles and types of artwork, past and present • art careers and resources in the community • types and functions of art in everyday life	Students are introduced to a variety of two- and three-dimensional artworks from different cultures and eras. They learn to think about artworks as the outcome of a process that involves many decisions by the artist. They learn to identify art in their home, school, and community and to think of their own creative work as art.	Students see and discuss styles and types of artwork from varied cultures and periods. They learn about places to see art in their community, where artists work, and the kinds of art they create. Students become aware of art in everyday life through lessons on architecture, clothing, and other environmental arts.	Students continue to learn about varied styles and types of art with greater emphasis on the cultural origin and functions of artworks. They expand their knowledge of types of artists, where they work and reasons people create or display art. Lessons on architecture and product design and related art forms focus attention on art in everyday life.
Informed Judgment Be able to: • describe sensory and design qualities in artworks • analyze themes and technical qualities of artworks • interpret the expressive meaning in artworks • cite criteria and offer reasons for judgments of artworks	Artworks are selected and introduced in ways that stimulate curiosity and interest in seeing them. Through structured questioning and conversations, students gain confidence in discussing features of artworks such as the subject matter, design qualities, and overall mood or feeling.	The process of looking at art is presented as an enjoyable and integral part of learning about art. Students learn to perceive and describe the subject matter, visual elements, and mood in their own art and the artwork of adults. Students learn to express their opinions about art and to respond thoughtfully to others' opinions.	Students continue to learn that looking at art is an enjoyable and thoughtful process. They perceive, compare, and contrast the subject matter and visual elements in artworks. They learn that judgments about art—their own and others'—should be based on features they perceive in the artwork.

Level 3	Level 4	Level 5	Level 6
Students become aware of and develop an ability to use different vantage points, e.g., side views, top views, for observing objects and scenes. They learn to perceive and describe subtle visual qualities such as lines, colors, shapes, textures, and patterns within the natural and constructed environment.	Increased visual awareness is developed as students learn to identify subtle visual qualities in the natural and constructed environment and artworks. Greater emphasis is placed on perceiving implied paths of movement, interactions of colors and shapes, moods of places at different times of day, and in different seasons or weather.	Students learn to apply and refine perceptual skills developed in earlier grades. They learn to identify and analyze more subtle and complex visual relationships such as how light affects our perception of colors, textures, and forms, and how we perceive space and distance.	Students apply skills and concepts acquired at previous levels. They learn to perceive more subtle interactions among qualities of color, line, shape, and other visual elements. They continue to perceive and identify underlying structures such as proportions, visual rhythms, and types of balance in the environment.
Students continue to create art based on imagination, recall, and observation. They learn to portray details, depict action, use different vantage points, and plan their use of visual qualities to express an idea, feeling, or non-verbal message. Activities develop flexibility and problem-solving skills in two- and three-dimensional media and art forms.	Students create more complex works of art and give greater attention to their expressive intentions. They use design concepts for specific purposes, such as color to express a mood and repetition to create visual rhythms. Efficient and inventive uses of media are emphasized to build skills and flexibility in creating expressive two- and three-dimensional art.	Students continue to create art in order to express what they see, know, feel, and imagine. They make sketches to develop ideas and to try out design concepts. Skills in using media are developed by problem-solving and planned experiments. Multi-step techniques are introduced in two- and three-dimensional media.	Students continue to use sketching and related techniques to generate ideas for artwork. They learn to incorporate principles of design such as balance, unity, and variety to create two- and three-dimensional artwork. Lessons emphasize efficient yet expressive uses of media.
Artworks are selected to help students appreciate themes, types, and styles of art. The functions, cultural origin and relative age of selected artworks are studied along with methods and reasons for creating art. The concept of living with art is developed in lessons about crafts, architecture, and related art forms.	Students contrast and compare the functions, cultural origin, and relative age of artworks from different eras. Students learn that creating and studying art can be a life-long pursuit or career. Lessons about innovative and traditional art reinforce the concept of art as a "living heritage" that brings artistry to daily life.	Students learn about selected styles and historical changes in art of the Americas as well as world cultures. They learn more about careers in art, the use of computers for art, and the role of museums. Lessons acquaint students with art in public places and 20th century art forms such as photography and filmmaking.	Students expand their knowledge of styles and eras of art, with a greater emphasis on recurrent themes—nature, myths, human needs, and activities—and the accomplishments of individual artists. They study the artistry involved in crafts, architecture, and mass-produced images such as posters and films.
Positive attitudes about the process of looking at art are reinforced and extended. Students learn to perceive more subtle visual qualities in their own art and the art of adults. They use art terms to describe, analyze, and interpret visual qualities of artworks. They develop skill in citing specific features in an artwork to explain their judgment of it.	Students learn to be art "detectives" who seek answers to questions such as: How is the work planned (designed)? What materials were used? What ideas or moods are expressed? Students learn that thoughtful judgments about art are related to qualities in the work and how they can be interpreted.	Students are introduced to the steps in art criticism: perceiving and discussing the artwork, analyzing it, and interpreting the "visual evidence." They learn that criteria for judgments of their own and others' work should be relevant to its general style or purpose—expressive, imaginative, representational, abstract, or functional.	Looking at art continues to be an integral part of the total process of learning about art. Students apply their skills in art criticism to analyze and judge works of art based on their perception of the subject, visual design, artist's use of materials, and other specific criteria.

Within any group of students you are likely to find a range of skills, abilities, and interests. Because children develop at different rates, it is essential to adapt instruction to meet individual needs.

Understanding Children's Artistic Development

A major goal of art education is to cultivate students' abilities to create original and expressive art. The artwork students create reflects their overall level of development—intellectual, emotional, social, physical—as well as their prior opportunities to create art. In order to set appropriate expectations and guide artistic growth, you should be familiar with the typical stages of development in creating artwork.

The illustrations and stages of artistic growth outlined below focus on skills in portraying space, proportions and movement or action. Each stage is typical of many children at a particular grade level; however, it is not unusual to find a range of developmental levels within a class or within the work of a single student during a year.

Similar variations can be expected in students' ability to respond thoughtfully to artwork. At each stage of development, some students will have greater interest and skill in responding to art than in creating art (or the reverse). Each lesson in *Adventures in Art* offers guidance to build on students' strengths and to expand the value they find in art experiences.

Responding to Students' Special Needs

All students benefit from a balanced program of creative work in two-and three-dimensional media and from the opportunity to try out different approaches to art. It is essential for you to encourage original thinking and authentically creative work.

Creativity is one of the most important considerations as you teach art and adapt instruction to meet the needs of individual students and groups who have special needs. Artwork that is traced, copied from adult art, or based on photocopied outlines does not involve the student in significant creative activity and should not be encouraged.

Talent plays a role in students' interest and skill in art, just as it does in other subjects. During the elementary and middle school years, encourage varieties of artistic accomplishment and understanding, not just skill in representational drawing. It is unwise to identify a few students as "class artists," or to compare students' artwork in a manner that discourages further interest. Always respect each student's unique effort and insights about art.

Students who are **blind or otherwise visually impaired** can respond to discussions of artwork, especially themes portrayed in artworks that are related to the student's experience. In studio work, provide materials to create tactile, kinesthetic artwork—clay, textured paper and cloth, small boxes or wood blocks to arrange.

Stage 1. Usually Grades K-2. *Children begin to create visual symbols to represent figures such as people, houses, trees. The figures often seem to "float" in space. Proportions are related to the importance of a feature in the child's experience. Movement is often suggested by scribble-like lines. Three-dimensional artwork reflects the level of prior instruction and practice in using media and the physical coordination students have developed.*

Stage 2. Usually Grades 1-3. *In picture-making, lines or borders are often used to represent the ground below and sky above. Figures may be placed along a line or at the lower edge of the paper. Proportions are shown through relative size—a house is larger than a person. Action is implied by the general position of lines and shapes, rather than subtle shifts in direction. Students who receive instruction will show general improvement in using three-dimensional media and applying design concepts as they work.*

Stage 3. Usually Grades 3-6. Students try out new ways to portray space in the pictures they draw and paint. These explorations often reflect remembered functional or logical relationships more than visual recall or observation. General proportions improve, as well as the use of diagonals to suggest action. Many students develop a strong affinity for three-dimensional work and are willing to try out new media and techniques that require several steps.

Stage 4. Usually Grades 4-6. In picture-making, students search for ways to portray recalled or observed space. Some students begin to use perspective to imply near and distant objects. Movement is suggested through more subtle angles and curves. Individual styles and preferences for two-or three-dimensional work become more evident, along with increased skill in applying design concepts to create expressive work.

Students who are **deaf or hearing impaired** respond slowly to verbal communication. Use nonverbal communication: Have students point out what they see or use pantomime to express responses. Present information through diagrams, charts and other visual aids. Non-verbal communication can be valuable for all students.

Students who are non-ambulatory or have otherwise **impaired mobility** may need to use alternate tools and materials for some activities. Rehabilitation specialists may help you solve unique problems. A number of special tools are available for students with physical impairments (scissors, a mouthpiece which holds a pencil or brush).

Students who are **developmentally disabled** often respond to art in a direct and insightful manner. They are often able to portray their ideas or feelings more successfully through art than through words. Simplify and separate into specific steps any especially difficult studio activities. Encourage independent thinking about the ideas to be expressed. (Discourage exact copies of any examples you have made). For more information on inclusion in the art classroom see *Exceptional Children, Exceptional Art: Teaching Art to Special Needs*, by David R. Henley (Davis, 1992).

Students **acquiring English** benefit from many of the same nonverbal teaching strategies already noted. Introduce the whole class to the arts and culture of the students. This will broaden the art background of all the students and help them communicate with each other.

Respect **cultural differences**. An important aspect of art education is learning about the arts of cultural groups. Identify individuals and groups in your community who can help familiarize students with unique cultural traditions in the arts and crafts. All students can benefit from learning about these examples of "living cultures" within their own community. Occasionally, parents or students may wish to have you offer alternative art lessons out of respect for their own cultural or religious values.

Learning styles of students differ because each person is unique. Many of the teaching methods you develop for students with special needs are likely to be just as valuable for other students or the whole class. Skilled teachers adapt their instruction to differences in learning styles by:

a) combining nonverbal and verbal communication,

b) offering concrete examples of abstract ideas,

c) providing "hands on" activities to make concepts vivid and give them personal meaning.

Notes on Teaching Art

To make the best use of the time devoted to art within the whole curriculum, your teaching must center on the student and also be goal-directed. Outlined below and on the next pages are general considerations in teaching art. More specific hints and suggestions for teaching "hands-on" studio projects are found on pages Reference 12–17. Additional suggestions for developing an appreciation of art are presented on page Reference 20.

Strategies for Teaching

Teaching should be based on methods appropriate to your students and the goals of the instructional process—the attitudes, skills, and knowledge that art education should develop. Some general teaching strategies are discussed below.

Nurturing Attitudes
Nothing creates positive attitudes toward art more effectively than your own positive attitude. Your enthusiasm and openness to learning about art should be evident to students. As you motivate, guide, and evaluate students' progress, keep these points in mind:

- Praise thoughtful and original responses. Never disparage a student's effort or artwork.

- Demonstrate your respect for each student's uniqueness and individual accomplishments in art.

- Show students that you regard learning about art as an adventure—a lifelong "voyage of discovery." Encourage this same attitude in students.

Developing Skills
Students acquire art skills by watching demonstrations, understanding why the skills are important, and having the opportunity to practice their skills in a variety of contexts. Keep these points in mind when teaching art skills:

- Anticipate the skills needed for an activity. Before you introduce a new art material or technique, always try out the steps and procedures students will use.

Photograph courtesy SchoolArts *and Paula Stevenson Hoglund, Appleton, Wisconsin.*

- Remember that in art, unlike many subjects, there often are several equally effective ways to interpret a theme, solve a problem or answer a question.

- Encourage development of skills by giving immediate praise to students, *while* they are displaying the appropriate behavior.

Teaching Concepts
Students' ability to master art concepts will vary in relation to their levels of development, prior instruction in art, and learning styles. In the early grades, always emphasize the specific, concrete, and practical meaning of concepts. In the upper grades, continue this emphasis but also introduce more abstract ideas (such as the principles of design).

- At all grade levels, provide visual examples of art concepts and terms. Point out familiar examples of the concepts (styles of art might be introduced by discussing clothing styles).

- At all grade levels, encourage students to apply their knowledge to new contexts and to their own creative artwork.

- Encourage role-playing, dramatization, and other ways of internalizing the meaning of concepts.

Strategies for Evaluation

Evaluation is an integral part of the teaching-learning process in art. General guidelines for evaluating students' growth in art are noted here.

Evaluating While You Teach
Important and subtle forms of evaluation occur while you are teaching.

- Focus on individual accomplishments—"Johanna's use of torn paper edges is inventive." "Tim has noticed the varieties of blue in this painting."

- Emphasize the process of learning, not just the final result—"You are learning to use diagonal lines to show action in your drawings of people." "Many of you are learning to be good 'art detectives' when you look at an artist's work."

- Examine ways to solve specific problems—"We took a long time for cleanup today. How could we do a better job and take less time?"

- Reinforce appropriate, yet different answers to a question or solutions to a problem—"Beth's work shows how a rainy day looks. Larry's suggests the gloomy feeling of a rainy day. Kim's work reminds us that rain can bring rainbows."

Involving Students in Assessment
Authentic and valid evaluations of performance require adequate records of learning.

- Prepare portfolios so students can save all sketches along with incomplete and complete artwork. Always have students sign and date their work so you and they can search for evidence of progress. Portfolios can be made from brown wrapping paper, folded and trimmed to hold the largest size of paper for artwork. See page Reference 14, "Keeping and Storing Portfolios," for tips on managing artwork.

- Storing and photographing three-dimensional work will help you and students contrast and compare their progress in creating two- and three-dimensional work. When you photograph artwork, prepare clear, large, name tags to place near each artwork. Place three to five artworks and name tags together in an alphabetical grouping. Take an instant-type photograph of the artworks for a record. Save small works in low, covered boxes.

- Have each student keep a sketchbook and journal. In the lower grades, you might write students' comments about their own work. Sketches and notes written by students provide insight into the quality of thought, imagination, and interest in art.

- Self-evaluation checklists can be used in the upper grades. Effective checklists combine questions related to the learning process as well as specific criteria for a lesson.

- Schedule conversational interviews with individual students at the end of each unit. Keep brief notes so you and the student can share information with parents or other mentors.

- Written assignments and reports should be introduced in connection with language arts or social studies and should always be evaluated for evidence of learning in art.

- Reproducible Assessment Masters, created for use with the *Adventures in Art* program, can be used as informal assessment activities, for assessment before starting a lesson or unit, or as the wrap-up of a unit or lesson. Completed activity sheets can become part of each student's portfolio as records of progress and for review at parent conferences.

Interpreting and Reporting Progress

Some general criteria for evaluating students' development in art are outlined below. A simple report for a student's progress in art, based on these criteria, is shown above.

Evaluating Attitudes. Positive attitudes toward art are an important indication of learning. Look for increasing evidence that the student:

- enjoys creating art and takes pride in having original ideas.

- is willing to experiment, try out new ways of using design elements and media.

- enjoys looking at art, sharing observations with others in class discussions.

Sample Evaluation Form

Name _____

Year _____
_____

Progress in Creating and Responding to Art

Is learning to:
____ find own ideas for art
____ refine, modify ideas for art
____ use media effectively
____ perceive, respond to varied art forms
____ interpret artworks
____ judge the value of art experience

Special Comments:

Learning About the Artistic Heritage

Is learning how and why:
____ artists find ideas for their work
____ artists refine, modify their ideas
____ artists use media
____ experts and others respond to art
____ experts and others interpret art
____ experts and others judge art

- respects informed judgments about art that may be different from his or her own.

- appreciates varieties of art and voluntarily seeks out opportunities to learn more about the subject.

Evaluating Skills. Individual growth in art skills will be reflected in students' responses to specific lessons. Look for evidence that the student:

- generates original ideas for artwork with increasing confidence and ease.

- shows increasing flexibility in using design elements and media to express ideas in art.

- perceives visual qualities and describes them with appropriate terms.

- makes good inferences about expressive meanings in artworks.

- offers reasoned judgments about art.

Evaluating Knowledge. The knowledge students gain about art can be evaluated by examining their artwork and the quality of their insights in discussions of art. You can also assess the knowledge students have acquired in relation to specific lesson objectives and more general understanding, such as:

- Art is created by people around the world for different purposes and in different styles.

- Artists of the past and present have explored a variety of subjects, design possibilities, and uses of media.

- Our judgments and interpretations of art should be informed by what we see in the work and by reflection on its meaning.

- Artistic skills—one's own and those of artists—are developed through practice, experimentation, and openness to new ideas.

Grading. Many school districts now require a written record of student progress during the year or the assignment of a letter grade in art. Most art educators believe that grades are potentially harmful to students' self-confidence and enjoyment of the process of learning about art. For this reason, written comments on each student's progress are recommended instead of letter grades.

To keep records of progress, most teachers invent a simple code that summarizes each student's response to specific lessons. This code can be of help when guiding students and making more formal reports on progress. One of many possible codes is outlined below.

S = Satisfactory progress. The student is achieving within the range of his/her ability.

+ = Special insight, progress, or achievement by this student.

I = Incomplete (Reminds you to follow up).

R = Review needed (Reminds you to offer extra guidance).

Guiding Creative Expression

When you teach students to create art and to understand how adult artists create art, follow the methods outlined below. Related methods are used in *Adventures in Art*.

Nurturing the Artistic Process

The methods presented here are based on research into the artistic-creative process and how students can become confident, skilled creators of art.

Photograph courtesy SchoolArts *and Paula Stevenson Hoglund, Appleton, Wisconsin.*

Generating Ideas

Introduce students to varied sources of ideas for art and provide vivid motivations. Many of the sources of inspiration that artists use are also appropriate for children. For example:

- Stimulate visual-kinesthetic recall of **personal experiences** at home, with friends, in the neighborhood, or on trips. "What is your favorite place to go after school? Is it inside or outside? What makes this place so special?"

- Observe the **natural environment** (changes in skies, seasons, weather, plant and animal life) and the constructed environment (the neighborhood, the view out the window, details such as telephone lines, fire hydrants).

- Explore imaginative, **fanciful ideas**: future-oriented or dream-like images, impossible or unusual combinations of ideas. Try topics such as "A city under the sea," "Transportation in the Year 3000," "My dream house."

- Introduce **broad themes** and topics that encourage reflection and personal interpretations. "A beautiful world," "Happiness," "Ugliness," "Carelessness."

Developing Ideas

Guide students to try different ways of visualizing what they see, feel, imagine, know. Many of the methods artists use to explore ideas visually are also appropriate for students. For example:

- Encourage **sketching** and the creation of small models to explore an idea or to try out design possibilities.

- Emphasize the process of **thinking** about the design of artwork—the planned used of visual qualities to express an idea. "What colors might help you express the idea of a spooky house at night?" "What lines and shapes might you use?"

- Cultivate **problem-solving skills**, flexibility in thinking. "What would happen if you made this shape brighter or larger?" "Are there other ways to create a repeated pattern?"

- Have students try out the same idea in **two- and three-dimensional media**; for example, draw a favorite animal, then create a sculpture of it in clay.

- Encourage students to consider the **purpose or function** of their work—especially when creating crafts, posters, or other useful art forms.

Exploring Media

Provide guided practice in using media. Learning to draw, paint, and use other art media requires time and guidance.

- Introduce and reinforce **procedures** for the efficient use of art tools and materials such as crayons, scissors, paste, clay.

- Stress **cause-effect thinking** about media—"Why should you wash and blot your brush before you choose a different color of paint?"

- Encourage **experiments** to allow for discovery of expressive possibilities. For example, contrast the effect of paint on wet paper with the effect on dry paper.

Evaluating the Process

- Focus on each student's **unique achievements**. "John has invented many textures for his sculpture. Maria's sculpture captures the sleek smoothness of a seal's body."

- Emphasize the **process of learning** about art, not just the final result. "You are *learning* to plan the lines, colors and shapes in your work."

- Encourage **self-evaluation**. Ask students to identify facets of their work which are visually effective. Have them consider how they might improve their work through additional effort or practice.

Displaying Artwork

Every school and classroom should have some space reserved for the display of student art as well as art reproductions or original art by local artists. Consult your local art museum or arts council for guidance on displaying original works by professional artists.

There are two major time periods during which you may wish to plan special exhibits and related activities to focus attention on the art program.

Youth Art Month. March has been designated Youth Art Month by the National Art Education Association. At this time, teachers in all schools are urged to make parents and the community aware of young people's enthusiasm for art and ways they are engaged in creating and studying art.

End-of-year exhibits. Near the end of the year, students are best able to demonstrate what they have learned. The last lesson in

Photograph courtesy SchoolArts *and Karen Watson-Newlin, Verona, Wisconsin.*

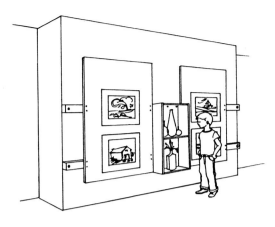

each level of *Adventures in Art* provides an opportunity for students to participate in a class art show. Coordinate the date with other teachers for a school-wide art show and invite parents and friends.

Recommendations. Displaying artwork should always be included as part of the process of learning about art. To emphasize what students are learning, include a title for the display, a brief description of relevant art concepts or skills, and artworks from many students or the entire class. In grades 1 to 6, it is not wise to feature only the work of talented students or to hold art competitions or award prizes.

For inexpensive mats around artwork, use large sheets of construction paper. Multi-level displays are best for sculpture and other three-dimensional work. Cover cardboard cartons with solid colors of paper. Stack the cartons to create shelves and pedestals for the work.

Extending the Learning Process

Help students appreciate relationships between their own creative art activity and the larger world of art.

- Emphasize the **variety of sources** artists use for their work—personal experience, observations of nature, imagination, and so on.

- Examine artists' sketches, preliminary studies, and variations on a theme. Emphasize the idea that a work of art may be the result of **several stages of exploration** and development.

- Invite **local artists** to discuss how they work, their preferred media, and idea sources. Arrange field trips to visit artists' studios or show films of artists at work.

- Set up **art learning centers**. Reserve part of the classroom for independent work by small groups or individual students. Arrange the space for studio work, study of artworks, or a combination.

Safety in the Art Class

Every teacher must be safety-conscious and teach students to be aware of safety. A few of the most common safety points are noted here.

- Always use art supplies that are certified to be **nontoxic** for children. The label should be coded AP (approved product) or CP (certified product).

- Teach **safety procedures**. Do not use glass containers or allow students to use blade-type paper cutters. Keep scissors closed when they are not in use.

- Dust-producing materials (chalk, water-based clay) should not be used by children

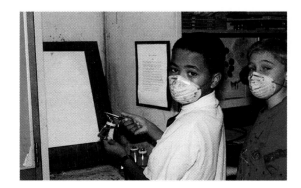

with dust allergies. **Provide substitutes** and a dust-free area for them to work.

- Provide a "towelette"—one-half of a damp paper towel—to help **keep hands clean** and reduce skin irritation. Do not allow children to place art tools or materials in their mouths or ingest them. Students who have open sores or skin rashes should not use materials that will irritate the skin or contribute to an infection.

- Have the **school kiln checked** annually for wiring, venting, other safety points. Do not attempt to fire clay unless you are trained in firing procedures.

- For **detailed safety guidelines**, write to: National Art Education Association, 1916 Association Drive, Reston, Virginia, 20191-1590.

Two additional sources of information are: Charles S. Qualley, *Safety in the Artroom.* Worcester, MA: Davis Publications, Inc., 1986 and Michael McCann, *Health Hazards Manual for Artists.* 3rd ed., NY: Lyons Books, 1985.

A voluntary testing and labeling program has been developed by the Art and Craft Materials Institute (ACMI, 715 Boylston St., Boston, MA 02116) to help teachers select art materials.

Products meeting ACMI standards are labeled in one of the three ways shown below. In general, products with the square health label should not be used by children under the age of twelve.

MEETS PERFORMANCE STANDARDS

Safety labels approved by the Art and Craft Materials Institute (ACMI)

Photograph courtesy School Arts *and John Richards, South Euclid, Ohio.*

Introducing Media and Techniques

An orderly system for introducing creative art activities promotes good work habits. This section offers additional information about art media and techniques that you can introduce in the elementary grades. Always introduce these media and techniques in ways that emphasize their creative use by students.

Technique Tips

Here are some brief descriptions of media suitable for students, and some hints on organizing the classroom for "hands-on" activities.

Drawing

Some of the most common drawing media are shown below. Chalk, pastels, and charcoal produce dust and should not be used by students who have dust allergies. Felt-tipped markers (water-based), oil pastels, and inks can produce stains that are difficult to remove from clothing. Permanent felt markers contain solvents that can irritate the lungs, eyes, and skin. They are not recommended for children.

Crayons. Use the point, side and flat surfaces. Mix colors. Try out hand movements such as a twist, dot and dash, and vary the pressure applied.

Photograph courtesy SchoolArts *and Vicki Evans, Houston, Texas.*

Oil pastels or wax-based pastels. Colors are easily mixed and blended without dust. Textures can be built up and lightly engraved with a pointed tool (pencil, paper clip).

Chalk or pastels. Use these like crayons, blending colors together with a tissue, erasing areas, applying chalk to damp paper or paper covered with diluted liquid starch.

Felt markers (water-based). Apply to damp or dry paper. Use a wet brush on top of lines, shapes, or textures to create effects similar to watercolor painting.

Pencils (graphite or colored), charcoal. Use techniques outlined for crayons. Blend with a tissue or eraser to create light and dark areas.

Inks. Introduce in the upper grades. Experiment with various pen points as well as brushes and sticks for drawing on wet and dry paper.

Painting

The most common paints for use in elementary schools are tempera and acrylic paint. Fingerpaints are best reserved for use in preschool or for simple monoprints. The following paints are not recommended as safe for use in grades 1 to 6: oil paints, house paints, lacquer, shellac, spray paints, many specialized craft stains, metallic paints, fabric paints.

Tempera. Available in several forms: powder (mix with water), compressed cakes (dry or semimoist) and liquid. When dry, tempera has a dull, chalky appearance.

Acrylic. Available in jars. It has a pudding-like consistency, can be diluted with water and when dry, has a slight sheen. Can be used to create glazes—semi-transparent layers of colors (allow each layer to dry)—or to create rich textures.

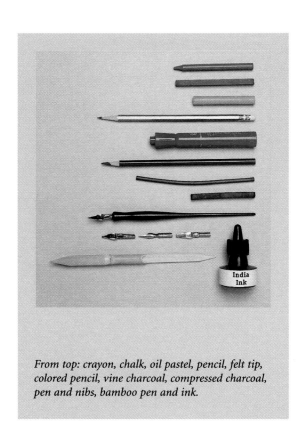

From top: crayon, chalk, oil pastel, pencil, felt tip, colored pencil, vine charcoal, compressed charcoal, pen and nibs, bamboo pen and ink.

Space savers

No sink? Use two buckets

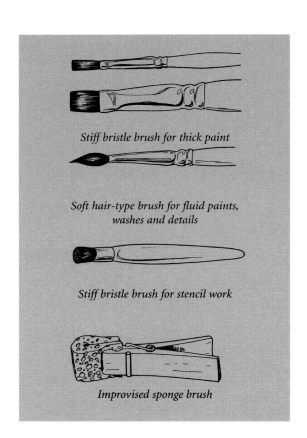

Stiff bristle brush for thick paint

Soft hair-type brush for fluid paints, washes and details

Stiff bristle brush for stencil work

Improvised sponge brush

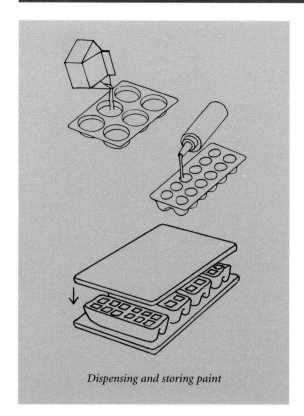

Dispensing and storing paint

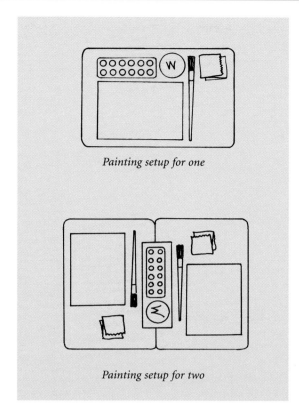

Painting setup for one

Painting setup for two

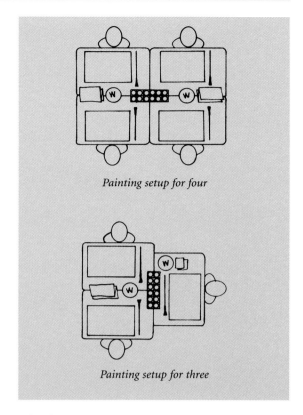

Painting setup for four

Painting setup for three

Watercolor. Available in sets with a brush and slender box with hinged lid. The lid of the open box is used as a palette to mix colors. Must be used with a wet brush. The transparent, fluid quality should be emphasized when introducing this medium.

Brushes. Have several sizes available.

Use nested plastic containers for water. Wash brushes in warm soapy water, rinse, blot, and store them upright. If a sink is not available, put clean water in one bucket, collect used water in another.

Tips and Techniques. Place powdered paint in an empty milk carton. Add water to make a thick, creamy paint. Close the carton and shake.

Use a funnel to dispense paint from large jars into nozzle-type containers. For a typical lesson, each student needs about two teaspoons each of white and yellow paint, one teaspoon each of other colors.

Students with impaired mobility should have non-spill paint containers with a brush for each color. Students with spastic disorders can be aided by placing Velcro strips on the drawing media or brush. Strap a second Velcro strip around the palm of the hand.

The desk arrangements shown above can be used for many activities. For easy cleanup, cover desks with newspapers. Use smocks or large shirts, sleeves cut at the elbow, to protect clothing.

Mixed Media and Processes
Many artists have explored techniques that combine media for drawing, painting, and collage. Only a few of the many possibilities are suggested here.

Collage. French for pasted paper. This art form developed most fully in the twentieth century. In addition to combining cut or torn paper with other media such as paint, artists may adhere fabrics and natural and constructed objects to a flat surface.

Crayon resist. Apply wax crayons or oil pastels with firm pressure; then use a wide brush and well-diluted tempera or ink to cover the entire paper. The paint or ink will resist or roll away from the wax crayon.

Tempera resist. Create a painting with thick tempera. Leave some areas of the paper unpainted. Allow the painting to dry; then apply waterproof India ink to the entire surface. Allow the ink to dry, then wash the entire painting under running water, gently rubbing it with a soft brush.

Chalk or oil pastel with tempera. Create a tempera painting. Allow it to dry. Add details and additional colors with chalk or oil pastels.

Tempera wash and ink. Dampen the entire paper with water. Brush diluted paint on the paper. Allow colors to blend and mix. Blot the "pools" of paint and study the contours or edges of shapes for an idea. Begin outlining some of the shapes with pen and ink. Add final details when the paint is dry.

Tissue collage "paintings." Cut or tear colored tissue paper for a collage. Brush diluted white glue on the entire paper and on each shape as it is glued down. Allow colors from tissue paper to bleed and blend.

Crayon and tempera "etching." Cover the paper with a thick layer of crayon or oil pastels (light colors). Cover the paper with a second layer of black tempera paint that has been mixed with a drop or two of liquid soap. Allow the paint to dry. Use a nail or other pointed tool to scratch away the black layer.

Manila
Oatmeal
White drawing
White typing bond
Newsprint
Bogus gray
Colored construction
Butcher or mural

PASTE

Distributing paste

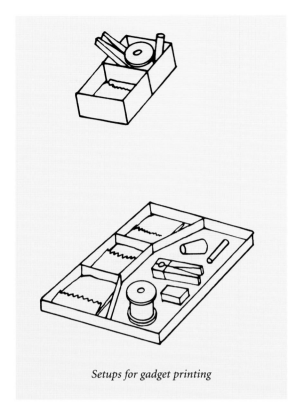

Setups for gadget printing

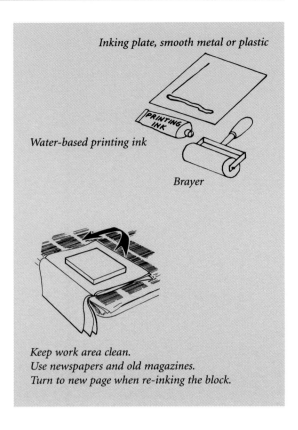

Inking plate, smooth metal or plastic

PRINTING INK

Water-based printing ink

Brayer

Keep work area clean.
Use newspapers and old magazines.
Turn to new page when re-inking the block.

Papers, Adhesives, Scissors

Provide a variety of **papers** for drawing, painting, and other artwork. Some of the most common are shown here.

For economy, order large jars of **paste**. For each student, put about one teaspoon of paste onto a small sheet of paper. Place the sheets on a tray to distribute quickly.

Use **white glue** in nozzle-type dispensers for three-dimensional work. Provide a "towelette"—one-half of a damp paper towel—to wipe hands while working.

Glue sticks are especially valuable for collage and for mounting artwork for display.

Round-tip scissors are best for grades 1 and 2 and for students who have severe coordination problems. Left-handed scissors should be available for left-handed children who are still learning to cut. Spring-type scissors may be helpful to students with physical disabilities.

Keeping and Storing Portfolios

Use large folders, one for each student's two-dimensional artwork. Place names on one edge, using the same location so the stack can be easily sorted and distributed.

Make sure names are on each artwork and that the artwork is dry when it is placed in the folder. (Place work unstacked on a counter or the floor until it dries.)

Teach students to sign and date their work, including sketches and incomplete work so the work can be referred to in evaluations.

Kerry Smith

ART FOLDERS

Save artwork

Printmaking

For most activities, two to four students can share supplies. Printing blocks can be made from a variety of materials—thin foam plastic from meat trays, layers of cardboard, clay slabs.

Create prints on an absorbent paper like newsprint, or try printing on colored or unusual papers such as a printed photograph in a magazine.

For **gadget printing**, use divided frozen dinner trays or trimmed milk cartons. To make stamp pads, place a thin sponge or layers of damp paper towels flat into the carton or divider and spread one teaspoon of paint on the top layer of the pad.

For **relief printing**, it is best to use water-based ink, brayers (special rollers), and a smooth inking plate, like a cookie sheet. Roll the brayer through the ink to cover it with a thin, even coat of ink. Then roll the inked brayer across the block to be printed. To make a substitute printing ink, mix several drops of glycerine (from the drugstore) with one tablespoon of thick tempera paint. Apply ink with a brush if brayers are not available.

Sculpture

Sculpture can be explored with a variety of media. Always consider the creative possibilities of the materials you have at hand.

Paper, clay, wood, wire, and combinations of these are appropriate at the elementary level. (Plaster is not recommended for grades 1 to 6 because it contains lime, a skin and lung irritant.)

Sculptural processes are usually grouped into four main categories: modeling, constructing/assembling, carving, and casting. Sometimes processes are grouped into two broader categories: additive and subtractive.

Clay. *Oil-based clay* is reusable and suitable for nonpermanent work. Place it in a warm area before the lesson to soften it. Cover desks with plastic mats or newspaper. Use tiles or 6 x 6" (15 x 15 cm) cardboard squares under the work.

Self-hardening or oven-bake clays are water-based, semipermanent, and suitable for sculpture (not for pottery containers).

Ceramic clay is water-based, and becomes permanent when fired in a kiln (a furnace-like oven). The fired clay can be decorated with glazes, then refired to make it waterproof. Use only nontoxic, lead-free glazes.

Photograph courtesy SchoolArts *and Shirley Jordan, Buena Park, California.*

Found objects. Cartons, tubes, plastic bottles, and other discarded objects can be used if they are clean and have no sharp edges. Assemble discarded items with white glue, tape, string, and rubber bands.

Paper. Stiff paper—construction paper or paper the weight of index cards—can be used to create a variety of three-dimensional forms. Some shaping techniques are shown below. Use white glue. To hold forms until the glue dries, use removable cellophane tape or paper clips.

Papier-mâché. Papier-mâché is made from a soupy mixture of wheat paste and paper. The paste-soaked paper becomes hard when it dries. Three methods are illustrated below. You must use nontoxic wheat paste. (Commercial wheat paste for wallpaper contains harmful chemicals and should not be used.) Newspapers can be used for armatures but all paper dipped in paste should be free of ink. (Newspaper ink is usually petroleum-based and can irritate skin.) Acrylic paint gives an excellent finish.

Wire and metal foil. Floral wire, pipe cleaners and stove-pipe wire can be bent and wrapped into sculptural forms. These forms can also be covered with papier-mâché or combined with string and straws.

When long wires are used, place corks or tape over the sharp pointed ends to prevent injury. Students should wear safety goggles and sit at a safe distance from each other. Metal foil can be embossed to create relief sculpture. Heavy-duty aluminum foil (kitchen-type) is best for grades 1 to 6. Heavier foil (36 gauge) sold in craft stores should be cut by the teacher. Put tape around the edges of the metal to prevent injury. Emboss the metal on a soft pad of newspapers or cloth.

Store artwork on trays

Clay tools and preparation

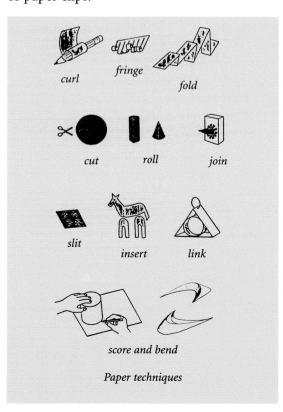

curl *fringe* *fold*

cut *roll* *join*

slit *insert* *link*

score and bend

Paper techniques

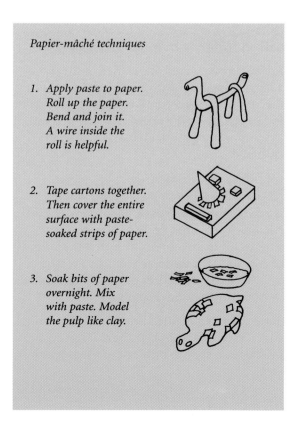

Papier-mâché techniques

1. *Apply paste to paper. Roll up the paper. Bend and join it. A wire inside the roll is helpful.*

2. *Tape cartons together. Then cover the entire surface with paste-soaked strips of paper.*

3. *Soak bits of paper overnight. Mix with paste. Model the pulp like clay.*

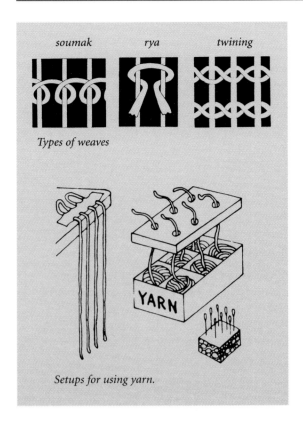

soumak rya twining

Types of weaves

YARN

Setups for using yarn.

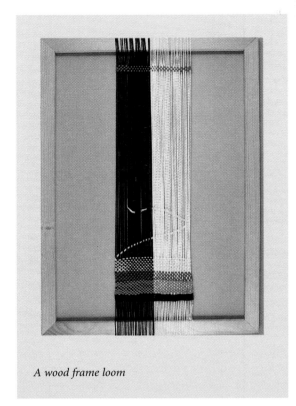

A wood frame loom

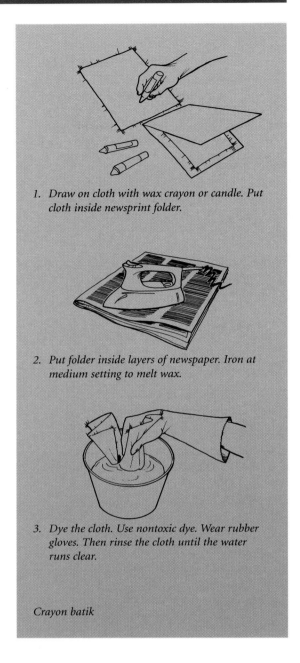

1. Draw on cloth with wax crayon or candle. Put cloth inside newsprint folder.

2. Put folder inside layers of newspaper. Iron at medium setting to melt wax.

3. Dye the cloth. Use nontoxic dye. Wear rubber gloves. Then rinse the cloth until the water runs clear.

Crayon batik

Fiber Arts

Fiber art is a general term for artwork created with thread, yarn, cloth and related materials. **Stitchery** is art created by sewing. Related arts are **embroidery** (fancy stitching), **appliqué** (stitching pieces of cloth to a background), **quilting** (stitching layers of cloth together to create a relief effect), and **soft sculpture** (a three-dimensional form).

Always provide guided practice in threading a large-eye needle with yarn, tying a knot at the end of the yarn, and making basic stitches in burlap. Stress the safe use of needles and the importance of making original, well-crafted designs.

Introduce **simple appliqué** with fabric pieces. Paste fabrics down before adding stitches. Display enlarged diagrams of basic stitches, knots and braids. Color-code the strands on the diagrams to match the strands of rope or yarn students will use. Provide step-by-step instruction until stitches, knots, or braids match the diagrams.

Store yarn in a divided box with holes from which yarn can be pulled. Store large-eye craft needles in a sponge or block of foam plastic.

To cut many lengths of yarn from a skein, wrap the yarn continuously around the back of a chair. Tape the yarn firmly to each upright edge of the chair. Cut the yarn near the tape. For shorter pieces, cut again near the other tape. For longer pieces, use two chairs, looping the yarn from one to the other. While students work, tape additional yarn to the edge of the desk.

Provide simple frame looms, yarn, string, and other fiberlike materials for **weaving activities**. Parents might help build looms similar to the one shown below.

Have students make small woven samplers to try out colors, textures, and patterns. Challenge students to weave wall hangings, table runners, belts, headbands, handbags, or baskets.

Allow time for practice and experimentation with various types of patterns and fibers (weft fibers can be long grass, thin sticks, ribbons, and the like).

Batik is dyed cloth with designs produced by the use of a wax or starchy resist medium.

The process is a traditional craft in Indonesia and parts of Africa.

In grades 1 to 6, tempera paints that stain cloth are a safe substitute for dyes, which can be harmful for students to use. Instead of using warm wax, which is also a hazardous medium, students should use a resist medium that can be removed with warm water, as described in specific lessons in *Adventures in Art*.

An alternative method, shown above, can be introduced if adults assume the responsibility for dyeing the cloth and using the warm iron.

Simple Light-Oriented and Photographic Media

Most children are fascinated by light and shadow. The process of developing a photographic image can be introduced through **blueprints or sun prints**. These are made on light-sensitive paper sold at nature shops and museums (for leaf prints). Check package instructions for procedures.

If **cameras** are available, introduce students to basic procedures for composing photographs and planning theme-based photographic essays.

Overhead projectors can also be used to explore light, color, and shadow. For example, collect a variety of natural and manufactured items that have unusual contours, open patterns, and transparent or translucent qualities. Have students place these on an overhead projector. Discuss the effects of the projected image.

For **handmade slides**, obtain plastic mounts for slides and blank 35 mm film (used to make "title" slides). Have students create slides using colored cellophane, felt markers, and tissue paper. Drawings and other materials must be on the inside "sandwich" of clear film and carefully placed in mounts.

Motion Pictures and Television

Adventures in Art introduces students to the arts of animated film and "flip" books to explore the illusion of motion. You can amplify these experiences by allowing students to create **handmade animated movies** by drawing on discarded movie film.

Soak the exposed film overnight in undiluted bleach to remove images. Rinse the film thoroughly and dry it. Use a rubber eraser or fine steel wool to lightly abrade the film. Draw on a 3' or 4' (1 m) piece of film with felt markers, pen and ink, or pencils. Use film-splicing tape to join film sections. Show the film with a taped sound track.

If equipment is available, have students produce **video programs**. Encourage them to develop original scripts. Emphasize the art concepts they use to create effective video productions.

Photograph courtesy SchoolArts *and Berniece Patterson, Denton, Texas.*

Computer Graphics

Introduce this field of art to students. If computers are not available, arrange field trips or other programs to acquaint students with the possibilities of this art form.

Demonstrate the "tools" available in software programs and how to use them. For rapid learning, have pairs of students collaborate and create an image to share with the class.

Set up a schedule for independent work. Emphasize originality, design qualities, and the discovery of new techniques. Challenge students to create computer images based on specific design concepts (symmetry, asymmetry), themes or problems (a book of original poems).

If computer programming is taught in your school, have students write programs that produce specific images: for example, repeated lines or shapes with even spaces between vs. the same image with progressive changes in spacing.

Graphic Design

Adventures in Art introduces students to some of the thought processes and skills needed by graphic designers—artists who plan the artwork for mass-produced posters, advertisements, books, and other printed materials.

You may wish to encourage additional work on the art of lettering and calligraphy (beautiful writing). There are many commercially available pen sets, types of ruled paper and guidebooks for practice.

Architecture, Interior Design and Community Planning

Students encounter these art forms in everyday life. The creation of small models—an activity in *Adventures in Art*—can be enriched by field trips to visit significant buildings, monuments, or spaces.

In addition, provide opportunities for students to change their own classroom—moving furniture into different groupings, adding a carpet, and placing artwork in new locations. Discuss the advantages and disadvantages of particular arrangements.

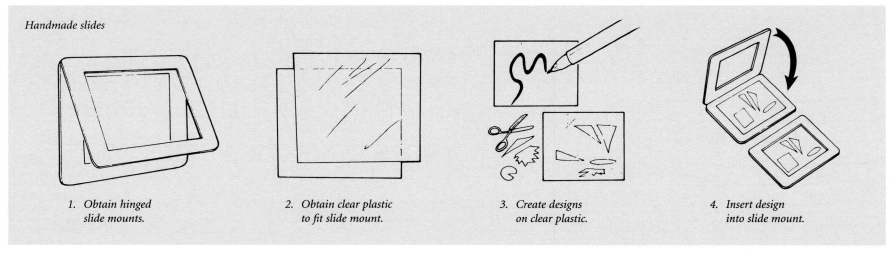

Handmade slides

1. Obtain hinged slide mounts.

2. Obtain clear plastic to fit slide mount.

3. Create designs on clear plastic.

4. Insert design into slide mount.

Art supplies are grouped by general category of use. **Quantities are for ten students for all lessons unless otherwise noted.** Quantities allow for typical extras needed during the year.

Purchase supplies in bulk or large sizes for economy. Use the nearest metric conversion of sizes and amounts as needed. Large paper can be cut in half or in quarters for some lessons. Compile supply lists for the whole school for greater savings.

Some items, such as old newspapers or magazines, can be obtained at little or no cost by asking students or parents to save them. Some schools have set up an "art resource team" to gather and organize donated supplies, and recycle discarded materials that can be used for art.

Students' Needs

crayons, wax, 8 colors	15 bxs.
erasers, soft pencil	15
markers, water-based, 8 colors	15 bxs.
notebook or sketchbook	15
oil pastels, 8 colors	15 bxs.
pencils, soft drawing	15
brushes, bristle, for tempera ¾", ¼"	12 ea. size
brushes, soft hair, for watercolor medium, large	12 ea. size
brushes, sponge or stencil	12
paint, tempera orange, green, violet, brown	½ pint
paint, tempera red, yellow, blue, black, white	1 quart
paint, watercolors, 8 color sets	12
glue, white, dries clear	1 pint
glue, white, stick-type	12
paper clips, large	2 bxs. per class
paste	1 pint
rubber bands, box	1 per class
rulers	12
scissors	12
cards, index, lined 3 x 5" pkg. of 100	1 per class
cards, index, unlined 3 x 5" pkg. of 100	1 per class
foil, aluminum, 36 ft. roll	1 per class
folders, clear plastic, notebook size	12
paper bags, large	12
paper, black construction, 9 x 12"	24
paper, blueprint, for school use, 6 x 9"	12
paper, calculator roll, 3 or 4" wide	3 per class

paper, colored construction, 12 x 18"	200
paper, colored construction, 18 x 24"	24
paper, colored lightweight, 12 x 18"	48
paper folders or portfolios for artwork	12
paper, for mounting artwork, 18 x 24"	12
paper, lined notebook	24
paper, manila, 12 x 18"	48
paper, manila, 18 x 24"	12
paper, mural or butcher, 36 or 48" wide	13 yds per class
paper, newsprint, 18 x 24"	12
paper, newsprint, 12 x 18"	200
paper or plastic tubes, cups, sm. boxes	30
paper plates	15
paper, stencil or substitute	12
paper, waxed	1 roll per class
paper, white drawing, 12 x 18"	276
paper, white typing bond	24
picture magazines to cut up	20
cardboard, 9 x 12" base for models	12
cardboard or floor tiles, 6 x 6"	12
cardboard squares, 3"	12
clay, ceramic or water-based	10 lbs.
clay, oil-based, reusable	5 lbs.
clay tools	15
fabric trims, buttons, lace, ribbon, fringe	30
facial tissues	1 bx. per class
foam plastic egg/meat cartons	12
gloves, disposable latex or plastic	12
mats for clay work	12
natural forms and small objects— twigs, shells, feathers, bolts, bottle caps, rope, wood scraps— for clay impressions and printing	15
plastic lids or frozen dinner trays	15
printing brayers	12
printing, inking slabs	12
printing ink, water-based, 4-oz. tubes	6
straws, soda	6 bxs. per class
swabs, cotton tip	12
textured papers, assorted scraps	24
thin sticks coffee stirs, tongue depressors	25
trays, stiff cardboard or cafeteria	12
toothpicks, box	1 per class

cloth, burlap, 12" squares 9 in 1 yard	24
cloth, cotton white or muslin, unsized, 9 x 12"	12
cloth, lightweight scraps, assorted	30
string, large ball	1 per class
thread, spools of assorted colors	12 per class
yarn, skeins of assorted colors	10 per class

Optional

objects, textured flat	15
rolling pins	6

Cleanup

newspapers for desks	large stack
paper towels, 100 in package	3 pkg.
paint cloths to blot brushes	15
smocks or old shirts	12
sponges	12
water containers	12

Teacher's Needs

flashlight	1
liquid detergent, bottle	1 per class
map, North America	1
map, world, or globe	1
paper cutter, in room or easy access	1
stapler and staples	1
tape, cellophane, large roll	1 per class
tape, masking, large roll	1 per class
tape, removable cellophane, large roll	1 per class
tape, removable white, 1" wide roll	1 per class
thumbtacks, box	2 per class

The following materials are recommended for demonstrations and to help teach concepts related to lessons:

Camera, to photograph 3-D artwork.

Chart for manuscript lettering and cursive writing.

Examples: books—Caldecott winners, poems and stories to illustrate.

Examples: contemporary or antique product designs—lamps, shoes, clothing, toys.

Examples: fiber arts—embroidery, weaving, batik, tie dyeing.

Examples: "glow in the dark" decorative items to illustrate qualitites similar to phosphorescent paint.

Examples: graphic design—stamps, posters, cards, package designs.

Examples: handcrafts from a variety of cultures.

Examples: highly creative alphabet books or alphabet cards.

Examples: mosaics.

Examples: patterned cloth or wrapping paper.

Examples: photographs of old and new architecture, landmarks—local, national, international.

Examples: photographs of the natural world—seasons, weather, plants, animals.

Examples: photography—film negative and a print made from it.

Examples: photography—section of motion picture film to show frames.

Old clothes and props for figure drawing poses.

Rubber stamp, with lettering to illustrate image reversals.

Unbreakable mirrors for self-portrait drawings.

Guiding Response and Appreciation

Developing students' appreciation of art and the visual world is a major aim for art education. On the following pages, you will find additional pointers for developing aesthetic perception, discussing artworks, and building an awareness of art in the environment.

Developing Aesthetic Perception

Aesthetic perception is marked by a feeling that ordinary things have extraordinary and often poetic qualities.

Nurture Sensory Awareness

Cultivate aesthetic awareness of the natural world by encouraging students to perceive beauty in such things as:

- the intricate detail and orderly repetition of large and small forms in a single stalk of wheat;

- the delicate lines and radial pattern of a spider web;

- the diamondlike sparkle of dew on the grass;

- the ever-changing forms and colors of the land caused by variations in light, seasons, and weather.

Encourage aesthetic perception of the constructed world—the things people have created and added to the natural world—by encouraging students to perceive beauty in:

- the shifting reflections of sky and clouds on tall glass-covered skyscrapers;

- the patterns formed by bricks, their textures (smooth or rough), their uniformity or variety in color;

- the sleek, shiny surfaces of chrome and paint on new cars;

- the dusky grays and browns in weathered lumber, soot-covered buildings.

Related Teaching Techniques

Aesthetic perception is often indelible—imprinted in our memory in a way that may lead us to recall details of an object or event many years later.

Adventures in Art encourages aesthetic perception in grades 1 to 6. Related activities, based on the following concepts, will expand students' sensitivity to what they perceive around them.

Multi-sensory associations. Enhance aesthetic perception by linking the sense of sight with the senses of touch, movement, sound. Encourage students to make sounds and movements that echo what they see: The whisper and gentle to and fro of fluttering leaves; the low roar and rhythmic crash of waves on a rocky shoreline.

Visual memory. Distribute to everyone an object of the same type but marked by subtle differences: old pencils, acorns, leaves, or pebbles from a stream. Have students look at the object and try to remember all its special features. Collect the objects and place them on a counter. Have students try to find their own unique object. Try the same experiment, having students draw the object as a way to remember its special visual features.

Imaginative seeing. Encourage imaginative associations. A familiar example is looking at the forms of clouds and "seeing" these as animals, faces, or landscapes. Cracks in a sidewalk may resemble branching rivers and streams.

Shifting point of view. Develop the ability to shift points of view—to imagine how the world might look from a bird's or an ant's eye view. Also try observing a common scene from more than one point of view, noting foreground and background elements, shifts in color and other visual relationships.

Photograph courtesy Cynthia Colbert, Lexington, South Carolina.

Personal identification. In aesthetic perception, we often relate visual qualities to human attributes and experiences. We may say that dark clouds look "threatening" or "angry," that the downward curves of a tree's branches make it look "droopy" or "forlorn." Have students search for words and phrases (especially adjectives and adverbs) that refer to the human feelings they associate with visual qualities.

Subtle comparisons and contrasts. Collect ordinary objects—natural or manufactured—to develop perception of subtle differences. For example, collect white papers that vary in texture and weight. Trim the papers into squares. Sort the papers into sequences from rough to smooth, lightweight to heavyweight, and so on.

Vocabulary games. Handmade flash cards can help make vocabulary words come alive. On one side of the card have students illustrate an art term. On the opposite side, have them write down one or two art terms that fit the illustration. Focus on adjectives and adverbs that describe related sensory qualities. Use a thesaurus to find words for colors and the like.

Discussing Works of Art

Develop students' enjoyment and skill in looking at works of art. The ability to have sustained and thoughtful encounters with art is a major goal for art education.

Emphasize Discovery and Reflection

Use the following discovery-based method to lead discussions of a single work of art. Similar procedures are used throughout *Adventures in Art*. Related procedures are often used by artists, art historians, critics, and other art experts.

Step 1. What did the artist want you to see? *Observe and describe* the most obvious features and qualities such as the art form, subject, or general theme. "I see many plants, people, hills…" Ask the students to be "art detectives." Identify more subtle features, such as how the artist has used the medium and the design elements. "The brushstrokes make swirling lines." "The colors in the sky are light blue and pink. They blend together, look smooth and still."

Step 2. How is the work planned? *Analyze* the work. Search for visual clues again, this time to discover the plan or design of the work. Use the principles of design as a guide to search for relationships between parts: "I see a hidden path of movement." "The proportions look exaggerated." "The symmetrical balance makes everything look still."

Continue to analyze the work. Search for clues that reveal what the artist emphasized. Compare elements: "The brightest colors are in the smallest shapes." Pace the discussion during steps 1 and 2, allowing ample time for students to gather "visual evidence" or "clues" to the mood and feeling of the work.

Step 3. What parts of the work give you a special feeling? *Empathize* with features in the work. Empathy is based on imaginative and kinesthetic response. Have students make gestures in the air similar to any paths of movement or visual rhythms. Assume a pose or expression analogous to that of persons or animals. Stand and stretch tall, echoing the upward thrust of shapes. Make sounds that seem to go with the color qualities.

Photograph courtesy SchoolArts *and Mari Evans, Yelm, Washington.*

Step 4. How does the work "speak" to you without using words? *Interpret* the work. An interpretation of the work is an inference about its meaning based on a process of "adding up" the visual evidence and reflecting on other clues—including one's own life experience. Encourage inferences and respect different interpretations. Art experts often interpret the same work in different ways.

A good interpretation refers to the expressive quality of an artwork using poetic language, rich in adjectives, adverbs, and analogies: "The artist wants you to see and feel the churning energy of the pounding waves." "The great spires and pointed windows seem to reach upward toward Heaven." An appropriate interpretation can often result from these four steps. Some works can only be interpreted if information is available on cultural symbols or the purpose of the work.

Step 5. Judge the work. Make sure students understand that a personal preference such as "I like it," or "I don't like it" is not the same as a critical judgment. In many respects, the process of judging art is no different from the process of judging anything else by the use of reasoning. You state the criteria that should be applied to the work, give reasons why the work does or does not meet the criteria, and cite evidence—qualities of the work—to support the judgment.

In the art world, standards depend on the purpose of making a judgment. For example, criteria are different if your purpose is to choose art for a restaurant rather than for an art museum. In the same way, when students judge their artwork, the most common purpose is to state what has been learned, not to decide if the work is a masterpiece in the history of art.

Judgments about art are most likely to be the same when people use the same process of judgment and have the same criteria for art. When people live in the same culture, have similar personal experiences and levels of expertise in art, they are more likely to judge art in the same way.

Related Teaching Techniques

Community resources and in-school activities can be used to stimulate interest in art.

Art games and puzzles. Play "I Spy" games. Display several reproductions. Call on a student to choose one of the artworks secretly and describe it, without mentioning the subject matter. Have the class guess which artwork is being described.

Play "Silent Description." Display several reproductions, coded by the letters A, B, C. On separate slips of paper (also coded A, B, C) have the students write one word or phrase to summarize the distinctive mood in each work. Collect the slips for each artwork. Read the words aloud or write them on the board. Discuss why the words do (or do not) seem to fit the works.

Field trips to see original art. Plan carefully for all trips to art museums and artists' studios, as well as tours of a city or neighborhood to study architecture, murals, public sculpture, and the like. Plan several lessons that focus on the purpose of the trip and what students should notice during it. Always follow district rules and procedures for trips beyond the school grounds.

Art museum programs for schools. Some museums offer an orientation to the museum prior to the first visit. Others introduce students to the process of seeing the differences between original works and reproductions.

Visiting experts in art. Invite local artists, craftsworkers, designers, and architects to school for special demonstrations. Seek help from your art supervisor or arts council.

In addition to cultivating students' aesthetic perception, your teaching should help students appreciate the many ways that art and design enter into everyday life.

The Constructed World

Many of the products students see and use are designed by people who are trained in art. Architecture—the design of homes and apartments, schools, hospitals, and other buildings—is one of the major forms of art we encounter in daily life.

Other examples can be seen in the design of: parks, playgrounds, communities; automobiles and other forms of transportation; appliances such as telephones, radios and television sets; home furnishings; signs, packages, labels, and related graphic images.

Environmental Awareness

When you make students aware of art and design in everyday life, help them discern the difference between well- and poorly-designed examples. Here are some hallmarks of well-designed products:

Careful crafting is indicated by attention to details in the design and manufacture or assembly of a building or product.

Attention given to human needs ensure that the building or product will meet our needs for comfort, efficiency, and ease of use.

Beauty is created by the designer, who considers the pleasure we may gain during the use of a product and the symbolic meaning it may have.

The following suggestions are but a few of many ways to expand on the lessons that *Adventures in Art* offers.

- Have students draw pictures of parts of their town which they consider "beautiful" and "ugly." Discuss the basis of their judgments. Then have them draw a picture of an imaginary town with features that make it beautiful.

- Save, and bring to class, empty laundry soap or cereal boxes. Discuss the lettering, images, colors, and overall package design. Ask students to offer explanations for similarities and differences in design.

Photograph courtesy Fashion Institute of Technology.

- Compare handcrafted and mass-produced versions of the same basic product—vases, jewelry, quilts, sweaters. Discuss the special qualities of design and advantages of each way of producing useful objects.

- Contrast products made from authentic materials (wood, metal, leather) with the many surface imitations of these materials (wood-grained contact paper, metallic foil or spray paint, leather-like vinyl).

- Arrange field trips or special in-school programs to make students aware of community development plans, historical preservation efforts, and landmarks that make your city or town distinctive. Engage students in making their own proposals for improving the quality of life and appearance of their community.

Careers in Art

Many students are unaware that careers in the arts are not limited to painting and sculpture. All your students should learn about occupations in art and the ways people may use art skills in occupations that are not directly related to art.

In many communities, there are arts councils which can help you arrange in-school visits by artists, designers, craftworkers, and architects. Consider planning field trips to artists' studios or to galleries and museums to acquaint students with people who devote most of their time to the study of art.

Many other occupations also involve the use of art skills and concepts. To make students aware of the many uses for art skills and concepts in daily life, it is sometimes helpful to use absurd or humorous illustrations. For example, ask them to consider what might happen if all the arrows and lines on streets were painted the same color as the street (instead of white or bright yellow), or to imagine how it would feel to go to a hospital where everything was painted black.

As you explore vocations which involve the use of art skills, you not only enrich students' awareness of art in everyday life, you also expand their appreciation of vocational opportunities for themselves.

Art in the Total Curriculum

Art is a distinct and important part of the total curriculum. Just as the study of art can enrich students' understanding of other subjects, so too can their studies of other subjects be linked to art. Each lesson in *Adventures in Art* suggests one or more specific activities to link art with other subjects. Additional possibilities are outlined here.

Language Arts

1. Develop students' art vocabulary.

- Write art terms and concepts on the board. Refer to them during the entire lesson.
- Develop lists of adjectives and adverbs to describe art elements and moods in artworks (lines can seem to be lazy, energetic, bold).
- Ask for complete and complex descriptions—"I see a large red square near the center of the painting."

2. Encourage reflective inquiry into art.

- Engage students in analysis and comparison—"This large simple form seems to balance this small patterned form." "This drawing has many more details than that one."
- Develop skills in reasoning. Ask for interpretations of visual evidence and explanations based on "visual facts." Encourage students to develop hypotheses about what an artist wants us to see, feel, imagine.

3. Have students read about art.

- Encourage oral and written reports on favorite artworks and artists.
- Create original art based on poems or stories.
- Study the arts of book illustration, the design of alphabets, and calligraphy (beautiful handwriting).

Social Studies

1. Teach students about the role of art in everyday life, past and present.

- Acquaint students with artistic traditions of cultural groups in their school and community. Arrange for students to do research projects on the cultural and artistic legacy of people who lived in your community or region long ago.
- Study the relationships of human needs—for food, clothing, shelter, and tools—to the development of art forms such as pottery, weaving, architecture, and industrial design.
- Develop connections between geography, history, and economics as these factors have influenced art. For example, with the growth of international trade and travel, including trade and travel related to art, some artists and art styles became internationally known.

2. Teach students about the rich heritage of art, past and present.

- In the lower grades, appreciation of varieties of art is more important than names, dates and other technical information. Stress the process of looking at art and reasons people around the world create art.
- In the upper grades, introduce art history as a parallel to social studies. Study the arts of specific cultures—North American Indian art, the arts of Africa, Japan, and other countries. Study art history as a facet of American history. Study world history with a strong emphasis on art (from cave art to the present).
- At all levels, make students aware of the artistic accomplishments of women and minority groups.

Science, Mathematics, Technology

1. Teach students how artists interpret the natural world and use scientific knowledge.

- Emphasize the importance of careful observation in art and in science—identifying things by their shape, size, texture, color, weight, and so on.
- Explore the many ways artists have expressed their ideas and feelings about the natural world—changing seasons, weather, the beauty of forms in nature.
- Have students create original artwork based on their observations of the subtle colors, textures, patterns, movement of natural forms—plants, animals, clouds.

2. Teach students how skills in mathematics and computer technologies apply to art.

- Emphasize how artists use their knowledge of measurement and geometric shapes and forms—in designing architecture, in planning beautifully proportioned vases and many other aspects of art.
- Arrange demonstrations and provide opportunities for students to use computers to create art.

Verbal and Performing Arts

A complete education in the arts will include studies of the visual arts along with the language arts (written and oral expression) and performing arts (music, dance and theater). Each art form provides a unique avenue for sharing ideas and feelings with others.

1. Teach concepts that apply to all the arts.

- In each art form, there are creative originators of ideas—composers of music, choreographers of dance, playwrights, poets, authors.
- All artists explore and master their chosen medium. Artists transform sounds into music; movements into dance; interactions of people into theater; qualities of paint into images; words into meaningful poems and stories.
- In all the arts, there is a planned composition, design, or arrangement of qualities of a medium. This unique plan explains why each artwork and each art form is unlike others.

2. Illustrate relationships among the arts.

- Note how terms from music are sometimes used to describe things we see—"loud" colors, "rhythmic" patterns of shapes, a "harmonious" design.
- Relate the qualities of movement in dance to actual or implied movement in visual art—a line may seem to "twist and turn" in space, as if it is "dancing."
- Have students create masks, puppets, plays. Discuss the visual qualities of masks, puppets, stage scenery, make-up and costumes as important facets of the art of theater.
- Help students appreciate how television and film, both major art forms of our time, uniquely combine other art forms—music, choreography, etc.

Thematic Units

If your school curriculum is organized around theme-based units which integrate all subjects, you can use the preceding concepts, along with specific lessons in *Adventures in Art*, to insure that art concepts are included in each unit.

Teaching About the Artistic Heritage

As a complement to the study of individual works of art, *Adventures in Art* introduces students to the rich heritage of world art.

Introducing Art History

Adventures in Art provides background information in a number of ways.

1. Cross-cultural comparisons and contrasts. Many lessons acquaint students with the purposes of an art form in different cultures. For example, in some lessons, students contrast and compare masks created by various cultural groups. They examine the functions of the masks and differences in the media or design as these relate to other aspects of the culture.

2. Ancient-modern comparisons. These lessons present comparisons that develop an awareness of chronological time and illustrate how art from "long ago" has influenced the art of today. For example, many of our sports arenas and colosseums are based on architectural ideas from ancient Rome.

3. Historical study and creative art. In this approach, students learn about art from long ago—the context in which artists worked and themes that were of special interest, such as portraits. They then create their own original art on a related but contemporary theme, such as a portrait of a classmate.

4. Individual artists. Biographies and examples of work by one artist help make students aware of relationships between an artist's general background of experience and changes or continuities in his or her style of artwork.

5. Variations within a culture, period or style. Lessons of this type help students become aware of artists' individual interpretations of their culture. For example, within the general style of Impressionism, students learn to see differences between the works of Monet and Seurat. Students are made aware of differences in the style of artists who share an African-American heritage.

6. Timelines. The timeline approach to studying art history can be introduced in the early grades, but it is best to refer to social studies instruction for guidance in chronological recognition. For example, in social studies, the distinction between BC and AD is not emphasized until grade 5. The development of concurrent civilizations in the Middle East, Africa and other regions is not emphasized until grade 6.

A Timeline of Artworks in the Student Text, Level 3

The following timeline presents common names for broad periods in art history with cultural or national identifications of the artworks in the student text. Exact dates of works are not always available.

Because history is based on inferences, cultural and national identifications for older works are sometimes disputed, even among experts. Some of the dates for North American Indian art and African art refer to the time they were collected for museums.

Note: The first lesson in every unit in *Adventures in Art* is known as the unit opener. In this timeline, unit openers are coded "U", plus unit number. Similarly, unit reviews are coded "R", plus unit number. Thus the Unit 4 Review would be coded R4.

Great Sphinx, ca. 2530 BC, Giza. Courtesy Rosenthal Art Slides.

A Timeline of Artworks in the Student Text, Level 3

Ancient		Lesson	Image
1370 BC	Africa-Egypt, el Amarna	55	B
1000 BC	Cyprus-Early Iron Age	53	A
800 BC	Iran-Assyrian	57	C
447–436 BC	Greece	44	A
300 BC	China	53	C
100 BC–250 AD	Mexico-Nayarit-Ixtian del Rio style	56	D
100	Africa-Egypt	27	B
118–128	Italy	44	C

Middle Ages: Spread of Christianity, Buddhism, Islam		Lesson	Image
547	Italy-Ravenna-Byzantine	40	B
700s	England	35	A
1100	China	35	B
1290	France	42	A
1200s	The Netherlands	43	B

14th to 16th Centuries: Voyages of Discovery, Beginning of Colonialism, Renaissance		Lesson	Image
1354	Iran-Isfahan	40	C
1456–70	Italy	39	A
1490–1520	Italy	57	D
1400s	Mexico-Aztec	53	B
1519–47	France	43	A
1590	India-Mughal School	21	A

17th Century: Aristocratic Rule, Rise of Colonialism, Growth in Knowledge		Lesson	Image
1643	The Netherlands	8	A

18th Century: Modern Era, Decline of Aristocracy, Industrial Revolution		Lesson	Image
1768–1809	United States	44	D

		Lesson	Image

19th Century: Growth in International Trade, Cross-Cultural Influences

Year	Place	Lesson	Image
1800–1900	Africa-Mali-Dogon	49	B
1830	United States	U4	D
1838	United States	20	B
1839	*England, photography invented*		
1839–1912	United States	44	B
1840–50	England	37	A
1855–56	France	1	B
1857	France	1	C
1864	France	20	A
1869–81	Germany	43	D
1872	France	19	C
1880s	France	18	C
1881–93	Russia	8	B
1882	The Netherlands	23	A
1885	France	13	A
1885	United States	23	B
1889	The Netherlands	R1	A
1889	United States	28	B
1890s	United States	17	B
1894	France	16	D
1800s	American Indian-Western Woodlands	47	A
1800s	France	1	A
1800s	Korea	46	C

20th Century

Year	Place	Lesson	Image
1900	American Indian-Hopi	58	B
1903	France	16	A
1907	Canada	17	A
1907	United States	27	A
1910	United States	25	A
1910	United States	R2	D
1911	United States	24	B
1913	United States	R2	A
1914–18	*World War I*		
1918	Canada	18	A
1918–50	United States	R1	C
1920–37	United States	44	E
1923	Russia	47	C
1924	Latin America	29	A
1924	Spain	2	C
1924	United States	23	C
1924	United States	23	D
1925	Germany	7	A
1929	Canada	15	A
1930	African-American	27	C
1930	Germany	12	B
1930	United States	15	D
1931	Mexico	11	C
1935	United States	11	A
1937	France	15	C
1937	Mexico	26	A
1938	The Netherlands	4	E
1939–45	*World War II*		
1939	United States	24	A
1939	United States	R2	E
1930s	United States	R2	C
1946	Canada	3	C
1949	Denmark	31	B
1940s	United States	R1	B
1950	African-American	25	B
1950	United States	45	A
1951	United States	56	A
1952	United States	14	A
1952	United States	29	B
1952	United States	54	A
1953	France	6	A
1954	United States	26	B
1958	African-American	59	A
1960	United States	14	B
1963	United States	28	A
1964	United States	54	C
1966	African-American	57	B
1967	United States	3	A
1969	African-American	60	B
1960s	Africa-Nigeria-Oshogbo	51	B
1960s	Australia-Port Keats Region	15	A
1960s	Japan-"Living Treasure"	48	A
1970–72	United States	58	A
1970	African-American	60	C
1970s	United States	34	C
1971	United States	2	A
1972	African-American	36	B
1974	African-American	59	C
1975	African-American	59	B
1977	United States	35	C
1978–82	Canada	31	D
1979–81	American Indian-Ottawa-Ontario	46	A
1979	Poland	36	D
1970s	Africa-Ashanti	U4	A
1970s	Japanese-American-Canada	U4	B
1980	United States	18	B
1980	United States	52	A
1982	United States	32	D*
1985	United States	51	A
1985	United States	34	A
1986–87	United States	38	A
1987	United States	30	A
1987	United States	30	B
1988	American Indian-Hopi-Choctaw	9	A
1988	United States	34	B
1989	United States	31	A
1989	United States	32	A
1989	United States	32	B
1989	United States	52	B
1980s	African-American	55	A
1980s	American Indian-Haida	49	A
1980s	Canada	41	A
1980s	Canada	41	B
1980s	United States	12	A
1980s	United States	31	C
1980s	United States	32	C
1980s	United States	41	C
1990s	American Indian	46	B
1990s	United States	42	B
1991	African-American	36	C
1991	Australia-North Queensland	U4	C
1991	Cuban-American	8	C
1992	Mexican-American	7	B

Introducing children to styles of art and cultures around the world is an important facet of art education. Brief background notes are provided here to help you teach about various art styles and traditions.

Introducing Styles and Style Terms

A style is the result of an artist's means of expression—the use of materials and techniques, design qualities, choice of subject, and the like. The style of an artwork helps identify it as similar to or different from other artworks.

Style terms may refer to a time, a culture, a trend artists follow, or changes in the work of one artist. Some artworks have no clear classification in relation to a style while others may be classified in several ways.

When you introduce style terms, help students to understand that style names are "invented," or coined, by artists, critics, historians, or others to help point out distinctive features in a group of works.

Students' understanding of styles of art will develop as they compare and contrast works of art created in different times and cultures by various artists. General style terms such as realistic and abstract are appropriate at all levels, but especially valuable in the early grades.

As students progress to the upper grades, more specific style terms, such as Surrealism or Impressionism, can be introduced, along with more information on cultural or historical influences.

Although style terms have been invented for many traditions of art around the world, students are most likely to encounter style terms associated with historical periods in Europe and North America. A few of these style terms are discussed below. Other commonly used style and historical terms are defined in the Glossary of the teacher's edition.

Common Periods and Styles: Western Culture

Prehistoric Art (25,000 BC–4000 BC) refers to the earliest known artworks. These range from representational carvings in bone to the well-known paintings in caves of Spain and France. Animals and hunting are the dominant themes. With the development of agriculture and settled communities, the arts of weaving, metalwork, and ceramics developed, along with architecture.

Ancient Art (4000 BC–400 AD) has been found on every continent. With the growth of centers of civilization, art forms became more diverse and coherent, both in style and cultural purpose. Concurrent centers of civilization developed in the Middle East and Egypt, as well as the Americas, India, and Asia.

Ancient Egyptian Art (3000–500 BC) combines representational elements with highly ordered compositions that depict the activities, attire, tools, and furnishings of daily life. These images, found in tombs such as the pyramids, were created for religious beliefs centered on the concept of an afterlife.

Ancient Greek Art (600–150 BC) evolved toward the classical style, marked by elegant proportions and a perfection of form, as seen in the Parthenon and other works devoted to goddesses and heros.

Ancient Roman Art (753 BC–476 AD) reflects ideas from Greece, with a greater interest in naturalistic detail and the use of art to serve practical or political purposes. The term classical refers to art influenced by Greek or Roman art, as seen in a perfection of form, proportion and detail, restraint in emotion, and idealized treatments of a subject.

Medieval Art (400–1400) reflects the growing dominance of Christianity and the beginning of cross-cultural exchanges through trade and conquest. Cathedrals became a major art form, along with paintings or mosaics. Illuminated manuscripts, tapestries, and fine metalwork were produced for the church. In general, naturalistic detail was less important than the symbolic expression of religious belief.

Byzantine Art (300–1500) is a blend of Roman, Greek and Asian influences. It developed in the Eastern Roman Empire (called Byzantium) and is marked by the rich use of color, flat, stiff figures, and religious themes.

Romanesque (1000–1200) is a style influenced by Roman art, seen especially in cathedrals featuring thick walls, rounded arches, and sculptural decorations.

Gothic Art (1100–1400) is a finer development of medieval art, seen in cathedrals with pointed arches, vertical forms, and the use of stained glass windows. Paintings and other works are more delicate or naturalistic and anticipate the Renaissance.

Renaissance Art (1400–1600) is marked by a renewed interest in naturalistic detail as well as the classical ideals for art, such as ideal proportions and the structural relationships that unify a work. Formal rules for perspective and other theoretical aspects of art developed.

Baroque (1600–1700) is a style marked by dramatic contrasts in light and shade, elaborate compositions, often with swirling curves, and rich colors and textures. It is an energetic yet orderly expression of Renaissance directions.

Rococo (1700–1800) is a style created for the French aristocracy that spread to other parts of Europe. Delicate colors, a playful use of line, and graceful movement are used to express the carefree life of the aristocracy.

Neoclassicism (1750–1875) is based on revived interest in the classical ideals of ancient Greek and Roman art and their use to express ideas about beauty, courage, sacrifice, and patriotism. The style developed as a reaction against Rococo art and helped establish a pattern of more rapid shifts in styles, often in reaction to others.

The Modern Era (1800–present) is typically described by style terms that apply primarily to painting and, in some cases, sculpture. Dates refer to customary beginning points of each style. Ending dates for the modern era, including twentieth century art, are not given because many of these styles continue to be explored and merged in contemporary art.

Romanticism (1815–) developed as a reaction against Neoclassicism. Themes focus on dramatic action, exotic settings, adventures, imaginary events, faraway places, or strong feelings.

Realism (1850–) is based on the concept that artworks should portray actual places, events, people, or objects. The style was developed by artists who rejected the formulas of Neoclassicism and the drama of Romanticism.

Impressionism (1875–) began in France, and emphasizes candid glimpses of various subjects, similar to snapshots, and the momentary effects of sunlight on color. Space and form are implied by varying the intensity of light and color.

Post-Impressionism (1880–) is a period of painting, immediately following Impressionism in France, in which various styles were explored, especially by Paul Cézanne (basic structures), Vincent van Gogh (emotionally strong brushwork), and Paul Gauguin (intense color and exotic themes).

Expressionism (1890–) is based on the concept that artworks should convey a strong mood, human emotion, or spiritual feeling. Brilliant colors and bold distortions are often used for expressive aims.

Twentieth Century Styles are numerous and reflect the high value placed on innovation in the art world. A few of the best-known styles are discussed here.

Cubism (1907–) is based on an interest in presenting multiple and partial views of objects on the flat surface of a paper or canvas. The result is an abstract, often puzzle-like design with fragmented elements. Picasso and Braque, who developed this style, also developed collage into a major medium. Many artists continue to explore variations on cubism.

Futurism (1909–) refers to an Italian movement in which artists expressed their interest in speed, force, and rapid change in an increasingly mechanized society. Although key artists died or changed styles during and after World War I, their interests and imagery influenced many other artists.

Dada (1915–) developed as a criticism of the culture in Europe before and after World War I. Artists explored "chance" as a principle for design and experimented with a variety of media and combinations of images. Some artists later explored Surrealism. "Dada" is a French word for hobbyhorse.

Nonobjective Art (1917–) is a general term for artworks with geometric or organic qualities and no recognizable subject matter. The works are an extreme form of abstraction in which the visual elements alone are sources of our response.

Surrealism (1924–) grew from interest in portraying dreams and fantasies related to the subconscious. Unrelated objects are often portrayed realistically in an illogical or unnatural setting.

Abstract Expressionism (1945–) refers to large paintings in which paint is freely and directly applied (dripped, splashed, spattered, brushed) with an intent to suggest abstract feelings or ideas.

Op Art (1950–) is based on optical illusions that heighten or intentionally confuse our normal response to color, pattern, and other visual elements.

Pop Art (1950–) is based on or is a parody of images popularized through advertising in a consumer-oriented society—comic strips, hot dogs, movie stars, etc.

Photo-Realism (1970–) includes a variety of art forms marked by photographic realism, including the odd distortions in color, scale, and detail associated with photographs.

Postmodernism is a phrase coined in 1960 and widely used since 1970 to describe trends in art and culture that have eroded traditional categories for art forms and styles. Contemporary artists borrow, adapt, and blend concepts from art history and continue to experiment with new media and art forms.

Traditional Arts of Cultural Groups

Brief notes are provided here to acquaint you with some characteristics of traditional arts in regions that, for thousands of years, were not influenced by art styles from Europe. In varying degrees, the artistic traditions of these regions are also reflected in contemporary work. In most regions of the world, there are intense efforts to preserve "living" artistic traditions, or historical evidence of "vanished" traditions.

Pre-Columbian Art

Pre-Columbian refers to art in the Americas before the Spanish conquests. North American Indians have a long history of distinctive art, reflecting a way of life and religious beliefs closely tied to nature.

In the Pacific Northwest region, wood is abundant and has been used to create plank houses, masks, household items, and large sculptured totem poles to honor ancestors.

In the Southwest, clay is a major medium for expression, not only in pottery but also in dwellings built of adobe (a mixture of clay and straw).

Bark-covered houses were built by groups living along the East Coast. Ceramics, metalworking, and weaving developed in all of these regions. In the Great Plains region, artists created small portable artifacts, many from animal hides, including decorated tents (tepees).

The ancient arts of Central and South America were also influenced by prevailing religious beliefs and social-political systems.

In Mexico and Meso-America, stone and adobe pyramids and earthen mounds were created for civic and religious rites. Images of animals and humans were often combined in designs for fabrics, ceramics, and metalwork.

The Olmec people of Mexico (1000–200 BC) created large stone sculptures of people and cat-like creatures. The Toltecs (900–1200) and Aztecs (1400–1521) developed storytelling carvings and illuminated manuscripts. In the Andes region of South America, the Incas (1200–1532) created planned communities (Machu Picchu), elaborate gold and silver artifacts and woven fabrics.

Africa and Middle Asia

The arts of ancient Egypt are major achievements in African history, and are widely studied as wellsprings of Western European culture.

In subequatorial Africa, the arts are distinct in many ways. Religious beliefs often center on powerful spirits—natural forces, ancestors, and guardians. Masks, sculptures, and body adornments are thought to embody such spirits or have the power to transform one's identity. All of the materials, style features, and procedures for making artifacts have many levels of meaning.

Representational art was created by people of the early Nok culture (500–200 BC) and by artists of the kingdoms of Ife (1200–1500) and Benin (1500–1600), where bronze casting was mastered.

The traditional arts of many Middle Asian groups reflect a shared heritage of Arabic culture. Much of the artwork is small and portable. The teachings of Islam, the dominant religion in this region, limit representations of the human figure to secular (court) life.

Islamic art is rich in geometric patterns and swirling lines related to the complexity of Arabic writing. Typical architectural forms have round and pointed arches, often decorated with inlaid or painted tiles and lacelike carved openings.

Asia

Much of the traditional art of Asia has been influenced by the Hindu, Buddhist, and Islamic religions.

In **India**, Hindu artworks are based on the concept of reincarnation and myths about Brahma (the creator), Vishnu (the preserver), and Siva (the destroyer). Siva is often shown entwined with snakes, or dancing in a circle of fire.

In Buddhist art, Buddha is often shown in a serene, meditative pose with a third "all-seeing" eye on his forehead. The lotus or water lily symbolizes purity.

Islamic influences are especially evident in work from the twelfth to sixteenth centuries.

Japanese art has been influenced by contacts with Korea, China, and Europe as well as Buddhist sects and Shinto beliefs, especially the veneration of ancestors.

During the so-called golden age (784–1192), temples, gardens, and crafts were developed for the purpose of living in harmony with others and contemplating beauty in the natural world.

The Kamakura period (1185–1392), a time of military rule, favored the creation of portraits, images of everyday life and military achievements. These themes continued during the Muromachi (1392–1568) and Momoyama (1568–1615) periods, with greater emphasis on court life.

During the Edo period (1615–1868), inexpensive woodcuts were produced for the growing middle class. Favored images were scenes of everyday life, popular myths and legends.

Buddhist themes—a deep respect for nature and ancestor worship—are prominent in the traditional arts of **China**. Bronze artifacts from 1100 BC have been found. During the Chou (1027–256 BC) and Han (206 BC–220 AD) dynasties, the Great Wall was built. Large tombs filled with clay sculptures of emperors and their armies were created.

The Tang dynasty (618–907) was a period of intense scholarship comparable to the European Renaissance. The arts of calligraphy, wood block printing, and ceramics flourished. Paintings of birds, flowers, and landscapes were highly developed.

During the Yuan (1279–1368) and Ming (1368–1644) dynasties, urban life flourished and art for export was created—especially ceramics and silk.

In the Quing dynasty (1644–1911), a more flamboyant, exotic, and highly decorative art emerged, comparable to Baroque art in Europe.

Oceanic Art

Oceanic art refers to the traditional arts of people who live in relative isolation in Southeast Asia, Australia, Micronesia, Polynesia, and Malaysia. Natural materials are commonly used for images that refer to local religious beliefs, myths, ancestors, heroes, and leaders.

Distinctive kinds of art are created in each area. For example, some aboriginal artists of Australia, who live in the desert, produce paintings on bark, often with images that refer to the importance of water in their lives. In Papua, New Guinea, brightly painted, decorated artifacts are used for ancestor worship. The Maori people (New Zealand) create elaborate unpainted, geometric wood carvings to honor their gods, chiefs, and heroes.

Alexandra Alaupovic (1921–) United States, sculptor. Born in Yugoslavia, Alaupovic works in clay and metal, blending contemporary and traditional influences. Nature is a dominant theme of her work. Her large works are always planned to fit their eventual site or location.

Josef Albers (1888–1976) United States, painter. Albers is known for his lifelong experimentation with color relationships, which established him as leader of the *Op art* style. In a well-known series of abstract works, *Homage to the Square,* he painted arrangements of squares in flat colors, often planning the interaction of hues and values to give the viewer an optical illusion of deep space or movement.

Leon Battista Alberti (1404–1472) Italy, architect and art theorist. Alberti was one of the leading architects and art theorists of the Renaissance. He emphasized the intellectual, rational and scientific aspects of all art, even works with religious importance. He was also an accomplished sculptor, playwright, painter, musician, mathematician and athlete.

John James Audubon (1785–1851) United States, painter, naturalist. Audubon was born in Haiti, educated in France, where he studied drawing. He moved to Pennsylvania as a teenager. Audubon was fascinated by ornithology. He painted remarkably accurate portraits of hundreds of species of birds and features of their habitats. The Audubon Society takes its name from this artist.

Tom Bacher (1951–) United States, painter. Bacher is fascinated with the effects of color and light. He developed a technique of mixing paint with crystals of calcium sulfite so the colors appear different under various lighting conditions. Each painting can be seen as a different artwork depending on the lighting.

Gordon Baer (20th century) United States, photographer. Baer is an internationally known photographer who works on his own projects as well as assignments. He is well-known for his photo essays including an award-winning book-length project documenting the lives of Vietnam veterans.

Richmond Barthé (1901–1989) United States, sculptor. Barthé was one of the most influential African-American sculptors of the twentieth century. He was the first African-American artist to have work included in the permanent collection of the Whitney Museum of American Art. His subjects include portraits of celebrities and sculptures that express the dignity and grace of African-American athletes and dancers.

Romare Bearden (1914–1988) United States, collage artist, painter. Bearden, an African-American, painted in oils and watercolor for many years and first explored collage in the 1960s. He is internationally recognized for his lifelong work on themes from the African-American experience and his innovative collages which combine drawings and painting with photographic images.

Gerald Beekenkamp (20th century) Canada, industrial designer. Beekenkamp revived a dying business in a Canadian town by designing a playground slide that is safe, colorful, durable in many climates, and easy to ship. The modular spiral unites can be packaged in small containers, saving distributors over fifty percent in shipping costs.

George Bellows (1882–1925) United States, painter, printmaker. Bellows is known for his portraits and paintings of ordinary people in urban activities. He worked in a realistic style but added drama to many works with strong highlights and expressive brushstrokes. Bellows was a superb athlete, and sports, especially boxing, became the subject matter for many of his paintings.

Lynda Benglis (1941–) United States, sculptor, mixed media artist. Benglis constantly experiments with materials, and is especially interested in the interactions among visual elements in different media. She is well-known for her abstract sculpture, using materials such as metal tubing and screens covered with plastic or cloth-like sheeting, which is pleated or folded, then cast or finished to resemble metal.

Sue Bevins-Ericsen (1941–) United States, sculptor. Bevins, an Inuit Indian, creates works in stone and other media. Her sculpture expresses the emotions associated with traditional Inuit activities such as fishing, hunting, and dancing. Bevins is noted for her ability to communicate memorable experiences through simple but powerful abstract forms.

Mel Bochner (1940–) United States, painter. Bochner uses geometric forms and other systems of measurement to plan his works. He is interested in the analysis of art and believes that it is important for his work to show the thought process he has used to create it.

Rosa Bonheur (1822–1899) France, painter, sculptor. Bonheur's best-known works are complex, action-filled paintings of horses and other animals. She sketched animals from life and studied their anatomy to ensure the accuracy of every detail. Her realistic paintings and sensitive bronze sculptures won many awards during her lifetime.

Pierre Bonnard (1867–1947) France, painter, designer, printmaker. Bonnard's work ranges in style from *Impressionism,* in which he captures the stunning bright light of scenes along the Riviera, to highly decorative paintings with flat subdued colors, an influence from seeing Japanese prints. He also created designs for books, stained glass and furniture.

Constantin Brancusi (1876–1957) France, sculptor. Brancusi, born in Romania, became a French citizen. His work was inspired by the simplicity of carved forms in African sculpture and Romanian folk art. He sought to create universal symbols of human experience by using exceptionally simple but expressive forms.

Charles Bulfinch (1763–1884) United States, architect. Bulfinch had no formal training in architecture, and learned about building through travel, research on Classical architecture, and consultations with masons and carpenters. He designed churches, public buildings and served as one of the architects of the United States Capitol in Washington, D.C.

Charles Burchfield (1893–1967) United States, painter. Burchfield's first paintings were based on childhood memories of scenes and emotional events. His later paintings have a strong symbolic quality with elements of fantasy. His expressive use of abstract design elements help to convey the moods and energies he associated with landscapes and with changes in seasons and weather.

Alexander Calder (1898–1976) United States, sculptor and painter. Calder's training as an engineer influenced his work as a sculptor. He is best known for his mobiles and stabiles. Some of his mobiles are motor-driven. Some of his sculptures are large outdoor works made from welded steel. Calder's work also includes textile designs, prints and paintings.

Emily Carr (1871–1945) Canada, painter. Carr studied art in San Francisco and later in Europe. Carr's work was influenced by other Canadian artists, known as the *Group of Seven,* who sought to capture the distinctive color, light and character of Canadian landscapes. She became well-known for her highly expressive paintings of British Columbia, especially Indian villages and rain forests.

Mary Cassatt (1844–1926) United States, painter and printmaker. Cassatt was born in Pennsylvania but spent most of her life in Paris, where she studied and exhibited with the *Impressionists.* She is renowned for her sensitive portrayals of women performing daily tasks, such as caring for children. She also advised many United States art collectors on purchases of artworks.

Elizabeth Catlett (1915–) United States, sculptor, painter, printmaker. Catlett was born in Washington, D.C., studied art in Mexico and eventually moved there. Her African-American heritage and the influences in her Mexican environment inspire much of her work. In her lifestyle and her artwork, Catlett seeks to affirm human dignity and protest against injustice.

Louisa Chase (1951–) United States, painter. Chase works with a variety of themes that include symbols of people and nature, often in unexpected combinations. She has described her work as "psychological cubism." This means that her work presents feelings and ideas in a design that reflects many points of view.

Ivan Chermayeff and Tom Geismar (20th century) United States, graphic designers. Chermayeff and Geismar are internationally known for their versatile and imaginative solutions to graphic design problems. Both have worked on logos for companies and organizations and designs for museum exhibits and international expositions. Chermayeff is also an illustrator and has designed posters and advertisements.

Helen Cordero (1915–1994) United States, sculptor, potter. Cordero is a Pueblo Indian who uses clay and natural pigments from her native New Mexico. She became well-known for her sculptures based on memories of her storyteller grandfather. Her sculptures are painted with a yucca needle and fired in an open cedar fire in Cordero's backyard.

Allan Rohan Crite (1910–) United States, painter. Crite, an African-American, is best known for his portraits and street scenes depicting everyday African-American life during the 1930s and 1940s. Later, he also painted religious themes. His black and white drawings of religious themes have been published in four books.

Barbara E. Cunha (20th century) United States, glass artist. Cunha creates custom-designed glass works in her studio. Most of her works are inspired by nature. Cunha is noted for her use of strong, bright colors and merging of traditional and modern designs.

Mino da Fiesole (1429–1484) Italy, sculptor. Da Fiesole's marble sculptures are portraits of Italians—some of his neighbors in Florence, others based on Classical figures. His reliefs have common characteristics: flat, irregular folds in the fabric, clearly modeled features, and subjects extending into the marble frame.

Leonardo da Vinci (1452–1519) Italy, painter, sculptor, architect, inventor. Da Vinci, one of the greatest Renaissance artists, is best known for the subtle naturalism and expressive gestures and poses in paintings such as the *Mona Lisa* and *The Last Supper*. His subtle gradations in color and precisely developed compositions influenced many artists. His sketchbooks record his tireless quest for knowledge, the extraordinary scope of his interests in the natural world, and his genius as an inventor.

Claire Darley (1949–) United States, painter. Darley has been interested in landscapes and animals since childhood. She explores varied subjects, giving special attention to color and space with the intent to evoke an emotional response in the viewer.

Robert Davidson (1946–) Canada, sculptor, artisan. Davidson, a Haida Indian, began carving stone when he was a teenager. He became an apprentice to Bill Reid, the master of Haida carving and work in metal. Davidson's jewelry and carvings are innovative variations on traditional Haida designs. As a young man, Davidson carved a 40–foot-tall totem pole, the first to be erected on his island in approximately 90 years.

Alexander Jackson Davis (1803–1892) United States, architect. Davis was founder of the American Institute of Architects and called himself an architectural composer. He designed many public buildings, including the Patent Office in Washington, D.C. and the state capitols of Indiana and North Carolina.

Stuart Davis (1894–1964) United States, painter and graphic artist. Davis first learned to paint in a realistic manner. After a visit to Paris, Davis' paintings became more abstract. He is known for his clean-edged, poster-like interpretations of his environment using bright bold colors and patterns. He compared his compositions to the planned improvisations of jazz.

Charles Demuth (1883–1935) France, painter. Demuth's early paintings, many in watercolor, included circus scenes and still lifes. He is best known for his paintings of industrial and architectural forms with a focus on simplified shapes and precise, clean-edged lines in a style known as *Precisionism*.

William Doriani (1891–date of death unknown) United States, painter. Doriani, a self-taught artist, was born in the Ukraine and came to the United States as a child. He returned to Europe to study opera and became interested in painting. His best known work, *Flag Day*, was inspired by the parade he saw on the day he returned to New York from Europe.

Arthur G. Dove (1880–1946) United States, painter. Dove began his career as an illustrator. After a visit to Europe, he developed a style of abstract art and became a leader of American abstract painting. He is best known for his interpretations of the moods and implied movements of natural forms.

Jean Dubuffet (1901–1985) France, mixed-media artist. Dubuffet was fascinated by the art of children and others who painted with untrained abandon and energy. He created sculptures with a variety of materials and built up rough surfaces on his canvas with plaster, sand, cement, glue and asphalt. His puzzle-like compositions often have recognizable subjects such as people, the city or landscapes.

Albrecht Dürer (1471–1528) Germany, painter, printmaker. Dürer is regarded as one of the most accomplished artists of the Renaissance. Dürer is well-known for his meticulous studies of nature, human proportions, and his expressive paintings of religious themes. He was the first painter of his time to gain much of his reputation from his prints.

Charles Eames (1907–1978) United States, industrial designer. Eames is best known for his innovative furniture designs using molded plywood, and later cast aluminum and fiberglass. He also became well-known for his exhibition designs, the design of his own house, and experimental films.

Mary Abastenia St. Leger Eberle (1878–1942) United States, sculptor, painter. Eberle's sculptures were based on direct observation of people and are noted for their sense of motion. She believed that artists have a responsibility to heighten the public's social awareness. Many of her works were inspired by her interest in poor people, especially women and children, who lived in urban slums.

Harold Edgerton (1903–) United States, photographer, inventor. Edgerton is known as the inventor of extremely high-speed photography with use of an electronic flash (strobe light). He worked on many refinements of the technique which enabled him to photograph previously unseen things such as the impact of a speeding bullet and the exact forms made by a single drop of milk as it splashes.

Louis Eilshemius (1864–1941) United States, painter. Eilshemius' paintings reflect his interest in impressionistic techniques and ability to use them in a dramatic style. His interest in dramatic landscapes was stimulated, in part, by his travels to Europe, Africa and the South Sea Islands.

James Ensor (1860–1949) Belgium, painter, printmaker. Ensor worked in several styles but is best known as a leading *Expressionist* painter whose use of bright colors and thick paint, applied quickly with a palette knife, helped to create a feeling of emotional intensity in many works. His subject matter ranged from city scenes and interiors to fantastic carnival themes and grotesque figures.

Arthur Erickson (20th century) Canada, architect. Erickson's designs reveal his concern for the symbolism of architecture and the beauty of land and water. For example, he designed a museum based on architecture of the Northwest Indians. It houses large totem poles and is oriented to the mountains and the water of Howe Sound. He has also designed a major civic center for downtown Vancouver which includes many park-like terraces and tiers of waterfalls.

Max Ernst (1891–1976) Germany, painter, sculptor, collage artist. Ernst is known as one of the most important *Surrealist* painters. His works were often based on childhood memories and imaginative uses of materials. Ernst invented a number of painting techniques, including frottage, a method for reproducing textures that is similar to crayon rubbing.

M.C. (Maurits Cornelius) Escher (1898–1972) The Netherlands, graphic artist. Almost all of Escher's prints are designed as optical illusions with manipulated perspectives and negative-positive patterns. His thoroughly planned and mathematically precise work is surrealistic in that it makes the impossible appear to be real. It is also related to the style called *Op art,* in which optical illusions are the major theme.

Henri Fantin-Latour (1836–1904) France, painter, printmaker. Fantin-Latour is noted for his luxurious paintings of flowers, still lifes and group portraits of artists of his day. Some of his paintings also interpret mythological subjects, a popular theme among nineteenth century artists.

Patricia J. Fay (20th century) United States, mosaic artist. Fay's artworks range from small, free-hanging mosaics to wall-size installations. She uses tile, wood, marble, metal and glass to create works with a variety of textures and colors.

Thomas Feelings (1933–) United States, illustrator, painter, sculptor, writer. Feelings, an African-American, has illustrated more than twenty books of stories based on his travel in Africa and contemporary African-American experiences. He has received two Caldecott Awards and many other honors. In the 1950s he wrote and illustrated a weekly comic strip for children on African-American history.

Marvin Finn (20th century) United States, sculptor. Finn, an African-American, is a self-taught artist who lives in Kentucky. He learned a few techniques for shaping wood from his father, but started making decorated sculptures as toys for his children. Most of his recent work is inspired by trips to the zoo and sold to collectors of folk art.

John B. Flannagan (1895–1942) United States, sculptor. Flannagan studied painting but became well-known for his sculpture. He preferred to work with field stones which he personally chose because their forms suggested the subject for a final sculpture. His approach to sculpture, known as direct carving, was to modify the existing form, letting the idea and plan be determined by the natural form of the material.

Helen Frankenthaler (1928–) United States, painter. Frankthaler investigates color combinations in stain painting, a technique in which paint is poured on unprimed canvas, thus eliminating any evidence of brushstrokes. She often adds titles to suggest a mood, quality or idea that she associates with the work. She is known as one of the leaders of *Abstract Expressionism* and its many variations.

Frank Furness (1839–1912) United States, architect. Furness, like many architects of his era, was fascinated by styles of art from many cultures. He is best known for his eclecticism—borrowing style elements from different times and cultures—to create highly decorative and imaginative sculptural facades, often with colorful bricks, textures, stone and other contrasting elements.

Thomas Gainsborough (1727–1788) Great Britain, painter. Gainsborough became well-known for his fashionable portraits of wealthy families. He preferred to paint idealized pastoral scenes and many portraits include landscapes in the background. One of his best-known paintings is *Blue Boy.* His sketches reveal his great skill and delight in recording subjects from life.

Rupert Garcia (1941–) United States, painter, printmaker. Garcia's artwork is influenced by his Mexican (Chicano) heritage and studies of mass media, especially posters with political and cultural content dealing with the oppression of minority groups. He devoted seven years of his career to creating such posters in a style influenced by *Pop art.* His recent work in pastels is a more personal and subtle expression of related themes.

Claude Gidman (20th century) Canada, industrial designer. Gidman has designed a variety of public transportation vehicles that accommodate the physical needs of the driver and passengers. One of Gidman's buses, The Orion II, can be adjusted to the level of the sidewalk, providing easy entrance for people in wheelchairs as well as other passengers.

William Glackens (1870–1938) United States, painter. Glackens, who began his career as a newspaper illustrator, became a member of the *Ashcan School,* a group of painters who wished to portray the lives of poor and middle-income people in urban settings. Many of his works focus on urban life as if it were a colorful spectacle, even among the people who live in a dreary, crowded environment.

Julio Gonzalez (1876–1942) Spain, sculptor and painter. Gonzalez began his career as a painter, but is known primarily for the realism of his work in bronze and innovative abstract sculpture. He was among the first artists to use industrial materials and techniques, including welding, to transform metal rods and sheets into sculpture.

Michael Graves (1938–) United States, architect. Graves is known for his development of buildings in a *Post-Modern* style. Post-Modern architecture is based on ideas from the past and present. It is intended to restore symbolic meaning to architecture and to provide viewers with decorative details through color contrasts, unusual shapes, and other features not found in the glass box buildings found in many cities.

George Grosz (1893–1959) United States, painter, illustrator. German-born Grosz became a United States citizen in 1938. While in Germany, he created many satirical drawings of German soldiers and politicians. His early works contrast the themes of affluence and consumption with poverty and disease. His later works include landscapes, still lifes and imaginary subjects.

Marsden Hartley (1877–1943) United States, painter. Hartley worked in a variety of styles but preferred abstract images based on landscapes or symbolic interpretations of people in various roles. He traveled extensively and often created work in pastels that he later interpreted in oil paintings. His last works were painted in the bold, direct style of *Expressionism.*

Carol Hartsock (20th century) fiber artist, painter. Harstock has worked as a fiber artist creating varied works including soft sculpture. She also creates paintings with a focus on portraits and views of the environment. These works have been inspired, in part, by her travel in Asia.

Robert Henri (1865–1929) United States, painter. Henri was the founder of the *Ashcan School,* a group of artists whose work portrayed the realities of American urban life, including slums. An influential teacher, Henri believed that artists should produce work that "creates a stir in the world." He was the first strong advocate for a popular democratic direction for art in the United States.

Ando Hiroshige (1797–1858) Japan, printmaker. Hiroshige was an artist associated with the *Ukiyo-e* movement. Ukiyo-e is Japanese for "pictures of the floating world" and refers to subjects preferred by printmakers in Japan from the seventeenth to nineteenth century. These subjects included everyday customs as well as fashion, and scenes from travel or the theater. The strong flat design in work by Hiroshige and other printmakers were admired by leading nineteenth century European artists and influenced their work.

Katsushika Hokusai (1760–1849) Japan, painter, printmaker. Hokusai worked as a painter and printmaker during the *Ukiyo-e* era (17th to 19th centuries). Ukiyo-e means "pictures of the floating world" and refers to artists' preferences for subjects related to everyday life and special scenes in Japan. The informal balance and flat patterns in works by Hokusai and other Ukiyo-e printmakers influenced nineteenth century artists in Europe to explore more abstract and symmetrical compositions.

Winslow Homer (1836–1910) United States, painter, graphic artist. Homer began his career as an illustrator and approached many works with an eye toward telling a story in a picture. His most powerful and original works portray the sea and events in the lives of fishermen. He was a master of watercolor as well as oil painting.

Richard Hunt (1935–) United States, sculptor, printmaker. Hunt, an African-American, cuts, shapes and welds sheets of different metals to make up a palette of colors for his abstract sculptures. He creates other colors through the use of heat and applied patina. The theme of most of his work is the harmony of natural and industrial elements of society.

Ictinus, Callicrates, and Phidias (ca. 440BC) Greece, architects. Between 447BC and 436BC, Ictinus, Callicrates and Phidias designed, decorated and supervised construction of the Parthenon, a temple to Athena, the goddess of wisdom. Although there are few records of how the work was divided, the architects were Ictinus and Callicrates. Phidias was general supervisor and created much of the sculpture, including the huge ivory and gold statue of Athena.

Robert Indiana (1928–) United States, painter, sculptor, graphic artist. Indiana's works are created in the *Pop art* style. Many works incorporate letters and common images from billboards and traffic signs. His images are usually painted with bright, clear colors and well-defined edges. He has also worked on poster designs and with a variety of two and three-dimensional media.

Alexander Young Jackson (1882–1974) Canada, painter. Jackson was an influential member of a group of Canadian landscape painters. Every year he made field trips to rural areas to sketch scenes that he later painted in his studio.

Arne Jacobsen (1902–1971) Denmark, architect, designer. Jacobsen summed up his design philosophy with the words "Economy plus function equal style." His architecture and designs for chairs combine a sculptural elegance with attention to details that are important to people who use his designs.

Thomas Jefferson (1743–1836) United States, architect. Jefferson, an amateur architect, studied in Europe and brought the organization, proportion and simplicity of the *Classical Revival* style to the United States. He designed the University of Virginia, the State Capitol at Richmond and his own home, Monticello, in Virginia.

Charles William Jefferys (1869–1951) Canada, illustrator, painter. Jefferys, born in England, was a muralist, landscape painter and historical illustrator for Canadian books and magazines. His watercolors and drawings have been used in numerous books about Canada, including history books for schools.

Phillip Johnson (1906–) United States, architect. Johnson is known for his sleek glass and steel buildings designed in the international style. The forms of many of his buildings are designed to provide a maximum amount of light on the inside and a least amount of decorative detail on the inside and outside.

Sargent Johnson (1887–1967) United States, sculptor, printmaker. Johnson, a versatile African-American sculptor, is noted for his dignified and sensitive sculptural portraits of African-Americans. He worked in a variety of sculptural media and completed several major commissions for murals in cast stone, mosaic and wood. His works are in major museums throughout the United States.

William Henry Johnson (1901–1970) United States, painter. Johnson, an African-American, studied art in Europe and traveled or lived there intermittently. He explored several styles but retained a strong and direct compositional framework throughout his career. His late paintings focused on religious themes, political history and African-American experiences. Over 1000 of his works are in the National Museum of American Art in Washington, D.C.

Wassily Kandinsky (1886–1944) Russia, painter. Russian-born Kandinsky spent much of his life working in Europe and Russia. His early paintings included images from Russian folk art, but between 1910 and 1920, he gradually eliminated all representational images from his paintings. He is widely known as the originator of *Nonobjective* art and wrote extensively on the relationship of visual art to spiritual feelings.

Lori Kammeraad (20th century) United States, textile artist. Kammeraad's textiles are created with her own custom-dyed wool that she weaves into abstract designs. Her artworks are often created for specific interior spaces, at the request of individuals or interior designers.

Ellsworth Kelly (1923–) United States, painter, sculptor. Kelly's work is known as *Hard Edge* painting. His compositions are based on sharp-edged geometric or curved shapes with flat bright colors. Kelly's painted sheet-metal sculptures have qualities related to his paintings.

Rose Williams Kimewon (20th century) Canada, artisan. Kimewon, an Ottawa North American Indian, is credited with leading the revival of porcupine quill box making. She developed a unique tufting technique for lids that are decorated with images of Canadian animals or with abstract star designs.

Kawanabe Kiosai (1831–1899) Japan, painter. Kiosai was a master of ink and brush painting. He is known for his unusual technique of painting on screens prepared with backgrounds of powdered gold. His work reflects a sensitive use of light and dark values and lively asymmetrical compositions.

Paul Klee (1879–1940) Switzerland, painter, printmaker. Klee's work does not fall into any clear category. He is regarded as one of the most gifted, intuitive and inventive artists of the twentieth century. His mature sense of design and sensitive use of media were often combined with themes and viewpoints that express humor, tragedy and subconscious feelings.

Keith Kleepsies (20th century) United States, painter, sculptor, graphic artist. Kleepsies is a versatile artist whose work is marked by humor and often irony. In addition to creating murals and environmental sculpture, he works on a variety of graphic design projects for publications and television.

Jacob Lawrence (1917–) United States, painter. Lawrence, an African-American, has become well-known for his narrative paintings depicting leaders and events in African-American history. He has developed a distinct abstract style by applying flat areas of paint to pencil drawings. He mixes one color at a time and applies it to other areas before mixing another color.

Linda Lomahaftewa (1947–) United States, painter, printmaker. Lomahaftewa is a Hopi-Choctaw Indian whose abstract acrylic paintings and monoprints are based on themes and symbols from her tribal heritage. Lomahaftewa has taught at the Institute of American Indian Arts in Santa Fe for over twelve years.

Morris Louis (1912–1962) United States, painter. Louis' paintings are described as *Color-field* paintings. Their main expressive purpose is to heighten one's appreciation of colors by surrounding you with a field of color. Louis' paintings are created by pouring thinned paint on unprimed canvas in bands of bright, overlapping colors. This technique was first used by Helen Frankenthaler, whose work Louis admired.

David Macaulay (1946–) United States, illustrator. Macaulay was born in England but lives and works in the United States. He has written and illustrated many books that explain the planning and construction processes for various inventions and types of structures, including cathedrals, castles and skyscrapers.

James Edward Hervey MacDonald (1873–1932) Canada, painter. Born in Great Britain, MacDonald was a founding member of the *Group of Seven*, Canadian painters who sought to capture the unique character and lighting of Canadian landscapes in different seasons and times of day.

Jock (J.W.G.) MacDonald (1897–1960) Canada, painter. MacDonald, born in Scotland, played an important role in the development of *Abstract* and *Surrealist* art in Canada. Throughout his career, he experimented with media for painting, often developing one color harmony or image through a series of works.

Édouard Manet (1832–1882) France, painter, graphic artist. Manet is often regarded as one of the most important influences on modern art. His work is marked by a direct, unidealized approach to his subjects and an obvious use of brushstrokes to define shapes and contrasts in color. The *Impressionists* looked to his work as a source of inspiration. Although Manet did not exhibit with the Impressionists, his later work, which is lighter and freer, reflects his association with them in the Parisian artworld.

John Marin (1870–1953) United States, painter, engraver. Marin is best known for his life-long interest in capturing the atmospheric effects and hidden energy of scenes in New York City and the Maine coast. His work combines abstraction and representation to capture what he called the "life and motion" of the whole environment—people, animals, clouds and even the "aliveness" of buildings and rocky coasts.

Marisol (Escobar) (1930–) United States, sculptor. Marisol, born in France of Venezuelan parents, was brought to the United States early in her life. She became well-known for her carved and assembled sculptures of people to which she often added ordinary objects such as necklaces and umbrellas as accessories or props. Some of her life-sized figures are satirical portraits of well-known people. These works are related to the *Pop art* style.

Henri Matisse (1869–1954) France, painter, sculptor. Matisse is widely recognized as one of the most influential artists of the twentieth century. His work emphasized the flatness of the picture space (rather than the illusion of depth and form). He developed line, pattern and color as abstract and decorative elements in his work. Late in life, he worked in collage using hand-painted papers and freely cutting shapes.

Melissa Miller (1951–) United States, painter. Miller, who grew up on a Texas ranch, has focused on animals in landscapes as a major theme for her paintings. Some works have a story element, but many are composed to suggest humorous, mysterious or puzzling relationships between animals, their environments, and people.

Jean-François Millet (1814–1875) France, painter, graphic artist. Millet is best known for his drawings and paintings of rural life and landscapes. He emphasized the dignity and hard labor of farm workers seeking "to make the trivial serve to express the sublime." His works were widely reproduced during the nineteenth century and often served as the basis for sermons or related moral instruction.

Joan Miró (1893–1983) Spain, painter. Miró is known as a leader of the *Surrealist* style. He believed that artists should allow themselves to work spontaneously and let unconscious ideas control the creative process. Many of the symbols in his work combine elements of remembered events, imaginary landscapes and invented shapes.

Amadeo Modigliani (1884–1920) Italy, painter, sculptor. Modigliani is best known for his portraits that have simple elongated forms, graceful linear elements and subtle shifts in color. His paintings and sculpture were strongly influenced by *Cubism* and the simplified abstract forms of African sculpture.

Claude Monet (1840–1928) France, painter. The *Impressionist* movement was named for a painting by Monet, *Impression: Sunrise,* which shows the misty atmospheric effects of the sun rising over water. Monet painted directly from nature to capture the immediate visual effects of color and light. He often created a series of paintings based on a single subject as seen at different times of day or seasons of the year.

Julia Morgan (1872–1957) United States, architect. Morgan was the first woman to be licensed architect in California. During her long career, she designed over 800 buildings. Her largest project was San Simeon, the castle-like residence of the publisher William Randolph Hearst.

Deborah Morrisey-McGoff (20th century) United State, painter. Morrisey-McGoff creates drawings and paintings that have subtle variations in textures and mixtures of colors. Her work has focused on landscapes, especially the mysterious interplay of light and shadow on three-dimensional forms.

Jessie Natkong (20th century) Canada, textile artisan. Natkong, a Haida North American Indian, is known for the tunics she sews. Traditionally, men wear these tunics at ceremonial events. Each tunic has at least one crest. The tunic shown in the text features the brown bear, the crest of the artist's adoptive father, and the leaping dog salmon, her personal crest. The artist created this tunic at the age of ninety.

Emile Nolde (1867–1956) Germany, painter, printmaker. Nolde, a deeply religious man, is known as an *Expressionist* painter. His paintings of flowers and landscapes reflect his emotional response both to his subject matter, and to the process of painting. His works are marked by bold lines, intense colors and distorted shapes. He is also well-known for his highly personal interpretations of Old and New Testament subjects.

Georgia O'Keeffe (1887–1986) United States, painter. O'Keefe's work was based on the natural appearances of objects, but she is known as one of the first artists in the United States to work in an abstract style. Her paintings portray modified, softened and simplified objects or enlarged elements of them which fill the canvas. Her subjects (flowers, bones, mountains, clouds and sky) were selected primarily because she found them visually intriguing. She often created a series of related works on the same subject.

José Clemente Orozco (1883–1949) Mexico, painter. Orozco was trained as an architect, but is best known for his large, narrative murals in fresco (fresh plaster) based on social, political and humanitarian themes. Orozco is credited with reviving the art of fresco painting in Mexico and in the United States where he worked on numerous murals.

Mary T. Osceola (20th Century) United States, artisan. Osceola, a Miccosukee Indian from Florida, caries on the traditional Seminole and Miccosukee craft of sewing patchwork clothing. The technique is related to quilting. Patchwork sewing was encouraged and developed by the sale of sewing machines in the early 1900s.

I.M. (Ieoh Ming) Pei (1917–) United States, architect. Chinese-born Pei is known for his elegant use of architectural materials to draw attention to the form of his buildings. He has designed commercial buildings, libraries, churches, and art museums including the East Wing of the National Gallery of Art in Washington, D.C.

Amado Peña (1943–) United States, printmaker. Peña works in serigraphy, a silkscreen process. His Hispanic and American Indian background is reflected in his choice of subjects and themes for his prints. Characteristic of his work is the use of strong patterns and multiple outlines that echo the major shapes.

Irving Penn (1917–) United States, photographer. Penn began his career as a photographer for *Vogue* magazine and is recognized for his portraits. He photographs his subjects, usually celebrities, in unusual and visually interesting environments.

Beatrice Perry (20th century) United States, sculptor. The landscape near her childhood home in Michigan has had a significant influence on Perry's work. She has also been inspired by the philosophy of the Bauhaus, a German art school that emphasized simplicity, lack of pretense, honesty with materials and art as a positive force in society.

Gábor Peterdi (1915–) United States, printmaker, painter. Peterdi was born in Hungary. He immigrated to the United States and, with other painters of the 1940s and 1950s, explored printmaking. Peterdi became well-known for his complex combinations of various printing techniques and processes. His major sources of ideas were the landscape, plants and the unseen growth process (seeds germinating).

Pablo Picasso (1881–1973) Spain, painter, sculptor, engraver. Picasso lived in Paris and experimented with many art styles and media during his long life. He developed *Cubism,* with its complex division of form and space. His paintings represent most of the twentieth century movements in art, from realistic to abstract. His sculpture is innovative and frequently humorous.

Camille Pissarro (1830–1903) France, painter, graphic artist. Pissarro was born in the West Indies and moved to Paris when he was twenty-five. He is known as a leader of the *Impressionist* movement, and influential teacher of other artists. He created paintings out of doors capturing the atmosphere and character of landscapes. His late works include scenes of Paris streets painted from windows of buildings.

François Pompon (1855–1923) France, sculptor. Pompon became well-known for his sculptures of animals. He created over 300 works in which the essential characteristics of species are portrayed in a lively yet dignified style.

Daniel Pressley (1918–1971) United States, sculptor. Pressley, an African-American, had no formal art training but drew, modeled clay and whittled from the age of seven. He kept a diary with sketches and comments about his life. He created about seventy-five relief sculptures which are today highly regarded by collectors.

Bill Reid (1920–) Canada, sculptor, artisan. Reid, a Haida Indian, began his career as a metalsmith working in gold and silver as his grandfather had done. Reid also studied the design and techniques in older Haida works that were in museums. Reid shares his knowledge of techniques and Haida design concepts through his own masterful work and through teaching, writing and films.

G.A. (George Agnew) Reid (1860–1947) Canada, painter. Reid's paintings reveal his interest in Canada's landscape and history. His paintings and murals are in many Canadian buildings and museums. He donated his collection of almost 500 works to the Ontario Department of Education.

Patricia A. Renick (1932–) United States, sculptor, painter, printmaker. Renick is widely known for her sculpture but she also creates paintings, drawings and prints. She prefers to maintain at least two directions for work at any given time so that ideas from one medium or theme can be contrasted with, or inspire, additional work.

Rembrandt van Rijn (1606–1669) The Netherlands, painter, printmaker, draughtsman. Rembrandt is known for his masterful techniques of painting, drawing and etching. In each art form, he captured the feeling of physical and spiritual presence of his subjects. His paintings have dramatic light and shade, rich textural effects and striking compositions. His subject matter ranged from portraits to religious subjects.

Alexander Rodchenko (1891–1956) Russia, painter, photographer, designer, sculptor. Rodchenko coined the term Nonobjectivism to describe his early drawings and paintings of geometric forms created with the aid of a ruler and compass, and without recognizable images. He also designed furniture, made films and photographs, and constructed sculptures to hang from ceilings. He was an important and early leader of experimental art in Russia.

Mark Rothko (1903–1970) United States, painter. Born in Russia, Rothko studied at Yale and the Art Students League and was a leader of the *Abstract Expressionist* movement. He was influenced by Surrealism, but developed his own style, surrounding soft-edged rectangles with related colors.

Henri Rousseau (1844–1910) France, painter.
Rousseau was a self-taught painter. His naïve and imaginative perspective, flattened colors and careful compositions of anmals, plants and figures were admired by *Post-Impresssionist* artists who were exploring new directions for art.

Betye Saar (1926–) United States, sculptor.
Saar, an African-American, is known for her assembled box sculptures made from found and natural materials such as wood, leather, fabric and shells. Saar often reworks and alters stereotypical images of African-Americans.

Lucas Samaras (1936–) Greek-American sculptor and experimental artist. Samaras has worked in a variety of sculptural media with the aim of redefining what sculptures are and how people respond to them. His sculptured book is one of many examples of a related theme in his work—that people should experience sculpture through the senses of touch or other physical interactions.

Siglinda Scarpa (20th century) United States, mosaic artist. Scarpa creates mosaics for interior and exterior walls, floors, windows, doors and fireplaces. Her style combines ancient Italian techniques with her own contemporary ideas.

Ben Shahn (1898–1969) United States, painter, printmaker, photographer, calligrapher. Born in Lithuania, Shahn came to the United States in 1906. His paintings included social concerns and satirical caricatures. He worked with Diego Rivera and later did murals of his own. His later work continued exploring social issues with directness and sometimes included written commentaries.

Charles Sheeler (1883–1965) United States, painter, photographer. Sheeler was a leader of a style known as *Precisionism*, in which objects are still recognizable but have geometric shapes and definite edges related to those in photographs. Sheeler said that he wanted to "reduce natural forms to the borderline of abstraction." Sheeler also explored photography as an art form. In both media, his favorite subject was architecture.

Li Shih-hsing (1283–1328) China, painter, calligrapher. Li Shih-hsing was the son of a government official and often traveled with his father. During these times, Li Shih-hsing met elders who taught him ancient Chinese painting and calligraphy techniques. Nature and old trees are common themes in his work.

Everett Shinn (1876–1953) United States, painter. Shinn was a member of the *Ashcan School*, a group of artists who realistically portrayed contemporary American urban life. Shinn's subject matter included theater and music hall activities. He also painted portraits and murals. He worked as an illustrator for newspapers and many childrens' books.

Skidmore, Owings and Merrill (20th century) United States, architects. Louis Skidmore, Nathaniel Owings and Edward Merrill established an architectural firm that became known world-wide for large projects designed in the *International* style. Characteristics of the International style include machine-like geometric forms made of concrete, steel, and glass usually with little decoration.

Moses Soyer (1899–1975) painter. Soyer was born in Russia. He emigrated to the United States. along with his twin, Raphael, who was also an artist. During the 1930s Depression, both artists painted portraits of their friends and realistically portrayed the social problems and the hopeless feelings of many people during the era.

Saul Steinberg (1914–) United States, painter, illustrator. Steinberg was born in Romania and trained as an architect. He is best known as a master of drawing in which calligraphy and humor are combined. He was a cartoonist for *The New Yorker,* but many of his works are also in museums around the world.

Joseph Stella (1877–1946) United States, painter. Italian-born Stella emigrated to the United States. Many of his paintings were inspired by his knowledge of the *Futurist* movement in Italy, which focused on the problem of expressing the motion, speed and energy of twentieth century life. Stella's paintings, based on scenes in and near New York City reflect his admiration for America as a "new civilization." He was especially awed by the Brooklyn Bridge, a subject in many of his paintings.

Varvara Stepanova (1894–1958) Russia, artist and designer. Stepanova worked with other Russian artists who were interested in the *Futurist* movement. She also designed textiles, stage sets, posters and type. Much of Stepanova's artwork is planned around geometric shapes, an influence from artists who admired the geometric elements in modern machinery.

Howard Storm (20th century) United States, painter. Storm is known for his paintings of landscapes, which are composed around unusual views and developed with strong color relationships. The landscapes are often visual metaphors for an intensive response he has had to the particular environment.

William Strickland (1788–1854) United States, architect. Although Strickland was best known as an architect, he was also a painter, engraver, illustrator, cartographer and scenery designer for the theater. In 1832, Strickland rebuilt and redesigned much of the 100 year-old Independence Hall using architectural ideas from England known as a *Georgian* style (for King George).

William Henry Fox Talbot (1800–1877) Great Britain, photographer. The Photographic Age began after the invention of the daguerreotype. This early process inspired Talbot to develop a way to make positive prints from paper negatives. He was one of the first to think of photography as an art medium. Talbot also used photography as a substitute for sketching landscapes.

Henry Ossawa Tanner (1859–1937) United States, painter. Tanner, an African-American, studied art in the United States and Europe, where he was influenced by the style of the *Impressionists* and first became well-known. Most of his works center on religious subjects or bring a spiritual and religious meanings to subject matter related to everyday life.

Wayne Thiebaud (1920–) United States, painter, filmmaker, graphic artist. Thiebaud began his career as a cartoonist and advertising art director in New York. His style is related to *Pop art*, with strong colors and stylized images set on a plain background. He is best known for his still lifes of cafeteria and convenience foods but has also portrayed animals and people in his work.

Tom Thomson (1877–1917) Canada, painter. Thomson is known as one of the first Canadians to concentrate on painting outdoors in the wilderness of Canada, attempting to capture the distinct character and color of the land. His spontaneous use of colors and brushstrokes as well as devotion to Canadian themes inspired the *Group of Seven*, Canadian landscape painters based in Toronto, who continued Thomson's ideas after his death.

Louis Comfort Tiffany (1848–1933) United States, designer. Tiffany is well-known for his work in glass. He contributed to the revival of interest in stained glass and the development of a new opalescent colored glass, or Tiffany glass. Tiffany stained glass windows, lamps and other decorations are widely copied.

Joaquín Torres-García (1874–1949) Uruguay, painter. Torres-García studied art in Spain and created murals for churches and public buildings. He later traveled to Paris and New York where he met artists who worked in a geometric style. As a result of their influence, he developed more geometric paintings, based on grids, which also included symbols from pre-Columbian and modern cultures.

Angelika Traylor (20th century) United States, glass artisan. Traylor creates one-of-a-kind stained glass lamps, panels and architectural installations. She is noted for the intricacy of her designs and for her use of bold, jewel-toned colors.

Martin Tucker (20th century) United States, painter, draftsman. Tucker is known for his expressive drawings and paintings of varied subjects in the environment. His drawings in color have a lively, painterly quality and his paintings have strong linear brushstrokes related to his style of drawing.

Vincent van Gogh (1853–1890) The Netherlands, painter. Van Gogh is known as a *Post-Impressionist* painter, which means he was influenced by *Impressionism* but developed his own style. Van Gogh is known for his expressive and symbolic use of color and thick paint applied with varied brush-strokes. His work was the inspiration for the development of many variations of the *Expressionist* style.

Jan (Joannes van der Meer) Vermeer (1632–1675) The Netherlands, painter. Vermeer is regarded as one of the greatest Dutch painters. He is known for his serene compositions and realistic depictions of everyday scenes. His paintings are small and in photographs, appear to have a smooth texture. The actual paintings have vibrant textures and translucent colors that have been aptly compared to "crushed pearls, melted together."

Marie Louise Élisabeth Vigée-Lebrun (1755–1842) France, painter. Vigée-Lebrun was a court painter in France, specializing in portraits of Marie Antoinette and others. During the French Revolution and Napoleonic regime, she traveled throughout Europe and continued to work for wealthy patrons. Her portraits were flattering, elegant and characteristic of the luxuriant sentiment in much *Rococo* art.

Maurice de Vlaminck (1876–1946) France, painter. Vlaminck is best known for his still life and landscape paintings with thick paint applied with energetic brushstokes. His early paintings were dominated by bright colors. His work is realistic but expressionistic in technique.

Erika Wade (1953–) United States, painter, fiber artist. Wade is an accomplished painter and fiber artist. She has created some weavings with stained painterly qualities and has recently created woven surfaces in which colored yarns are interlocked with strips of painted paper.

Thomas Ustick Walter (1804–1887) United States, architect. Walter was one of a number of architects who were responsible for developing the *Greek Revival* style in which elements from ancient Greek architecture are used. Walter, one of many architects of the United States Capitol, was largely responsible for designing its great dome, rotunda and flanking wings.

Andy Warhol (1926–1987) United States, painter, graphic designer, filmmaker. Warhol, a commercial artist, became a leader of *Pop art*, a style that recycled images from popular culture. His best-known works are brightly-colored, silk-screened or painted images of mass-produced objects (soup cans), celebrities (Marilyn Monroe) and events reported in the mass-media (Vietnam war).

Laura Wheeler Waring (1887–1948) United States, painter. Waring, an African-American, studied art in the United States and Europe. Her painting style combines realistic and impressionistic techniques to express the individual character of her subjects. Waring was commissioned to paint portraits of many distinguished African-Americans.

George Washington, (1732–1799) United States, architect. The first President of the United States, like many well-educated people of his time, had enough knowledge of architecture to design much of his family estate, Mount Vernon.

Beverly Willis (1928–) United States, architect, designer. Willis has architectural offices in New York and San Francisco. Her practice centers on designs for art centers and housing which ranges from individual homes to mass housing for the U.S. Army. She has received numerous awards for her sensitive combinations of old and new architectural concepts and for her attention to the social purposes of architecture. She also designs furniture, paints and sculpts in wood.

Frank Lloyd Wright (1867–1959) United States, architect. Wright is internationally recognized as a major twentieth century architect. During his seventy years of work, he designed hundred of buildings—homes, hotels, museums, churches, businesses. He is known for "breaking up the box" (as he put it) and developing open, free-flowing spaces in buildings. He made technical improvements in construction and imaginatively combined materials. His last major project, completed after his death, was the Solomon R. Guggenheim Museum in New York.

Takeo Yamaguchi (1902–) Korea, painter. Yamaguchi, who studied in Europe and lived in Japan, is noted for his paintings of abstract shapes, often derived from Japanese hieroglyphics and enlarged on a solid colored background. Yamaguchi's work inspired other Japanese artists to explore *Abstract* art.

Mahonri Young (1877–1957) United States, sculptor. Young studied sculpture in the United States and in Paris where he first became well-known. His sculptures of workmen, cowboys, horses and prize-fighters won many awards. He is also well-known for a large commemorative sculpture of his Mormon heritage, and for a portrait of his grandfather, Brigham Young.

Bibliography for Teachers

Books: Teaching Art

For teachers who wish to expand their general understanding of art in education, the following professional books are recommended.

Adams, James L. *The Care and Feeding of Ideas: A Guide for Encouraging Creativity.* Reading, MA: Addison-Wesley, 1986.

Arnheim, Rudolph. *Visual Thinking.* Berkeley, CA: University of California Press, 1980.

Brommer, Gerald and Joseph Gatto. *Careers in Art: An Illustrated Guide.* Worcester, MA: Davis Publications, 1984.

Chapman, Laura H. *Approaches to Art in Education.* San Diego, CA: Harcourt Brace Jovanovich, 1978.

Chapman, Laura H. *Teaching Art.* Worcester, MA: Davis Publications, 1989.

Chapman, Laura H. *Instant Art, Instant Culture: The Unspoken Policy for American Schools.* New York: Teachers College Press, 1982.

Clements, Claire and Robert Clements. *Art and Mainstreaming: Art Education for Exceptional Students in Regular School Classes.* Springfield, IL: Charles C. Thomas, 1983.

Cobb, Virginia. *Discovering the Inner Eye.* New York: Watson-Guptill, 1988.

Gardner, Howard. *Artful Scribbles: The Significance of Children's Drawings.* New York: Basic Books, 1982.

Henley, David. *Exceptional Children, Exceptional Art: Teaching Art to Special Needs.* Worcester, MA: Davis Publications, 1991.

Hurwitz, Al and Michael Day. *Children and Their Art: Methods for the Elementary School.* 5th ed. New York: Harcourt Brace Jovanovich, 1991.

Hurwitz, Al. *The Gifted and Talented in Art: A Guide to Program Planning.* Worcester, MA: Davis Publications, 1983.

Johnson, Andra, ed. *Art Education: Elementary.* Reston, VA: National Art Education Association, 1992.

Lowenfeld, Viktor and W. Lambert Brittain. *Creative and Mental Growth.* 8th ed. New York: Macmillan, 1987.

National Art Education Association. *Essentials of a Quality Art Program.* Reston, VA: National Art Education Association, 1981.

National Endowment for the Arts. *Toward Civilization: A Report on Arts Education.* Washington, DC, 1988.

Peterson, Bryan. *Learning to See Creatively.* New York: Watson-Guptill, 1988.

Qualley, Charles A. *Safety in the Artroom.* Worcester, MA: Davis Publications, 1986.

Young, Bernard, ed. *Art, Culture, and Ethnicity.* Reston VA: National Art Education Assoc., 1991.

For additional information on contemporary art education in schools, write for a list of publications from:

National Art Education Association, 1916 Association Drive, Reston, VA. 20191-1590.

Art Reference Books for Teachers

Art History Surveys

Arnason, H. H. *History of Modern Art: Painting, Sculpture, Architecture,* 3rd ed. Englewood Cliffs, NJ: Prentice-Hall, 1986.

Brommer, Gerald. *Discovering Art History,* 3rd ed. Worcester, MA: Davis Publications, 1997.

De la Croix, Horst. *Art Through the Ages,* 9th ed. San Diego, CA: Harcourt Brace Jovanovich, 1990.

Feldman, Edmund Burke *The Artist,* 1982; *Thinking About Art,* 1985; *Varieties of Visual Experience,* 3rd ed., 1987. Englewood Cliffs, NJ: Prentice-Hall.

Gombrich, E. H. *The Story of Art,* 14th ed. Englewood Cliffs, NJ: Prentice-Hall, 1985.

Hobbs, Jack A. *Art in Context.* 4th ed. San Diego, CA: Harcourt Brace Jovanovich, 1990.

Honour, Hugh, and John Fleming. *The Visual Arts: A History.* 2nd ed. Englewood Cliffs, NJ: Prentice-Hall, 1986.

Hughes, Robert. *The Shock of the New.* Westminster, MD: Alfred A. Knopf, 1990.

Artistic Traditions

Asian

Stanley-Smith, Joan. *Japanese Art.* New York: Thames and Hudson, 1984.

Lee, Sherman. *A History of Far Eastern Art,* 4th ed. New York: Harry N. Abrams, 1982.

African and African-American

Center for African Art. *Art/Artifact.* New York: Center for African Art, 1988.

Driskell, David C. *Hidden Heritage: Afro-American Art.* San Francisco, CA: The Art Museum of America, 1985; *Two Centuries of Black American Art.* Westminster, MD: Alfred A. Knopf/Los Angeles County Museum of Art, 1976.

Lewis, Samella. *Art: African American.* Los Angeles: Hancraft Studios, 1990.

Willett, Frank. *African Art.* New York: Thames and Hudson, 1985.

Chanda, Jaqueline. *African Arts and Cultures.* Worcester, MA: Davis Publications, 1993.

Americas

Bronx Museum of the Arts. *The Latin American Spirit: Art and Artists in the United States, 1920–1970.* New York: Harry N. Abrams, 1988.

D'Alleva, Anne. *Native American Arts and Cultures.* Worcester, MA: Davis Publications, 1992.

Emmerich, André. *Art Before Columbus.* New York: Simon & Schuster, 1983.

Highwater, Jamake. *Arts of the American Indians: Leaves from the Sacred Tree.* New York: Harper Collins, 1985.

La Duke, Betty. *Compañeras: Women, Art and Social Change in Latin America.* San Francisco: City Lights Books, 1985.

Paz, Octavio, et al. *Mexico: Splendors of Thirty Centuries.* Boston: Bulfinch Press, 1990.

Folk Art

Rosenak, Chuck and Jan. *Museum of American Folk Art Encyclopedia of Twentieth-Century American Folk Art and Artists.* New York: Abbeville Press, 1991.

Schuman, Jo Miles. *Art from Many Hands.* Worcester, MA: Davis Publications, 1981.

Siporin, Steve, *American Folk Masters: The National Heritage Fellows.* New York: Harry N. Abrams, 1992.

Themes and Purposes of Art

Elsen, Albert E. *Purposes of Art,* 4th ed. New York: Holt, Rinehart and Winston, 1981.

Kris, Ernst, and Otto Kurz. *Legend, Myth, and Magic in the Image of the Artist: A Historical Experiment.* New Haven, CT: Yale University Press, 1979.

Smeets, René. *Signs, Symbols and Ornaments.* New York: Van Nostrand Reinhold, 1982.

Women Artists

Harris, Ann. *Women Artists: 1550–1950.* Westminster, MD: Alfred A. Knopf, 1977.

Heller, Nancy G. *Women Artists: An Illustrated History.* New York: Abbeville Press, 1987.

Munro, Eleanor. *Originals: American Women Artists.* New York: Simon & Schuster, 1982.

Petersen, Karen, and J. J. Wilson. *Women Artists: Recognition and Reappraisal from the Early Middle Ages to the Twentieth Century.* New York: HarperCollins, 1976.

Remer, Abby. *Pioneering Spirits: The Life and Times of Remarkable Women Artists in Western History.* Worcester, MA: Davis Publications, 1997.

Rubinstein, Charlotte Streifer. *American Women Artists: From Early Indian Times to the Present.* Boston: G. K. Hall, 1982.

Van Wagner, Judy K. Collischan. *Women Shaping Art: Profiles in Power.* Westport, CT: Greenwood Publishing Group, 1984.

Watson-Jones, Virginia. *Contemporary American Women Sculptors.* Phoenix, AZ: Oryx Press, 1986.

Aesthetics and Art Criticism

Atkins, Robert. *Artspeak: A Guide to Contemporary Ideas, Movements and Buzzwords.* New York: Abbeville Press, 1990.

Battin, Margaret, et al. *Puzzles About Art: An Aesthetics Casebook.* New York: St. Martin's Press, 1989.

Berger, John. *Ways of Seeing.* New York: Viking Penguin, 1977.

Goodman, Nelson. *Languages of Art.* 2nd ed. Indianapolis, IN: Hackett Publishing, 1976.

The Creation of Art

Artist's Quotes/Writing

Goldwater, Robert and Marco Treves, eds. *Artists on Art: From the 14th to the 20th Century.* New York: Pantheon Books, 1974.

Herbert, Robert L. *Modern Artists on Art: Ten Unabridged Essays.* Englewood Cliffs, NJ: Prentice-Hall, 1964.

Johnson, Ellen H., ed. *American Artists on Art from 1940 to 1980.* New York: HarperCollins, 1982.

Roskill, Mark, ed. *The Letters of Vincent Van Gogh.* New York: Macmillan, 1963.

Biographies of Artists

Anderson, Nancy K. and Linda S. Ferber. *Albert Bierstadt: Art and Enterprise.* New York: Hudson Hills Press, 1991.

Castro, Jan Garden. *The Art and Life of Georgia O'Keeffe.* New York: Crown Publications, 1985.

Hammacher, A.M. and Renilde. *Van Gogh.* New York: Thames and Hudson, 1990.

Levin, Gail. *Edward Hopper: The Art and the Artist.* New York: W. W. Norton, 1980.

Mattison, Robert Saltonstall. *Grace Hartigan: A Painter's World.* New York: Hudson Hills Press, 1990.

Rubin, William, ed. *Pablo Picasso: A Retrospective.* New York: Harry N. Abrams/Museum of Modern Art, 1980.

Shadbolt, Doris. *The Art of Emily Carr.* Seattle: University of Washington Press, 1988.

Elements and Principles of Design

Bevlin, Marjorie E. *Design Through Discovery,* 5th ed. Fort Worth, TX: Holt, Rinehart & Winston, 1989.

Landa, Robin. *An Introduction to Design.* Englewood Cliffs, NJ: Prentice-Hall, 1983.

Lauer, David A. *Design Basics.* Fort Worth, TX: Holt, Rinehart & Winston, 1990.

Martinez, Benjamin and Jacqueline Block. *Visual Forces: An Introduction to Design.* Englewood Cliffs, NJ: Prentice-Hall, 1988.

Roukes, Nicholas. *Design Synectics.* Worcester, MA: Davis Publications, 1987.

Samuelson, Jerry and Jack Stoops. *Design Dialogue,* rev. ed. Worcester, MA: Davis Publications, 1985.

Specific Art Forms

Architecture

Busch, Akiko. *The Art of the Architectural Model.* New York: TAB Books, 1991.

Fletcher, Sir Banister. *A History of Architecture,* 19th ed. Stoneham, MA: Butterworth-Heinemann, 1987.

Lacy, Bill. *100 Contemporary Architects.* New York: Harry N. Abrams, 1991.

Scully, Vincent. *Modern Architecture,* rev.ed. New York: Braziller, 1974.

Smith, G.E. Kidder. *Looking at Architecture.* New York: Harry N. Abrams, 1990.

Crafts

Lucie-Smith, Edward. *The Story of Craft: The Craftsman's Role in Society.* Oxford, England: Phaidon, 1981.

Margetts, Martina, ed. *International Crafts.* New York: Thames and Hudson, 1991.

Nelson, Glenn C. *Ceramics: A Potter's Handbook,* 5th ed. Forth Worth, TX: Holt, Rinehart & Winston, 1984.

Sayer, Chloë. *Arts and Crafts of Mexico.* San Francisco: Chronicle Books, 1990.

Sprintzen, Alice. *Crafts: Contemporary Design and Technique.* Worcester, MA: Davis Publications, 1987.

Topal, Cathy Weisman. *Children, Clay and Sculpture.* Worcester, MA: Davis Publications, 1983.

Drawing

Betti, Claudia, and Teel Sale. *Drawing: A Contemporary Approach,* 3rd ed. Forth Worth, TX: Holt, Rinehart & Winston, 1992.

Brommer, Gerald. *Exploring Drawing.* Worcester, MA: Davis Publications, 1988.

Chaet, Bernard. *The Art of Drawing,* 3rd ed. Forth Worth, TX: Holt, Rinehart & Winston, 1983.

Enstice, Wayne and Melody Peters. *Drawing: Space, Form and Expression.* Englewood Cliffs, NJ: Prentice-Hall, 1990.

Gatto, Joseph. *Drawing Media and Techniques.* Worcester, MA: Davis Publications, 1987.

Godfrey, Tony. *Drawing Today.* New York: Phaidon Universe, 1990.

Larsen, Karl V. *See & Draw.* Worcester, MA: Davis Publications, 1992.

Mugnaini, Joseph. *Expressive Drawing: A Schematic Approach.* Worcester, MA: Davis Publications, 1988.

Nicolaides, Kimon. *The Natural Way to Draw: A Working Plan for Art Study.* Boston: Houghton Mifflin, 1990.

Environmental Design

Alexander, Christopher, et al. *A Pattern Language: Towns, Buildings, Construction.* New York: Oxford University Press, 1977.

Bacon, Edmund N. *Design of Cities.* New York: Viking Penguin, 1976.

Graphic Design and Computer Graphics

Gatta, Kevin, et al. *Foundations of Graphic Design.* Worcester, MA: Davis Publications, 1991.

Greh, Deborah. *Computers in the Artroom.* Worcester, MA: Davis Publications, 1991.

Richmond, Wendy. *Design and Technology.* New York: Van Nostrand Reinhold, 1990.

Roth, Laszlo. *Package Design.* Englewood Cliffs, NJ: Prentice-Hall, 1981.

Painting

Brommer, Gerald. *Exploring Painting.* rev. ed., 1995; *Understanding Transparent Watercolor,* 1993. Worcester, MA: Davis Publications.

Chaet, Bernard. *An Artist's Notebook: Techniques and Materials.* Fort Worth, TX: Holt, Rinehart and Winston, 1979.

Goldstein, Nathan. *Painting: Visual and Technical Fundamentals.* Englewood Cliffs, NJ: Prentice-Hall, 1979.

Topal, Cathy Weisman. *Children and Painting.* Worcester, MA: Davis Publications, 1992.

Photography, Film, Video

Newhall, Beaumont. *The History of Photography: From 1839 to the Present Day,* 5th rev. ed. Boston: Bulfinch Press/Museum of Modern Art, 1982.

O'Brien, Michael and Norman Sibley. *The Photographic Eye,* rev. ed. Worcester, MA: Davis Publications, 1995.

Patterson, Freeman. *Photography and the Art of Seeing.* San Francisco: Sierra Club Books, 1990.

Rosenblum, Naomi. *A World History of Photography,* rev. ed. New York: Abbeville Press, 1989.

Printmaking

Acton, David. *A Spectrum of Innovations; Color in American Printmaking 1890–1960.* New York: W.W. Norton & Co., 1990.

Ross, John, Tim and Clare Romano. *The Complete Printmaker.* New York: The Free Press/Macmillan, 1990.

Toale, Bernard. *Basic Printmaking Techniques.* Worcester, MA: Davis Publications, 1993.

Sculpture

Mills, John. *The Encyclopedia of Sculpture Techniques.* New York: Watson-Guptill, 1990.

Nigrosh, Leon. *Sculpting Clay.* Worcester, MA: Davis Publications, 1991.

Peck, Judith. *Sculpture as Experience.* Radnor, PA: Chilton Book Co., 1989.

Roukes, Nicholas. *Sculpture in Paper.* Worcester, MA: Davis Publications, 1993.

Verhelst, Wibert. *Sculpture: Tools, Materials and Techniques.* Englewood Cliffs, NJ: Prentice-Hall, 1988.

Williams, Arthur. *Sculpture: Technique, Form and Content,* rev. ed. Worcester, MA: Davis Publications, 1995.

Wolfe, George. *3-D Wizardry: Design in Papier-Mâché, Plaster and Foam.* Worcester, MA: Davis Publications, 1995.

Bibliography for Students

Art Resource Books

Aesthetics and Appreciation

Belves, Pierre, and Mathey, François. *Enjoying the World of Art*; *How Artists Work: An Introduction to Techniques of Art*. Scarsdale, NY: Lion Books, 1968.

Blizzard, Gladys S. *Come Look with Me: Enjoying Art With Children*. Charlottsville, VA: Thomasson Grant, 1990.

Franc, Helen M. *An Invitation to See: 125 Paintings from The Museum of Modern Art*. New York: Harry N. Abrams/Museum of Modern Art, 1973.

Greenberg, Jan and Sandra Jordan. *The Painter's Eye*. New York: Delacorte Press, 1991.

Sullivan, Charles, ed. *Children of Promise: African-American Literature and Art for Young People*. New York: Harry N. Abrams, 1991.

Art History

Aardema, Verna. *Why Mosquitoes Buzz in People's Ears: A West-African Tale*. New York: Dial Books for Young Readers, 1978.

Janson, H.W. *History of Art for Young People*, 3rd ed. New York: Harry N. Abrams, 1987.

Musgrove, Margaret. *Ashanti to Zulu: African Traditions*. New York: Dial Books for Young Readers, 1976.

Smith, Bradley. *Mexico: A History in Art*. New York: Doubleday & Co., 1971.

Taylor, Barbara Howland. *Mexico: Her Daily and Festive Breads*. Claremont, CA: Ocelot Press, 1969.

Individual Artists

Goldstein, Ernest. *Let's Get Lost in a Painting* Series. Dallas, TX: Garrard Publications, 1984.

Howard, Nancy Shrayer (series) *Jacob Lawrence: American Scenes, American Struggles,* 1996; *Helen Cordero and the Storytellers of Cochiti Pueblo,* 1995; *William Sidney Mount: Painter of Rural America,* 1994. Worcester, MA: Davis Publications.

Locher, J. L., ed. *The World of M. C. Escher*. New York: Harry N. Abrams, 1988.

Rockwell, Norman. *Norman Rockwell: My Adventures As An Illustrator*. New York: Harry N. Abrams, 1988.

Venezia, Mike (series). *Getting to Know the World's Greatest Artists*. Chicago: Children's Press.

Subjects and Themes in Art

Lerner Publications, Minneapolis, MN: Series: *The Horse in Art; Kings and Queens in Art; Sports and Games in Art; Musical Instruments in Art; The Ship and the Sea in Art; The Warrior in Art: The Cat in Art; Demons and Beasts in Art; Medicine in Art; The Self-Portrait in Art; The Worker in Art; The Old Testament in Art; The New Testament in Art.*

Elements and Principles of Design

O'Neill, Mary. *Hailstones and Halibut Bones: Adventures in Color*. New York: Doubleday & Co., 1990.

Selleck, Jack, Joseph Gatto, Albert Porter, Gerald Brommer and George Horn (series). Part I: *Elements of Design* ; Part II: *Principles of Design*. Worcester, MA: Davis Publications.

Yanawine, Philip (series). *Shapes, Lines, Colors, Stories*. Canada: Delacorte Press /Museum of Modern Art, 1991.

Specific Art Forms

Architecture/Design in Everyday Life

Crouch, Dora P. *History of Architecture: Stonehenge to Skyscrapers*. New York: McGraw-Hill, 1985.

Macaulay, David (series) *Cathedral, City, Pyramid, Castle, Unbuilding, Underground*. New York: Macmillan.

McAlester, Virginia and Lee. *A Field Guide to American Houses*. Westminster, MD: Alfred A. Knopf, 1984.

Taylor, Anne, George Blastos and Alison Marshall. *Architecture and Children*. Seattle, WA: Architecture and Children Institute, 1991.

Camera/Electronic Arts

Bruandet, Pierre. *Photograms*. New York: Watson-Guptill, 1973.

Laybourne, Kit. *The Animation Book: A Complete Guide to Animated FilmMaking—From Flip-Books to Sound Cartoons*. New York: Crown Publications, 1988.

O'Brien, Michael F. and Norman Sibley. *The Photographic Eye*, rev. ed. Worcester, MA: Davis Publications, 1995.

Computer Software

Cricket Draw, Computer Graphics Software, Malvern, PA: Cricket Software (Disc).

Fontographer, Computer Fonts, Plano, TX: Altsys Corp (Disc).

Kid Pix, Broderbund Software, San Rafael, CA.

Kid Works 1 & 2, Davidson & Associates, Inc., Torrance, CA.

MacDraw, MacPaint, Claris Corporation, Santa Clara, CA.

Pixel Paint, Computer Graphics Software, San Diego, CA: Silicon Beach Software (Disc).

Thunderscan, Optical Scanner and Software, Orinda, CA: Thunderware (Hardware and Disc).

Video Works, Computer Animation Software, Chicago, IL: MicroMind (Disc).

Crafts

Ceramics

Birks, Tony. *Pottery*. Asheville, NC: Lark Books, 1988.

Nigrosh, Leon. *Claywork: Form and Idea in Ceramic Design,* 3rd ed. Worcester, MA: Davis Publications, 1995.

Sapiro, Maurice. *Clay: Hand Building;* 1979; *Clay: The Potter's Wheel;* 1977. Worcester, MA: Davis Publications.

Fibers

Brown, Rachel. *The Weaving, Spinning, and Dyeing Book,* 2nd ed. Westminster, MD: Alfred A. Knopf, 1983.

Leeming, Joseph. *Fun with String*. New York: Dover Publications, 1974.

Other Crafts

Flower, Cedric, and Alan Fortney. *Puppets: Methods and Materials*. Worcester, MA: Davis Publications, 1983.

Rump, Nan. *Puppets and Masks: Stagecraft and Storytelling*. Worcester, MA: Davis Publications, 1996.

Solga, Kim. *Draw! Paint! Make Prints! and Make Gifts!* Cincinnati, OH: Northlight Books.

Tejada, Irene. *Brown Bag Ideas From Many Cultures*. Worcester, MA: Davis Publications, 1993.

Toale, Bernard, *The Art of Papermaking*. Worcester, MA: Davis Publications, 1983.

Drawing

Gatto, Joseph. *Drawing Media and Techniques*. Worcester, MA: Davis Publications, 1986.

James, Jane H. *Perspective Drawing: A Point of View,* 2nd ed. Englewood Cliffs, NJ: Prentice-Hall, 1988.

Painting and Collage

Brommer, Gerald. *The Art of Collage.* 1978; *Understanding Transparent Watercolor,* 1993. Worcester, MA: Davis Publications.

Porter, Al. *Expressive Watercolor Techniques*. Worcester, MA: Davis Publications, 1982.

Topal, Cathy Weisman. *Children and Painting*. Worcester, MA: Davis Publications, 1992.

Printmaking

Brommer, Gerald. *Relief Printmaking*. Worcester, MA: Davis Publications, 1970.

Toale, Bernard, *Basic Printmaking Techniques*. Worcester, MA: Davis Publications, 1993.

Sculpture

Hall, Carolyn Vosburg. *Soft Sculpture*. Worcester, MA: Davis Publications, 1981.

Wolfe, George. *3-D Wizardry: Design in Papier-Mâché, Plaster and Foam*. Worcester, MA: Davis Publications, 1995.

Zelanski, Paul. *Shaping Space*. Fort Worth, TX: Holt, Rinehart & Winston, 1987.

Periodicals on Art

The following list contains titles only. Addresses can be found in your library's copy of *Reader's Guide to Periodical Literature*. Write for sample copies to see which might be valuable additions to your artroom resource center, your school library or your own office.

African Arts
American Artist
American Arts
American Craft
American Indian Art
Art Direction
Art Education
Art in America
Art News
Arts and Activities
Artweek
Arts Canada
Arts Magazine
Arts of Asia
Camera
Ceramics Monthly
Communication Arts
Design
Design for Art Education
Fiber Arts
Graphic Design
Historic Preservation
Industrial Design (ID)
Interiors
Landscape Architect
Print
SchoolArts
Shuttle, Spindle and Dyepot
Sculpture
Smithsonian

Print and Audio Visual Resources

The Extension Program of the National Gallery of Art lends a variety of materials free of charge to educational institutions and community groups. The following are categories of available materials: Color slide programs, films, video cassettes, curriculum guides. To order materials, or for more information, write to:

Department of Extension Programs
National Gallery of Art
Washington, DC 20565

The Metropolitan Museum of Art and J. Paul Getty Trust have set up and maintain an international index of over 17,000 films and videos on art, for a small fee—you can obtain a list of resources that exactly match your needs in relation to age/grade level, artists' names, art forms, style or period, materials or techniques, geographic region, ethnic or gender identification of artists, concepts (art and mathematics), and other criteria. For more information, write to:

Program for Art on Film at Columbia University
2875 Broadway
New York, NY 10025

Other A-V Resources

Annotation codes:
F= Films
FS = Film strips
S = Slides
P = Prints, reproductions
V = Video
CD = Software, CD ROM

Agency for Instructional Television, Box A, Bloomington, IN 47402 **V, S**

American Crafts Council, Research and Education Department, 40 West 53rd St., New York, NY 10019 **FS, S**

American Institute of Architects, 1735 New York Ave, NW. Washington, DC 20006 **F**

American Library Color Slide Collection, 222 West 23rd St., New York, NY 10011 **S**

Art Now, Inc. 320 Bonnie Burn Road, Scotch Plains, NJ 07076 **S, FS**

Art Resource, 65 Bleecker St., New York, NY 10012 **S, FS**

Arts America, 9 Benedict Place, Greenwich, CT 06830 **V**

Audio Visual Center, Indiana University, Bloomington, IN 47401 **F, B, FS, V**

BBC-TV Enterprises, Manulife Centre, 55 Bloor St. W., Suite 510, Toronto, Ontario M4W 1A5 **V**

Budek Films and Slides, 1023 Waterman Ave., East Providence, RI 02906 **F, S,FS**

Canadian Film Institute, 303 Richmond Rd., Ottawa, Ontario K1Z 6X3 **F**

Castelli-Sonnabend Tapes and Films, 420 W. Broadway, New York, NY 10012 **F, V**

Center for Humanities, Inc., 2 Holland Ave., White Plains, NY 10603 **S, FS, V**

Centre Productions, 1800 30th St., Suite 207, Boulder, CO 80301 **FS,V**

Crystal Productions, Box 12317, Aspen, CO 81612 **FS, P, V**

Davis Publications, 50 Portland St., Worcester, MA 01608 **FS, S, P, V**

Department of the Interior, Bureau of Indian Affairs, P.O. Box 345, Brigham City, UT 84302 **S**

Educational Audio Visual, Inc., 17 Marle Ave., Pleasantville, NY 10570 **S, F, FS, V**

Educational Dimensions Group, Box 126, Stamford, CT 06904 **S, FS**

Grolier Enterprises, 845 Third Ave., New York, NY 10022 **FS, S**

G. K. Hall, Sandak, 70 Lincoln St., Boston, MA 02111 **S, FS**

Harry N. Abrams, 110 East 59th St., New York, NY 10022 **P**

Hester and Associates, 11422 Harry Hines Boulevard, Dallas, TX 75229 **F, FS**

Imaginus, Inc., R. R. 1, Box 552, Lee, MA 01238 **P**

International Film Bureau, 332 South Michigan Ave., Chicago, IL 60604 **F, FS**

Kentucky Educational Television, Lexington, KY 40506 **V**

Konrad Prothmann, 2378 Soper Ave., Baldwin, NY 11510 **P**

Life Filmstrips, Time & Life Building, New York, NY 10020 **FS**

Miller-Brody Productions, Inc., 342 Madison Ave., New York, NY 10017 **V, FS**

Miniature Gallery, 2 Birds Hill Rise, Oxshott Surrey, KT 220SW **S, FS**

Museum of Modern Art, 11 West 53rd St., New York, NY 10019 **ALL**

My Weekly Reader, Art Gallery Education Center, Columbus, OH 43216 **P**

National Film Board of Canada, Customer Services, P.O. Box 6100, Station A, Montréal, Québec, H3C 3H5, Canada **F**

New York Graphic Society, 140 Greenwich Ave., Greenwich, CT 06830 **P**

NIT Bureau of Audio Visual Education, School of Education, Indiana University, Bloomington, IN 47401 **F, V**

Prothmann Associates, Inc., 2795 Milburn Ave., Baldwin, NY 11510 **FS, S, P**

Rosenthal Art Slides, 50 Portland St., Worcester, MA 01608 **S**

Saskia Limited, P.O. Box 621109, Littleton, CO 80123 **S**

Shorewood Reproductions, Inc., 724 Fifth Ave., New York, NY 10019 **P**

Society for Visual Education, Inc., 1345 Diversy Parkway, Chicago, IL 60614 **S, FS**

The Software Source, 1750 Brielle Ave., A-2, Ocean, NJ 07712 **CD**

UNESCO Publications Center, 650 First Ave., New York, NY 10016 **P**

United CD ROM, 800 United CD ROM Dr., Urbana, IL 61802 **CD**

Universal Color Slide Company, 1221 Main St., Suite 203, Weymouth, MA 02190 **S**

University Prints, 21 East St., Winchester, MA 01890 **P**

VRI, Inc., P.O. Box 45734, Los Angeles, CA 90045 **S, FS**

Warner Educational Productions, Box 8791, Fountain Valley, CA 97208 **FS, V**

Warren Schloat Productions, 150 White Plains Road, Tarrytown, NY 10591 **FS**

Wilton Art Appreciation Programs, P.O. Box 302, Wilton, CT 06897 **FS, P, V**

Internet Resources

Check with your librarian for a current directory of Internet addresses for art and art education. The following sites provide an interactive format for questions about arts education:

ArtsEdNet
http://www.artsednet.getty.edu/

National Art Education Association
http://www.naea-reston.org

Literature Link Bibliography, Level 3

A = Artwork links to lesson
S = Story line links to lesson
I = Information links to lesson

U1 Seeing and Creating Art
Sky Tree by Thomas Locker with Candace Christiansen. HarperCollins, ©1995. **A**
Fox Song by Joseph Bruchac. Illustrated by Paul Morin. Philomel, ©1993. **A**
Reflections by Ann Jonas. Greenwillow, ©1987. **A**

1 Drawing People Who Pose
Miranda's Smile by Thomas Locker. Dial, ©1994. **S**
My Ballet Class by Rachel Isadora. Greenwillow, ©1980. **A**
Bill Peet: An Autobiography by Bill Peet. Houghton Mifflin, ©1989. **I**

2 Drawing Imaginary Places
Roxaboxen by Alice McLerran. Illustrated by Barbara Cooney. Lothrop, ©1991. **S**
A Day with Wilbur Robinson by William Joyce. HarperCollins, ©1990. **S**
Free Fall by David Wiesner. Lothrop, ©1988. (Mulberry, 1991) **S**

3 Lines to Show Motion
The Flame of Peace: A Tale of the Aztecs by Deborah Nourse Lattimore. HarperCollins, ©1987. (Harper Trophy, 1991) **A**
Old Black Fly by Jim Aylesworth. Illustrated by Stephen Gammell. Holt, ©1992. **A**

4 Shapes and Spaces
The Trek by Ann Jonas. Greenwillow, ©1985. **A**
Opt: An Illusionary Tale by Arline and Joseph Baum. Viking, ©1987. (Puffin, 1989) **A, S**
Visual Magic by David Thomson. Dial, ©1991. **A**

5 Spaces with Shapes
The Amazing Book of Shapes by Lydia Sharman. Dorling Kindersley, ©1994. **I**
Ed Emberley's Picture Pie 2: A Drawing Book and Stencil by Ed Emberley. Little, Brown, ©1996. **A, I**
The Animals: Selected Poems by Michio Mado. Translated by the Empress Michiko of Japan. Illustrated by Mitsumasa Anno. Margaret K. McElderry, ©1992. **A**

6 Balance and Rhythm
The Mountain That Loved a Bird by Alice McLerran. Illustrated by Eric Carle. Simon & Schuster, ©1985. **A**
The Stone-cutter: A Japanese folk tale adapted by Gerald McDermott. Viking, ©1975. (Puffin, 1978) **A**

7 Seeing and Touching Textures
Where the Forest Meets the Sea by Jeannie Baker. Greenwillow, ©1987. **A**
Red Leaf, Yellow Leaf by Lois Ehlert. Harcourt, ©1991. **A**
Snowsong Whistling by Karen E. Lotz. Illustrated by Elisa Kleven. Dutton, ©1993. **A**

8 Invented Textures
The Eagle's Song: A Tale from the Pacific Northwest adapted by Kristina Rodanas. Little, Brown, ©1995. **A**
Animals should definitely not wear clothing by Judi Barrett. Illustrated by Ron Barrett. Atheneum, ©1970. (Aladdin, 1989) **A**
Animals should definitely not act like people by Judi Barrett. Illustrated by Ron Barrett. Atheneum, ©1980. (Aladdin, 1989) **A**

9 Prints About Animals
Dancing Teepees: Poems of American Indian Youth selected by Virginia Driving Hawk Sneve. Illustrated by Stephen Gammell. Holiday House, ©1989. **A**
Star Boy retold by Paul Goble. Macmillan, ©1983. (Aladdin, 1991) **S**
Moon Song by Byrd Baylor. Illustrated by Ronald Himler. Scribner's, ©1982. **A**

10 Plans for Patterns
The Leopard's Drum: An Asante Tale from West Africa by Jessica Souhami. Little, Brown, ©1995. **A**
The Amazing Book of Shapes by Lydia Sharman. Dorling Kindersley, ©1994. **I**

11 Picture a Crowd
Yankee Doodle by Dr. Richard Shackburg. Illustrated by Ed Emberley. Simon & Schuster, ©1965. (Half Moon Books, 1994) **A**
Yankee Doodle by Steven Kellogg. Simon & Schuster, ©1996. **A**
The Great Migration: An American Story by Jacob Lawrence. HarperCollins, ©1993. **A**

12 Color Families
The Night of the Whippoorwill by Nancy Larrick. Illustrated by David Ray. Philomel, ©1992. **A**
The Way To Start a Day by Byrd Baylor. Illustrated by Peter Parnall. Scribner's, ©1978. (Aladdin, 1986) **A**

13 Mixing Colors of Paint
Claude Monet by Peter Harrison. Sterling, ©1996. **I, A**
Linnea in Monet's Garden by Christina Bjork. Illustrated by Lena Anderson. R & S Books, ©1985. **I, A**
Nate the Great by Marjorie Weinman Sharmat. Illustrated by Marc Simont. Coward-McCann, ©1972. (Dell, 1977) **S**

14 Experimenting with Paint
Over the Green Hills by Rachel Isadora. Greenwillow, ©1992. **A**
Cherries and Cherry Pits by Vera B. Williams. Greenwillow, ©1986. (Mulberry, 1991) **A**

15 Exploring Brushstrokes
Zomo the Rabbit: A Trickster Tale from West Africa by Gerald McDermott. Harcourt, ©1992. **A**
Morgan and the Artist by Donald Carrick. Clarion, ©1985. **S**
The Little Painter of Sabana Grande by Patricia Maloney Markun. Illustrated by Robert Casilla. Bradbury, ©1993. **S**

R1 Review Unit 1
Painting the Wind by Michelle Dionetti. Illustrated by Kevin Hawkes. Little, Brown, ©1996. **A, S**
Vincent Van Gogh by Peter Harrison. Sterling, ©1996. **A, I**

U2 How Artists Work
Knoxville, Tennessee by Nikki Giovanni. Illustrated by Larry Johnson. Scholastic, ©1994. **A**
Brown Angels: An Album of Pictures and Verse by Walter Dean Myers. HarperCollins, ©1993. **A**

16 Paintings About Cities
Claude Monet by Peter Harrison. Sterling, ©1996. **I, A**
Punch in New York by Alice Provensen. Viking, ©1991. **S**
My New York by Kathy Jakobsen. Little, Brown, ©1993. **A**

17 When the Wind Blows
Reflections by Ann Jonas. Greenwillow, ©1987. **A**
One White Sail by S.T. Garne. Illustrated by Lisa Etre. Simon & Schuster, ©1992. **A**
Mirandy and Brother Wind by Patricia C. McKissack. Illustrated by Jerry Pinkney. Knopf, ©1988. **S**

18 Seasons and Spaces
Sky Tree by Thomas Locker with Candace Christiansen. HarperCollins, ©1995. **A**
Mother Earth by Nancy Luenn. Illustrated by Neil Waldman. Atheneum, ©1992. (Aladdin, 1995) **A**
In for Winter, Out for Spring by Arnold Adoff. Illustrated by Jerry Pinkney. Harcourt, ©1991. **A**

19 Details in Landscapes
Where the River Begins by Thomas Locker. Dial, ©1984. **A**
The Boy Who Held Back the Sea retold by Lenny Hort. Illustrated by Thomas Locker. Dial, ©1987. **A**

20 Animal Expressions
Turtle in July by Marilyn Singer. Illustrated by Jerry Pinkney. Macmillan, ©1989. **A**
The Ice Horse by Candace Christiansen. Illustrated by Thomas Locker. Dial, ©1993. **A**
Whale by Judy Allen. Illustrated by Tudor Humphries. Candlewick, ©1992. **A**

21 Imaginary Creatures
The Shelf-Paper Jungle by Diana Engel. Macmillan, ©1994. **S, A**
Matthew's Dragon by Susan Cooper. Illustrated by Jos. A. Smith. Margaret K. McElderry, ©1991. (Aladdin, 1994) **S**
The Great Ball Game: A Muskogee Story retold by Joseph Bruchac. Illustrated by Susan L. Roth. Dial, ©1994. **A**

22 Small Creatures
My Son John by Jim Aylesworth. Illustrated by David Frampton. Holt, ©1994. **A**
Tracks in the Wild by Betsy Bowen. Little, Brown, ©1993. **A**

23 Drawing People
Vincent Van Gogh by Peter Harrison. Sterling, ©1996. **A, I**
People by Philip Yenawine. Delacorte, ©1993. **A**
The Young Artist by Thomas Locker. Dial, ©1989. **S**

24 People Outdoors
The Green Lion of Zion Street by Julia Fields. Illustrated by Jerry Pinkney. Margaret K. McElderry, ©1988. (Aladdin, 1993) **A**
Market Day by Eve Bunting. Illustrated by Holly Berry. HarperCollins, ©1996. **A**
My Little Island by Frané Lessac. HarperCollins, ©1984. (Harper Trophy, 1987) **A**

25 A Crowded Scene
The Great Migration: An American Story by Jacob Lawrence. HarperCollins, ©1993. **A, I**
Take Me Out to the Ballgame by Maryann Kovalski. Scholastic, ©1992. **A**

26 Faces of People
Miranda's Smile by Thomas Locker. Dial, ©1994. **S, A**
The Gentleman and the Kitchen Maid by Diane Stanley. Illustrated by Dennis Nolan. Dial, ©1994. **S**

27 Portraits and Self-Portraits
The Young Artist by Thomas Locker. Dial, ©1989. **S**
The Rough-Face Girl by Rafe Martin. Illustrated by David Shannon. Putnam's, ©1992. **A**

28 Still Lifes of Food
Yum, Yum, Yum by Andy Warhol. Little, Brown, ©1996. **A**
A Fruit & Vegetable Man by Roni Schotter. Illustrated by Jeanette Winter. Little, Brown, ©1993. **A**

29 City Spaces
Street Music: City Poems by Arnold Adoff. Illustrated by Karen Barbour. HarperCollins, ©1995. **S**
My New York by Kathy Jakobsen. Little, Brown, ©1993. **A**
Town and Country by Alice and Martin Provensen. Crown, ©1984. **A**

30 A City at Night
Night on Neighborhood Street by Eloise Greenfield. Illustrated by Jan Spivey Gilchrist. Dial, ©1991. **S**
Citybook by Shelley Rotner and Ken Kreisler. Photographs by Shelley Rotner. Orchard, ©1994. **A**

R2 Review Unit 2
Bridges by Ken Robbins. Dial, ©1991. **I**
Crossing the New Bridge by Emily Arnold McCully. Putnam's, ©1994. **S**
Tar Beach by Faith Ringgold. Crown, ©1991. **S, A**

U3 Art in Your World
Visiting the Art Museum by Laurene Krasny Brown and Marc Brown. Dutton, ©1986. (Puffin, 1990) **I**
Disney's Art of Animation: From Mickey Mouse to Beauty and the Beast by Bob Thomas. Hyperion, ©1991. **I, A**

Puddle Jumper: How a Toy Is Made by Ann Morris. Photographs by Ken Heyman. Lothrop, ©1993. **I**

31 Industrial Design
Sneakers: The Shoes We Choose! by Robert Young. Dillon Press, ©1991. **I**
How Does Soda Get Into the Bottle? by Oz Charles. Messner, ©1988. (Silver Burdett Press, 1993) **I**

32 Graphic Design
The Sign Painter's Dream by Roger Roth. Crown, ©1991. **S**
The Signmaker's Assistant by Tedd Arnold. Dial, ©1992. **S**
The Sign Painter's Secret: The Story of a Revolutionary Girl by Dorothy and Thomas Hoobler. Illustrated by Donna Ayers. Silver Burdett Press, ©1991. **S**

33 Picture Writing
Puff . . . Flash. . . Bang! A Book About Signals by Gail Gibbons. Morrow, ©1993. **I**
You Don't Need Words! A Book about Ways People Talk Without Words by Ruth Belov Gross. Illustrated by Susannah Ryan. Scholastic, ©1991. **I**

34 Picturing an Alphabet
The Z was Zapped by Chris Van Allsburg. Houghton Mifflin, ©1987. **A**
The Graphic Alphabet by David Pelletier. Orchard, ©1996. **A**
Alphabetics by Sue MacDonald. Simon & Schuster, ©1986. (Aladdin, 1992) **A**

35 Making a Book
Breaking into Print: Before and After the Invention of the Printing Press by Stephen Krensky. Illustrated by Bonnie Christensen. Little, Brown, ©1996. **I**
Go In and Out the Window: An Illustrated Songbook for Young People by Dan Fox. Holt, ©1987. **A**
A Book Takes Root: The Making of a Picture Book by Michael Kehoe. Carolrhoda, ©1993. **I**

36 Illustrating Stories
Daydreamers by Eloise Greenfield. Illustrated by Tom Feelings. Dial, ©1981. **A**
Something on My Mind by Nikki Grimes. Illustrated by Tom Feelings. Dial, ©1978. **A**

37 Photography
Click: A Book about Cameras and Taking Pictures by Gail Gibbons. Little, Brown, ©1997. **I**
The Science Book of Light by Neil Ardley. Harcourt, ©1991. **I**
Light and Shadow by Myra Cohn Livingston. Photographs by Barbara Rogasky. Holiday House, ©1992. **S**

38 Pictures That Move
Disney's Art of Animation: From Mickey Mouse to Beauty and the Beast by Bob Thomas. Hyperion, ©1991. **I, A**
That's a Wrap: How Movies Are Made by Ned Dowd. Photographs by Henry Horenstein. Silver Burdett Press, ©1991. **I**
Ed Emberley's 3 Science Flip Books by Ed Emberley. Little, Brown, ©1994. **A**

39 Shapes in Buildings
What It Feels Like To Be a Building by Forrest Wilson. The Preservation Press, ©1988. **A**
Architects Make Zigzags: Looking at Architecture from A to Z by Diane Maddex. Illustrated by Roxie Munro. The Preservation Press, ©1986. **A**

40 Colorful Mosaics
Cleopatra by Diane Stanley and Peter Vennema. Illustrated by Diane Stanley. Morrow, ©1994. **A**
The Romans and Pompeii by Philip Steele. Dillon Press, ©1994. **A**
Jerusalem by Saviour Pirotta. Dillon Press, ©1993. **A**

41 Spaces and Lighting
Night on Neighborhood Street by Eloise Greenfield. Illustrated by Jan Spivey Gilchrist. Dial, ©1991. **S**

Night of the Moonjellies by Mark Shasha. Simon & Schuster, ©1992. **A**
On a Starry Night by Natalie Kinsey-Warnock. Illustrated by David McPhail. Orchard, ©1994. **A**

42 A Colorful Window
Light, Color, & Lenses by Pam Robson. Franklin Watts, ©1992. **I, A**
Disney's The Hunchback of Notre Dame. Walt Disney, ©1996. **S, A**
Disney's The Hunchback of Notre Dame Stained Glass Kit. Disney Press, ©1996. **A, I**

43 A Model of a Castle
The Truth about Castles by Gillian Clements. Carolrhoda, ©1990. **I**
A Medieval Feast by Aliki. HarperCollins, ©1983. (Harper Trophy, 1986) **I, A**
A Tournament of Knights by Joe Lasker. HarperCollins, ©1986. (Harper Trophy, 1989) **A**

44 Styles of Buildings
Thomas Jefferson: A Picture Book Biography by James Cross Giblin. Illustrated by Michael Dooling. Scholastic, ©1994. **S, A**
Monticello by Catherine Reef. Dillon Press, ©1991. **I, A**

45 Landscape Architecture
Linnea in Monet's Garden by Christina Bjork. Illustrated by Lena Anderson. R & S Books, ©1985. **S**
Roxaboxen by Alice McLerran. Illustrated by Barbara Cooney. Lothrop, ©1991. **S**
Miss Rumphius by Barbara Cooney. Viking, ©1982. (Puffin, 1985) **S**

R3 Review Unit 3
The Little House by Virginia Lee Burton. Houghton Mifflin, ©1969. **S**
Town and Country by Alice and Martin Provensen. Crown, ©1984. **S**

U4 Kinds of Art, Past and Present
Kente Colors by Debbi Chocolate. Illustrated by John Ward. Walker, ©1996. **A**
Tonight Is Carnival by Arthur Dorros. Dutton, ©1991. **A**
Lion Dancer: Ernie Wan's Chinese New Year by Kate Waters and Madeline Slovenz-Low. Photographs by Martha Cooper. Scholastic, ©1990. **I**

46 Art in Containers
How Raven Brought Light to People retold by Ann Dixon. Illustrated by James Watts. Margaret K. McElderry, ©1992. **S**
The Piñata Maker/El Piñatero by George Ancona. Harcourt, ©1994. **I**
Hannah's Fancy Notions by Pat Ross. Illustrated by Bert Dodson. Viking, ©1988. (Puffin, 1992) **S**
Go In and Out the Window: An Illustrated Songbook for Young People by Dan Fox. Holt, ©1987. **A**

47 Art in Clothing
Powwow by George Ancona. Harcourt, ©1993. **A**
Her Seven Brothers by Paul Goble. Bradbury, ©1988. **S, A**
Powwow: Festivals and Holidays by June Behrens. Photographs by Terry Behrens. Childrens, ©1983. **A**

48 Art for Comfort
The Badger and the Magic Fan: A Japanese Folktale adapted by Tony Johnston. Illustrated by Tomie dePaola. Putnam's, ©1990. **S**
The Boy of the Three-Year Nap by Dianne Snyder. Illustrated by Allen Say. Houghton Mifflin, ©1988. **A, S**
The Tale of the Mandarin Ducks by Katherine Paterson. Illustrated by Leo & Diane Dillon. Lodestar, ©1990. **A, S**

49 Art for Special Times
Masks by Meryl Doney. Franklin Watts, ©1995. **I, A**
Raven's Light: A Myth from the People of the Northwest Coast retold by Susan Hand Shetterly. Illustrated by Robert Shetterly. Atheneum, ©1991. **S, A**

50 Weaving and Unweaving
Annie and the Old One by Miska Miles. Illustrated by Peter Parnall. Little, Brown, ©1971. **S**
Unraveling Fibers by Patricia A. Keeler and Francis X. McCall, Jr. Atheneum, ©1995. **I, A**

51 Batik Designs on Cloth
Dia's Story Cloth: The Hmong People's Journey of Freedom by Dia Cha. Illustrated by Chue and Nhia Thao Cha. Lee & Low, ©1996. **A**
Som See and the Magic Elephant by Jamie Oliviero. Illustrated by Jo'Anne Kelly. Hyperion, ©1995. **A**
Kente Colors by Debbi Chocolate. Illustrated by John Ward. Walker, ©1996. **A**

52 Fiber Arts
Dia's Story Cloth: The Hmong People's Journey of Freedom by Dia Cha. Illustrated by Chue and Nhia Thao Cha. Lee & Low, ©1996. **A**
Tonight Is Carnival by Arthur Dorros. Dutton, ©1991. **A**
Life Around the Lake by Maricel E. Presilla and Gloria Soto. Holt, ©1996. **A, I**

53 An Imaginary Animal
Animals That Ought To Be: Poems About Imaginary Pets by Richard Michelson. Illustrated by Leonard Baskin. Simon & Schuster, ©1996. **S**
Animals in Art by Louisa Somerville. Marshall Cavendish, ©1996. **A**
Totem Pole by Diane Hoyt-Goldsmith. Photographs by Lawrence Migdale. Holiday House, ©1990. **A**

54 Found Object Sculpture
Stay Away from the Junkyard by Tricia Tusa. Macmillan, ©1988. (Aladdin, 1992) **A**
The Sweet and Sour Animal Book by Langston Hughes. Oxford, ©1994. **A**

55 Creating a Form
Toys by Meryl Doney. Franklin Watts, ©1995. **A, I**

56 People in Action
Marie in Fourth Position: The Story of Degas' "The Little Dancer" by Amy Littlesugar. Illustrated by Ian Schoenherr. Philomel, ©1996. **A, S**
Henry Moore: From Bones and Stones to Sketches and Sculptures by Jane Mylum Gardner. Four Winds Press, ©1993. **I**

57 A Relief Sculpture
The Story of Money by Betsy Maestro. Illustrated by Giulio Maestro. Clarion, ©1993. (Mulberry, 1995) **A**

58 A Standing Figure
The Storyteller by Joan Weisman. Illustrated by David P. Bradley. Rizzoli, ©1993. **S**
Pueblo Storyteller by Diane Hoyt-Goldsmith. Photographs by Lawrence Migdale. Holiday House, ©1991. **A, I**
Pueblo Boy: Growing Up in Two Worlds by Marcia Keegan. Dutton, ©1991. **I**

59 African-American Sculptors
African American Art For Young People: Volume 1 by Samella Lewis. Unityworks, ©1991. **A, I**

60 Meet the Artist
Walt Disney: His Life in Pictures by Russell Schroeder. Disney Press, ©1996. **I**
Bill Peet: An Autobiography by Bill Peet. Houghton Mifflin, ©1989. **I**
Self-Portrait: Trina Schart Hyman by Trina Schart Hyman. HarperCollins, ©1981. **I**

R4 Review Unit 4
Visiting the Art Museum by Laurene Krasny Brown and Marc Brown. Dutton, ©1986. (Puffin, 1990) **I**
Aunt Lilly's Laundromat by Melanie Hope Greenberg. Dutton, ©1994. **S**
Jamaica Louise James by Amy Hest. Illustrated by Sheila White Samton. Candlewick, ©1996. **S**

Glosario

Este glosario incluye una serie de términos artísticos que no se usan en el texto de los estudiantes, pero que pueden servir cuando usted enseña los medios, técnicas, estilos y otros aspectos de arte.

abstracción Obra de arte abstracto que se basa generalmente en un tema identificable, en la cual el artista omite detalles, simplifica o reorganiza los elementos visuales. Las obras de arte abstracto que no tienen un tema identificable se llaman arte no objetivo. *(abstraction)*

abstracto Ver abstracción. *(abstract)*

acolchar Un proceso de costura mediante el cual se unen dos capas de tela colocando un relleno entre las capas. *(quilting)*

acrílico Pintura en la que se usa acrílico plástico líquido como aglutinante para los pigmentos. El acrílico tiene muchas de las características del óleo, pero el acrílico es soluble en agua antes de secarse. *(acrylic)*

activo Que expresa movimiento. Es lo opuesto a estático. *(active)*

acuarela Una pintura transparente hecha con la mezcla de colores en polvo, un aglutinante y agua. El término también se refiere a una pintura hecha con acuarela. *(watercolor)*

aglutinante En pintura, una sustancia tal como la cera, el aceite, la goma o el plástico líquido que hace que las partículas del pigmento se adhieran. *(binder)*

aguada Pigmento pulverizado en agua y mezclado con un aglutinante para formar una acuarela opaca. La aguada se parece a la témpera o a la pintura para carteles. *(gouache)*

aguafuerte Un proceso de grabado. La imagen se crea cuando se cubre la superficie de una plancha de metal y se hacen incisiones a través de esta capa, para luego sumergir la plancha en un ácido. El ácido quema a través de las líneas incisas, haciendo ranuras en el metal. Estas ranuras retienen la tinta. *(etching)*

aguatinta Un proceso de grabado en el que una placa de metal se prepara con pequeñas partículas de resina. Las partículas se adhieren dejando pequeñas aperturas al calentarse la plancha. Luego se graba la lámina sumergiéndola bajo ácido durante un lapso de tiempo mayor o menor, produciendo de este modo diferentes tonos. *(aquatint)*

alfarería Ollas, platos, vasos y otros objetos que se modelan en arcilla húmeda. *(pottery)*

altorrelieve Escultura en la que desde una superficie plana se proyectan superficies hacia afuera. *(high relief)*

ambiguo Cualquier imagen o elemento visual que parece tener más de un significado. *(ambigous)*

ampliación Una imagen que se ha agrandado más que otra versión suya. *(enlargement)*

análogos Colores que están estrechamente relacionados porque tienen un color en común. Por ejemplo, el azul, el azul violeta y el violeta contienen todos el color azul. Los colores análogos aparecen yuxtapuestos en la escala cromática. *(analogous)*

animación Forma de cine. Se toman fotos individuales de una serie de dibujos u otras imágenes. Cada imagen contiene un pequeño cambio. Cuando los dibujos se muestran rápidamente en sucesión, se crea la ilusión de movimiento. *(animation)*

apagado(a)/pálido(a) Matiz/tono/color de baja intensidad. Una superficie que no es brillante. *(dull)*

aplique Proceso por el cual se pespuntea y/o pega tela sobre un fondo, similar al collage. *(appliqué)*

arcilla Un material natural de la tierra compuesto principalmente de minerales finos. Cuando se humedece se le puede moldear fácilmente; cuando se le somete a cocción a altas temperaturas se endurece permanentemente. *(clay)*

arcilla cruda Obra de arte en arcilla y/o cerámica, seca y sin hornear. *(greenware)*

arcilla de modelar Un material plástico usado para modelar que por lo general contiene arcilla natural, aceite, glicerina y color. No se usa en cocción ni para objetos permanentes. *(modeling clay)*

arco En arquitectura, una estructura da o en punta que soporta el peso de materiales sobre un espacio abierto tales como un puente, o una entrada a una casa o edificio. *(arch)*

arco gótico Un arco acabado en punta, desarrollado para lograr mayores alturas en edificios y ventanas grandes en iglesias góticas. *(Gothic arch)*

arco romano Un arco cuya parte superior está redondeada (medio círculo). Lo usaron extensamente por primera vez en la Roma antigua. *(Roman arch)*

armazón Una estructura escueta que se usa para sostener otros materiales. *(armature)*

armonía La disposición de los elementos de una composición hecha de tal forma que crea un sentimiento de unidad agradable a la vista, similar a una armonía agradable en música. *(harmony)*

arquitectura El arte de diseñar o planear la construcción de edificios, ciudades y puentes. *(architecture)*

arte fantástico Obra artística que tiene como intensión ser imaginativa, irreal, extraña u onírica. *(fantasy art)*

arte islámico 600–900 d.C. Un período de rápida difusión de las influencias artísticas y culturales musulmanas que se extendieron hasta el siglo xvii en Asia y África. *(Islamic Art)*

arte popular/folclórico Arte tradicional hecho por gente que no ha tenido entrenamiento formal o cuyo estilo y técnica de arte han sido transmitidas de generación en generación. *(folk art)*

artefactos Objetos creados o adaptados por la gente y que generalmente no son considerados como obras de arte. *(artifacts)*

artesanías Obras de arte decorativas o útiles, que se hacen con destreza, a mano. *(crafts)*

artesano(a) Una persona experta en crear objetos hechos a mano. *(artisan)*

artífice Una persona con una gran destreza en la creación manual de obras de arte útiles y decorativas. Un artista que diseña y crea objetos útiles tales como textiles, cerámicas y joyas. *(craftsworker)*

artistas que utilizan fibra Artistas que usan materiales largos y delgados similares a una hebra para crear obras de arte. *(fiber artists)*

asimétrico Una clase de equilibrio visual en el que los dos lados de la composición son diferentes y aún así están en equilibrio; iguales visualmente sin ser idénticos. Se le llama también equilibrio informal. *(asymmetrical)*

asunto/tema Un tema o idea representada en una obra de arte, especialmente algo reconocible, tales como un paisaje o animales. *(subject)*

autorretrato Cualquier obra de arte en la que un artista se representa a sí mismo(a). *(self portait)*

bajorrelieve Una forma de escultura en la que partes del diseño sobresalen ligeramente sobre el fondo. *(bas-relief)(low-relief)*

barbotina Arcilla que se ha hecho menos espesa con agua o vinagre, para formar un líquido espeso. La barbotina se usa en las muescas para unir pedazos de arcilla. *(slip)*

barro cocido Cerámica burda y porosa, usualmente beige o rojiza, que ha sido cocida a baja temperatura. *(earthenware)*

batik Un método de teñido de tela en el que se usa la cera para repeler la tintura. La cera se aplica a partes del diseño que no se quieren teñir. *(batik)*

bellas artes Arte valorado por las cualidades de su diseño y por sus ideas y su expresividad, y no sólo por su excelencia técnica o su uso. *(fine art)*

bidimensional Obra de arte plana que se mide en dos dimensiones: altura y anchura. *(two dimensional)*

bizcocho Artículo de cerámica que ha sido cocido una vez pero no ha sido vidriado. *(bisque)*

boceto pequeño Un boceto de pequeñas dimensiones. Generalmente se hace más de uno en una página. *(thumb-nail sketch)*

bordado Diseños decorativos hechos sobre tela con una aguja e hilo o lana. *(embroidery)*

bosquejo Un dibujo hecho rápidamente para captar las características de un tema. También, un dibujo que puede ser usado para ensayar una idea o planear otra obra. *(sketch)*

brillante Una superficie que brilla. Una superficie que refleja mucha luz. *(glossy)*

bronce Una aleación metálica hecha de estaño y cobre. Una obra de arte hecha de bronce. *(bronze)*

budismo Una religión basada en las enseñanzas de Gautama Buda (546–480 a.C.), quien enseñó que el sufrimiento es parte de la vida, pero que la autodisciplina mental y moral pueden producir la iluminación; una forma de existir libre de sufrimiento y sin perturbaciones causadas por los problemas materiales de la existencia. *(Buddhism)*

busto Una escultura que reproduce la cabeza, cuello y pecho de una persona. *(portrait bust)*

calco Técnica mediante la cual se transfiere la textura de una superficie sobre un papel. El papel se coloca sobre la superficie y se frota con crayón, tiza o lápiz. *(rubbing)*

calco con crayón Un diseño hecho calcando con un crayón sobre un papel que ha sido colocado sobre una superficie con relieve. El calcado con el crayón muestra la textura. *(crayon rubbing)*

caligrafía Líneas que fluyen, hechas con pinceladas similares a la escritura oriental. El arte de escribir letras y palabras en un estilo hermoso y ornamentado usando plumas o pinceles. *(calligraphy)*

capa/aguada Un baño muy fino de pintura. Un color que ha sido rebajado con agua (o aguarrás si la pintura es de aceite) de tal forma que cuando se pinta sobre un papel, un lienzo o una tabla, la superficie que está debajo todavía se puede ver. *(wash)*

carboncillo Medio blando para dibujar, hecho de madera calcinada, lianas o carbón comprimido. *(charcoal)*

caricatura Un dibujo en el que los rasgos distintivos de una persona o animal, tales como la nariz, las orejas, o la boca, se distorsionan o exageran con propósito cómico o crítico. Las caricaturas se usan a menudo en los editoriales. *(caricature)*

cemento blanco Un cemento fino o yeso usado para llenar los espacios entre teselas en un mosaico. *(grout)*

cerámica El arte de hacer objetos de arcilla, vidrio u otros materiales no metálicos por medio de la cocción en un horno a altas temperaturas. También los productos así producidos. *(ceramics)*

claro Un matiz relativamente puro. *(bright)*

clásico Un término de historia del arte para designar cualquier forma de arte que se cree inspirada o influenciada por el arte de Grecia o Roma antigua, especialmente trabajos que se distinguen por su perfección en la forma y las proporciones, dominio de las emociones y el tratamiento idealizado del asunto o tema. *(classical)*

cocción En cerámica, el proceso de exponer objetos de arcilla a altas temperaturas, generalmente en un horno, con el propósito de endurecerlo permanentemente. *(firing)*

"colágrafo" Un grabado hecho de una superficie que ha sido construida como un collage. *(collagraph)*

collage Una obra de arte que se crea pegando pedazos de papel, tela, retazos, fotografías u otros materiales sobre una superficie plana. *(collage)*

color Ver matiz. *(color)*

color atmosférico Color percibido por el observador debido a un efecto atmosférico o luz inusual en el color real. *(optical color)*

color complementario dividido Una combinación de color que se basa en un matiz, y en los matices que están a cada lado de sus complementarios en la escala cromática. El naranja, el azul-violeta y el azul-verde son colores complementarios divididos. *(split complement)*

color intermedio Un color creado al mezclar un color secundario con un color primario. El azul verde, el amarillo verde, el amarillo naranja, el rojo naranja, el rojo violeta y el azul violeta son colores intermedios. *(intermediate color)*

color neutro Un color que no se asocia con un matiz, tal como el negro, el blanco o el gris. Los arquitectos y los diseñadores consideran como neutras las ligeras variaciones del negro, blanco, marrón y gris porque muchos otros colores se pueden mezclar con ellos en combinaciones de colores agradables. *(neutral color)*

color primario Uno de los tres colores básicos (rojo, amarillo y azul) que no pueden ser creados mezclando colores y que sirven como base para mezclar otros colores. Con referencia a la luz, los colores primarios son el rojo, el verde y el azul. *(primary color)*

color secundario Un color que se logra mezclando partes iguales de dos colores primarios. Verde, naranja y violeta son los colores secundarios. El verde se hace mezclando azul y amarillo. El naranja se hace mezclando rojo y amarillo. El violeta se hace mezclando rojo y azul. *(secondary color)*

colores cálidos A los colores cálidos se les da este nombre porque a menudo se les asocia con el fuego y el sol, y le recuerdan a la gente lugares, cosas y sentimientos cálidos. Los colores cálidos están relacionados y van desde el rojo hasta los naranjas y los amarillos. *(warm colors)*

colores fríos Colores que a menudo se asocian con lugares, cosas o sentimientos fríos. Es aquella familia de colores que comprende desde el verde hasta los azules y violetas. *(cool colors)*

colores puros Colores intensos (espectrales) que se ven en el arco iris o cuando la luz pasa por un prisma. Son el rojo, el naranja, el amarillo, el verde, el azul y el violeta. *(pure colors)*

colores relacionados/análogos Colores que se encuentran el uno al lado del otro en una escala cromática. También llamados colores análogos. *(related colors)*

combinación de colores (plan) Un plan para la combinación o selección de colores. Las combinaciones comunes de colores incluyen: los cálidos, los fríos, los neutros, los monocromáticos, los análogos, los complementarios, los complementarios divididos, las tríadas. *(color scheme)*

complementarios Colores que están directamente opuestos en la escala cromática, tales como el rojo y el verde, el azul y el naranja, el violeta y el amarillo. Cuando los colores complementarios se mezclan forman un marrón neutro o gris. Cuando se yuxtaponen en una obra de arte, crean contrastes fuertes. *(complementary)*

composición La creación, formación o diseño de algo por medio del arreglo de distintas partes para crear un todo unificado. *(composition)*

composición gráfica El arreglo de las letras y de las ilustraciones en el proceso de diseño gráfico. *(layout)*

con ritmo de jazz Una forma de ritmo o movimiento visual que tiene una estructura compleja, similar al ritmo de la música de jazz. *(jazzy)*

cóncavo Una forma que cuenta con un área hueca o una depresión, análoga al interior de un tazón. *(concave)*

contemporáneo(a) El tiempo o época actual. *(contemporary)*

contenido El significado de una obra de arte, expresado por medio de sus cualidades a un observador inteligente e instruido. *(content)*

contorno Una línea que representa o describe los bordes, las protuberancias, o perímetro de una figura o forma. *(contour)*

contraste Una diferencia apreciable entre dos cosas: por ejemplo, áspero y suave, amarillo y morado, luz y sombra. Los contrastes generalmente le añaden entusiasmo, dramatismo e interés a las obras de arte. *(contrast)*

convexo Una forma que cuenta con un área levantada o una superficie elevada, análoga a la parte exterior de un tazón o una colina. *(convex)*

copia fotostática/ferroprusiato Una imagen hecha en papel de color azul intenso desarrollada por medio de gases de amoníaco líquido. También llamada ferroprusiato. *(photogram)*

crayón indeleble Un dibujo hecho con crayón de cera y cubierto con una aguada. Debido a que la cera repele el agua, la pintura no llega a cubrir el área dibujada con el crayón. *(crayon resist)*

creativo Que es capaz de diseñar o hacer algo nuevo y original, usando la imaginación en vez de imitar algo. *(creative)*

créditos Información que identifica una obra de arte impresa en una publicación. Los créditos incluyen usualmente el nombre del artista, el título de la obra, el año en que fue terminada, medio, tamaño, localización, dueño o donante. *(credit line)*

criterios para juzgar el arte Normas que se usan para juzgar el arte y que se pueden comunicar a otras personas. Las normas no son fuertes opiniones personales o vagas preferencias. *(criteria for judging art)*

crítica de arte El proceso y el resultado del pensamiento crítico acerca del arte. La crítica de arte comprende la descripción, el análisis y la interpretación del arte. No siempre incluye la estipulación de un juicio de valor o mérito. *(art criticism)*

cualidades expresivas Los sentimientos, la disposición de ánimo y las ideas comunicadas al observador a través de la obra de arte. *(expressive qualities)*

cualidades formales Las cualidades estructurales de una obra de arte generalmente descritas en relación a los principios de diseño. *(formal qualities)*

cualidades sensorias Cualidades particulares de línea, color, forma y otros elementos visuales. Por ejemplo, una línea irregular tiene una cualidad sensoria que se diferencia de una línea suave. *(sensory qualities)*

cualidades técnicas La cualidades y efectos visuales creados por la manera especial mediante la que el artista usa los materiales y técnicas. *(technical qualities)*

cúpula Bóveda hemisférica o techo sobre un espacio circular. Se eleva sobre la parte central de un edificio. Algunas veces se eleva aún más cuando se coloca sobre un tambor circular. *(dome)*

desvanecerse Moverse hacia el fondo o distanciarse. *(recede)*

dibujo asistido por computadora Un dibujo terminado con la ayuda de una computadora. *(computer-assisted drawing)*

dibujo gestual Un dibujo hecho rápidamente que capta el movimiento. gesture drawing)*

difuminado En arte bidimensional, figuras con contornos borrosos que tienen una cualidad suave o fluida. *(soft-edge)*

dinámico Se refiere a fuerzas de movimiento reales o implícitas. *(dynamic)*

dinastía Un período durante el cual un grupo de gente es dirigido o gobernado por una misma familia y sus herederos. *(dynasty)*

diseño El plan, organización o composición de elementos en una obra de arte. *(design)*

diseño decorativo El enriquecimiento ornamental de la superficie de un objeto o material. El diseño puede ser parte de la estructura del material (como en un tejido) o puede aplicarse a la superficie (como en un aplique). *(decorative design)*

diseño estructural Las cualidades de diseño que resultan de la manera como se construye una obra de arte en vez de las decoraciones que se añaden a su superficie. *(structural design)*

diseño gráfico Un término genérico para designar obras de arte en las que las formas de las letras (escritura, tipografía) son un elemento visual importante y cuidadosamente localizado. *(graphic design)*

disposición de ánimo/humor/sentimiento El sentimiento o humor creado por una obra de arte. *(mood)*

distorsionar Cambiar la manera como algo se ve por medio de la modificación o exageración de algunos de sus rasgos. *(distort)*

dominante La parte más importante o impactante de una obra de arte o que tiene la mayor influencia sobre el observador. *(dominant)*

edición En grabado, el número total de impresiones hechas en un solo tiraje, de la misma plancha o bloque, e impresas de la misma manera. *(edition)*

elemento subordinado Cualquier elemento de una obra de arte que ayuda al observador a notar otros elementos más dominantes. *(subordinate element)*

elementos de arte/diseño Los elementos son los nombres de categorías correspondientes a las principales cualidades sensoriales del arte. Entre los elementos (categorías) se incluyen el color, el valor, la línea, la figura, la forma, la textura y el espacio. *(elements of art/design)*

empaste Una aplicación muy gruesa de pintura que crea texturas. *(impasto)*

énfasis Áreas en una obra de arte que dominan la atención del observador. Estas áreas por lo general tienen tamaños, formas, colores u otros rasgos distintivos que contrastan. *(emphasis)*

enmarcar Sujetar o pegar una imagen, pintura, grabado, etc. a una superficie de papel o cartón, dejando un borde ancho alrededor. *(mount)*

ensamblaje Una obra de arte tridimensional que consiste en muchas piezas unidas. Obra de arte que se hace combinando en una sola unidad un grupo de objetos tridimensionales. *(assemblage)*

equilibrio Un principio de diseño que describe la distribución de las partes de una obra de arte y que crea un sentido de igualdad, interés o estabilidad en la importancia visual. Muchos tipos de equilibrio son simétricos, asimétricos y radiales. *(balance)*

equilibrio formal Obra de arte en la cual las partes están arregladas en ambos lados casi de la misma manera, como en una imagen reflejada. Se le llama también diseño simétrico. *(formal balance)*

equilibrio informal Ver diseño asimétrico. *(informal balance)*

escala La proporción entre dos conjuntos de dimensiones. Por ejemplo, si una imagen es dibujada a escala, todas sus partes son igualmente más pequeñas o más grandes que las partes del original. *(scale)*

escala cromática Un gráfico circular que organiza los colores del espectro visible. Se usa comúnmente como ayuda para recordar la relación entre los colores que se aplican a los pigmentos. *(color wheel)*

escultura Una obra de arte con tres dimensiones: altura, anchura y profundidad. Esta clase de obra puede ser tallada, modelada, construida o fundida. *(sculpture)*

escultura cinética Una escultura que se mueve o que tiene elementos que se mueven. El movimiento puede ser producido por la fuerza del aire, la gravedad, la electricidad, etc. *(kinetic sculpture)*

escultura ensamblada Cualquier escultura cuyas partes han sido unidas para completar la obra. *(constructed sculpture)*

espacio Un elemento de arte que se refiere al área vacía o abierta en medio, alrededor, arriba, abajo o adentro de los objetos. Las figuras y las formas están definidas por el espacio alrededor y dentro de ellas. El espacio a menudo se describe como tridimensional o bidimensional, como positivo (ocupado por una figura o forma) o negativo (que rodea una figura o forma). *(space)*

espacio/forma positivo Las figuras o espacios principales en una obra de arte, no el fondo ni el espacio circundante. *(positive space/shape)*

espacio/forma negativa El espacio que circunda figuras o formas sólidas en una obra de arte. *(negative shape/space)*

espectro cromático Una banda de colores que se produce cuando la luz blanca pasa a través de un prisma y se divide en diferentes longitudes de onda. Los colores visibles aparecen siempre en el mismo orden, de acuerdo con la longitud de onda, desde la más larga hasta la más corta, así: rojo, naranja, amarillo, verde, azul y violeta. Una escala cromática muestra aproximadamente el espectro visible dispuesto en un círculo. *(color spectrum)*

estático(a) En apariencia inactivo o sin movimiento. *(static)*

estatua Una escultura que se asemeja principalmente a una persona o animal y que se mantiene erecta por sí sola. *(statue)*

estilo Un estilo es el resultado de los medios de expresión de un artista; el uso de materiales, cualidades del diseño, métodos de trabajo, el tema escogido y otros similares. En la mayoría de los casos, estas selecciones revelan las cualidades únicas de un individuo, una cultura o una época. El estilo de una obra de arte ayuda a reconocer en qué difiere de otras obras de arte. *(style)*

estudio El sitio de trabajo de un artista o diseñador. *(studio)*

expresionismo Término usado para denominar un estilo de arte en el cual la idea central consiste en comunicar una disposición de ánimo o sensación definitiva o fuerte. Cuando se escribe con la E mayúscula en inglés, se refiere a un estilo particular de arte, sobre todo en Alemania, entre 1890 y 1920. *(Expressionism)*

fachada El frente o entrada de un edificio. A menudo está diseñada para anticiparle al visitante el espacio arquitectónico que se encuentra en el interior. *(facade)*

fibra Cualquier material delgado similar a una hebra al que se le puede dar forma o unir para crear arte. Generalmente se le asocia con el hilo y las telas tejidas. *(fiber)*

figura Forma plana que se crea cuando se juntan líneas implícitas o reales que cierran un espacio. Un cambio de color o una sombra pueden definir una figura. Las figuras se pueden dividir en varios tipos: geométricas (cuadrado, triángulo, círculo) y orgánicas (contornos irregulares). *(shape)*

figurativo Semejante a la forma como se ve un objeto o escena. *(representational)*

foco de atención Aquella parte de una obra de arte hacia la que el ojo del observador es atraída en forma inmediata o consistente. Generalmente es la parte más importante de la obra de arte. *(center of interest)*

fondo Partes de una obra de arte que parecen estar en la distancia o detrás de objetos que se encuentran en primer plano. *(background)*

forma Cualquier objeto tridimensional. Una forma puede ser medida de arriba abajo (altura), de lado a lado (anchura) y de adelante hacia atrás (profundidad). Es además un término que se refiere a la estructura o diseño de una obra. *(form)*

forma libre Un término usado para designar figuras o formas que no se pueden describir fácilmente refiriéndolas a simples figuras o medidas. *(free-form)*

fresco Una técnica de pintura en la que los pigmentos se aplican a una capa delgada de yeso húmedo para que se absorban, volviéndose la pintura parte de la pared. *(fresco)*

fuente de luz Una fuente de luz real o implícita que explica algunos de los efectos de luz y sombra que vemos en una obra de arte. *(light source)*

galería de arte Un lugar donde ocasionalmente se venden y se exhiben temporalmente obras de arte. Una galería puede también referirse a un museo o sección de un museo donde se exhiben obras de arte. *(art gallery)*

geométrico Término que se refiere a objetos de apariencia o forma mecánica, y a aquellos descritos por medio de fórmulas matemáticas en la geometría: figuras tales como círculos, cuadrados, rectángulos, triángulos y elipses; formas tales como conos, cubos, cilindros, bloques, pirámides y esferas. *(geometric)*

glaseado/vidriado En pintura, una capa delgada de pintura transparente. En cerámica, una capa delgada de minerales que se funde a la arcilla por medio de la cocción en un horno. El glaseado o vidriado forma una superficie permanente y vidriosa sobre la arcilla. *(glaze)*

grabado Una figura o marca hecha con un bloque o plancha de impresión u otro objeto cubierto con tinta y al que se le aplica presión contra una superficie plana, tal como papel o tela. La mayor parte de los grabados se pueden repetir una y otra vez, entintando nuevamente el bloque o plancha de grabado. *(print)*

grabado al crayón Una técnica en la que se aplica abundantemente el crayón sobre una superficie y luego se cubre con más crayón o una tinta o pintura opaca. El diseño se registra a través de la capa de material que cubre el crayón hasta llegar a éste en la capa inferior. *(crayon etching)*

grabado de estampas/en dulce Es el proceso de hacer un diseño al cortar o hacer incisiones con un instrumento afilado en un material, comúnmente metal. También, un proceso de grabado basado en la creación de muescas directamente en la superficie del metal o madera. *(engraving)*

grabado en madera Una clase de grabado en relieve, en el que las áreas del bloque de madera son talladas; la superficie que queda se entinta y se imprime en un papel cuando se le aplica presión. *(woodcut)*

grabado en relieve Un grabado que se obtiene mediante un proceso en el cual las partes realzadas en el bloque o plancha reciben tinta. *(relief print)*

grabado por medio de plancha/bloque El proceso de grabado que se logra al crear un diseño resaltado en una superficie plana. El diseño se entinta o se cubre con color y se estampa en una superficie como el papel o la tela. *(block printing)*

gradación Un cambio suave y gradual desde luminoso a oscuro, de áspero a suave, de un color a otro y variaciones similares. *(gradation)*

"Harlem Renaissance" 1920–1940. Nombre dado a un periodo y a un grupo de artistas que trabajaron en una variedad de formas de arte para expresar su experiencia y herencia como afroamericanos. Vivieron en Harlem, en la ciudad de Nueva York. *(Harlem Renaissance)*

heráldica El arte de diseñar insignias. *(heraldry)*

horizontal Línea o figura paralela al borde superior e inferior de una superficie. *(horizontal)*

horizonte La línea donde el agua o la tierra parecen terminar y donde el cielo parece comenzar. Está normalmente al nivel de los ojos del observador. Si el horizonte no se puede ver, se debe imaginar su lugar. *(horizon line)*

horno Aparato que sirve para trabajar y transformar con la ayuda del calor las sustancias minerales. Usado para cocer objetos de cerámica o para fusionar metales a vidrio, o a esmaltes. *(kiln)*

ícono Una pintura o imagen sagrada. En las gráficas de computadora, simplemente un símbolo visual que se refiere a un conjunto de cálculos (instrucciones) para la computadora. *(icon)*

idealizado(a) Más perfecto de lo que se encontraría ordinariamente en cualquier ejemplo específico. *(idealized)*

ilusión espacial El uso de recursos artísticos, especialmente sistemas de perspectiva, para producir una semblanza de espacio tridimensional en una superficie plana. *(illusion of space)*

ilustrador independiente Un artista que crea ilustraciones por su cuenta. *(free-lance illustrator)*

ilustrador(a) Un artista que crea dibujos para explicar algo, para mostrar una parte importante de un cuento, o para añadirle un elemento decorativo a un libro, una revista u otro trabajo impreso. *(illustrator)*

imagen Una representación mental que corresponde a algo que se ve o de lo que se puede hacer una representación mental aun cuando no se encuentre frente a nuestros ojos. *(image)*

importancia visual El interés o la atracción que para el observador tienen ciertos elementos de una obra de arte. A la importancia visual la afectan factores tales como el tamaño, el contorno, la intensidad del color, el color cálido o frío, el contraste de los valores, la textura y la posición. *(visual weight)*

impresión Cualquier marca o huella hecha por presión. En grabado, una estampa que resulta del contacto de una superficie entintada con la superficie de un papel. *(impression)*

intaglio Un proceso de grabado en el cual la imagen está incisa debajo de la superficie. Las líneas acanaladas contienen la tinta. *(intaglio)*

intensidad La brillantez u opacidad de un color. Un color puro se considera un color de alta intensidad. Un color apagado (un color mezclado con su complementario) se le considera un color de baja intensidad. *(intensity)*

interacción de los colores Una ilusión óptica en la que los colores cambian debido a su relación con otros colores. *(color interaction)*

irregular Líneas, formas y figuras que no son geométricas. *(irregular)*

joyas Ornamentos que la gente lleva puestos, como anillos, collares, brazaletes o aretes. *(jewelry)*

juicio estético Juicio artístico que se basa en la capacidad que tiene la obra para crear, o no, una respuesta estética. Ver percepción estética. *(aesthetic judgement)*

labor de aguja Un término genérico para obras de arte creadas con agujas, hebras o hilos y tela. Una puntada es un movimiento hacia adentro y hacia afuera de una aguja con hilo. *(stitchery)*

lienzo Tela fuerte que desde el Renacimiento han usado muchos artistas como superficie para pintar. *(canvas)*

línea Una huella continua con longitud y dirección, creada por un punto que se mueve a lo largo de una superficie. Una línea puede variar en longitud, anchura, dirección, curvatura y color. Una línea puede ser bidimensional (una línea a lápiz sobre papel), tridimensional (alambre), o implícita. *(line)*

líneas convergentes Líneas reales o imaginarias que parecen moverse hacia el foco de atención en el espacio. Una técnica relacionada con la perspectiva lineal. *(converging lines)*

litografía Un método de impresión que se lleva a cabo preparando una superficie plana pétrea o metálica, basado en el principio de que la grasa y el agua se repelen. Se hace un dibujo sobre la piedra o la plancha con una sustancia grasosa y luego se baña con agua. Cuando se le aplica una tinta grasosa, ésta se adhiere a la grasa del dibujo pero se desliza fuera de la plancha sobre la superficie húmeda, con lo que se obtiene la impresión del dibujo. *(lithography)*

logotipo Un símbolo visual que identifica un negocio, club u otro grupo. *(logo)*

loza/bloque/tabla Una forma que es sólida, plana y gruesa. Un trozo grueso y parejo de arcilla, piedra, madera o materiales similares. *(slab)*

mano alzada Dibujo hecho sin instrumentos para trazar o dibujar, tales como una regla o un compás. *(freehand)*

manuscrito iluminado Un manuscrito decorado o ilustrado, popular durante el medioevo, en el cual las páginas usualmente se pintaban con plata, oro y vistosos colores. *(illuminated manuscript)*

maqueta Modelo a escala de una escultura más grande. *(maquette)*

marca Cuando se hace presión con un instrumento puntiagudo en un papel o cartulina sin atravesarlo, creando una línea por donde se dobla fácilmente. Cuando se trabaja con arcilla, los artistas marcan muescas o rayan la superficie de la arcilla por donde ésta se va a juntar. *(score)*

marina Obra de arte que muestra una escena del mar, del océano, un paisaje costero o un gran lago. *(seascape)*

mate Una superficie que exhibe una textura opaca. No lustrosa o brillante. *(matte)*

materiales encontrados Cualquier objeto natural (tal como piedras u hojas) u objetos manufacturados desechados que se usan con un propósito nuevo en arte. *(found materials)*

matiz/tono/color El nombre común de un color en o relacionado al espectro, tal como amarillo, amarillo anaranjado, azul violeta, verde. *(hue)*

medio húmedo Un medio en dibujos y pinturas en el que hay un componente fluido o líquido. *(wet media)*

medio(s) Los materiales y técnicas que el artista usa para producir una obra de arte. Se puede referir también al líquido en el cual los pigmentos en polvo se mezclan para hacer una pintura. *(medium) (media)*

medios mixtos Cualquier clase de arte en la que se usa más de un medio artístico. *(mixed media)*

medios secos Lápiz, tiza, crayón u otros medios que se usan sin líquidos. *(dry media)*

método por substracción Un método para la ejecución de esculturas mediante el cual se crea una forma cortando, esculpiendo o removiendo material de cualquier otra forma. *(subtractive method)*

mezzatinta/grabado a media tinta/grabado al agua tinta Un proceso de grabado en el que se crea una textura sobre la superficie de una plancha metálica por medio de una herramienta con púas metálicas finas, llamada graneador. La tinta se mantiene en las pequeñas depresiones que han sido creadas con el graneador. *(mezzotint)*

miniatura Muy pequeño en relación con el tamaño de la figura humana. *(miniature)*

molde Una forma ahuecada que se llena con un material como el yeso o metal y que se saca cuando el material se endurece después de tomar la forma del molde. Un molde se usa para hacer una o muchas copias de un objeto. *(mold)*

monocromático(a) Consistente en un solo color o matiz, lo cual incluye sus matices y sombras. *(monochromatic)*

monograbado Un proceso de grabado que por lo general resulta en un solo grabado en vez de muchos. *(monoprint)*

"montage" Una clase especial de collage, hecho con pedazos de fotografías u otras imágenes. *(montage)*

monumental Grande o excepcionalmente grande en relación al tamaño de la figura humana. *(monumental)*

mosaico Obra de arte hecha juntando teselas; pedazos pequeños de vidrio coloreado, o azulejos, piedras, papel u otros materiales. *(mosaic)*

móvil Una escultura suspendida, con partes que pueden moverse, especialmente mediante corrientes de aire. *(mobile)*

movimiento Una forma de combinar elementos visuales para producir la ilusión de acción, o causar que la mirada del observador recorra la obra de una manera determinada. *(movement)*

mural Una pintura u obra de arte grande diseñada generalmente para crearla sobre una pared o el cielo raso de un edificio público. *(mural)*

muralistas mexicanos 1910–1940. Artistas mexicanos que revivieron el arte del fresco en la pintura mural. *(Mexican Muralists)*

museo de arte Un edificio donde se guarda, se exhibe y se mantiene una colección permanente de arte. *(art museum)*

Naïf/pintura ingenuista Arte ejecutado por artistas autodidactas con poco o ningún entrenamiento en técnicas de arte. *(naive art)*

naturaleza muerta Arte que se basa en una composición de objetos que no están vivos o que no se mueven, tales como frutas, flores o botellas. Los elementos se seleccionan a menudo como símbolos de ideas abstractas; un libro puede ser el símbolo del conocimiento. Una naturaleza muerta generalmente se representa en un escenario interior. *(still life)*

nearika Un tipo de arte que se originó en los comienzos de México, en el que hilo o pita de colores se pega a un fondo formando diseños sólidos. *(nearika)*

óleo Una pintura que se seca lentamente, hecha de pigmentos mezclados con una base de aceite. Cuando el aceite se seca se convierte en una película dura que protege el brillo de los colores. *(oil paint)*

opaco Que no permite que la luz lo atraviese. No se puede ver a través de un objeto o material que es opaco. Lo opuesto a transparente. *(opaque)*

orgánico Que tiene una cualidad que se asemeja a las cosas vivas. *(organic)*

original Obra de arte que parece muy diferente de otras obras de arte; que no ha sido copiada. También cualquier obra de arte auténtica e inalterada, contraria a su reproducción. *(original)*

paisaje Una obra de arte que muestra un escenario natural, tal como las montañas, los valles, los árboles, los ríos, y los lagos. *(landscape)*

paisaje urbano Una obra de arte en la que se usan elementos de la ciudad (edificios, calles, almacenes) como tema. *(cityscape)*

paleta Bandeja o tabla en la que se mezclan los colores. *(palette)*

papel "maché" Del francés para "papel molido." La pulpa de papel maché es un material de modelado que se hace mezclando pequeños pedacitos de papel con agua y pasta líquida. Es bastante fuerte cuando se seca. *(papier-mâché)*

pastel Una tiza parecida al crayón hecha de colores finamente molidos. Un retrato hecho al pastel. También un término para tonos de colores. *(pastel)*

patrón Las líneas, colores o figuras que se han escogido y que se repiten una y otra vez de acuerdo con un plan. Puede ser también un modelo o guía para hacer algo. *(pattern)*

patrones repetidos Un diseño realizado con partes que se repiten una y otra vez en forma regular y concebida para crear un ritmo visual u armonía. *(repeated pattern)*

pellizcado Un método usado para hacer cerámica o escultura que consiste en presionar, halar o pellizcar arcilla u otro material blando. *(pinch method)*

percepción estética Respuesta al arte o al medio ambiente que unifica en forma intensa y positiva los pensamientos, las sensaciones y los sentimientos. *(aesthetic perception)*

perfil Representación de algo cuando se le ve de lado. *(profile)*

perímetro/contorno Una línea que muestra o crea el borde externo de una figura o forma. También llamado contorno. *(outline)*

perspectiva Una técnica para crear la ilusión de profundidad en una superficie bidimensional. *(perspective)*

perspectiva aérea Llamada también perspectiva ambiental. Método que expresa el efecto de la luz, el aire y la distancia en una superficie plana. Se logra generalmente usando azules, y luz, con colores apagados para los objetos distantes. *(aerial perspective)*

perspectiva ambiental La ilusión de profundidad y distancia en una obra de arte bidimensional que se crea generalmente usando colores apagados y detalles vagos en los objetos distantes. *(atmospheric perspective)*

perspectiva lineal Un sistema de dibujo o pintura que se usa para crear la ilusión de profundidad en una superficie plana. Las líneas de los edificios u otros objetos están inclinadas hacia adentro, haciéndolas aparecer como si se extendieran hacia atrás en el espacio. Si las líneas se alargan se encuentran en un punto colocado sobre una línea horizontal imaginaria que representa el nivel de los ojos. Al punto en el cual se encuentran las líneas se le llama el "punto de fuga." *(linear perspective)*

pictograma Simples símbolos visuales que representan cosas, ideas o historias. *(pictograph)*

pigmento Cualquier material colorante, generalmente un polvo fino que se mezcla con un líquido o un aglutinante para hacer pintura, tinta o crayón. *(pigment)*

piñata Una vasija decorada, hecha en papel maché, y llena con dulces y regalos. Se cuelga en fiestas y celebraciones mexicanas para que los niños la rompan como parte de un juego. *(piñata)*

pintura sobre corteza Pinturas hechas sobre cortezas que se han desprendido de los árboles, con pigmentos generalmente naturales, con tonos en la gama del marrón al beige. *(bark painting)*

placa/bloque de entintado Una superficie pulida no absorbente sobre la cual se esparce tinta con un rodillo de gelatina. *(ink slab)*

plancha/bloque En grabado, un pedazo de material plano de madera, linóleo o metal que se ha preparado para hacer un grabado. En escultura, cualquier material sólido que se puede usar para tallarlo. *(block)*

plano Cualquier superficie plana . La mayoría de las superficies tridimensionales están compuestas por muchos planos pequeños que se juntan para formar superficies angulares o curvadas más extensas. *(plane)*

plano intermedio Partes de una obra de arte que parecen estar entre los objetos que están en primer plano y los objetos del fondo. *(middle-ground)*

polímero Líquido que se usa en la pintura acrílica para diluir o dar un acabado. Es relativamente impermeable cuando se seca. *(polymer medium)*

preservación histórica Actividades arquitectónicas dirigidas a conservar y usar de nuevo importantes edificios históricos. *(historical preservation)*

primer plano En una escena u obra de arte, la parte que parece estar más cercana al observador. Además, trabajo de arte o punto de vista en una escena en la cual los objetos parecen estar muy cerca del observador. *(foreground)(close-up view)*

principios de arte/diseño Directrices que ayudan a los artistas a componer diseños y a controlar la manera cómo los observadores puedan reaccionar ante las imágenes. El equilibrio, el contraste, la proporción, el patrón, el ritmo, el énfasis, la unidad y la variedad son principios de diseño. *(principles of art/design)*

proceso aditivo Proceso de crear una escultura usando materiales que se modelan, adicionan, combinan o construyen. *(additive process)*

proceso/material repelente Un proceso en el que se usan materiales tales como el aceite o la cera, porque éstos no se mezclan con el agua. El material repelente se usa para bloquear ciertas áreas de una superficie que el artista no quiere que sean afectadas por la tintura, pintura, barniz, ácido, u otra sustancia. *(resist)*

proporción La relación entre objetos respecto al tamaño, la cantidad, el número o el grado. *(proportion)*

punta seca Un método de grabado en el que la imagen se incide sobre la superficie de la plancha de grabado con una aguja de acero. Las líneas y los tonos en la imagen impresa tienen a menudo una apariencia aterciopelada. *(dry-point)*

punteado Una técnica de marcar una superficie con puntos, usada a menudo para sugerir sombreado. *(stipple)*

punto de fuga En un dibujo en perspectiva, uno o más puntos en el horizonte donde las líneas paralelas que se pierden en la distancia parecen encontrarse. *(vanishing point)*

puntos de vista Los lados y ángulos desde los que se puede ver un objeto. Si se pone una taza y platillo sobre una mesa se puede caminar alrededor de la mesa para observar las diferentes vistas de la taza y el platillo. *(viewpoints)*

radial Una clase de equilibrio en el que líneas o figuras irradian desde un punto central. *(radial)*

realista El arte realista representa un tema reconocible en colores, texturas, sombras, proporciones y otros elementos similares que parecen vivos. *(realistic)*

realzado El área de cualquier superficie que refleja más luz. *(highlight)*

regionalismo norteamericano Década de los años treinta. Término usado en la historia del arte para designar aquellos pintores cuyo trabajo se inspiró en la vida de las áreas rurales y de los poblados de la región central de los EE.UU. *(American Regionalism)*

relieve Una forma tridimensional, diseñada para ser vista por un solo lado, en la que superficies se proyectan desde un fondo. *(relief)*

repetición rítmica Forma rítmica visual creada en la obra artística por medio de la repetición de dos o más elementos diferentes que se yuxtaponen. *(alternating)*

réplica Una reproducción o facsímil de una forma de arte tridimensional. *(replica)*

reproducción Copia de una imagen o trabajo de arte hecha usualmente por medio de un proceso fotográfico o de grabado. *(reproduction)*

repujado En metalistería, un proceso en el cual el diseño se hace por medio de presión o golpecitos en el metal por su reverso. *(repoussé)*

retrato Cualquier forma de expresión artística que se asemeja a una determinada persona o animal. *(portrait)*

ritmo Principio de diseño que se refiere a un tipo de movimiento visual o real en una obra de arte. Un ritmo se crea usualmente con la repetición de elementos visuales. El ritmo se describe a menudo como regular, repetitivo, fluido, progresivo o de jazz. *(rhythm)*

ritmo progresivo Un patrón o ritmo que se desarrolla paso a paso desde lo más grande hasta lo más pequeño o desde lo más brillante hasta lo más apagado. *(progressive rhythm)*

rodillo de gelatina Un rodillo pequeño de caucho para distribuir manualmente la tinta de grabado, en forma uniforme, sobre una superficie antes de imprimirla. *(brayer)*

rosetón Gran ventana circular de vitrales, usado a menudo en las catedrales góticas. *(rose window)*

"sans-serif" Tipo y letra escrita sin coletillas. *(sans-serif)*

"serif" Tipo de letra con coletilla. *(serif)*

serigrafía Un grabado que se logra forzando tinta sobre un papel a través de una matriz de seda similar a una criba. *(serigraphy)(silkscreen)*

silueta Un contorno de un objeto sólido que se ha rellenado, como con una sombra, sin detalles en el interior. *(silhouette)*

silueteado Un dibujo en el que se usan solamente líneas de contorno. *(contour drawing)*

símbolo Algo que representa otra cosa; especialmente una letra, figura o signo que representa un objeto o idea real. Un corazón rojo es un símbolo común para representar al amor. *(symbol)*

simetría aproximada Casi simétrico. *(approximate symmetry)*

simétrico(a) Una clase de equilibrio en el cual el contenido a ambos lados de una línea central es exactamente o casi el mismo, como una imagen reflejada en un espejo en la que las cosas a ambos lados de una línea central son idénticas. Por ejemplo, las alas de una mariposa son simétricas. Se le conoce también como "equilibrio formal." *(symmetrical)*

sin soporte Una escultura que no necesita de una base o plataforma especial que la soporte. *(free-standing)*

sombra Cualquier valor oscuro de un color que se logra generalmente añadiendo negro. *(shade)*

sombra proyectada Una área oscura creada en una superficie cuando una fuente de luz es bloqueada por una figura o una forma. *(cast shadow)*

sombreado Un cambio gradual de la luz a la oscuridad. El sombreado es una manera de hacer aparecer una pintura más realista y tridimensional. *(shading)*

sombreado con trazos finos El efecto que se crea en una textura colocando líneas yuxtapuestas. *(hatch)*

sombreado de líneas entrecruzadas La técnica que consiste en dibujar líneas muy juntas en direcciones opuestas para crear áreas oscuras en un dibujo o grabado. *(cross-hatch)*

stencil/matriz Un papel o cualquier otro material plano con un diseño recortado que se usa para imprimir. Tinta o pintura se aplica a través del diseño recortado sobre la superficie que se imprime. *(stencil)*

superficie en relieve Cualquier superficie sobre la que una textura o diseño se eleva desde el fondo. *(raised surface)*

superficie pictórica La superficie de una obra de arte bidimensional. *(picture plane)*

supuesto Una serie de puntos separados o bordes de figuras que el observador tiende a ver como conectados. *(implied)*

táctil Las cualidades y sensaciones experimentadas por el sentido del tacto. *(tactile)*

tallar Crear una forma tridimensional quitando las partes que no se necesitan de un bloque de madera, piedra u otro material duro. *(carve)*

tamaño natural Del mismo tamaño de algo natural, real u original; la escultura de tamaño natural de un camello. *(life-sized)*

tambor En arquitectura, la pared cilíndrica que sostiene una cúpula y que generalmente eleva la cúpula a una posición que sobresale sobre la estructura principal del edificio. *(drum)*

tapiz Una tela densamente tejida en la que se crean figuras irregulares tejiendo el hilo de la trama parcialmente a lo largo del ancho de la tela. *(tapestry)*

técnica La forma como un artista usa los materiales de arte para lograr el efecto deseado. Una técnica puede ser la manera particular mediante la que un artista crea su obra de arte (un tipo especial de pincelada) o un procedimiento estándar (la técnica para crear un crayón indeleble). *(technique)*

técnicas de grabado Cualquiera de las técnicas que se usan para hacer múltiples copias de una imagen. Algunos ejemplos son: grabado en madera, aguafuerte, colágrafo y serigrafía. *(printmaking)*

tejer El proceso de tramar dos hilos paralelos, o materiales semejantes a las fibras, que generalmente están colocados en ángulo recto en un telar, para crear una tela. *(weaving)*

telar Un bastidor o soportes relacionados para tejer telas. Algunos hilos son soportados por el telar mientras otros hilos se tejen a través de ellos. *(loom)*

tema La interpretación del artista de un motivo o asunto en una obra de arte. Por ejemplo, un paisaje puede tener un tema relacionado con el deseo de conservar la naturaleza, o conquistarla. Un tema amplio como el amor, el poder, el respeto, se puede expresar mediante una variedad de motivos. La frase "tema y variaciones" se refiere comúnmente a varias interpretaciones o versiones de una idea. *(theme)*

témpera Una pintura opaca, soluble en agua y ligeramente terrosa. Se hace mezclando pigmentos con una goma o con una yema de huevo (témpera al huevo) u otro aglutinante. La pintura para cartón de dibujo escolar es un tipo de témpera. La témpera al huevo fue popular antes de la invención de la pintura al óleo. *(tempera)*

témpera al huevo Medio usado en pintura en el que la yema de un huevo mantiene juntos los pigmentos. *(egg tempera)*

tesela Pequeños pedazos de vidrio, azulejo, piedra, papel u otros materiales que se usan para hacer mosaicos. *(tesserae)*

textil Obras de arte hechas de tela o fibras, tales como el hilo. Las técnicas textiles incluyen el tejido, la tapicería, el bordado, el aplique, el acolchado y los textiles impresos. *(textile)*

textura La textura se percibe por medio del tacto y la vista. La textura se refiere a la manera como una superficie se experimenta al tacto (textura real) o a la vista (textura simulada). Las texturas se describen con palabras como burda, sedosa, de guijarro. *(texture)*

textura simulada El uso de un patrón bidimensional para crear la ilusión de una textura o superficie tridimensional. *(simulated texture)*

textura visual La ilusión tridimensional de una superficie con relieve, la apariencia ante la vista de una superficie con textura (opuestamente al tacto). *(visual texture)*

tintura Un líquido coloreado que penetra un material y lo tiñe. *(dye)*

tipografía El arte de diseñar y usar artísticamente las formas del alfabeto. *(typography)*

títere a contraluz Una clase de títeres que se mueven detrás de una cortina iluminada, de tal forma que sólo se pueden ver los movimientos de las sombras. *(shadow puppet)*

título El nombre que se le da a una obra de arte, inclusive la expresión "sin título." "Sin título" puede referirse al hecho de que: a) no se conoce un título de la obra o, b) la decisión deliberada del artista de no darle un título a la obra. *(title)*

tono/matiz Un valor suave o una variación de un color puro que usualmente se logra agregando blanco. Por ejemplo, rosado es un tono del rojo. *(tint)*

torno de alfarero Un disco plano giratorio sobre el que se coloca arcilla blanda para moldearla a mano. *(potter's wheel)*

tótem Un objeto o imagen que sirve de símbolo o emblema de una familia, persona, idea, leyenda o experiencia. Los tótems por lo general toman la forma de un pilar de madera o piedra esculpido y pintado que tiene por propósito preservar la historia o las tradiciones de un grupo. *(totem)*

trama En tejido, hilos u otros materiales similares a una fibra, que se tejen a través de una urdimbre de un lado para el otro. *(weft)*

trama tafetán El tejido más básico, creado cuando la trama corre alternativamente por debajo y por encima de la urdimbre. *(plain weave[tabby])*

translúcido Que trasmite luz difusa. Los colores y detalles de un objeto más allá o detrás de una superficie translúcida no se pueden ver claramente. *(translucent)*

transparente Que permite que la luz la atraviese de tal forma que los objetos que están debajo se pueden ver. Lo opuesto a opaco. Son transparentes las ventanas de vidrio, el celofán y las acuarelas. *(transparent)*

traslapo Cuando una parte cubre todo o parte de otras partes. *(overlap)*

trayectoria del movimiento Cualquier elemento de arte que parece dirigir la vista de un lugar a otro. *(path of movement)*

tríada cromática Una combinación de colores basada en tres colores cualesquiera, que están espaciados equidistantemente en la escala cromática. *(color triad)*

tridimensional Obra de arte que se puede medir en tres sentidos: altura, anchura y profundidad o espesor. Obra de arte que no es plana. Cualquier objeto que tiene altura, anchura y profundidad. *(three-dimensional)*

unidad Sensación de que todas las partes de un diseño funcionan como un conjunto. *(unity)*

urdimbre Una serie de cuerdas tensas que se extienden a lo largo en un telar, a través de las que se teje la trama. *(warp)*

vaciado El proceso de reproducir un objeto, tal como una escultura o una joya, por medio de un molde en el que se vierte yeso líquido, concreto o metal fundido. También el objeto producido por medio de este proceso. *(cast)*

vacío Un espacio vacuo. *(void)*

valor Elemento de arte que se refiere a la oscuridad o luminosidad de una superficie. El valor depende de la cantidad de luz que refleja una superficie. Los tintes son los valores luminosos de un color puro. Las sombras son los valores oscuros de un color puro. El valor puede ser también un elemento importante en las obras de arte en las que el color está ausente o es muy sutil, tales como en dibujos, grabados y fotografías. *(value)*

variación Un cambio de forma, figura, detalle o apariencia que vuelve diferente a un objeto de otros. Como un principio de diseño, es el uso de diversas líneas, figuras, texturas, colores y otros elementos de diseño para suscitar interés en una obra de arte. *(variation)*

variedad Ver variación. *(variety)*

visor Una ventanilla en una máquina fotográfica (o un rectángulo cortado en un pedazo de papel) a través del cual un observador mira con el fin de ver o planear la composición de una pintura. *(viewfinder)*

vitral Pedazos de vidrio coloreados y brillantes, unidos por tiras de plomo para formar un dibujo o diseño. Los vitrales fueron usados inicialmente en iglesias románicas y se volvieron una característica prominente de las catedrales góticas. *(stained glass)*

Zen Una rama del budismo, especialmente en Japón, en la que la creación de obras de arte es vista como un camino hacia la iluminación. Una obra de arte se crea como una forma de meditación, autocontemplación, con el uso de la intuición. *(Zen)*

Glossary

This glossary includes a number of art terms that are not used in the student text but may be helpful as you discuss media, techniques, styles and other aspects of art.

abstract *See* abstraction.

abstraction An abstract artwork is usually based on an identifiable subject, but the artist leaves out details, simplifies or rearranges visual elements. Abstract works that have no identifiable subject are called nonobjective art.

acrylic A paint which uses liquid acrylic plastic as a binder for the pigments. Acrylic has many qualities of oil paint, but acrylic is water soluble before it dries.

active Expressing movement. Opposite of static.

additive process The process of making sculpture by modeling, adding, combining or building up materials.

aerial perspective Also called atmospheric perspective. A method of showing the effect of light, air and distance on a flat surface. It is usually achieved by using blues, and light, dull hues for distant objects.

aesthetic judgment A judgment of art based on whether or not it produces an aesthetic response. *See* aesthetic perception.

aesthetic perception A response to art or the environment in which thoughts, sensations and feelings are unified, intense and positive.

alternating A form of visual rhythm created in artwork by repeating two or more different elements beside or near each other.

ambiguous Any visual element or image that seems to have more than one meaning.

American Regionalism 1930s. Art history term for painters whose work was inspired by life in rural areas and small towns in the Midwest United States.

analogous Colors that are closely related because they have one hue in common. For example, blue, blue-violet and violet all contain the color blue. Analogous colors appear next to one another on the color wheel.

animation A form of motion picture. A series of drawings or other images are photographed individually. Each image shows a small change in movement. When the pictures are shown quickly, one after the other, the illusion of motion is created.

appliqué A process of stitching and/or gluing cloth to a background, similar to collage.

approximate symmetry Almost symmetrical.

aquatint In printmaking, an intaglio, etching process. A metal plate is prepared with small particles of resin. When the plate is heated, the particles adhere, leaving tiny openings. By timed etching of the metal in acid, varying tones are produced.

arch In architecture, a curved or pointed structure supporting the weight of materials over an open space such as a doorway or bridge.

architecture The art of designing and planning the construction of buildings, cities and bridges.

armature A skeleton-like framework used to support other materials.

art criticism The process and the result of critical thinking about art. Art criticism involves the description, analysis and interpretation of art. It does not always include a stated, explicit judgment of worth or merit.

art gallery A place where artwork is temporarily shown and is sometimes sold. A gallery can also refer to a museum or section of a museum where artworks are displayed.

art museum A building where a permanent collection of artwork is housed, displayed and cared for.

artifacts Objects, created or adapted by people, which are not usually regarded as art.

artisan A person skilled in creating handmade objects.

assemblage A three-dimensional work of art consisting of many pieces assembled together. Art made by combining a collection of three-dimensional objects into a whole.

asymmetrical A type of visual balance in which the two sides of the composition are different yet balanced; visually equal without being identical. Also called informal balance.

atmospheric perspective The illusion of depth and distance in a two-dimensional artwork, usually created by using dull colors and hazy details in distant objects.

background Parts of artwork that appear to be in the distance or behind the objects in the foreground.

balance A principle of design that describes the arrangement of parts of an artwork to create a sense of equality in visual weight, interest or stability. Major types of balance are symmetrical, asymmetrical and radial.

bark painting Paintings created on bark removed from a tree, usually with natural earth pigments.

bas-relief Also called low relief. A sculptural form in which portions of the design protrude slightly from the background.

batik A method of dyeing cloth which involves the use of wax to resist dye. Wax is applied to parts of the design where the color of a dye is not desired.

binder In paint, a substance such as wax, oil, glue or liquid plastic that causes the particles of pigment to cling together.

bisque Ceramic ware that has been fired once but not glazed.

block In printmaking, a piece of flat material, such as wood, linoleum or metal, prepared to make a print. In sculpture, any solid material that can be used for carving.

block printing The process of making prints by creating a raised design on a flat surface. The design is inked or covered with color and stamped on a surface such as paper or cloth.

brayer A small, hand-held rubber roller used to spread printing ink evenly on a surface before printing.

bright A relatively pure hue.

bronze A metal alloy made of tin and copper. An artwork made of bronze.

Buddhism A religion based on the teachings of Gautama Buddha (566–480 BC), who taught that suffering is a part of life but that mental and moral self-discipline can bring about enlightenment and a state of being free of suffering and undisturbed by the problems of material existence.

calligraphy Flowing lines made with brushstrokes similar to Oriental writing. The art of writing letters and words in a beautiful, ornamental style using pen or brushes.

canvas A strong cloth which, since the Renaissance, many artists have used as a surface for painting.

caricature A picture in which a person's or an animal's distinctive features, such as nose, ears or mouth, are distorted or exaggerated for a comical or critical intent. Caricatures are often used in editorial cartoons.

carve To create a three-dimensional form by cutting away unwanted parts from a block of wood, stone or other hard material.

cast The process of reproducing an object, such as sculpture or jewelry, by means of a mold into which liquid plaster, concrete or molten metal is poured. Also the object produced by this process.

cast shadow A dark area created on a surface when a source of light is blocked by a shape or form.

center of interest The part of an artwork to which the viewer's eyes are most immediately or consistently drawn. Usually the most important part of a work of art.

ceramics The art of making objects from clay, glass or other nonmetallic minerals by firing them at high temperatures in a kiln. Also the products so produced.

charcoal A soft drawing medium made of charred wood, vines or compressed charcoal.

cityscape An artwork that uses elements of the city (buildings, streets, shops) as subject matter.

classical An art history term for any art form thought to be inspired or influenced by ancient Greek or Roman art, especially works marked by a perfection of form and proportion, restraint in emotion and idealized treatment of a subject or theme.

clay A natural material from the earth, composed mainly of fine minerals. When moist, it is easily shaped; when fired at a high temperature, it becomes permanently hard.

close-up view Artwork or a viewpoint on a scene in which objects appear to be very near to the viewer.

collage A work of art created by gluing bits of paper, fabric, scraps, photographs or other materials to a flat surface.

collagraph A print made from a surface that has been constructed in the manner of a collage.

color *See* hue.

color interactions An optical sensation that colors are changed by their relationship to other colors.

color scheme A plan for selecting or organizing colors. Common color schemes include: warm, cool, neutral, monochromatic, analogous, complementary, split-complementary, triad.

color spectrum A band of colors produced when white light passes through a prism and is broken into separate wavelengths. Visible colors always appear in the same order, by wavelength, from longest to shortest: red, orange, yellow, green, blue, violet. A color wheel shows the approximate visible spectrum arranged in a circle.

color triad A color scheme based on any three colors spaced an equal distance apart on the color wheel.

color wheel A circular chart organizing colors of the visible spectrum. It is commonly used as an aid in remembering color relationships that apply to pigments.

complementary Colors that are directly opposite each other on the color wheel, such as red and green, blue and orange, violet and yellow. When complements are mixed together, they form a neutral brown or gray. When they are used side by side in a work of art, they create strong contrasts.

composition To create, form or design something by arranging parts to create a unified whole.

computer-assisted drawing A drawing completed with the aid of a computer.

concave A form that has a hollow area or depression, analogous to the interior of a bowl.

constructed sculpture Any sculpture in which parts are joined together to complete the work.

contemporary Of the present time.

content The meaning of an artwork, as conveyed by the qualities of the work, to a perceptive and educated viewer.

contour A line which represents or describes the edges, ridges or outline of a shape or form.

contour drawing A drawing in which contour lines alone are used.

contrast A large difference between two things: for example, rough and smooth, yellow and purple, light and shadow. Contrasts usually add excitement, drama and interest to artworks.

converging lines Actual or implied lines that seem to move toward a central point in space. A technique related to linear perspective.

convex A form that has a raised area or elevated surface, analogous to the exterior of a bowl or hill.

cool colors Colors often associated with cool places, things or feelings. The family of colors ranging from the greens through the blues and violets.

crafts Works of art, decorative or useful, that are skillfully made by hand.

craftsworker A person highly skilled in creating useful or decorative artwork by hand. An artist who designs and creates useful objects such as textiles, ceramics and jewelry.

crayon etching A technique in which crayon is applied heavily to a surface, then covered with additional crayon or an opaque ink or paint. Designs are scratched (etched) through the covering material to the crayon below.

crayon resist A drawing made with wax crayon and covered with a wash. Since wax repels water, the paint will not cover the crayoned part.

crayon rubbing A design made by rubbing a crayon over a paper that has been placed on a textured surface. The crayon rubbing shows the textures.

creative Able to design or make something new and original, using the imagination rather than imitating something else.

credit line Information identifying a work of art shown in a publication. A credit line usually includes the artist's name, the title of the work, year completed, medium, size, location, owner or donor.

criteria for judging art Standards for judging art that you can state to others. The standards are not strong personal opinions or vague preferences.

cross-hatch The technique of placing lines close together in opposite directions to create dark areas in a drawing or print.

decorative design The ornamental enrichment of the surface of an object or a material. The design may be part of the structure of the material (as in weaving) or it may be applied to the surface (as in appliqué).

design The plan, organization or arrangement of elements in a work of art.

distort To change the way something looks by altering or exaggerating some of its features.

dome A hemispherical vault or ceiling over a circular opening. It rises above the central part of a building. Sometimes it is elevated further by being placed on a circular drum.

dominant The part of an artwork that is most important, powerful or has the most influence on the viewer.

drum In architecture, the cylindrical wall supporting a dome and usually raising the dome to a position above the main building.

dry media Pencil, chalk, crayon and other media that do not require the use of a fluid.

dry-point A method of intaglio printing in which the image is scratched into the surface of the printing plate with a steel needle. The print is also called a dry-point. The lines and tones in the printed image often have a velvety appearance.

dull A hue of low intensity. A surface that is not glossy.

dye A colored liquid that sinks into a material and stains it.

dynamic Refers to actual or implied forces of movement.

dynasty A period of time in which a group of people are led or governed by a single family and heirs to that family's name.

earthenware A coarse, porous pottery, usually buff or reddish, that has been fired at a low temperature.

edition In printmaking, the total number of impressions made at one time from the same block or plate and printed in the same way.

egg tempera A painting medium in which pigments are bound together with the yolk of an egg.

elements of art/design Elements are names of categories for the main sensory qualities of art. The elements (categories) include color, value, line, shape, form, texture and space.

embroidery Decorative designs sewn on cloth with a needle and thread or yarn.

emphasis Areas in a work of art which dominate the viewer's attention. These areas usually have contrasting sizes, shapes, colors or other distinctive features.

engraving The process of cutting or incising a design into a material, usually metal, with a sharp tool. Also, an intaglio printmaking process based on cutting grooves directly into a metal or wood surface.

enlargement A picture that has been made larger than another version of it.

etching An intaglio printmaking process. The image is made by coating the surface of a metal plate, scratching through the coating, then submerging the plate in acid. The acid burns through the scratched lines, making grooves in the metal that can hold the ink.

Expressionism A style term for artwork in which the main idea is to convey a definite or strong mood or feeling. If written with a capital E, it refers to a definite style of art, primarily in Germany, from about 1890 to 1920.

expressive qualities The feelings, moods and ideas communicated to the viewer through a work of art.

facade The front or entrance side of a building. It is often designed to prepare the visitor for the architectural space found inside.

fantasy art Artwork that is meant to look imaginative, unreal, strange or dream-like.

fiber Any thin, thread-like linear material that can be shaped or joined to create art. Usually associated with yarn and woven fabrics.

fiber artists Artists who use long, thin, thread-like materials to create artwork.

fine art Art that is valued for its design qualities and ideas or expressiveness, not just for its technical excellence or use.

firing In ceramics, the process of exposing a clay object to high heat, usually in a furnace-like oven called a kiln, in order to harden it permanently.

folk art Traditional art made by people who have not had formal art training or whose art styles and techniques have been handed down over the generations.

foreground In a scene or artwork, the part that seems near or close to you.

form Any three-dimensional object. A form can be measured from top to bottom (height), side to side (width) and front to back (depth). Also a general term that refers to the structure or design of a work.

formal balance Artwork in which the parts are arranged in about the same way on both sides, as in a mirror image. Also called "symmetrical design."

formal qualities The structural qualities of an artwork, usually described by referring to the principles of design.

found materials Any natural object (such as stones or leaves) or discarded manufactured item that is used for a new purpose in art.

free-form A term for irregular and uneven shapes or forms, not easily described by reference to simple shapes or measurements.

free-lance illustrator An artist who creates illustrations and is self-employed.

freehand A drawing done without tracing paper or drawing aids such as a ruler or compass.

freestanding A sculpture that does not require a special base or platform to support it.

fresco A technique of painting in which pigments are applied to a thin layer of wet plaster so that they will be absorbed and the painting becomes part of the wall.

geometric Refers to mechanical-looking shapes or forms and those described through mathematical formulas in geometry: shapes, such as circles, squares, rectangles, triangles and ellipses; forms such as cones, cubes, cylinders, slabs, pyramids and spheres.

gesture drawing A drawing done quickly and to capture movement.

glaze In painting, a thin layer of transparent paint. In ceramics, a thin coating of minerals that is fused to clay by firing the work in a kiln. The glaze forms a thin, permanent, glassy surface on clay.

glossy A shiny surface. A surface that reflects much light.

Gothic arch A pointed arch, developed to allow greater height in building and huge window spaces in Gothic churches.

gouache Pigments ground in water and mixed with a binder to form an opaque watercolor. Gouache resembles school tempera or poster paint.

gradation A gradual, smooth change from light to dark, from rough to smooth, from one color to another and the like.

graphic design A general term for artwork in which letter forms (writing, typography) are an important and carefully placed visual element.

greenware Dry, unfired artwork or pottery made of clay.

grout A fine cement or plaster used to fill the spaces between tesserae in a mosaic.

Harlem Renaissance 1920–1940. A name given to a period and to a group of artists who worked in a variety of art forms to express their experience and heritage as African-Americans. They lived in Harlem, New York City.

harmony The arrangement of elements of a composition in a way that creates a feeling of unity pleasing to the eye, similar to a pleasing harmony in music.

hatch The textural effect produced by placing lines next to each other.

heraldry The art of designing insignia.

high relief Sculpture in which areas project far out from a flat surface.

highlight The area on any surface which reflects the most light.

historical preservation Activities in architecture aimed at preserving and reusing historically important buildings.

horizon line A level line where water or land seems to end and the sky begins. It is usually on the eye level of the observer. If the horizon cannot be seen, its placement must be imagined.

horizontal A line or shape that is parallel to the top and bottom edges of a surface.

hue The common name of a color in or related to the spectrum, such as yellow, yellow-orange, blue-violet, green. Hue is another word for color.

icon A sacred painting or image. In computer graphics, a simple visual symbol that refers to a set of calculations (instructions) for the computer.

idealized More perfect than you would ordinarily find in any particular example.

illuminated manuscript A decorated or illustrated manuscript, popular during the Medieval period, in which the pages are often painted with silver, gold and rich colors.

illusion of space The use of artistic devices, especially perspective systems, to produce a likeness of three-dimensional space on a flat surface.

illustrator An artist who creates pictures to explain a point, to show an important part of a story, or to add decoration to a book, magazine or other printed work.

image A mental picture that corresponds to something you actually see or can mentally picture even if it is not presented to the eye.

impasto A very thick application of paint that creates textural effects.

implied A series of separate points or edges of shapes that the viewer tends to see as connected.

impression Any mark or imprint made by pressure. In printmaking, a print resulting from an inked surface making contact with a paper surface.

informal balance *See* asymmetrical.

ink slab A smooth, nonabsorbent surface on which printing ink is rolled out with a brayer.

intaglio A printmaking process in which the image is recessed below the surface. The recessed lines hold the ink.

intensity The brightness or dullness of a hue. A pure hue is called a high-intensity color. A dulled hue (a color mixed with its complement) is called a low-intensity color.

intermediate color A color made by mixing a secondary color with a primary color. Blue-green, yellow-green, yellow-orange, red-orange, red-violet and blue-violet are intermediate colors.

irregular Lines, forms and shapes that are not geometric.

Islamic Art AD 600–900. A period of rapid spread of artistic and cultural influences from Moslems, continuing into the 1600s in Asia and Africa.

jazzy A form of visual rhythm or movement that has a complex structure, similar to the rhythms in jazz music.

jewelry Ornaments that people wear, like rings, necklaces, bracelets or earrings.

kiln The furnace-like oven used for firing ceramic objects or for fusing glass or enamels to metal.

kinetic sculpture A sculpture that moves or has moving parts. The motion may come from the forces of air, gravity, electricity, etc.

landscape An artwork that shows natural scenery such as mountains, valleys, trees, rivers and lakes.

layout The arrangement of type and illustrations for a graphic design.

life-sized Of the same size as a natural, real or original item—a life-sized sculpture of a camel.

light source An actual or implied source of light that explains some of the effects of light and shade that we see in a work of art.

line A continuous mark with length and direction, created by a point that moves across a surface. A line can vary in length, width, direction, curvature and color. Lines can be two-dimensional (a pencil line on paper), three-dimensional (wire) or implied.

linear perspective A system of drawing or painting used to create the illusion of depth on a flat surface. The lines of buildings and other objects in a picture are slanted inward, making them appear to extend back into space. If lengthened, these lines will meet at a point along an imaginary horizontal line representing the eye level. The point at which the lines meet is called a "vanishing point."

lithography A method of printing, from a prepared flat stone or metal plate, based on the principle that grease and water repel each other. A drawing is made on the stone or plate with a greasy substance and then washed with water. When greasy ink is applied, it sticks to the greasy drawing but runs off the wet surface, allowing a print to be made of the drawing.

logo A visual symbol that identifies a business, club or other group.

loom A frame or related support for weaving cloth. Some threads are held by the loom while other threads are woven through them.

low-relief *See* bas-relief.

maquette Scale model of a larger sculpture.

matte A surface that appears to have a dull texture. Not glossy or shiny.

media Plural of medium.

medium The materials and techniques used by the artist to produce a work of art. It may also refer to the liquid with which powdered pigments are mixed to make paint.

Mexican Muralists 1910–1940. Mexican artists who revived the art of fresco mural painting.

mezzotint An intaglio printing process in which the surface of a metal plate is textured by means of a tool with fine metal spikes, called a rocker. The ink remains deposited in the small depressions cut by the rocker. The print is also called a mezzotint.

middleground Parts of an artwork that appear to be between objects in the foreground and the background.

miniature Very small relative to the size of the human figure.

mixed media Any artwork that uses more than one medium.

mobile A suspended sculpture with parts that can be moved, especially by air currents.

modeling clay A plastic material used for modeling, usually containing natural clay, oil, glycerine and color. It is not used for firing or for permanent objects.

mold A hollow shape that is filled with a material such as plaster or metal and removed when the material hardens into the shape of the mold. A mold is used to make one or many copies of an object.

monochromatic Consisting of only a single color or hue, including its tints and shades.

monoprint A printing process that usually results in one print rather than many.

montage A special kind of collage, made from pieces of photographs or other pictures.

monumental Large or exceptionally large in relation to the size of a human.

mood The feeling created by a work of art.

mosaic Artwork made by fitting together tesserae—tiny pieces of colored glass or tiles, stones, paper or other materials.

mount To attach a picture to a larger piece of paper or cardboard, leaving a wide border all around it.

movement A way of combining visual elements to produce the illusion of action or to cause the viewer's eye to sweep over the work in a definite manner.

mural A large painting or artwork, generally designed for and created on the wall or ceiling of a public building.

naive art Art made by self-taught artists with little or no training in techniques of art.

nearika A kind of art that originated in early Mexico in which colored yarn or string is glued on a background to form a solid design.

negative shape/space The space surrounding shapes or solid forms in a work of art.

neutral color A color not associated with a hue—such as black, white or gray. Architects and designers refer to slight variations on black, white, brown and gray as neutral because many other hues can be combined with them in pleasing color schemes.

oil paint A relatively slow-drying paint made from pigments mixed with an oil base. When the oil dries, it becomes a hard film, protecting the brilliance of the colors.

opaque Not allowing light to go through. You cannot see through an object or a material that is opaque. The opposite of transparent.

optical color Color perceived by the viewer due to the effect of atmosphere or unusual light on the actual color. Also called atmospheric color.

organic Having a quality that resembles living things.

original Artwork that looks very different from other artwork; not copied. Also any unaltered authenticated work of art, rather than a repro-duction of it.

outline A line that shows or creates the outer edges of a shape or form. Also called a contour.

overlap One part covers up all or some of other parts.

palette A tray or board on which colors of paint are mixed.

papier-mâché French for "chewed" or "mashed paper." Papier-mâché pulp is a modeling material made by mixing small bits of paper in water and liquid paste. It is quite strong when it dries.

pastel A chalk-like crayon made of finely ground color. A picture made with pastel crayons. Also a term for tints of colors.

path of movement Any element of art that seems to lead the eye from one part to another.

pattern A choice of lines, colors or shapes, repeated over and over in a planned way. Also, a model or guide for making something.

perspective Techniques for creating the illusion of depth on a two-dimensional surface.

photogram An image on blueprint paper developed by fumes from liquid ammonia.

pictograph Simple visual symbols representing things, ideas or stories.

picture plane The surface of a two-dimensional artwork.

pigment Any coloring matter, usually a fine powder, that is mixed with a liquid or binder to make paint, ink, dyes or crayons.

piñata A decorated papier-mâché container filled with candies and gifts. It is hung up at Mexican parties and celebrations, to be broken open by children in a game.

pinch method A method of hand-building pottery or sculpture by pressing, pulling and pinching clay or other soft materials.

plain weave (or tabby) The most basic weave, created when the weft alternately travels under and over the warp.

plane Any surface that is flat. Most three-dimensional surfaces are made up of many tiny planes that join to form larger angular or curved surfaces.

polymer medium A liquid used in acrylic painting as a thinning or finishing material. It is relatively waterproof when dry.

portrait Any form of art expression which resembles a specific person or animal.

portrait bust A sculptured likeness of a person's head, neck and chest.

positive space/shape The main shapes or spaces in a work of art, not the background or the space around them.

potter's wheel A flat, spinning disc on which soft clay is placed and shaped by hand.

pottery Pots, dishes, vases and other objects modeled from wet clay. Also, a potter's workshop.

primary color One of three basic colors (red, yellow and blue) which cannot be produced by mixing colors and which serve as the basis for mixing other colors. In light, the primary colors are red, green and blue.

principles of art/design Guidelines that aid artists in composing designs and controlling how viewers are likely to react to images. Balance, contrast, proportion, pattern, rhythm, emphasis, unity and variety are principles of design.

print A shape or mark made from a printing block or other object that is covered with ink and then pressed on a flat surface, such as paper or cloth. Most prints can be repeated over and over again by re-inking the printing block.

printmaking Any of several techniques for making multiple copies of a single image. Some examples are woodcuts, etchings, collagraphs and silkscreen prints.

profile A representation of something as seen from a side view.

progressive rhythm A pattern or rhythm that develops step-by-step—from larger to brighter to duller.

proportion The relation of one object to another with respect to size, amount, number, or degree.

pure colors Intense (spectral) colors seen in the rainbow or when light passes through a prism: red, orange, yellow, green, blue, violet.

quilting A process of stitching together two layers of cloth with padding between the layers.

radial A kind of balance in which lines or shapes radiate from a center point.

raised surface Any surface in which a texture or design stands up from a background.

realistic Realistic art portrays a recognizable subject with lifelike colors, textures, shadows, proportions and the like.

recede To move back or become more distant.

related colors Colors that are next to each other on a color wheel. Also called analogous colors.

relief A three-dimensional form, designed to be viewed from one side, in which surfaces project from a background.

relief print A print resulting from the printing process in which the raised portions of the block or plate receive ink.

repeated pattern A design with parts that are used over and over again in a regular or planned way, usually to create a visual rhythm or harmony.

replica A reproduction or facsimile of a three-dimensional art form.

repoussé In metalworking, a process in which the design is made by pressing or tapping the metal from the reverse side.

representational Similar to the way an object or scene looks.

reproduction A copy of an image or a work of art, usually by a photographic or printing process.

resist A process in which materials such as oil or wax are used because they will not mix with water. The resist material is used to block out certain areas of a surface that the artist does not want to be affected by dye, paint, varnish, acid or another substance.

rhythm A principle of design that refers to a type of visual or actual movement in an artwork. A rhythm is usually created by repeating visual elements. Rhythms are often described as regular, alternating, flowing, progressive or jazzy.

Roman arch An arch with a rounded top (half circle). It was first used extensively by the ancient Romans.

rose window Large circular windows of stained glass often used in Gothic cathedrals.

rubbing A technique for transferring the textural quality of a surface to paper. Paper is placed over the surface. The top of the paper is rubbed with crayon, chalk or pencil.

sans-serif Type and handlettering without tags.

scale The proportion between two sets of dimensions. For example, if a picture is drawn to scale, all of its parts are equally smaller or larger than the parts in the original.

score To press a pointed instrument into but not through paper or thin cardboard, creating a line where it will bend easily. In clay work, artists score grooves or make scratches into surfaces of clay that will be joined together.

sculpture A work of art with three-dimensions: height, width and depth. Such a work may be carved, modeled, constructed or cast.

seascape Artwork that shows a scene of the sea, ocean, a coastal environment or a large lake.

secondary color A color made by mixing equal amounts of two primary colors. Green, orange and violet are the secondary colors. Green is made by mixing blue and yellow. Orange is made by mixing red and yellow. Violet is made by mixing red and blue.

self-portrait Any work of art in which an artist portrays himself or herself.

sensory qualities Particular qualities of line, color, shape and other visual elements. For example, a jagged line has a sensory quality that differs from a smooth line.

serif Type or lettering with tags.

serigraphy A print, also known as a silkscreen print, that is made by forcing ink through a stencil and silkscreen to paper below.

shade Any dark value of a color, usually achieved by adding black.

shading A gradual change from light to dark. Shading is a way of making a picture appear more realistic and three-dimensional.

shadow puppet A type of rod puppet that is moved behind a lighted screen so that only the action of the puppet's shadow can be seen.

shape A flat figure created when actual or implied lines meet to enclose a space. A change in color or shading can define a shape. Shapes can be divided into several types: geometric (square, triangle, circle) and organic (irregular in outline).

silhouette An outline of a solid shape filled in completely, like a shadow, with no inside details.

silkscreen *See* serigraphy.

simulated texture The use of a two-dimensional pattern to create the illusion of a three-dimensional texture or surface.

sketch A drawing done quickly to catch the important features of a subject. Also, a drawing that may be used to try out an idea or to plan another work.

slab A form that is solid, flat and thick. A thick, even slice of clay, stone, wood or similar material.

slip Clay, thinned with water or vinegar, to form a thick liquid. Slip is used on scored areas to join pieces of clay together.

soft-edge In two-dimensional art, shapes with fuzzy, blurred outlines that have a soft or fluid quality.

space Element of art referring to the empty or open area between, around, above, below or within objects. Shapes and forms are defined by space around and within them. Space is often described as three-dimensional or two-dimensional, as positive (occupied by a shape or form) or negative (surrounding a shape or form).

split complement A color scheme based on one hue and the hues on each side of its complement on the color wheel. Orange, blue-violet and blue-green are split complementary colors.

stained glass Pieces of brightly colored glass held together by strips of lead to form a picture or design. Stained glass was first used in Romanesque churches and became a major feature of Gothic cathedrals.

static Inactive or motionless in appearance.

statue A sculpture, especially a likeness of a person or animal, that stands up by itself.

stencil A paper or other flat material with a cutout design that is used for printing. Ink or paint is applied through the cutout design onto the surface to be printed.

still life Art based on an arrangement of non-moving, nonliving objects, such as fruit, flowers or bottles. The items are often selected as symbols for abstract ideas—a book may be a symbol for knowledge. A still life is usually portrayed in an indoor setting.

stipple A technique of marking a surface with dots, often used to suggest shading.

stitchery A general term for artwork created with needles, thread or yarn, and cloth. A stitch is one in-and-out movement of a threaded needle.

structural design The design qualities that result from the way an artwork is constructed rather than the decorations added to its surface.

studio The workplace of an artist or designer.

style A style is the result of an artist's means of expression—the use of materials, design qualities, methods of work, choice of subject matter and the like. In most cases, these choices reveal the unique qualities of an individual, culture or time period. The style of an artwork helps you to know how it is different from other artworks.

subject A topic or idea represented in an artwork, especially anything recognizable, such as a landscape or animals.

subordinate element Any element of a work of art that helps you to notice other, more dominant elements.

subtractive method A method of making sculpture in which a form is created by cutting, carving away or otherwise removing material.

symbol Something that stands for something else; especially a letter, figure or sign that represents a real object or idea. A red heart shape is a common visual symbol for love.

symmetrical A type of balance in which the contents on either side of a center line are exactly or nearly the same, like a mirror image in which things on each side of a center line are identical. For example, the wings of a butterfly are symmetrical. Also known as "formal balance."

tactile The qualities and feelings experienced from the sense of touch.

tapestry A heavy woven cloth in which irregular shapes are created by weaving the weft thread only part of the way across the width of the fabric.

technical qualities The visual qualities and effects created by an artist's special way of using a medium.

technique An artist's way of using art materials to achieve a desired result. A technique can be an artist's unique way to create artwork (a special kind of brushstroke) or a fairly standard step-by-step procedure (the technique of creating a crayon-resist).

tempera A slightly chalky, opaque, water-soluble paint. The paint is made by mixing pigments with a glue or egg yolk (egg tempera) or another binder. School poster paint is a type of tempera. Egg tempera was popular before the invention of oil painting.

tesserae Small pieces of glass, tile, stone, paper or other materials used to make a mosaic.

textile Artworks made from cloth or fibers such as yarn. Textile techniques include weaving, tapestry, stitchery, appliqué, quilting and printed textiles.

texture Texture is perceived by touch and sight. Texture refers to the way a surface feels to the sense of touch (actual texture) or how it may appear to the sense of sight (simulated texture). Textures are described by words such as rough, silky, pebbly.

theme The artist's interpretation of a subject or topic in a work of art. For example, a landscape can have a theme related to the desire to preserve nature, or to conquer nature. A broad theme—love, power, respect—can be expressed through a variety of subjects. The phrase "theme and variations" usually refers to several interpretations or versions of one idea.

three-dimensional Artwork that can be measured three ways: height, width, depth or thickness. Artwork that is not flat. Any object which has depth, height and width.

thumb-nail sketch A small sketch. Several are usually made on one page.

tint A light value or variation of a pure color, usually achieved by adding white. For example, pink is a tint of red.

title A name given to an artwork, including the phrase "untitled." Untitled may refer to the fact that: a) no title is known for the work, or b) the artist's deliberate decision not to title the work.

totem An object or image that serves as a symbol or emblem of a family, person, idea, legend or experience. Totems often take the form of a carved and painted pillar of wood or stone intended to preserve the history or traditions of a group.

translucent Transmitting diffused light. The exact colors and details of objects beyond or behind a translucent surface cannot be clearly seen.

transparent Allowing light to pass through so that objects can be clearly seen underneath. The opposite of opaque. Window glass, cellophane and watercolors are transparent.

two-dimensional Artwork that is flat or measured in two ways: height and width.

typography The art of designing and artistically using alphabet forms.

unity A feeling that all parts of a design are working together as a team.

value Element of art that refers to the darkness or lightness of a surface. Value depends on how much light a surface reflects. Tints are light values of pure colors. Shades are dark values of pure colors. Value can also be an important element in works of art in which color is absent or very subtle, such as drawings, prints and photographs.

vanishing point In a perspective drawing, one or more points on the horizon where receding parallel lines seem to meet.

variation A change in form, shape, detail or appearance that makes an object different from others. As a principle of design, the use of different lines, shapes, textures, colors and other elements of design to create interest in a work of art.

variety *See* variation.

viewfinder A small window in a camera (or a rectangle cut into a piece of paper) that an observer looks through in order to see or plan the composition of a picture.

viewpoints The sides and angles from which an object can be seen. If you put a cup and saucer on a table you can move around the table to see different views of the cup and saucer.

visual texture Illusion of a three-dimensional textured surface, the appearance of a textured surface to the eye (as opposed to touch).

visual weight The interest or attraction that elements in a work of art have for the viewer. Visual weight is affected by factors such as size, contour, intensity of colors, warmth and coolness of colors, contrast in value, texture and position.

void An empty space.

warm colors Warm colors are so called because they are often associated with fire and the sun, and remind people of warm places, things and feelings. Warm colors are related and range from the reds through the oranges and yellows.

warp A series of taut threads extending lengthwise on a loom, through which the weft is woven.

wash A very thin coat of paint. A color which has been thinned with water (or turpentine, if the paint is oil) so that when it is brushed on the paper, canvas or board, the surface beneath can still be seen.

watercolor A transparent paint made by mixing powdered colors with a binding agent and water. The term also refers to a painting done with watercolors.

weaving The process of interlocking two sets of parallel threads or fiber-like materials, usually held at right angles to one another on a loom, to create a fabric.

weft In weaving, thread or other fiber-like materials that are woven across the warp from side to side.

wet media Drawing and painting media in which there is a fluid or liquid component.

woodcut A type of relief printing in which areas of the wood block are chiseled away; the remaining surface receives the ink and is printed onto paper when pressure is applied.

Zen A branch of Buddhism, especially in Japan, in which creating art is seen as a path to enlightenment. Artwork is created as a form of meditation, self-contemplation, and through the use of intuition.